Saving the World
Through Science Fiction

CRITICAL EXPLORATIONS IN SCIENCE FICTION AND FANTASY
(a series edited by Donald E. Palumbo and C.W. Sullivan III)

1 *Worlds Apart? Dualism and Transgression in Contemporary Female Dystopias* (Dunja M. Mohr, 2005)

2 *Tolkien and Shakespeare: Essays on Shared Themes and Language* (ed. Janet Brennan Croft, 2007)

3 *Culture, Identities and Technology in the* Star Wars *Films: Essays on the Two Trilogies* (ed. Carl Silvio, Tony M. Vinci, 2007)

4 *The Influence of* Star Trek *on Television, Film and Culture* (ed. Lincoln Geraghty, 2008)

5 *Hugo Gernsback and the Century of Science Fiction* (Gary Westfahl, 2007)

6 *One Earth, One People: The Mythopoeic Fantasy Series of Ursula K. Le Guin, Lloyd Alexander, Madeleine L'Engle and Orson Scott Card* (Marek Oziewicz, 2008)

7 *The Evolution of Tolkien's Mythology: A Study of the History of Middle-earth* (Elizabeth A. Whittingham, 2008)

8 *H. Beam Piper: A Biography* (John F. Carr, 2008)

9 *Dreams and Nightmares: Science and Technology in Myth and Fiction* (Mordecai Roshwald, 2008)

10 Lilith *in a New Light: Essays on the George MacDonald Fantasy Novel* (ed. Lucas H. Harriman, 2008)

11 *Feminist Narrative and the Supernatural: The Function of Fantastic Devices in Seven Recent Novels* (Katherine J. Weese, 2008)

12 *The Science of Fiction and the Fiction of Science: Collected Essays on SF Storytelling and the Gnostic Imagination* (Frank McConnell, ed. Gary Westfahl, 2009)

13 *Kim Stanley Robinson Maps the Unimaginable: Critical Essays* (ed. William J. Burling, 2009)

14 *The Inter-Galactic Playground: A Critical Study of Children's and Teens' Science Fiction* (Farah Mendlesohn, 2009)

15 *Science Fiction from Québec: A Postcolonial Study* (Amy J. Ransom, 2009)

16 *Science Fiction and the Two Cultures: Essays on Bridging the Gap Between the Sciences and the Humanities* (ed. Gary Westfahl, George Slusser, 2009)

17 *Stephen R. Donaldson and the Modern Epic Vision: A Critical Study of the "Chronicles of Thomas Covenant" Novels* (Christine Barkley, 2009)

18 *Ursula K. Le Guin's Journey to Post-Feminism* (Amy M. Clarke, 2010)

19 *Portals of Power: Magical Agency and Transformation in Literary Fantasy* (Lori M. Campbell, 2010)

20 *The Animal Fable in Science Fiction and Fantasy* (Bruce Shaw, 2010)

21 *Illuminating* Torchwood*: Essays on Narrative, Character and Sexuality in the BBC Series* (ed. Andrew Ireland, 2010)

22 *Comics as a Nexus of Cultures: Essays on the Interplay of Media, Disciplines and International Perspectives* (ed. Mark Berninger, Jochen Ecke, Gideon Haberkorn, 2010)

23 *The Anatomy of Utopia: Narration, Estrangement and Ambiguity in More, Wells, Huxley and Clarke* (Károly Pintér, 2010)

24 *The Anticipation Novelists of 1950s French Science Fiction: Stepchildren of Voltaire* (Bradford Lyau, 2010)

25 *The* Twilight *Mystique: Critical Essays on the Novels and Films* (ed. Amy M. Clarke, Marijane Osborn, 2010)

26 *The Mythic Fantasy of Robert Holdstock: Critical Essays on the Fiction* (ed. Donald E. Morse, Kálmán Matolcsy, 2011)

27 *Science Fiction and the Prediction of the Future: Essays on Foresight and Fallacy* (ed. Gary Westfahl, Wong Kin Yuen, Amy Kit-sze Chan, 2011)

28 *Apocalypse in Australian Fiction and Film: A Critical Study* (Roslyn Weaver, 2011)

29 *British Science Fiction Film and Television: Critical Essays* (ed. Tobias Hochscherf, James Leggott, 2011)

30 *Cult Telefantasy Series: A Critical Analysis of* The Prisoner, Twin Peaks, The X-Files, Buffy the Vampire Slayer, Lost, Heroes, Doctor Who *and* Star Trek (Sue Short, 2011)

31 *The Postnational Fantasy: Essays on Postcolonialism, Cosmopolitics and Science Fiction* (ed. Masood Ashraf Raja, Jason W. Ellis and Swaralipi Nandi, 2011)

32 *Heinlein's Juvenile Novels: A Cultural Dictionary* (C.W. Sullivan III, 2011)

33 *Welsh Mythology and Folklore in Popular Culture: Essays on Adaptations in Literature, Film, Television and Digital Media* (ed. Audrey L. Becker and Kristin Noone, 2011)

34 *I See You: The Shifting Paradigms of James Cameron's* Avatar (Ellen Grabiner, 2012)

35 *Of Bread, Blood and* The Hunger Games: *Critical Essays on the Suzanne Collins Trilogy* (ed. Mary F. Pharr and Leisa A. Clark, 2012)

36 *The Sex Is Out of This World: Essays on the Carnal Side of Science Fiction* (ed. Sherry Ginn and Michael G. Cornelius, 2012)

37 *Lois McMaster Bujold: Essays on a Modern Master of Science Fiction and Fantasy* (ed. Janet Brennan Croft, 2013)

38 *Girls Transforming: Invisibility and Age-Shifting in Children's Fantasy Fiction Since the 1970s* (Sanna Lehtonen, 2013)

39 Doctor Who *in Time and Space: Essays on Themes, Characters, History and Fandom, 1963–2012* (ed. Gillian I. Leitch, 2013)

40 *The Worlds of* Farscape: *Essays on the Groundbreaking Television Series* (ed. Sherry Ginn, 2013)

41 *Orbiting Ray Bradbury's Mars: Biographical, Anthropological, Literary, Scientific and Other Perspectives* (ed. Gloria McMillan, 2013)

42 *The Heritage of Heinlein: A Critical Reading of the Fiction* Television Series (Thomas D. Clareson and Joe Sanders, 2014)

43 *The Past That Might Have Been, the Future That May Come: Women Writing Fantastic Fiction, 1960s to the Present* (Lauren J. Lacey, 2014)

44 *Environments in Science Fiction: Essays on Alternative Spaces* (ed. Susan M. Bernardo, 2014)

45 *Discworld and the Disciplines: Critical Approaches to the Terry Pratchett Works* (ed. Anne Hiebert Alton and William C. Spruiell, 2014)

46 *Nature and the Numinous in Mythopoeic Fantasy Literature* (Christopher Straw Brawley, 2014)

47 *J.R.R. Tolkien, Robert E. Howard and the Birth of Modern Fantasy* (Deke Parsons, 2014)

48 *The Monomyth in American Science Fiction Films: 28 Visions of the Hero's Journey* (Donald E. Palumbo, 2014)

49 *The Fantastic in Holocaust Literature and Film: Critical Perspectives* (ed. Judith B. Kerman and John Edgar Browning, 2014)

50 Star Wars *in the Public Square:* The Clone Wars *as Political Dialogue* (Derek R. Sweet, 2016)

51 *An Asimov Companion: Characters, Places and Terms in the Robot/Empire/Foundation Metaseries* (Donald E. Palumbo, 2016)

52 *Michael Moorcock: Fiction, Fantasy and the World's Pain* (Mark Scroggins, 2016)

53 *The Last Midnight: Essays on Apocalyptic Narratives in Millennial Media* (ed. Leisa A. Clark, Amanda Firestone and Mary F. Pharr, 2016)

54 *The Science Fiction Mythmakers: Religion, Science and Philosophy in Wells, Clarke, Dick and Herbert* (Jennifer Simkins, 2016)

55 *Gender and the Quest in British Science Fiction Television: An Analysis of* Doctor Who, Blake's 7, Red Dwarf *and* Torchwood (Tom Powers, 2016)

56 *Saving the World Through Science Fiction: James Gunn, Writer, Teacher and Scholar* (Michael R. Page, 2017)

Saving the World Through Science Fiction
James Gunn,
Writer, Teacher and Scholar

BY MICHAEL R. PAGE

Foreword by Christopher McKitterick

CRITICAL EXPLORATIONS IN
SCIENCE FICTION AND FANTASY, 56
Series Editors Donald E. Palumbo *and* C.W. Sullivan III

McFarland & Company, Inc., Publishers
Jefferson, North Carolina

LIBRARY OF CONGRESS CATALOGUING-IN-PUBLICATION DATA

Names: Page, Michael R., 1967– author. | McKitterick, Christopher, writer of foreword.
Title: Saving the world through science fiction : James Gunn, writer, teacher and scholar / Michael R. Page ; foreword by Christopher McKitterick.
Description: Jefferson, North Carolina : McFarland & Company, Inc., Publishers, 2017. | Series: Critical explorations in science fiction and fantasy ; 56 | Includes bibliographical references and index.
Identifiers: LCCN 2017005058 | ISBN 9781476663098 (softcover : acid free paper) ∞
Subjects: LCSH: Gunn, James E., 1923– | Gunn, James E., 1923– Criticism and interpretation. | Novelists, American—20th century—Biography. | Science fiction, American—History and criticism.
Classification: LCC PS3513.U797 Z83 2017 | DDC 813/.54 [B] —dc23
LC record available at https://lccn.loc.gov/2017005058

BRITISH LIBRARY CATALOGUING DATA ARE AVAILABLE

ISBN (print) 978-1-4766-6309-8
ISBN (ebook) 978-1-4766-2822-6

© 2017 Michael R. Page. All rights reserved

No part of this book may be reproduced or transmitted in any form or by any means, electronic or mechanical, including photocopying or recording, or by any information storage and retrieval system, without permission in writing from the publisher.

Front cover: James Gunn, 2007; background images © 2017 iStock

Printed in the United States of America

McFarland & Company, Inc., Publishers
  Box 611, Jefferson, North Carolina 28640
    www.mcfarlandpub.com

Contents

Acknowledgments	ix
Foreword: "Science Fiction's Dad" Christopher McKitterick	1
Preface	9
One. James Gunn: A Life in Science Fiction	17
Two. Early Stories to *This Fortress World* and *Star Bridge*	77
Three. *The Joy Makers* to *The Burning*	132
Four. *The Listeners* to *Crisis!*	188
Five. *The Joy Machine* to the *Transcendental* Trilogy	225
Six. The Scholarship	252
Chapter Notes	261
Bibliography	269
Index	273

Acknowledgments

First and foremost I want to thank James Gunn for his hospitality (I stayed at his home on a number of visits to Lawrence), for access to materials in his files, for answering all my questions, for sharing stories and anecdotes, and for reading the manuscript in draft and offering suggestions and correctives. And for asking me to go along for his Science Fiction and Fantasy Hall of Fame induction in Seattle. It's not often that one has so much direct access to his subject. For all of that, and probably more, thanks, Jim.

I'd also like to thank Christopher McKitterick, director of the Gunn Center for the Study of Science Fiction, for providing a foreword to the volume. Chris continues to do great work in making Jim's mantra "Let's save the world through science fiction" a reality by developing new ways that the Gunn Center can interconnect with science fiction writers, scholars, teachers, readers, and fans. Chris is a wonderful teacher, writer, and colleague, someone who I am proud to have as a friend. Thanks also go to Chris's KU colleague Kij Johnson for words of encouragement and to all the folks that make up the Young Gunns who make the trek to Lawrence every summer for the Writers' Workshop and the Campbell Conference. To the intrepid Lydia Ash for saying hey (and providing keys) during my research trips to Lawrence. I need to say a special thanks to Amanda Hemmingsen, who took charge of the World Con Academic Track programming when Chris and I were embedded in our various projects. She did a stellar job!

A number of others have contributed to this project in various ways. First, thanks to Elspeth Healy and the librarians at the Kenneth Spencer Research Library at the University of Kansas for their assistance in accessing the James Gunn materials they currently hold on deposit. The Spencer Library has an extraordinary collection of original archival materials. I encourage other scholars to investigate their holdings. You'll be amazed.

I'd like to thank Noël Sturgeon and the Theodore Sturgeon Literary Trust for permission to quote from letters Ted Sturgeon exchanged with Jim Gunn in 1951 and 1952 regarding the story "Breaking Point." Thanks to the Chair of my department at the University of Nebraska, Marco Abel, for financial support, an overall enthusiasm for my work, and his hearty collegiality. To Steve Behrendt, my friend and mentor, for timely advice and commiseration. And to my retired colleague and friend Bob Stock, who again read chapters as they were in draft and offered helpful encouragement, as well as allowed access to his pulp magazine collection. I'd also like to thank my colleagues in the departmental office for help on various things and for filtering out some of the minor summer office business so I could write: Mirhuanda Meeks, Leann Messing, Barbara Starks, Sue Hart, Edie Schleiger, Erin Chambers, Brad Cain, Erica Thomas, and Kelly Payne. Erica especially for her copying! You all do a terrific job!

Finally, to my family. My wife Susan for putting up with another summer of 24/7 obsession and for going to *Star Trek Beyond* and the Psychedelic Furs at timely moments when I needed a break, and for just being herself. To Mary, our Labrador retriever, now eleven; this will be her third book! To my mom, Joyce, and our almost daily calls. Lastly, to my brother, Ken (he'll always be Ken to me), who gave me a copy of *The Science Fiction Hall of Fame* back in 1981 and introduced me to the glories of science fiction.

Foreword:
"Science Fiction's Dad"
Christopher McKitterick

Mentor. Scholar. Teacher. Friend. *Dad.*
James Gunn has meant so many things to so many who, together, comprise this community we call "science fiction." Though he's not as well-known as, say, Isaac Asimov (about whom Jim is considered the premier scholar), few have influenced the field more than James Gunn.
About that last one—I'll get back to that in a minute. First I want to frame this book a bit.

* * *

What you're holding (or viewing on a screen) is the first full-length study of the life and work of science fiction Grand Master James Edwin Gunn. I'm so pleased that Michael R. Page has written such an impressive, thoroughly researched book on a man who has meant so much to both of us. I first met Mike about ten years ago when he passed through Lawrence on his way home to Nebraska after a research trip to the Jack Williamson Library at Eastern New Mexico University, where he was accessing the Williamson archive for the collection, *The Man with the Strange Head and Other Early Science Fiction Stories* by Miles J. Breuer he was editing.
That summer and the next, Mike came down for the Gunn Center for the Study of Science Fiction's annual Intensive Institute on the Teaching of Science Fiction (when Jim was still leading the class). Since then, Mike has become a regular feature at the Campbell Conference we host each summer (usually in Lawrence), sandwiched between my and Kij Johnson's specific writing workshops for the two weeks prior, and the Institute and our "Repeat Offenders" workshops during the two weeks after. As

Mike has become more invested in our activities, I made him Affiliate Faculty and a Research Fellow of the Center, where he's helped plan the last two Campbell Conferences—including 2016's special event in conjunction with MidAmeriCon II in Kansas City, which served as the academic-programming track for the WorldCon.

When Mike asked me to write this foreword, I felt honored to share my enthusiasm about James Gunn and what he's meant to me and the field. Where to begin? I started reading through the dozens of introductions and articles I've written or presented about Jim, searching for something new I could say here about the man, the SF Center he founded, and my relationship with him, as a sort of introduction to Mike's study.

But Mike covers most of what I've said elsewhere, and much more, better than I can. What's left to say here? I began trying to fill in the blanks. Mike asked me to write this because I've known and worked closely with Jim since 1992, when I was accepted into Jim's Science Fiction Writers Workshop. At its most comprehensive, this Foreword was more than 6,000 words long. But none of it really captured the essence of James Gunn.

I needed to share why Jim means so much to *me*, and why.

So I put aside the research microscope and decided to just chat with you for a few minutes about the man I've known as "Jim" since before grad school, who has served as my mentor and role model for almost as long as I've been an adult.

I first encountered Gunn's work through his seminal anthology and history, *The Road to Science Fiction, Volume 3*. Not only was it full of Golden Age gems (and I was at "The Golden Age," myself, twelve or thirteen years old), but he also placed each story and author in context of the broader conversation that is science fiction. This was the first book I bought new with my own money, because I couldn't imagine a better anthology.

So when I learned he offered a writing workshop, I immediately applied. I'd just spent a year surrounded by the vast, quiet beauty of the Montana Badlands, teaching in a tiny school, writing, and discovering the limits of my understanding. In my application letter, I mentioned that I wasn't sure what I'd be doing afterwards, except that I wanted to write SF, and I couldn't imagine anyone better to learn from than James Gunn. He told me that he was retiring from full-time teaching in a year, so if I wanted to *really* study with him, I'd best apply for grad school at the University of Kansas. On Gunn's recommendation, I was accepted into KU's creative writing program.

My future fell into focus.

I moved to Lawrence, Kansas, to study under *James Gunn*. This decision proved pivotal, launching a decades-long relationship with the University of Kansas, the Gunn Center for the Study of Science Fiction, and the man himself.

In that first workshop, I was astounded to discover that I had the privilege to work not only with Gunn but also Frederik Pohl, whose work I had admired for as long as I'd been reading SF. At that year's Campbell Conference, two "Young Gunns" (what many of his students, and the students of his students, call ourselves)—Bradley Denton and John Kessel—were honored with the Campbell and Sturgeon awards, and spent time with the workshoppers for days beforehand. There I also met scholars like Betty Anne Hull, editors like Ellen Datlow, and lots of serious writers and fans.

It was magical. Enjoying the focused attention of literary heroes set me upon a path that led to a career in SF.

Because he now had a critical mass of grad students studying SF, Jim resurrected all the literature, scholarship, and writing courses he'd ever offered. I wrote a 200,000-word novel for him as my thesis project. I sold my first few short stories, an article or two, and, eventually, that novel.

After graduating in 1995, I moved to Seattle. There I wrote freelance and for-hire, and later worked in the high-tech and gaming industries. But for two to four weeks each summer, I returned to science fiction's gravitational center, apprenticing under Jim. His summer program provided the unique opportunity to study under a diverse, ever-changing series of SF scholars and authors that later included Brian Aldiss, Paolo Bacigalupi, Stephen Baxter, Cory Doctorow, Andy Duncan, Kathleen Ann Goonan, Joe Haldeman, Nancy Kress, Geoffrey Landis, Ian MacLeod, Jack McDevitt, China Miéville, James Morrow, Pamela Sargent, Robert Sawyer, Charles Sheffield, Dan Simmons, Joan Slonczewski, Vernor Vinge, Robert Charles Wilson, George Zebrowski, and many other guests of the Center. The magic continued.

I returned every summer not just because of the exciting and educational SF-related things I got to do, but because I respect, appreciate, and love the man.

I feel more fortunate than I can express in having been granted these opportunities. It's why, when Jim asked me to take on more and more duties for the Center (manage the Sturgeon Award process, develop the Center's website, manage the Conference, and a thousand other things), I was honored to do so.

When KU began recruiting me to teach writing and SF full-time in 2002, it was an easy decision to drop a lucrative career in beautiful Seattle and move back to Kansas. I got to co-teach the summer program with Jim until he *really* retired in 2010, when I succeeded him as the Center's director and took over his courses. I get to see Jim often, and we and Kij (now the Center's associate director) still have breakfast together every Saturday. As Jim had, now I get to invite the nation's best SF writers and scholars to the annual Campbell Conference and as guest author-instructors of my Speculative Fiction Writing Workshop and the SF Institute. And I get to direct where we focus the gravity waves of the Gunn Center.

Jim has influenced both me and my writing in countless ways. His critiques can, in just a few words, get to the heart of what's wrong with a story and suggest what they need to sing. He treats workshop materials as if they had been submitted to an editor for publication, just as he treats requests for personal advice with all the attention of a therapist, but with none of the preamble. He treats his students as potential peers, welcoming us into the community of SF scholars and writers.

The summer of 1992 changed my life. I felt I must do my best to become a *real* SF writer and scholar in order to deserve such access and attention. Being treated seriously by such greats in the field is why I fell in love with the Center and have dedicated my life to SF.

No one can be Jim, but he inspires our absolute best.

* * *

Who is James Gunn? In this book you'll learn about his scholarship, teaching, and writing. He's received the highest honors the field offers for all those things. But to me and the Young Gunns, he's so much more.

He's a gentleman, endlessly courteous to even the most difficult human beings; polite, thoughtful, and generous with his time, energy, intelligence, gentle wisdom, and money. In order to help "save the world through science fiction," he helped found AboutSF, the Center's educational-outreach program whose mission is to make the future a better place through helping others teach SF. He's leaving most of his savings to found a Professorship of Science Fiction at KU. And a thousand other such generosities. Most of us will never get to meet a true gentleman, and I suspect they were nearly as rare in the past.

He's a good friend to many, always warm and welcoming and ready to apply his deep understanding in whatever way he can to help others. When you first meet Jim, you could ask him to come speak at your school or library half way across the country, health allowing. On his request, dozens of science fiction's luminaries have made the trek to Kansas to do interviews or talks for his *Literature of Science Fiction* film series or his classes. Fred Pohl and Betty Anne Hull came down for the Workshop and Teaching Institute for more than twenty years.

He's a full-time mentor. When he was teaching—and for at least a decade after retiring—Jim would go to his office each day and write there, door open to passers-by. If anyone had a question, he'd pause in his work and welcome their questions. I once asked him if I had what it takes to become a writer, because it's a difficult and painful calling. He asked me why I keep doing it if I felt that way. I said that if I don't write, I get grumpy and unhappy, and then went on to excitedly explain what I was trying to say in my newest story. As I spoke, he smiled, then nodded and said, "Anyone who can be discouraged from becoming a writer should be. The rewards are small and delayed, few people will ever care about your work, and there are no guarantees. Only those who cannot be discouraged find success. You have what it takes."

His advice was never solely scholarly in nature: In response to a question about how he, a handsome, best-selling author who attended conventions without his wife (who suffered social anxiety), avoided unwanted advances from fans, he chuckled and said, "A gentleman doesn't *notice* unwanted attention." He's patiently offered advice on relationships, work, and a thousand other things, then calmly returned to work.

Mentoring is his approach to life. Everything Jim does is to help others, and he expects others to do the same, and helps guide those who listen into becoming better people through service to the greater good. His rationality and intellectualism stem from deep emotional investment in the betterment of the human species. His devotion to the field inspires the SF community to reach higher, grow deeper, and become ever more humane.

Tireless dedication to not only writing or teaching, but to mentoring and building community, defines him. This form of mentorship—his warm, open helpfulness—is, I believe, the essence of James Gunn, and why so many of us think of him as *Dad*.

* * *

What I realized after recognizing this—what set me to starting over with this piece—is that Jim's genius arises from "Gunn's Law," which states, simply, "Sell it twice." Ostensibly, this advice for writers derives from how he worked for most of his career. Jim would write a short piece, publish it, and then later collect it with others into a larger volume of scholarship or fiction, updated to best serve the larger work's function. I despise when critics mock novels like this as mere "fix-ups." It's tough enough to write a good short story. It's even more difficult to write a good novel. And it's *really* challenging to do both well. Jim is a master of writing and teaching each and both.

"The magic happens in revision," he says. That's true in all aspects of life.

There are a lot of great writers out there, great teachers, great scholars, and so forth. Very few are great across the board, and fewer still who also possess his admirable personal qualities. He's smarter and more knowledgeable and has more experience in the field than most anyone, kind, thoughtful and generous, patient, and able to guide and inspire his students toward becoming the best we can hope to be.

Jim is *Dad* because he's everything that the writers and teachers he's mentored aspire to be when we grow up. He's the father of modern science fiction. Not a flashy Dad, the kind who seeks publicity or fame, but the kind who does everything in his power to help his kids do their best. And he has a lot of such kids, and grandkids, and now great-grandkids.

* * *

H.G. Wells said that the world was in a race between education and catastrophe, and called for an "open conspiracy" of people of good will to create a better world. Jim has always seen science fiction as central to that education, and has devoted his career to not only writing with this in mind, but also propagating his understanding. He has profoundly influenced the field through his humanistic approach, emphasizing in his writing, teaching, scholarship, and public service how humanity could better respond to change. During more than sixty years of nonstop effort, Jim has touched the lives of almost everyone in science fiction, from the millions who have read his stories and books (or listened to or watched adaptations thereof) to the thousands who were his students. Many of the Young Gunns have gone on to enjoy success as authors, editors, agents, librarians, scholars, and educators in their own right (notables include Pat Cadigan, Bradley Denton, Kij Johnson, John Kessel, and Gary Wolfe).

This, more than anything, is the measure of Jim's influence: He has taught so many teachers, scholars, and educators that his reach is immeasurable. Jim's mentoring has shaped the genre into what we enjoy today, making him one of the most influential figures in SF. His is a life devoted to science fiction, and without him, the field would not be the same, nor the world as aware of both the peril and potential of human endeavor.

In recent years, Gunn has been signing his emails and letters with the sentence "Let's save the world through science fiction." About this, he says: "It's hyperbole, of course: I'm not sure the world is in danger of destruction, though it may be, and if it is I'm not sure anyone or anything can save it. But I think we need to try, not in any specific way but in the spreading of SF's capabilities as far as we can. From my earliest contacts with SF, I recognized important qualities: a realization of the continuity of existence from the remote past to the distant future, the relationship of present decisions and actions to the futures we and our descendants will inhabit, a recognition of mutual humanity that emphasizes species concerns above those of individuals or tribes or nations, a willingness to work together for a better world, and general good will." If SF is a living community, we want to do all we can to preserve and grow its heart and soul; to maintain its roots from the time before it was even "Scientifiction," through its exciting expansion, and into its mature years—especially important now that SF's core community is only part of what its larger corpus, and as society is *becoming* SF, and because tomorrow's society will be ever-as-different from today as the Golden Age was from the days of Gilgamesh.

This is exciting and inspiring, and I believe more than ever that the best hope for the future of humankind lies in what Jim has nurtured. Not just in the specifics, like the classes and awards and conference and AboutSF and all the rest (though, yes, those things too), but in the ineffable heart of the community, the vision for a future world better than today's, where our worst human attributes might well be driven to extinction not just by good intentioned, rational people, but by eradicating the poisonous mental memes that have been passed down since humans first began to talk.

If SF serves as no more than inoculation against societal diseases, it is the noblest profession we can serve. James Gunn seems to have been immune to the toxic ideas that plagued the twentieth century. Like the best antibodies, he has helped immunize hundreds of his mind-children directly—and thousands more, as we pass on his antibodies to new generations, who then pass them on again, and so on.

Kij Johnson, multiple-award-winning author and our colleague at the Gunn Center, wrote this as a sort of private tribute to Jim in her newest book, *The Dream-Quest of Vellitt Boe*: "Some people change the world. And some people change the people who change the world."

Jim has been the most influential person in my life, and everything I do is in service of our shared vision of SF's potential.

Our best mentors guide us to fresh mental perspectives, be they a clearing in the chaos of revolution or a station orbiting far above this pale blue dot. They encourage silence and reflection, so that we may step outside of our mundane points of view to gain new ways to glimpse underlying patterns and examine what really matters. Once we reach that place of SFnal clarity, we can share what we've discovered through our own writing, or teaching, or conversations.

Jim's is a life devoted to science fiction. Without him, the field would not be as deeply thoughtful or self-aware, nor the broader world as mindful of both the promise and peril of human endeavor. We are all beneficiaries of his legacy.

I am deeply grateful to my mentor, Grand Master James Gunn. Thank you for everything.

I hope this personal perspective helps lend another dimension to the subject of this book.

Christopher McKitterick is the director of the Gunn Center for the Study of Science Fiction at the University of Kansas, where he also teaches science fiction, technical communication and creative writing.

Preface

Science fiction has grown old. Although it still remains a vibrant and important cultural force, perhaps more now than ever before, nevertheless, it is fair to say that science fiction—and here I date science fiction's beginnings (its *origins* date back further) as a self-aware cultural category to 1926 when Hugo Gernsback launched *Amazing Stories*—is no longer just a phenomenon of contemporary culture, it is also an *historical* phenomenon. Most of the writers of science fiction's golden era of the 1940s and 50s, the writers I and others of my generation and the generation before us grew up reading, are no longer with us. There are a few still around: Brian Aldiss, Harlan Ellison, Robert Silverberg—and James Gunn. But no longer are writers like Asimov, Heinlein, Clarke, Simak, Sturgeon, Van Vogt, Pohl, and Williamson—the writers of the Golden Age—the gateways through which new readers universally discover the genre. Often new readers encounter these greats, if at all, after entering the genre via other avenues: contemporary genre writers, YA fiction, movies and video games, the classroom, etc. Yet, when I teach my science fiction class at the University of Nebraska, there is always a handful of students who have some familiarity with what Gardner Dozois once called "the good old stuff": Herbert's *Dune*, Asimov's *Foundation*, Niven's *Ringworld*.... Often these students say they were introduced to this book or that author by a parent or teacher; another indicator of science fiction's historicity, as it has achieved the generational.

My own gateway into the genre began with H. G. Wells, Jules Verne, and Edgar Rice Burroughs (although more accurately, it was probably *Star Trek* and the *Planet of the Apes* franchise). But this was just a prelude. I didn't really become an SF reader, I didn't really *know* that there was this contemporary, living, intellectually stimulating, and exciting literary genre until I read *The Science Fiction Hall of Fame Volume IIA*, containing Campbell's "Who Goes There?," Heinlein's "Universe," Williamson's "With

Folded Hands," Sturgeon's "Baby Is Three," and six other Golden Age masterpieces, over the Christmas holiday in 1981 when I was fourteen. A fortuitous trip to the local thrift store in Lincoln, Nebraska, before school started again yielded collections and novels by Sturgeon, Van Vogt, Asimov, Heinlein, Clarke, Bradbury, and Healy and McComas's *Adventures in Time and Space*. From then on, I was hooked. Soon after I discovered *Analog* magazine and the Science Fiction Book Club.

And at some point that summer I discovered James Gunn. Gunn's story "The Anti-Nuclear Conspiracy" appeared in the August 1982 issue of *Analog*, the third issue of my subscription. In retrospect, it's a minor story, but at the time it was certainly topical, and for a kid growing up during the era of Three Mile Island and in the early years of the Reagan administration it was memorably revelatory. But "New Blood," the first of *The Immortals* stories, which I read that fall in Barry Malzberg's elegiac anthology *The Fifties: The End of Summer*, was of a different order of magnitude. With its compelling narrative about a young drifter who donates what turns out to be regenerative blood and the ensuing hunt to find him by the egotistical financier Weaver and the well-intentioned Dr. Russell Pearce, coupled with Gunn's succinct verisimilitude of hospital practices and procedures, "New Blood" instantly became one of my favorite stories. My youthful science fiction reading was, however, hit-and-miss, not systematic; the books I read depended on what I found in thrift stores and used book shops. Living in the country, I'd lost touch with the benefits of the public library, where, I realized years later, one could dip deeply into the catalog of a favorite writer.

Oddly, I didn't find a copy of *The Immortals*—or anything else by Gunn—until about a decade later. What I did find was a copy of the first volume of Gunn's monumental historical anthology *The Road to Science Fiction* in the paperback rack at the back of my tenth grade English classroom. From it I learned of the historical origins of SF, as Gunn traces early ancestors from Lucian of Samosata to Francis Bacon to Nathaniel Hawthorne and Fitz-James O'Brien, ending the volume with Wells's remarkable story "The Star." I must confess that I didn't get much past Lucian at the time. But I did read Gunn's fourteen-page introduction many times over, and the genre definitions he provides therein became the centerpiece of my high school research paper the following year and again a few years later when I took a college science fiction class with L. David Allen, whose book *Science Fiction Reader's Guide* I'd read in high school, at the University of Nebraska, the class I now teach.

As my early reading in science fiction continued, my next encounter with the work of James Gunn came over the Christmas break of 1983 when his story "End of the World" appeared in the January 1984 issue of *Analog*. That issue included a Jay Kay Klein "Biolog" feature on Gunn, where I learned that Gunn was a Professor of English at the University of Kansas, only two hundred miles south of where I grew up. I might have entertained the possibility of going to KU and studying with Gunn at the time, but never far enough to actually pursue it. A road not (then) taken.

A few years later as an undergraduate I suspect I vaguely considered looking into Gunn's summer programs—a hazy memory suggests that I may have asked Allen about it—but at that time I was a pretty vague young man, and it never occurred to me that I could study science fiction with a well-known writer and scholar, let alone actually speak with or write to him. This was long before the internet simplified communication. Another road not taken. And, lastly, as I recall, upon returning to Lincoln in 1992 after a difficult year and a half in Los Angeles trying to vaguely make it in the film industry, I again contemplated making contact with Gunn and inquiring about graduate studies at KU, after attending a local mini-science fiction convention at the public library during a time when I made some vague attempts to become a science fiction writer. But that was another road not taken. Coincidentally, as you read in my dear friend Christopher McKitterick's foreword, that is precisely the road he took in 1992 when he journeyed from Minnesota to Kansas for Gunn's summer Science Fiction Writers Workshop and then entered KU's graduate program to study with Gunn, eventually to become his assistant and then to succeed him as Director of the Gunn Center for the Study of Science Fiction.

Fortunately, the road to science fiction eventually leads to James Gunn. Jump ahead fifteen years. After spending most of the nineties working in the public library in Lincoln and immersively reading through literary criticism, philosophy, the western canon, modernism and postmodernism, and some science fiction, I went back to graduate school in English, focusing my work, at first, on the interconnections between nineteenth-century British literature and emerging scientific and technological discourses, particularly evolutionary theory. There were a few years where I hardly read any science fiction at all. But once I immersed myself in the poetry, fiction, and essays of the British Romantic period, I began to see affinities that Romanticism has with the ideas and *zeitgeist* of science fiction. After all, Mary Shelley's *Frankenstein* is, as Brian Aldiss has famously claimed and as I have strongly argued elsewhere, the first real science fiction novel. These connections were further extended while taking a class on the fin de siècle, where I focused my seminar paper on the ghost stories of M. R.

James, Arthur Machen, and Algernon Blackwood—Blackwood's work, especially, sits in a weird balance between horror and science fiction—which, in turn, led to another holiday break of immersive reading of the science fiction anthologies in our university library I rediscovered while searching the stacks for Machen, Blackwood, and other late Victorian writers of the fantastic. This immersive reading continued during the spring semester at which time I read Gunn's history of the genre *Alternate Worlds*, and was reminded that he was in nearby Lawrence. Those two hundred miles didn't seem quite as far away as they once did.

I was a star student, slightly older than most of my peers, and the next year I was awarded a year-long fellowship for the third year of my doctoral studies. In addition to dissertation work, I spent the year putting together a collection of stories by the early genre pioneer Miles J. Breuer, *The Man with the Strange Head and Other Early Science Fiction Stories*, who happened to have been a physician in Lincoln in the 1920s and 30s when he was writing for Gernsback's *Amazing*. In those early days of magazine science fiction, the older Breuer had collaborated with a young Jack Williamson on a story called "The Girl from Mars" and a novel called *The Birth of a New Republic*, which had some later influence on Robert A. Heinlein. I had the pleasure of exchanging email with the ninety-eight-year-old Williamson a few months before he died in the fall of 2006 as I got the Breuer project underway. The following spring, I trekked south to the Williamson Library at Eastern New Mexico University in Portales to access Williamson's correspondence with Breuer. On the way back home, I took a slight detour east to Lawrence, Kansas, where I met James Gunn for the first time. Over the next few months I read through a good part of Gunn's oeuvre, re-read *The Road to Science Fiction* anthologies, and that July participated in Gunn's Intensive Summer Institute on the Teaching of Science Fiction. At age forty, I'd doubled-back onto the road to science fiction and I've been happily traveling on that road ever since.

As the years went by and my scholarly work increasingly shifted from nineteenth-century British literature and science to twentieth-century science fiction, and as my connection to James Gunn and the Gunn Center for the Study of Science Fiction grew, I began thinking about doing some scholarly work on Gunn and his contributions to the field. I had already presented a conference paper on the history of science fiction teaching, "Science Fiction Goes to College: Jack Williamson, James Gunn, and the Teaching of Science Fiction," for the 2008 Science Fiction Research Association Conference, held that year in Lawrence. To honor Jim's ninetieth birthday in 2013, I organized a panel including Chris McKitterick, Nate

Williams, and Marleen Barr, celebrating his achievement at the joint Eaton/SFRA conference in Riverside, California. We were pleased that Jim decided to join us. I set up a similar panel, including former students Gary Wolfe, John Kessel, and Kij Johnson for the World Science Fiction Convention in San Antonio that summer, where Jim was Guest of Honor. Meanwhile, I signed a contract with the University of Illinois Press to write a book on Gunn's longtime friend and associate Frederik Pohl for their new *Modern Masters of Science Fiction* series. James Gunn was instrumental in helping me connect with Pohl, whom I had met only briefly the last two times he came to Lawrence for the Campbell Conference, and I was able to interview Fred and his wife Betty Hull in his Chicago-area home a few months before he died. Betty has since become a treasured friend. As the Pohl project neared completion in the summer of 2014, Chris McKitterick and Kij Johnson, the Gunn Center's associate director, invited me to read from the work-in-progress at that year's Campbell Conference, and Chris and I began talking about doing a collaborative book on Jim. Once the Pohl book had gone to press, I began putting together a proposal, and needless to say I was thrilled when series editor Donald Palumbo and the folks at McFarland responded with enthusiasm. Over the course of the next year and a half, I immersed myself in the works of James Gunn and took a number of trips to Lawrence to pour through the Gunn papers at the Kenneth Spencer Research Library and Jim's personal files at his home and campus office. This included many delightful hours conversing with Jim at his home where he graciously invited me to stay during my visits. Admittedly, being Jim Gunn's houseguest is a memory I will treasure for the rest of my life. Due to the heavy demands Chris has as Director of the Gunn Center and his devotion to the summer writing workshops founded by Gunn, and because of my own obsessive tendencies when it comes to literary analysis, Chris's role in this project was reduced to his beautifully rendered foreword, but his enthusiasm and encouragement along the way has been greatly appreciated.

The result is what you have here. This is the first full-length critical study of the science fiction of James Gunn, one of the major figures who shaped the field of science fiction through his writing, his teaching, and his scholarship. I begin with a biographical chapter that details Gunn's early development as a science fiction reader—he saw H. G. Wells speak in Kansas City at age fourteen in 1937—his formative education, and his experiences during World War II. Interested readers can find more details of Gunn's early years in his memoir, which McFarland will also publish. I then examine Gunn's post-war college experience, his early years as a writer, and his experiences working for Western Printing and the Dell paperback line. The Gunn archival material at the Spencer Library, including correspondence with Isaac Asimov, Frederik Pohl, Robert Sheckley, Theodore Sturgeon, Jack Williamson, and others, places Gunn within the context of the professionalization of the field in the early 1950s when he emerged as a writer and when he made one of the first forays into the field of academic science fiction criticism with his master's thesis *Modern Science Fiction: A Critical Analysis*, part of which was published in the pulp science fiction magazine *Dynamic* in 1953–54. The biographical sketch goes on to trace Gunn's writing career during the fifties and sixties till the present, his experiences as a university administrator at the University of Kansas, and his later experiences since the 1970s as one of the key founders of the teaching of science fiction and of the genre's now bountiful body of literary criticism.

Chapters Two through Five provide detailed analysis and commentary on Gunn's fiction and frame this work within the context of Gunn's life experiences, his growing involvement with the science fiction community of writers and fans (and later scholars), the ongoing megatext of science fiction, and the social, political, and cultural contexts of the times. Chapter Two considers Gunn's early short stories, including his first major work, the novella "Breaking Point," and the classic psi novella "The Reluctant Witch." The chapter concludes with detailed readings of his first two novels, the space operas *This Fortress World* and *Star Bridge*, his extraordinary collaborative novel with Jack Williamson. Chapter Three examines Gunn's major works of social science fiction from the 1950s, including *The Joy Makers*, *Station in Space*, and *The Immortals*, and a number of stories illustrative of the "*Galaxy*-school," culminating in a discussion of Gunn's fierce warning of political demagoguery *The Burning*. Chapter Four explores Gunn's return to science fiction after a decade in university administration, with detailed analysis of his classic alien-contact novel *The Listeners*, his scintillating near-future academic satire *Kampus*, the proto-cyberpunk novel *The Dreamers*, and the *Crisis!* sequence of stories from *Analog*. Chapter Five looks at Gunn's fiction following his official retirement from the University of Kansas in 1993 (although he continued his daily trek to his campus office for nearly twenty years thereafter), including the *Star Trek* novel *The Joy Machine*, based on an unproduced script written by Gunn's longtime friend Theodore Sturgeon; *The Millennium Blues*, Gunn's underappreciated attempt at a mainstream novel with science fictional overtones; *Gift from the Stars*, in part a response to Carl Sagan's *Contact*, which itself had been influenced by *The Listeners*; and the recent *Tran-*

scendental trilogy, culminating in an analysis of the third volume *Transformation*, which should be out from TOR about the time this study is published. I end this study with a brief overview of Gunn's contributions to the academic study and criticism of the science fiction genre.

I hope that this study expands readers' understanding and appreciation of the life, career, and work of James Gunn, a man who has contributed so much to the field he has devoted his life to. Further, I hope readers find it a useful addition to their overall understanding of the historical development of the science fiction genre. James Gunn's vision that science fiction can serve a positive purpose in our troubled world, that we *can* "save the world through science fiction," is not only inspirational, it is a call to action. A call to work out our problems, here on Earth and beyond, and to avoid the catastrophes he warns us of in his dystopian nightmares, such as *The Joy Makers*, *The Immortals*, and *Kampus*. These texts, and Gunn's other fiction, *teach* us: teach us that there are potential consequences to technological innovation; teach us to avoid the apocalyptic scenarios that come when our dreams turn into nightmares; teach us to envision a better world; teach us to be better people. In his foreword, Chris McKitterick argues that James Gunn is "science fiction's dad," alluding to H. G. Wells's designation as science fiction's father. But I would add that James Gunn, Jim, is not only "dad" to many of us, he is also "teacher." Gunn's role as teacher has somewhat overshadowed the importance of his fiction. In what follows in this study, I hope to convey the significance of his body of work to the overall history of science fiction and to introduce (or reintroduce) readers to the thought-provoking pleasures of James Gunn's science fictional imagination.

One

James Gunn: A Life in Science Fiction

Having just celebrated his ninety-third birthday at the time of this writing, James Gunn is still going strong and contributing to the field of science fiction in each of the three areas in which he has been a major and foundational contributor. He's just completed *Transformation*, the third novel in his latest series, and it will be published in 2017. As I write, he's been working with participants in the short story group at the Summer Speculative Fiction workshops at the University of Kansas and is a guest at a writers' retreat in Gunnison, Colorado, where he was presented with the *Writing the Rockies* Lifetime Achievement Award. He continues to regularly peer review academic manuscripts and he'll be actively taking part at the 74th World Science Fiction Convention in Kansas City. Gunn is a member of First Fandom and his formative experiences in SF date to that era when science fiction became a significant part of American culture.

James Edwin Gunn was born in Kansas City in the family home at 3416 East 10th Street on July 12, 1923, the second son of J. Wayne and Elsie Gunn. His brother Richard was just nineteen months older and the two brothers were very close. It was a happy childhood for both boys. Upon Richard's death in 2002, his estate endowed the J. Wayne and Elsie Gunn Center for the Study of Science Fiction at the University of Kansas in honor of their parents. Another Kansas City native, Robert A. Heinlein, grew up in a house four miles from the Gunn home. Heinlein turned sixteen five days before Gunn's birth, although he spent the entire month of July in 1923 hiking in Colorado with his friend Stanley Moise.[1] Interested readers can find Heinlein's vivid recreation of the Kansas City of the era in his final novel *To Sail Beyond the Sunset*.[2]

While growing up, Gunn was influenced by the literary and political ambitions of his uncle John, who wrote for *The Appeal to Reason*, a socialist newspaper published in the small town of Girard, Kansas, where Gunn's grandparents lived. At its peak, *The Appeal* mailed out half a million copies a week. In an anthology of *Appeal* articles, *"Yours for the Revolution": The Appeal to Reason, 1895–1922*, a number of John Gunn's contributions are included.³ While writing for *The Appeal*, John Gunn met Emanuel Julius (later Haldeman-Julius), who would launch the *Little Blue Books*, low-priced, staple-bound paperback books intended to bring great works of literature and philosophy to the working class. John became Haldeman-Julius's best friend and worked as an editor and writer on the *Little Blue Books* for many years. Gunn has his uncle's collection of *Little Blue Books* in his home library.

Like many science fiction writers, notably Frederik Pohl, Raymond Palmer, Robert Silverberg, and Jack Williamson,⁴ James Gunn experienced a childhood illness, contracting scarlet fever during his kindergarten year, causing him to miss the entire spring semester,⁵ and this contributed to Gunn becoming a reader. As Gunn reflects, "I remember much of my childhood spent with books, and many of the great moments I remember were found in books."⁶ Gunn's first major reading discovery was the Frank Merriwell adventures, a popular series about a robust Yale student and sportsman that his father had tucked away in a closet.⁷ Aside from the bout with scarlet fever, Gunn was a relatively healthy and active child, spending his time, when not reading, playing games and sports with his brother and neighborhood children. He enjoyed school, but also looked forward to the holidays and the summers.

It seems like whenever science fiction people (fans, writers, editors, scholars, etc.) get together, the conversation swings around to the question: when did you first discover science fiction? Many of Gunn's contemporaries have described that moment in their autobiographical writings. Arthur C. Clarke's memoir, *Astounding Days*, begins with fond reminiscences of the March 1930 issue of *Astounding Stories* and the November 1928 issue of *Amazing Stories*, which initiated him into the genre as a youngster.⁸ For Jack Williamson, it was the November 1926 issue of *Amazing* that a friend loaned to him in Portales, New Mexico.⁹ Frederik Pohl's grand discovery was the Summer 1930 issue of *Wonder Stories Quarterly* at age ten.¹⁰ On many occasions, Isaac Asimov delighted in telling the story about how he talked his father into letting him read issues of *Amazing* and *Science Wonder Stories* in the family's candy store in 1929.¹¹

Gunn's experience was equally revelatory. His road to science fiction began with Tarzan. As he has written recently in a foreword to a study of

Burroughs' work, "I couldn't believe my good fortune. In the back closet of my grandmother's house in the small, southeastern Kansas town of Girard, I came upon a stack of books bound, as I recall, in green cloth. I was seven or eight probably—maybe as young as six.... They had been consigned to the oblivion of the closet and the dismissal of being stacked and not shelved, but my heart beat faster as I picked up one of them and began to read. Probably it was *Tarzan of the Apes*; under it were half a dozen, maybe more, of Tarzan's later adventures. One by one I took them from their hiding place and home with me to Kansas City."[12] For Gunn, Tarzan was "my magic door into the world of popular imagination."[13] Gunn's development as a science fiction reader expanded further when he was ten years old and his father brought home the second issue of the new Hero Pulp *Doc Savage*, featuring a novel called *Quest of the Spider*. In *Cheap Thrills*, Ron Goulart calls *Doc Savage* "Frank Merriwell and his chums updated."[14] The Hero Pulps combined the do-gooder hero aesthetic epitomized by Frank Merriwell with the super-science inventor-hero found in science fiction like "Doc" Smith's Seaton and Crane and John W. Campbell's Arcot, Morey, and Wade. Henceforward, Gunn was a constant reader of the Hero Pulps—until he graduated to the science fiction magazines—devouring every issue of *Doc Savage, The Shadow, The Spider, Operator #5*, and *G-8 and His Flying Aces* that came his way. *Doc Savage* was the one he liked best and he still maintains a complete collection of the paperback reprints in his home library.

A year later, when Gunn was old enough to take the bus to downtown Kansas City, he discovered a used magazine store called Andy's, where he found such magazines as *Amazing Stories, Wonder Stories*, and *Astounding Stories of Super-Science*: "I was immediately enthralled and gladly traded two of my hero pulps for one of this new breed of pulp magazine with stories as filled with adventure as the others but offering something that they had little of: not only science but ideas, speculation and what Sam Moskowitz later called the 'sense of wonder,' a feeling of awe at scope and concept and possibilities that I had never before considered."[15] This parallels Robert Silverberg's later experiences as a teenager in 1950 in a similar store in Brooklyn, which he describes as his "Aladdin's Cave."[16] From there, Gunn sought out books in the public library in search of more stories that conveyed that experience of wonder. There he found H.G. Wells, Jules Verne, and Rider Haggard, a pattern of discovery paralleling that of many of his contemporaries, such as Frederik Pohl.[17] As he grew into his teens, Gunn also was impacted by works of contemporary literature, especially the novels of Thomas Wolfe, Hemingway, Raymond Chandler and Dashiell Hammett.

Later, when Gunn was in high school, he "became entranced in 1939 by a new magazine that came out, *Famous Fantastic Mysteries*."[18] It is interesting that Gunn's early influences were the Hero Pulps and the reprint magazine *FFM*, since these magazines often stood on the border between science fiction and fantasy, and in his later theoretical work Gunn carefully distinguishes the difference between the two. Nevertheless, from this early reading we can deduce Gunn's interest in the history and origins of the science fiction field as it emerged from a broader tradition of the fantastic. Indeed, that first issue of *FFM* contained A. Merritt's "The Moon Pool," which Gunn included in his monumental historical teaching anthology *The Road to Science Fiction*.

In 1937, Gunn had one of those formative experiences that can shape the life of a writer. That fall his Uncle John took him and Richard to see H.G. Wells, who was speaking in downtown Kansas City during his American lecture tour. Wells mentions his stop in Kansas City in an appendix article titled "The Fall in America, 1937" in his essay collection *World Brain*—"Kansas City looked amazingly fine and handsome"[19]—and this essay appears to be a revision of a piece titled "New Americans" in the February 5, 1938 (in *World Brain* it's wrongly dated as January 28) issue of *Collier's*. In the *Collier's* version, Wells wrote that he was impressed by the youth he encountered: "I found a new generation, alert and interrogative.... They seem to be facing the American problem in something like its real distinctness and complexity."[20] That generation of youth would include Gunn and his fellows of the generation of science fiction writers of the Golden Age. For Gunn, seeing Wells in person was both monumental and deflating: "I remember that the great man (and founding father of the genre to which I would devote much of my life) was short and stout and spoke in a squeaky, high-pitched voice, but I was impressed anyway and pushed forward (I was fourteen) to shake his hand as he made his way out through the crowd. But he brushed past me without noticing."[21]

John Kessel, who was Gunn's student in the 1970s, obliquely captures some of Gunn's experience in his classic story "Buffalo." In the story, Kessel imagines an encounter between his father, Jack Kessel, a young man from Buffalo, New York, working at a CCC camp in Washington, D.C., in 1934, and Wells, his "spiritual" father as the foundational figure of SF, in Washington for his first visit with President Roosevelt to discuss his notion of an "'Open Conspiracy' of rational thinkers that would culminate in a world socialist state."[22] The story is a beautiful reflection on Kessel's origins, family and professional, and although not directly alluded to in the story, Gunn (as Kessel has himself told me), Kessel's third father-figure, and his experience encountering Wells in 1937, lurks in the background of the story.

Gunn entered high school soon after seeing Wells, attending Northeast High School where he excelled as a student, especially in English. It was during high school that Gunn learned touch-typing, "a skill that has been more important in my career than any other I may have learned. It was as liberating as learning to read."[23] When he graduated, Gunn was the top male student out of a class of five hundred and gave a commencement address, his first try at public speaking, in the Municipal Auditorium. As a child Gunn had difficulty with a stammer and he reflects back on those speech difficulties in his memoir: "There is some irony in the fact that I became something of a public speaker in my adult years, speaking to student, faculty, and alumni gatherings at KU and overseas for the U.S. Information Agency in Yugoslavia, Romania, Poland, Denmark, Sweden, and the Soviet Union in Europe, in Iceland, and in Japan, Taiwan, and Singapore in the Far East. And I have been paid as much as $6,500 to lecture in the U.S."[24] Those who know Gunn as a teacher and scholar can attest to his powerful and eloquent speaking voice.

Gunn finished high school in 1940 and that fall attended Kansas City, Missouri, Junior College, with the ambition of becoming an engineer. But he quickly learned that he didn't have the aptitude for geometry and chemistry that is essential for engineering. Instead, he excelled at English, and when he transferred across the river to Kansas City, Kansas, Junior College the following year, he focused on humanities courses. While Gunn was enrolled at KCKJC, the Japanese bombed Pearl Harbor on December 7, 1941. The following summer Gunn enlisted in the Navy Air Corps, with a deferment until after he completed his junior year. He spent that year as a student at the University of Kansas in Lawrence, and although Lawrence was a mere forty miles from Kansas City, this was the first time that Gunn had been away from home. For Gunn, that first year in Lawrence was "one of the great years of my life."[25] The landscape between the two cities—river valley, followed by rolling hills, and then flat plains—was to become a central image in much of Gunn's later work. At the time, the University of Kansas had only 4,000 students (now enrollments are around 30,000) and the city of Lawrence was a modest 15,000 (now Lawrence is slightly over 90,000). During that first year at KU, Gunn got involved with the student paper the *University Daily Kansan*, writing columns and feature stories.

Gunn's university experience was cut short as he had to fulfill his commitment to the Navy. By May 1943 the United States was fully mobilized and young men were being shuttled from place to place across the country for training. Gunn went through basic training at Cornell College in Mount Vernon, Iowa, then flight training in Las Vegas, New Mexico, and from there to Athens, Georgia, where at a drug store he discovered Donald Wollheim's *Pocket Book of Science-Fiction*, which he repeatedly read throughout the war.[26] Following Athens, Gunn went to the Naval Air Station in Memphis for pilot training. He soon washed out as a navy pilot, in part due to an absence of wind on the day of his test flight; it had been gusty all spring during his lessons. In retrospect, he was glad it worked out that way: "After a month in Memphis I was shipped off for reassignment to the Great Lakes Naval Station north of Chicago. It was another turning point in my life: my wartime experience would have been far different if I had completed pilot training."[27] From the Great Lakes, Gunn then transferred to Asbury Park, New Jersey, for pre-midshipman school and then was sent to Notre Dame University in South Bend, Indiana, for midshipman's training. He was next assigned to Boulder, Colorado, for intensive Japanese language courses; the idea being that there would be a need for Americans who could read and speak Japanese as the war continued. Although Gunn did not become fluent in Japanese, he learned valuable lessons about intensive education, which would later serve when he developed the Intensive Summer Institute for the Teaching of Science Fiction at the University of Kansas.[28] Those who have taken Gunn's Summer Institute, which covers as many as twenty-five novels in those three weeks, can attest to the value of such a fully immersive learning experience. From Boulder he went to Stillwater, Oklahoma, some months after his later colleagues Frederik Pohl and Jack Williamson were in weather training at nearby Enid. Gunn's military merry-go-round next sent him to Miami for Advanced Line Officers Training, where he was stationed when news of the atomic bomb dropped on Hiroshima was announced. Because he was a science fiction reader, Gunn understood what the bomb meant: "I had knowledge not shared by my fellows; but I also had special apprehensions. Some of the stories had suggested that the atom bomb might set off a chain reaction in the Earth's crust, and I wondered if something like this had happened how long it would take for the reaction to reach the United States."[29] Soon the fighting ended and though Gunn had bounced from one stateside training facility after another during the hostilities, he would serve overseas in the aftermath. He received orders to report to San Francisco for duty in the Pacific, first at Guam and then on Truk Island, where he was assigned to be adjutant to the commanding general. Gunn spent eight months in the Pacific, returning stateside in

June 1946. He was a dutiful soldier in the office, where he managed the mail, among other duties, and he had an aptitude for managerial and administrative work, skills which would serve him well later when he took an administrative post at the University of Kansas. Gunn chuckles at the fact that he only broke protocol once while handling the mail: "My only infraction was to keep a copy of *Astounding* that had come to a sailor who had been returned to the States. That copy brought back so many great reading experiences that I couldn't bring myself to let go of it, so I told myself it probably would have gotten lost in the mail anyway."[30] Since Gunn left Truk in late May 1946, receiving his discharge in San Francisco that June, it is possible that the issue at hand was perhaps the August 1945 issue containing the first installment of Van Vogt's *The World of Null-A* or the November 1945 issue launching Asimov's two-part *Foundation* novella *The Mule*, although Gunn does not recall the specific issue.[31] Both works would later become central to Gunn's teaching and scholarship.

Once discharged in San Francisco Gunn traveled by train to Los Angeles, before heading home to Kansas City. Soon after, he made the short trip to Lawrence to look into re-enrolling at the university, and was immediately offered an editorial position at the *Daily Kansan*. This offer had to be approved by the paper's student board, which was chaired by a young woman named Jane Anderson. As Jane Anderson was soon to become Mrs. Gunn, this was a significant moment in Gunn's life.[32]

Gunn returned to the University of Kansas for the fall semester 1946, taking advantage of the funding provided by the G.I. Bill. He began dating Jane Anderson, who was from the small town of Osborne in the central part of the state; Jane was entering her senior year studying journalism: "I asked Jane Anderson if she'd like to go with me to a play. It was a couple of months into the semester, and Jane said later that she'd been sitting behind me in Law of the Press trying to send me a mental message." (Shades of Gunn's psi-powers story "The Reluctant Witch"?) As Gunn further reflects, "It was not much of a date. The play, as I recall, was a comedy, and afterwards I took Jane to the bus stop and said I had to go back to the news room and write a review. But it was the beginning of a romance that would culminate in a wedding in KU's Danforth Chapel on February 6, right after finals."[33] Jane and Jim would live happily together for the next sixty-five years until Jane's death in 2012.

Gunn thrived at college, becoming an active member of the student community and honing his writing skills in journalism and in playwriting. The most important class Gunn took during the fall semester was a playwriting class with Allen Crafton, who had built the KU theater program and had written a number of books on acting, directing, and stage production. For the final project students wrote a play. Perhaps inspired by the Yuletide time of year, Gunn wrote a daring play called *Thy Kingdom Come*: "It was about the second coming of Christ, who is convinced to run for president, but everyone turns against him and he is crucified again. My idea was that Christ's doctrine was too extreme for those who call themselves Christians."[34] *Thy Kingdom Come* was produced during the spring 1947 semester. Gunn further honed his skills as a writer during that year in Lawrence and got his first taste of writing for pay by selling an article about Allen Crafton and a sonnet to the *Kansas City Star*, the same paper that nurtured the early writing of Ernest Hemingway, for $15 and $10, respectively.

One of Gunn's close friends during this second period at KU was Reverdy "Rev" Mullins, a slightly older, worldly air force pilot who had served in the Aleutian Islands. Gunn would transform Rev into Rev McMillen, the heroic pilot who "makes" the first orbit of Earth in the story "The Cave of Night." Gunn and the other returning veterans took their college work seriously and, like Gunn, many of them quickly moved into active professional lives soon after graduation. As Gunn sums it up, "The returning veterans and the G.I. Bill transformed higher education in many ways. They not only contributed to doubling the enrollment, they brought a new seriousness and an urgency about getting on."[35]

After finishing his B.S. in Journalism in the spring of 1947, Gunn was accepted into the playwriting graduate program at Northwestern University in Evanston, Illinois. On the train to Evanston that summer, Gunn immersed himself in the best science fiction published during the war years, "whiling away the day-time trip by reading copies of the two great postwar anthologies, Healy and McComas's *Adventures in Time and Space* and Groff Conklin's *The Best of Science Fiction*."[36] Spending most of his time learning stagecraft and painting sets instead of writing, Gunn decided that he'd had enough after just two quarters at Northwestern, although he did take a valuable course in radio writing. With the possibilities of radio writing in mind and since neither he nor Jane looked forward to the prospects of another Chicago winter, they packed up and returned to Kansas City, taking a small "garret" attic apartment where Gunn embarked on a plan to write radio dramas on Kansas City history for local radio. No station was interested, but the radio plays did serve as good practice for when Gunn began writing science fiction stories, and, indeed, when he wrote the first version in script form of his first major novella "Breaking Point." Gunn's curiosity about the possibilities of radio writing may have been stimulated by his reading of Frederic Wakeman's 1946 novel *The Hucksters* and the Clark Gable film the following year.

Despite this setback, Gunn didn't give up on his plans to make it as a writer. So he turned to science fiction and began work on his first stories. The first was a story called "Paradox," which he completed in the summer of 1948 and sent to John W. Campbell at *Astounding*. Campbell promptly rejected it, but sent an encouraging letter asking Gunn to send more stories. Undeterred, Gunn sent the story to other magazines and was delighted to receive an acceptance letter from Sam Merwin, Jr., the editor of *Thrilling Wonder Stories*, in late July. Gunn reflects that it was "a letter that changed my life: Merwin said he liked my story and would pay me eighty dollars for it."[37]

This first sale stimulated Gunn to start "writing stories as fast as I could."[38] After a little over a year of freelancing he had written eleven stories, ten of which would find publication in the next few years, listed here in order of composition: "Paradox" (*Thrilling Wonder* October 1949), "Mask of Peace" (*Future* September 1951), "Slaves of Venus"—Gunn's more sober original title, "Freedom, Inc." is much better—(*Planet Stories* September 1952), "Communications" (*Startling* September 1949), "Slave Psychology" (*Future* January 1951), "These Things Are Sirius" (*Thrilling Wonder* August 1951), "The Sun Came Up Last Night" (*Science Fiction Quarterly* August 1951), "Open Warfare" (*Galaxy* May 1954, in a heavily revised version), "Private Enterprise" (*Astounding* July 1950), and "The Man with Common Sense" (*Amazing* July 1950). The only one that didn't sell was his fourth story, "Sane Asylum," an ambitious novelette that Gunn first tried to sell to mainstream fiction magazines; it eventually appeared in the first of *The Unpublished Gunn* booklets in 1992. These early stories appeared under the byline Edwin James because Gunn wanted to preserve his own name for other writing. Not until 1952, when his story "The Misogynist" appeared in *Galaxy*, did Gunn put his own name on his stories.

Gunn admits that most of his early stories were "competently written but derived largely from my reading of science fiction."[39] It was not until later that Gunn would draw inspiration from other sources, including his observations of contemporary society and his university experience, and truly find his own voice within the field. Here Gunn raises an interesting point about the nature of science fiction: much science fiction is in dialogue with other stories, with the author's immersive reading in the genre. This is the great conversation that is science fiction; illustrated much later—and conspicuously—in Gunn's own work when Carl Sagan was inspired by Gunn's *The Listeners* (which was itself inspired by Sagan's early writings on extraterrestrial intelligence) for his bestselling novel *Contact*, to which Gunn responds in his novel *Gift from the Stars*.

In the spring of 1949 Gunn also forged a connection with Lloyd Smith, editorial director at Western Printing & Lithographing of Racine, Wisconsin, a printing company that produced Dell paperbacks and comic books. Smith had worked in Girard with Uncle John for the Haldeman-Julius *Little Blue Books* and, likely prompted by John, was sounding Gunn out about doing some freelance work for Dell. Smith asked Gunn to write him about his background and said he would send any "fantasy fiction" manuscripts Gunn's way for review, although Dell, at the time, wasn't interested in getting into the science fiction/fantasy field. Smith also offered Gunn the opportunity to write scenarios for the *Dick Tracy Monthly* comic book.[40] Gunn's first scenario, "Dick Tracy and the Moon Rocket," was too much science fiction for editor Albert Stoffel, but Stoffel did accept Gunn's story involving a bubble gum chewing con artist: "I came up with something I called 'Dick Tracy and the Restless Swindler.' I had noticed that the chief variable in the comic books was some identifying characteristic for the villain of the month. I had him blow bubblegum. Western published it as 'Dick Tracy and Bubbles,' and paid me $100."[41] Oddly, Stoffel was flabbergasted by the idea of a grown man chewing bubble gum—"No adult in his right mind would chew bubble gum for enjoyment or recreation—I've got a couple of kids who chew it—and I know!"[42]—but nonetheless took the story. Gunn's scenario was published in the December 1949 issue. In Gunn's archives, there are notes for a number of other scenarios he pitched to Stoffel, including one called "Dick Tracy and the Case of the Staring Eyes," which Stoffel promptly rejected. Interestingly, Stoffel comments that "the golf course chase is not a bad angle. However, it does not carry the rest of the story."[43] A few months earlier Gunn had completed the first version of the robot-golf story later published in *Galaxy* as "Open Warfare." But Stoffel was a tough sell and before Gunn could submit any more scenarios, Stoffel informed him that *Dick Tracy Monthly* was being discontinued. Gunn's story appeared in the final Dell issue, although the comic was soon resurrected by Harvey Comics and ran for another decade. The first instance, as Gunn quips, that he helped kill a magazine.

As this first year of full-time writing concluded, Gunn soon learned that freelance writing wasn't particularly lucrative, and more so, at a penny a word, it was hardly enough income to support a family. And a family was on its way, as Jane was expecting their first child. So Gunn decided to take another shot at graduate school. He once again enrolled at the University of Kansas in the summer of 1949 in the English department "just in time for a summer Writers' Workshop and my first introduction to the literary culture."[44] One of his classmates was Evan S. Connell, who later became famous for his novel *Mr. and Mrs. Bridge.* But while Connell would later find his place in the world of literary fiction, Gunn was the one who was already making a mark in his chosen field of science fiction. Indeed, as Gunn's published stories began to appear on the newsstands that fall, he soon discovered that he "was the only graduate student in English who was a published author."[45] Gunn would focus on the developing science fiction genre as the subject for his Master's Thesis, which would be one of the first academic studies of the genre accepted for an advanced degree. Gunn had written an article for the *Kansas City Star* about the history of science fiction during his freelance year, which "earned me a thank-you letter from Hugo Gernsback and got me a place on his Christmas-card list,"[46] which had stimulated his thinking about the budding genre's history.

Once again Gunn took to his college work with enthusiasm—and to fatherhood: his first son Christopher, "Kit," was born in September as the fall semester got underway. Gunn recalls studying "Chaucer while jiggling his bassinet with my foot and Old English while rocking him."[47] After taking a course on Modern Drama, taught by Carroll Edwards, the founder of the journal *Modern Drama,* Gunn wrote a science fiction play titled "Breaking Point" for an independent study project, with the idea that he could later turn the play into a marketable story. Over the summer of 1950 he revised the play into a short novel and sent it to Horace Gold who had just launched a new magazine called *Galaxy.* Gold called Gunn at home and said that he liked "Breaking Point" but thought it was too long, and he wanted Theodore Sturgeon to cut it down. In truth, as Sturgeon told Gunn later, Gold wanted Sturgeon to do a complete rewrite. This first contact with Gold was Gunn's gateway into the brotherhood of science fiction writers: not only did it trigger correspondence with Gold and Sturgeon, but Gold also told Fred Pohl about the story, which led to a letter from Pohl offering to become Gunn's agent. Hence the beginnings of a robust professional relationship with Gold and long friendships with Sturgeon and Pohl.

Only a few days after Gunn first mailed "Breaking Point" to Gold, he received another letter from Lloyd Smith at Western Printing. Smith asked if Gunn was interested in doing some work for Western "in the nature of some reading research."[48] The game had changed and the publisher was now interested in plunging into the science fiction market. Smith wanted to see if Gunn was interested in reviewing science fiction manuscripts under consideration for Dell paperbacks. On October 5, Smith sent Gunn the manuscript of Isaac Asimov's *Pebble in the Sky* and asked for a reader's report that gave Gunn's assessment, told him something about the plot, and whether he thought it would have wide enough appeal for "200,000 or 300,000 readers."[49] If Gunn produced a satisfactory review, then they would make an arrangement by which Gunn would review subsequent manuscripts for $5 per report. Smith also requested that Gunn be on the lookout for SF stories and novellas, as they were considering trying the anthology market. Gunn sent in his report the following week. The report indicates a keen analytical mind, a savvy understanding of the as yet, but soon to be, booming science fiction paperback marketplace, and a discerning critical approach:

> First, as to Isaac Asimov's *Pebble in the Sky*, I would say that Asimov is one of the best writers in the science fiction field and in one of the higher (if not, however, the highest) brackets of popularity.... The problem of publishing *Pebble in the Sky* has points on both sides. The novel is one of the most mature expressions yet written within the field itself (excluding from consideration such basically science fiction books as Stewart's *Earth Abides* and Orwell's *1984*).... On the other hand are facts which seem to argue against the publication of the novel at this time, although this may be a misinterpretation on my part of the facts and psychology of publishing and selling. The original edition of *Pebble*, for instance, was published only a year or so ago. The edition you sent me seems to be a dollar reprint. In addition, in what seems to me a somewhat unusual procedure, *Pebble* did not appear first in magazine form as most science fiction works do.[50]

Although Gunn appears to advise caution here with regard to Asimov's novel, he is less circumspect about the possibilities of science fiction as a paperback venture:

> As for the future of science fiction itself, it seems from my strictly non-professional viewpoint that its expansion has passed the stage where it could be termed a fad and that it will go on to become a solid, popular, worthwhile addition to the literary field.... Science fiction, it seems to me, satisfies a basic need of today.... Science fiction, in one of its attributes, seeks to orient the only too confused citizen in the ever-expanding, ever more baffling, technological, scientific, philosophic, ethical, social world of today and tomorrow, the entire gamut of the world's communications facilities have failed to fulfill. Its scope, moreover, is as limitless as the universe, as unbounded as the human imagination, and it is becoming increasingly more consciously literate, more mature, more aware of its own possibilities.[51]

Notably, Gunn mentions in the same letter having written the first half of his thesis the previous spring, and his vision for the possibilities of science fiction and its contributions to culture and thought, which he has championed for over sixty-five years, are apparent in the above assessment.

Ultimately, Dell passed on Asimov's novel, and it didn't see paperback publication until Bantam brought it out in 1957. As *Pebble in the Sky*, and Asimov's work in general, has sold in the millions over the years, this was, perhaps, an unwise decision. For his part, Gunn suggested they consider Van Vogt's *Slan* instead, which Dell did end up publishing in paperback in 1953. The correspondence between Gunn and Smith provide a fascinating glimpse into how science fiction became part of the developing paperback industry in the early 1950s. Dell's caution is telling here. A number of the books Gunn recommended were to become successful ventures for other firms.

Throughout his second year in graduate school Gunn did a number of reports for Dell, not just limited to books in the science fiction field. In a letter dating from January 1951, Smith mentions to Gunn an idea to bring out ten cent pocket editions. Later, when he was working in the Western offices in Racine, Gunn edited an edition of Heinlein's "Universe" for this series. In that same letter, Smith sent Gunn three more books for commentary: Edgar Rice Burroughs' *Pirates of Venus*, Anthony Boucher's *Rocket to the Morgue*, and A. E. Van Vogt's *The Voyage of the Space Beagle*. The following month, Smith proposed that Gunn send him monthly reports on what's happening in the science fiction field for an additional $10 a month. A few days later Gunn replied with what is essentially an application letter. Gunn soon heard back from Smith telling him that they would likely have an editorial position in Racine waiting for him in June, after graduation, and a few days later sent another letter inviting Gunn to come to Racine for a job interview. Gunn interviewed in Racine on March 28 and was offered a position via letter the following day, with plans for him to start in June as a junior editor.

Gunn also heard from Don Ward, who was editing *Zane Grey's Western Magazine*, published by Dell, and working on the paperback line. Ward had been trying to get Smith to consider science fiction for years and had managed to talk him into two H.G. Wells novels and an anthology, *Invasion from Mars: Interplanetary Stories*, "selected" by Orson Welles (Ward did the compiling).[52] In his first letter, Ward confirmed that Heinlein's "Universe" was being planned as a ten cent paperback. Gunn's monthly reports were also going to Ward, and in his reply to Ward's letter, Gunn's assessment of Ray Bradbury, whose novella "The Fireman" (the basis of *Fahrenheit 451*) had just appeared in *Galaxy*, is priceless: "The burning of the books stories (which includes his novelette in *Galaxy*, 'The Fireman') go too far in their symbolism and the characters become allegorical figures and the stories allegorical fantasy—it is Bradbury's style carried too far. Bradbury, also, it seems to me, has a rather limited popular appeal."[53]

Ward was also a friend of Theodore Sturgeon, who had written some stories for *Zane Grey's*, and who was, presumably, at work on making the cuts on "Breaking Point" at this time. But Gunn hadn't heard anything from Gold for some time and expressed his frustration to Ward: "I was interested to learn that Ted Sturgeon was a friend of yours. Coincidentally, he is (or is supposed to be) doing a shortening job on a short novel of mine that *Galaxy* has contracted for. It has been, however, six months since Gold called me about the story in the first place and suggested that Sturgeon do it, and two or three months since Sturgeon wrote me requesting permission and apologizing for the delay. But, no check; I suppose that there has been some sort of delay on Sturgeon's part. If he doesn't get going on the job he said would take no more than a week, he's likely to be no friend of mine."[54] Ward wrote back with some information about Sturgeon's situation: "Ted Sturgeon's got a full-time job circulation-promoting for *Time*, writes only in spare time now; Gold shouldn't have asked him, probably; he shouldn't have consented."[55] Sturgeon and Gunn were, of course, to become treasured friends in later years; Sturgeon participated in Gunn's summer courses until his death in 1985 and the University of Kansas is now the repository of the Sturgeon papers.

A month later, after Gunn's job interview, Ward wrote that Heinlein was too busy to write an introduction for "Universe" and that the task would be Gunn's instead, once he arrived in Racine. Not allowing for his degree completion to get in the way of his new editorial job, Gunn wrote the "Universe" introduction during the week of his oral exams. "Universe" is one of the quintessential SF classics of "Conceptual Breakthrough," a term developed by Peter Nicholls to describe stories in which a protagonist questions the reality of their world and experiences a paradigm-shifting revelation when it proves their insular experience is part of a much greater reality.[56] In this early piece of criticism, Gunn makes headway towards Nicholls's later formulation of Conceptual Breakthrough:

> "Universe" describes how these men look at their circumstances and how a unified explanation of things is built up to satisfy their need for security and stability ... "Universe," for instance, describes the way truth is lost and the way it is regained. For it is not the truth about the nature of the universe we want as much as an explanation that satisfies our need for order and peace and, occasionally, beauty.... But sometimes a world does not know when it is ready for a new view of the universe; sometimes it takes a single man to blast aside the old conventions. Galileo was such a man, insisting against the established view of the Church, that

it was the earth that moved and not the sun and the stars.... And, finally, are we sure that our view of the universe is the final truth? Or shall we, too, like Hugh, step out onto the "Captain's Veranda" and see—the stars?[57]

Ward was a good mentor for Gunn, prior to his coming to Racine and once he got there, coaching him on the expectations of the mass paperback marketplace. On April 17, Ward wrote Gunn with some suggestions about how he should evaluate the marketability of a particular work. Interestingly, the story under discussion was Sturgeon's novella "Maturity." Ward advised Gunn "to depart from the scholarly viewpoint in judging the appeal of fiction for the mass market" and cautioned him not to be "over-analytical, in a scholarly-academic sense."[58] Gunn wrote back, agreeing but also advocating literary standards: "You're probably right about the necessity of modifying my viewpoint for the mass market; I hope to learn a great deal more about the psychology of that market when I join you in June. It seems to me, however, that the more that can be offered in a story, the better it will be for the mass market."[59] A few days later, Ward responded, suggesting that they would be comrades-in-arms once Gunn arrived: "Frankly, I'll be glad when you get here, and can take up the s-f battle."[60]

But before the Gunns could pack up and move to Racine, Gunn had to submit his thesis for graduation in May. Gunn's master's thesis, a book length work totaling 231 pages titled *Modern Science Fiction: A Critical Analysis*, was a study of the development of science fiction. In the spring of 1950, Gunn sent the first chapter to John W. Campbell for comment: "It represents, I believe, a beginning of what science fiction very badly needs at this time—a summation of what it has been trying to say during the last ten to twenty years and an indication of the possibilities ahead."[61] Campbell's response was positive, although he wasn't interested in publishing it in *Astounding*. Later, when Pohl was representing Gunn's work, he managed to sell it to his old Futurian pal Bob Lowndes, who published portions of the thesis in three installments in *Dynamic Science Fiction*, one of the magazines he was editing during the boom year of 1953. *Dynamic* folded before finishing the serialization. Pohl also tried to interest a number of book publishers, but at that time publishers didn't quite know what to do with science fiction, let alone a study of the field. Ultimately, Gunn's complete thesis would remain unpublished, but this early grappling with SF from a scholarly perspective would certainly contribute to Gunn's later scholarly works, such as *Alternate Worlds* and *The Road to Science Fiction* anthologies, and the parts that did appear in *Dynamic* undoubtedly influenced the development of scholarly discourse concerning the field in the coming decades.

With degree in hand, Jim, Jane and baby Kit moved to Racine, a small Wisconsin city located between Chicago to the south and Milwaukee to the north. One of Gunn's first editorial assignments was to work up material for the *Disney* magazine. In the Gunn archives, there are delightful drawings of Mickey Mouse and Goofy that presumably Gunn sketched, along with a number of detailed story scenarios. Like the earlier Dick Tracy material, Gunn imagined ways to get Mickey and Goofy to the Moon or involved in other science fictional scenarios, which, ultimately, didn't fly with the magazine's senior editors. Gunn also proposed a comic book called *Zip Foster, Spaceman*, which got as far as some mock up illustrations to go with initial scenarios. Zip Foster is similar to such fifties era space heroes as Tom Corbett and Rocky Jones. *Tom Corbett, Space Cadet*, which had been inspired by Heinlein's 1948 juvenile novel *Space Cadet*, had first appeared on CBS television in the fall of 1950, before moving to ABC, and a daily comic strip began in September 1951. So one can surmise that Zip Foster was conceived as a potential rival. However, rather than develop Zip Foster, Dell apparently acquired the rights to Tom Corbett and began a comic book series in early 1952. Interestingly, Jack Williamson's daily comic strip *Beyond Mars* began appearing in the *New York Daily News* in the same month that Dell launched the Tom Corbett comic. Six months later, Gunn would make Williamson's acquaintance at the World Science Fiction Convention in Chicago and subsequently collaborate with him on the novel *Star Bridge*.

As a junior editor, Gunn also wrote blurb lines for the front and back covers of paperback detective novels and westerns. His most ambitious project was a joke book. *Funny Side Up* can be considered Gunn's first (unofficial) book, as his name does not appear as editor. Billed by its front cover blurb, presumably supplied by Gunn, as "a laugh-loaded collection of the funniest cartoons and gags of the year," it is a sampling of the jokes of the period culled from such periodicals as *Collier's, Cosmopolitan, The American Magazine*, and elsewhere. Most of the jokes have lost their humorous context over the years and many raise a smirk by their mid-century chauvinism, but some still hold up and are good for a laugh.

The friendship with Ward that started in their spring correspondence continued at the Racine offices. But Gunn was disappointed when, around a year later, Ward and another young editor, Allan Barnard, were transferred to New York when Dell decided to do more of its editing there: "Don told me later that he asked for me to go along, too, but was turned down. I'm not sure how that would have worked out. When I had an offer of a job at *Galaxy* a year and a half later, Jane said that I could take the position if I wanted but that she refused to live in New York."[62] Many years later, Ward attended one of the early Intensive Teaching Institutes, to which he "brought a sign we posted in the dormitory lounge we used as a classroom: 'Science fiction is spoken here!'"[63]

After Ward's departure, Gunn wasn't sure how long he wanted to stay with Western. His unease is expressed in an undated letter, probably from early spring 1952, to his friend Rev Mullins, in which Gunn enquires about a job possibility in Lawrence: "Work here at Western is light and varied but not exactly the kind of thing I was thinking of when I came. Editorial work on the Dell pocket reprint line was transferred to New York about the first of the year, and since then it has largely been a matter of finding odd jobs for me to do—and that includes everything but sweeping out the place at night.... I even edited a joke book (413 jokes, 117 cartoons—counted 'em today for some ad material) which should come out in June or July. It's called *Funny Side Up*; don't know if it will have my name on it or not—Western is funny that way."[64] By May, Gunn was sending inquiries to Kansas City area schools about teaching positions, although nothing opened up and Gunn stayed with Western throughout the summer. In the evenings Gunn began work on his first novel *This Fortress World*, working up the first fifty pages before getting stuck until he later was inspired to change the viewpoint from third person to first.

Gunn's life was to change dramatically when he convinced Smith to send him to the 1952 World Science Fiction Convention in nearby Chicago over Labor Day weekend. There Gunn met several of the leading writers and editors in the field for the first time and forged many new friendships; friendships which would last for decades. Gunn recalls those he met: "A great many writers were there, including Clifford Simak, with whom I had a drink at the bar (and found out later that it was his first World Con, too), Mack Reynolds, with whom I formed a friendship that lasted for a couple of decades (he tried to persuade me later to move to San Miguel de Allende in Mexico, where a writer could live in comfort on a writer's income), Richard Matheson (that may have been his last, as well, since I never saw him again), Bob Bloch, a man named Davis who advertised himself a citizen of the world, and many others."[65] In addition, he met Jack Williamson, L. Sprague de Camp, John W. Campbell, Anthony Boucher, Raymond Palmer, Evelyn Gold, and his agent Fred Pohl. For Western Gunn wrote a report on the proceedings, but as he later reflected, "The report didn't include the most important aspects of the occasion: the instant rapport I felt with these readers, writers, editors, publishers, and agents that I was meeting for the first time. I discovered a brotherhood linked together with ties stronger than family; we shared a love of what we read, and faith in the future and in the power of the written word to change it."[66] Thus Gunn's full initiation into the world of science fiction. Henceforth Gunn would take an active part in the correspondence and camaraderie of the writers of his generation. Like many who enter the world of science fiction through the convention tradition, Gunn was reinvigorated with new energy and wanted to get back to serious writing: "I took the train back to Racine, filled with renewed enthusiasm about a writing career and a deep sense (that I took back from every later convention) that I wanted to work harder and write better to earn the right to belong to this wonderful group, who were dedicated not just to literary pursuits but to its vision of a better world."[67] Here we see the seeds of Gunn's idea of "saving the world through science fiction," his version of Wells's Open Conspiracy. Christopher McKitterick, now director of the Gunn Center for the Study of Science Fiction, enthusiastically articulated the "saving the world" concept in a 1996 article for *Analog*: "Science fiction readers must spread the SF way of thought because SF offers choices and alternative futures; it encourages the adventurous spirit and faith in human ingenuity. At the same time it provides excitement and an escape from a life that sometimes feels unendurable, SF replaces despair with dreams and offers—or at least illuminates—hope."[68]

Gunn was especially pleased by news he heard from his agent Frederik Pohl. Pohl had placed several of Gunn's stories in recent weeks: "Survival Policy" with *Astounding*, "The Misogynist" and "Open Warfare" with *Galaxy*, and "The Boy with Five Fingers" with *Thrilling Wonder*. On the strength of this affirmation of his work, Gunn quit his editing job at Western and returned first to rural Kansas, and then to Kansas City to take up full-time writing. As he later reflected on this momentous decision: "I decided, on the feeble evidence of Fred's announcement, that I would quit my job and return to full-time writing. I went into Lloyd's office and told him; he didn't raise any objections but said that he had hoped I would start a science-fiction line. If he had told me that earlier, it might have made my time at Western more meaningful."[69] They left Racine just before the November elections and Gunn proudly remembers "casting an absentee ballot against Senator Joseph McCarthy."[70] Gunn's distaste for the notorious Senator from Wisconsin is evident in some of his work from the period, especially the novella "Witches Must Burn" (*Astounding* August 1956), which imagines a McCarthy-like demagogue at the head of a fundamentalist movement that destroys the universities.

Soon after the Gunns moved back to Kansas City, where they lived at his parents' house rent free, Gunn took the train to New York where he made the rounds of the SF community, stopping by editorial offices, meeting with Pohl, and having after hours bull sessions with some of the writers he met in Chicago. And he received a memorable offer from Horace Gold. Gold tried to convince Gunn to become his assistant editor at *Galaxy* and the story has become a central part of Gunn lore:

> "How would you like to be assistant editor of *Galaxy*?" he asked. I probably asked him how much the position paid. The salary may have been $75 a week, which didn't seem like a living wage in New York.
> "You can sell me stories," Horace said.
> "I'm not sure my wife would like living in New York," I replied.
> "That's all right," Horace said. "There's lots of women."[71]

Needless to say, Gunn did not take Gold's offer. However, Gunn would go on to place a number of stories with Gold over the next few years, in *Galaxy* and its short-lived fantasy companion *Beyond*. Gunn was impressed by the aesthetic promoted by Gold in both magazines and made *Galaxy* and *Beyond* his primary target market for the next few years. Gunn later said of *Galaxy*: "It was a new magazine which already had published stories like Fritz Leiber's "Coming Attraction," Pohl and Kornbluth's *Gravy Planet*, and Alfred Bester's *The Demolished Man*—different stories all, but all the kind of stories I wanted to write. For the next four years *Galaxy* would get first look at what I wrote."[72] As evidenced by the handling of "Breaking Point," where Gold talked Gunn into letting Theodore Sturgeon make some cuts, which, in truth, meant he wanted a rewrite, and then still turning the story down, Gold was an editor who was hard to pin down. His mercurial personality, idiosyncratic quirks, and micromanagement of stories often created distance between the two. Recently introducing a Gunn story Gold rejected, Robert Silverberg sums up Gold's quirks: "Gold was a difficult editor to understand: sometimes he rejected stories that seemed perfectly attuned to his magazine, perhaps because he thought they were *too* perfectly attuned to it."[73] Nonetheless, despite Gold's quirks, Gunn admired him for his curious mind and dynamic energy and found Gold a congenial host when visiting his apartment on his trips to New York. Many years later, Gunn encountered Gold at a party at Forrest J. Ackerman's Hollywood mansion, where it was apparent that Gold's dynamism had waned. And a few years after that, Gold tried to enlist Gunn to help him with a project: "He telephoned me with a request that I write up his psychotherapy theories. He never had psychological training, but he had, he said, been very successful in personal counseling sessions and thought his methods ought to be made available to others. I told him I was too busy with my own writing."[74] Like his rivals John W. Campbell and Raymond Palmer, Gold apparently fancied himself an amateur psychologist.

Gunn also stopped by the offices of Street and Smith to see John W. Campbell, where Campbell discoursed on the latest he'd read on psychic phenomena, demonstrating his own penchant for off-beat psychology: "He talked with me for the better part of an hour, most importantly about a recent discovery by the British Psychical Society that poltergeist phenomena happened around disturbed adolescents. On the train ride back to Chanute, a plot came to me that turned into a novella I called 'Happy Is the Bride.'"[75] Ironically, the novella was later published by Gold in *Galaxy* after a great deal of back-and-forth as "Wherever You May Be," then again retitled "The Reluctant Witch" in Gunn's 1970 collection *The Witching Hour*.

Upon his return to Kansas City, Gunn took a job in civil defense, reporting every day to City Hall, a towering building overlooking downtown Kansas City: "In those days of nuclear war concerns, civil defense was still an issue. I mostly worked on budgets, but there was a Civil Defense emergency drill that I participated in. My service in civil defense lasted only three months."[76] Although Gunn didn't contribute a nuclear war story during this time when it was one of the primary focuses of science fiction—think, Merril's *Shadow on the Hearth*, Bradbury's *The Martian Chronicles*, Tucker's *The Long Loud Silence*, and Dick's "The Defenders"—his visions of an apocalyptic Kansas City in such stories as "Deadly Silence," *The Immortals*, and *The Burning* certainly draw from this period of civil service. This was the period of nuclear hysteria portrayed in multiple science fiction scenarios, not only in the literature but on television and in the movies as well. The fact that Gunn, for this brief period, worked directly in civil defense may have influenced him to take his stories in other apocalyptic directions.

At this time Gunn received news from Abelard Press offering him a contract for his first novel *This Fortress World*. Abelard was producing a few hardcover SF books and was being supplied by Pohl; the first SF-related book they published was *It's Your Atomic Age: An Explanation in Simple Everyday Terms of the Meaning of Atomic Energy to the Average Person* (1951) by Pohl's client and friend Lester Del Rey; and they had just published Cyril Kornbluth and Judith Merril's *Outpost Mars*.

Gunn also began corresponding with veteran writer Jack Williamson, whom he had met at World Con. Just before Gunn went on his New York sojourn, Williamson wrote to him: "I want to say again that getting to know you was one of the best things about the convention for me, and I feel that we're already good friends. Everything else aside, we seem to have very much the same attitudes toward science fiction."[77] Like Gunn, Williamson lived in the middle of the country—on the southwestern edge of the Great Plains in Portales, New Mexico, even further away from the hustle-bustle of the agents and editors in New York—and was currently scripting the daily newspaper comic strip *Beyond Mars*. But Williamson was suffering from writer's block and was struggling to complete projects. He was hoping that Gunn might be willing to collaborate on a novel that he'd stalled out on. After reading Williamson's materials and coming up with some new ideas, the two agreed to collaborate on what became the novel *Star Bridge*. Williamson and Gunn began corresponding about ideas, but the writing—mostly done by Gunn—would have to wait until the completion of *This Fortress World*.

Gunn set to work on his second period of full-time freelance science fiction writing and was enormously productive in the ensuing months, producing the seeds for a number of his major works. Rather than writing at home, Gunn worked at his brother's house while Richard was at his medical office: "I set up a simple office in a basement room of my brother's house and began commuting there five days a week; I wanted to work at writing like a job and to have a place I did nothing but write. I showed up about 8 a.m., wrote for four hours, my mother fixed me some lunch—usually a bowl of soup and a sandwich—and I went back to write for four more hours. During the next two years I wrote about ten pages a day, revised it once while I wrote a final draft, and sent it off, averaging a 6,000-word short story every week, or a 12,000-word novelette every two weeks, or a 20,000-word novella every four weeks."[78] The stories came in a flurry over the course of the next three years and together they make a significant portion of Gunn's overall fiction oeuvre. Three of the first five stories didn't sell; a novella titled "Tiger! Tiger!" did, to *Planet Stories*, but before it was published *Planet* folded and the story did not see publication until a fan publisher named Chris Drumm brought it out as a booklet in 1984 with an introduction by Gunn. Pohl sold the next story, "The Man Who Owned Tomorrow," to the mainstream slick magazine *Argosy*. Gunn completed a consumerist satire in the Pohl-Kornbluth vein, "Ad Infinitum," presumably targeted for Gold at *Galaxy*, a few weeks after Christmas. When Robert Silverberg reprinted it in a 2012 *Super-Science* retrospective anthology, he noted that the story had all the qualities of a good *Galaxy* story: "the brisk pace, the glossy surface, the hard-edged satire of American consumerist life in the Eisenhower era."[79] But Gold didn't take it. Instead it sold to Lester Del Rey at *Space*, but like *Planet Stories*, *Space* folded before Gunn even got a check; it was eventually published as "Every Day Is Christmas" in *Super-Science Fiction* February 1957. Ironically Silverberg earlier had dismissed this same story in a review of Gunn's collection *Future Imperfect* in *Amazing* in 1964, remarking that it "didn't even click at the intended market."[80] After "Ad Infinitum" Gunn completed his aforementioned breakthrough novella "Happy Is the Bride," which features a psychokinetic hillbilly waif, drawing landscape background material from a vacation the Gunns had enjoyed in the Ozarks during the first period of freelancing in the late forties. It was the lead novella in the May 1953 issue of *Galaxy* under the title "Wherever You May Be." Gunn followed it up with a 4,000-word short titled "The Stranger," published as "The Reason Is with Us" some years later in *Satellite* April 1958, before spending the next several months completing *This Fortress World* and corresponding with Jack Williamson about their collaboration on *Star Bridge*.

Meanwhile, the stories Pohl had sold that prompted Gunn to depart from Western began appearing under the James Gunn byline. "Survival Policy," which appeared in the October 1952 issue of *Astounding*, still was credited to Edwin James, but "The Misogynist" appeared the next month in *Galaxy* as by James E. Gunn. The delightful little mutant story "The Boy with Five Fingers" appeared in the January 1953 issue of *Startling Stories*. And Gunn's most ambitious story to that point "Breaking Point"—Sturgeon now having completed the rewrite—appeared in the March 1953 issue of *Space*.

Things were in flux in New York, however, as Pohl was struggling to keep his agency above water and his writers were getting nervous. Gunn was one of the writers who suffered from Pohl's financial troubles at the agency. As Pohl admits in *The Way the Future Was*, he was around $30,000 in debt, an enormous amount for 1953.[81] But behind some of this debt were good intentions: Pohl would often advance money for unsold stories to keep writers afloat while they worked to produce quality work. However, Gunn was never the beneficiary of such advances, perhaps because he was more remotely located. In correspondence with Williamson, Robert Sheckley, and Gunn's new agent Harry Altshuler, the difficulties writers were having with Pohl is revealed. As early as the letter Williamson sent to Gunn before the New York trip, Williamson voiced some of his concerns and asked Gunn to report back to him if he found anything out: "I'd appreciate any information or impressions about his position and prospects that you happen to pick up while you are in New York City."[82] Upon his return home, Gunn reported back to Williamson: "I could never work the conversation around to Fred Pohl's financial position gracefully and came back little better informed than I want.... Consequently I did not sever relationships, particularly when Fred informed me of two sales he had made for me. If I experience any repetition of this summer's long delay in informing me of sales and payment for stories, I shall procrastinate no longer. I suggested as much to Fred, although not as bluntly as I would have liked to, having no guts for this kind of thing.[83] The frustrations mounted, but both Gunn and Williamson stayed connected with Pohl. At one point, Williamson talked to him face-to-face in New York with the intention of severing ties, but they came to an agreement and Williamson sent him "half a million words of manuscripts—mostly novels that I had abandoned unfinished"—this presumably included what was to become *Star Bridge*, the Pohl-Williamson *Undersea* juvenile series, and the early versions of the Pohl-Williamson *Starchild Trilogy*, which developed from an idea Williamson had worked up called the "iron-collar man."[84] In April, Gunn wrote Williamson in frustration that no money from Pohl was forthcoming: "Fred is up to his old tricks. I haven't heard from him since before you passed through K.C. on your way home: no confirmation on the Abelard novel contract or details, no payment for 'Breaking Point,' 'The Saddest Man in the World,' or further word on 'Tiger! Tiger!' What an agent!"[85]

Meanwhile, the collaboration on *Star Bridge* got underway and by early May Gunn had completed the first few chapters. He wrote Williamson as to whether they should forward them to Pohl to start sending around to publishers or whether they should get more of the manuscript finished: "The only thing that would hold me back is Fred. After sending him a telegram and a long, strongly worded letter over two weeks ago, I still haven't had an answer from him. I have come to the conclusion that I can't hope to make a go of freelance writing, full-time, with someone as undependable as Fred. I have almost made up my mind to change agents when I go to New York in August, if not before. Certainly, if I don't hear from Fred soon, something is going to pop."[86] Williamson commiserated, but cautioned Gunn: "I have usually found out that he had been doing a better job than I thought he was, and I'm still hoping that he'll turn out to be a pretty good agent, if I can make sufficient allowances for his way of doing business."[87] Indeed, Williamson still believed that Pohl was the best in the business and in retrospect, some years later, Williamson reflected that Pohl "has always known science fiction better than nearly anybody; he's an inventive creator of new opportunities in fiction or out of it; he can be a most persuasive salesman. His clients, for a few exciting years, were writing most of the best science fiction, and he sold it well."[88]

Gunn felt the same way, reflecting that "he was a good agent, and he sold a lot of stories for me," although admitting that "Fred was a better agent than a businessman."[89]

Pohl's difficulties came to a head during the summer as he sent a letter to all of his clients that he was closing the agency. Williamson wrote Gunn as soon as he received the news on July 20.[90] At Gunn's end, he had yet to hear from Pohl (although his letter from Pohl, dated July 21, was undoubtedly in the mail when Gunn received the news from Williamson), who still owed him around $1,000 and he immediately wrote Williamson back with unusual steam:

> I got your letter today. The news about Fred came as a complete surprise. Not only have I not been informed about his getting out of the agent business, I haven't heard from him at all for over two months. I imagine my feelings about it are the same as yours. I rather welcome the opportunity to change to a *good* agent. But mixed with that is uneasiness about the sizable (for me) amount of money Fred owes me and an uncomfortable awareness of the possible difficulties. I'd like to know why Fred decided to quit (for a better job, because of financial reasons, or what?) and whether the money he owes us will be forthcoming without fail. It was with some difficulty that I kept myself from taking off immediately for New York instead of a month from now as I have planned. After cooling off a little I guess I'll wait and hope for a letter from Fred clarifying the situation.[91]

A few days later Gunn wrote Williamson again, with his decision to take the diplomatic approach: "In spite of the way I feel about Fred, I am trying to close things out with him on a friendly basis. Who knows? Hard words might come home to roost. The way it has ended is no doubt for the best. If I can collect from him, I'll consider it a happy ending."[92] Gunn's decision not to exchange hard words with Pohl at the time illustrates a Gunn character trait that served him well in his later period as a university public relations officer.

Gunn wasted no time seeking another agent. He wrote Harry Altshuler, who had been recommended to him by Ted Sturgeon. Altshuler wrote back promptly on July 31, 1953 (promptness would be a happy characteristic of Gunn's relationship with Altshuler for the next fifteen years) with some news that must have made Gunn even more tense; Altshuler had heard from James Blish that Pohl's checks were bouncing.[93] Gunn took the train to the World Con in Philadelphia over Labor Day Weekend, where he met Willy Ley, whose *Collier's* articles on the conquest of space would inspire the *Station in Space* sequence, and, for the first time, the youthfully exuberant Harlan Ellison, who was telling everyone about his first story sale. From there, Gunn went on to New York, where he was reassured by Isaac Asimov that Pohl would settle his affairs: "Isaac Asimov seems to be his big creditor, to the tune of several thousand, but Isaac didn't seem broken up about it."[94] At World Con, Gunn had also become acquainted with another young writer who was making a name for himself in the pages of *Galaxy* with sharp, pungent humorous stories: Robert Sheckley. In a letter to Sheckley at the end of the month, Gunn indicates that Blish's warnings had come true: "I incidentally have been initiated into that exclusive club: THE POHLARIZED, or, SEE HOW THEY BOUNCE. The check Fred graciously handed me in New York (cleverly, on Friday after the banks had closed) came back with much attached memoranda from sundry officials, chiding one and all for miscalculation or connivery (little do they know!). Then, wonder of wonders, Fred wired the money with an additional twenty-five bucks he had forgotten to include."[95]

I have gone to some length to reveal the relationship between Gunn and Pohl at this time to show, from letters, that there is much truth to the difficulties writers were having with Pohl at this time. But let me, as the author of a recent book on Pohl, make this clear: this is not intended as an indictment of Pohl's character, as some other studies of the period have made it out to be. Countless writers and fans have testified to Pohl's generous spirit and kindness, editorial acumen, and support over the ensuing years. Nonetheless, to fully understand what James Gunn was experiencing during this period of his most fertile creativity, it is important to understand the disquietudes he was having with Pohl and how that fed the creative relationship he had with Jack Williamson, and the friendships he forged with other writers. To testify to all this, that although Gunn and Williamson were frustrated with Pohl at this time (as were a host of other writers), it should be emphatically reaffirmed that the three were to become—and remained—great friends in later years. By 1957, Pohl was able to settle up with Williamson, who wrote Gunn that "as my confidant, in the course of my sometimes disheartening affairs with Fred Pohl, you will possibly be interested as well as surprised to know that he has finally settled up in full."[96] And he also settled with Gunn and the other writers he represented, though it took him nearly a decade to clear all his debt.[97]

Ironically, Gunn had finished *This Fortress World* just a few days before Pohl's announcement that he was closing up shop and mailed the manuscript to Pohl on July 21, the very same day that Pohl wrote Gunn about closing the agency. Pohl may have been the one who sent it on to Abelard, but Altshuler began dealing with the publisher from then on. By late November Gunn got the copyedited manuscript back from Abelard, and he was furious. The copyeditor had taken a bludgeon to Gunn's manuscript, making numerous changes Gunn considered "style-deaf and prudish," and he was particularly angered by the presumptuous notes scrawled on the box, suggesting that the copyeditor was being paid by the change.[98] Having spent a year at Western and having by then published well over a dozen stories, Gunn felt this was an affront to his professionalism. This prompted Gunn to pen a long, angry letter to Abelard, which he wisely didn't send. Instead, he wrote to Altshuler voicing his grievances. Altshuler, in turn, informed Gunn that Abelard had botched a book by Charles Dye and that he didn't "see any reason for you to play along with them if you don't have to."[99] The book was pulled from Abelard and Altshuler quickly made a new deal with Marty Greenberg of Gnome Press. Altshuler reported to Gunn that Greenberg "claims to have s-f sales and distribution second only to Doubleday.... And though he is beset by all the small publishers' problems, he is reasonably reliable, I think."[100] Altshuler's confidence was soon tested. The contract with Greenberg was to prove a more frustrating arrangement than anything Gunn had ever experienced with Pohl. As late as 1960, Altshuler was still trying to get unpaid royalties for the novel.[101] Nonetheless, Greenberg did get the book published and it appeared in hardcover in the fall of 1955, followed by a paperback reprint by Ace in 1957 in an Ace Double edition with Robert Silverberg's second novel *The Thirteenth Immortal*.

Before his trip to World Con that September Gunn finished the story "A Monster Named Smith," and then in the post-convention euphoria and after his dealings with Pohl, he finished the novella "Beauty Is a Witch," about a convention of practitioners of the dark arts at a hotel, which Gold later published in *Beyond* as "Sine of the Magus." Gunn would later expand the story into the 1976 novel *The Magicians*. The rest of the fall was spent finishing up *Star Bridge*.

While working on *Star Bridge* Gunn and Williamson discussed further collaboration. For instance, in the fall of 1953, they exchanged a substantial amount of material for a collaborative novel called *Witch Hunt*, but this never materialized for either writer, although the title, at least, may have worked its way into Gunn's "Witches Must Burn." They also brainstormed over one of Williamson's abandoned ideas called *The Mindsmith*—some of this eventually worked its way into the Pohl-Williamson *Starchild Trilogy*. Ultimately, Gunn felt that further collaboration wasn't financially feasible no matter how congenial it was to work with the good-natured Williamson. At the beginning of 1955, Gunn wrote Williamson to tell him he couldn't afford to continue to collaborate. Williamson wrote back: "I, too, am very regretful to end our collaboration. I think *Star Bridge* is a good novel, and I'm sure that we could have turned out more and better ones, if the circumstances had been a little more favorable."[102]

Both *This Fortress World* and *Star Bridge* were released in 1955 by Gnome. Although Gunn completed *This Fortress World* first, *Star Bridge* was the first to see publication, probably because Williamson was already a well-established writer. Gunn soon found that getting earnings forwarded from Greenberg was more difficult than getting them from Pohl. After writing these first two novels for very little money and then waiting for overdue payment, Gunn formulated "Gunn's Law": "Nothing is worth writing unless you can use it at least twice."[103] From here on Gunn conceived most of his novels as story sequences, which he could first sell as individual stories to the magazines before packaging them for the book market. Gunn explains the sell-it-twice concept in the introduction to *Some Dreams Are Nightmares*: "I was convinced that the best length for science fiction was the novelette and that the way to obtain the greatest immediate return (not, perhaps, the greatest final return) on my investment of time and thought was by writing the shorter form, but I felt that a novel-length idea treated in this way made possible artistic effects not available in the novel.... I would not be forced, I thought, to provide any specious solutions to any eternal problems. I could deal with an idea over a considerable span of time and over the lifetimes of several characters. I could dramatize, show the impact of the idea on individual lives, show how it works out for them, and allow the idea itself to complete its destiny, clarified but unresolved, after the book had ended."[104] *The Joy Makers, Station in Space, The Immortals*, and later, *The Burning, The Listeners, The Dreamers, Crisis!*, and *Gift from the Stars* were written in this way.

Gunn also determined to write in the near-future instead of in the far future of the space opera genre. Until he returned to space opera with his new *Transcendental* series, Gunn consistently addressed the possibilities and consequences of technological and social change extrapolated from current trends. For Gunn, science fiction could be a vehicle by which to address such outcomes: "I was noticing the very real problems in the world around me and I was feeling a need to contribute to their solution, if I could, and a sense of the power of science fiction to change the world."[105] At this time Gunn tried his hand at a few conventional mainstream stories—perhaps as a way to transition from space opera to near-future social science fiction—which almost led him astray, but after a few encouraging rejection slips from *Collier's* and *This Week*, he decided not to spend time working on stories that weren't likely to sell.[106] As another warm up to his shifting focus, shortly after completing *Star Bridge* at the end of January 1954, Gunn wrote a comedic fantasy set in a brewery (he "toured" the Blatz Brewery for research) titled "The Beautiful Brew" for *Beyond*, likely prompted by a letter from Gold requesting stories for the magazine. Gunn then began work on the first novella of *The Joy Makers*, "The Hedonist," published in *Thrilling Wonder* as "Name Your Pleasure," which makes up section two of the novel. Over the course of the next four months, Gunn finished the second *Joy Makers* novella, "Hedonics, Inc." (published as "The Unhappy Man"), "The Cave of Night" (the first story in the *Station in Space* series), "New Blood" (the first in *The Immortals* series), the short "Without Portfolio," which Campbell bought for *Astounding*, and "Shill," a 22,000- word novella picked up by *If*. Gunn was on his way to becoming one of the brightest new stars in the science fiction field.

"The Cave of Night" was inspired by a series of articles in *Collier's* by Willy Ley, illustrated by Chesley Bonestell, about the building of a space station and the coming conquest of space. Gunn had hoped one of the slicks would take the story, but *Collier's* turned it down. Instead, it went to *Galaxy*, and the story probably had a better life because of its association with that magazine than it ever would have in one of the slicks, which have proved much more ephemeral to the cultural consciousness than have the SF magazines. Gold sent the story to the NBC radio program *X Minus One*, which was dramatizing *Galaxy* stories. *X Minus One* went on to do three more Gunn stories: "Wherever You May Be," "Open Warfare," and "Tsylana." Contemporary listeners can now find the broadcasts online at various webpages. "The Cave of Night" was reprinted in the April 2 and 16, 1957, issues of *Science World*, a magazine for high school students, a sign that educators were taking the prospect of a space future seriously and saw Gunn's story as topically relevant. They also ran an abridged version of the second story "Hoax." At the end of the fifties, "The Cave of Night" was adapted into an hour-long television drama for Desilu Playhouse, retitled *Man in Orbit*, starring Lee Marvin and E.G. Marshall, airing on May 11, 1959. Although the story was significantly altered, it still had its admirers, including Isaac Asimov: "I watched *Man in Orbit* on the Desilu Playhouse and was proud and pleased. I was proud because I could bask in the reflected glory of having a friend of mine contribute a major drama on television."[107] Asimov later selected "The Cave of Night" for the anthology *Where Do We Go from Here?*

The Gunns' second son, Kevin, was born on June 13, 1954, a month before Gunn mailed "New Blood" to Altshuler. In "Medic," the second story written in the series, Gunn named the young medic Dr. Flowers, in honor of the resident physician at Kevin's birth at the KU Medical Center.

At this time, after having endured several wrangles with Gold, Gunn felt that Campbell was the best market, writing to Williamson on June 17, 1954: "I think that if there's anything significant being done in science fiction, John Campbell is doing it. Horace would scoff at a mission for science fiction, maybe rightly, and John goes off on some wild hobby horses of his own and ends up in right field sometimes. But still I want my science fiction to mean something and say something, and I give John credit for presenting that type of story consistently and being tremendously fertile with speculative ideas."[108] From these remarks, the further development of Gunn's "saving the world" concept, that science fiction contributes significantly to the cultural dialogue and has the potential to shape it, aligning Gunn with Wells's concept of the Open Conspiracy, is apparent, and he would continue to develop his aesthetic in this direction.

That summer, Gunn participated in the Kansas Writers' Conference, an experience he discussed with Williamson: "Though, rationally, I'm afraid that the art of writing can't really be picked up by any kind of osmosis from the presence of people who possess it, there is still something stimulating about meeting a few of them now and then."[109] Williamson responded in kind: "I agree that writing can't be taught. My experience is that it can only be learned by doing; the more you write the better you can write. Some things can be taught, though—the use of tools, mostly."[110] As both were to become university creative writing teachers, these early reflections are notable for their uneasiness with the process.

At the 1954 World Con in San Francisco, Gunn met veteran writer A.E. Van Vogt and newcomer Philip K. Dick, who stayed in the hotel lobby because he was too shy to enter the convention. He reported his impressions of Dick in a letter to Sheckley: "Young, nice-looking, nervous, and very shy; suffers from complaints like Horace—never goes out. Although he lives in Oakland, he didn't come to the convention until lured over the next to last day."[111] Gunn spent a good deal of time at the convention with Evelyn Gold, who would attend conventions as surrogate for her agoraphobic husband; unlike Horace, Mrs. Gold was charming and gregarious and Gunn recalls her leading an entourage of writers to San Francisco's opera bars.[112]

Gunn finished eight more stories during the second half of the year, including the second *Immortals* story, "Medic"; "The Last Word," a sequel to "The Misogynist" from the wife's point of view; a long novella set in Kansas City called "Shhhh!" later published in *Fantastic Universe* as "Deadly Silence" in 1958; the second *Station in Space* story, "Hoax"; "Pill Roller," which appeared in *The Saint Mystery Magazine*; and three stories that didn't find markets—although one of these three, "Teddy Bear," was picked up in 1970 by Lester Del Rey for *Fantasy* magazine.

Gunn continued to write productively during the first half of 1955, writing another ten stories before the end of July. The first was "Donor," the third story in *The Immortals* series. Gunn had much difficulty placing this story—which is ironic given the fact that *The Immortals* would eventually become the first science fiction book transformed into a television series. "Donor" was followed by the extraordinary conclusion of *The Joy Makers*, "The Angry Man," which appeared as "The Naked Sky" in the final issue of *Startling Stories*. The short "Feeding Time" sold to *Astounding*; "Little Orphan Android," "The Gravity Business," and "Tsylana" to *Galaxy*; "The Stilled Patter" to *Infinity*; and the third *Station in Space* story, "The Big Wheel," to *Fantastic Universe*. The only story that didn't sell was the short-short, "Kindergarten," which Gunn dusted off and sold to *Galaxy* in 1970. The most ambitious story following "The Angry Man" was the novella "Witches Must Burn," which sold to John W. Campbell. Reflecting on the disastrous demagoguery and anti-intellectualism of Joseph McCarthy, Gunn wanted to examine what would happen if the forces of anti-intellectualism, anti-science, and the religious right gained an overwhelming foothold in American cultural and political life. Notably, this is one of Gunn's first stories to be centered on the campus of the University of Kansas (although the university had played a prominent role at the conclusion of "Wherever You May Be"). Gunn spent the rest of the year trying to come up with a sequel to "Witches Must Burn," but couldn't make it work. He came back to it a decade later, when he returned to writing after a long hiatus, and completed two additional novellas that make up the novel *The Burning*.

There was another reason why Gunn's writing slowed during the second half of 1955. Late that summer the Gunns moved back to Lawrence after two-and-a-half years in Kansas City. They bought a ranch-style house with the financial help of Jane's parents and moved in in August. Gunn fully intended to continue freelancing, but once in town, he visited the English Department to renew old acquaintances. It was a fortuitous visit: he was offered a job to teach two English courses that semester. In part, Gunn accepted the job because they would provide him an office where he could work without the distractions of two little boys at home. He wrote Sheckley at the beginning of August about the opportunity: "I'll probably be teaching a couple of classes of freshmen or sophomore English at the University of Kansas (which is at Lawrence) this fall, which should be stimulating as a change of climate and may even improve my production."[113] Gunn had discussed the possibilities of going into teaching as a path to a more stable income as early as 1953 in a letter to Williamson: "I have a deal pending which, if it materializes, may be an ideal set up. Got a letter from the University of Kansas Extension Service, which has adult classes in Kansas City, Kansas. They are interested in getting me to teach. If I could get a part-time evening job teaching a class or two which paid enough to buy groceries, I'd quit this job [the Civil Defense job] so quick—!"[114] Around midterm, Williamson wrote enquiring how Gunn liked teaching: "I'll be interested to know how you enjoy your part-time teaching job. Sometimes I'm tempted to qualify myself for the same sort of thing in the university here."[115] It appears that Gunn's experiences might have been the impetus for Williamson's own pursuit of advanced degrees in higher education. Williamson finished his B.A. in the spring of 1957, and then his M.A. that fall at his local campus Eastern New Mexico University in Portales and also began teaching classes. At age 50 in 1958 Williamson began Ph.D. work at the University of Colorado, returning to a faculty position at Eastern New Mexico following completion of his degree.[116]

Before the fall term began, however, Gunn went to New York to meet with editors and publishers prior to the 1955 World Con in Cleveland, and then rode with Marty Greenberg, Sheckley, Asimov, and Evelyn Gold to the Con. Greenberg wrote an enthusiastic note as they made preparations: "Will have a long chat with you when you hit NY. This is just to let you know you have a ride to Cleveland with Asimov, Sheckley, Gold, and myself. Be warned."[117] In Cleveland, Gunn gave a speech titled "The Function of Science Fiction"—later he wrote Altshuler about perhaps getting a PhD in English with a dissertation on "Science Fiction and Modern Society": "The idea being that science fiction is a real and significant outgrowth of modern society and serves a valuable purpose in it."[118] At the convention banquet Gunn sat with Mark Clifton, Judith Merril, Mildred Clingerman, and Frank Riley and family—this was the year that Clifton and Riley's novel *They'd Rather Be Right* won the Hugo. A photo of the dinner appears on page 193 of *Alternate Worlds*.[119] Gunn also fondly recalls sitting with Asimov on a sofa in the lobby and Asimov observing, "'Why is it we spend all our time among strangers who don't know what we do and don't care so that we can spend a few days a year among the people we love.'"[120] Years later, Fred Pohl made a similar observation, telling Gunn, "Conventions never end; they just adjourn to another venue."[121] On the trip home, Gunn sat with Forrest J. Ackerman on the train to Chicago. Ackerman wrote of their journey in a column for the February 1956 issue of *If:* "Riding back from Cleveland to Chicago I had the good fortune to have as a companion

James E. Gunn, one of the newer voices in science fiction who's going places. Jim gave one of the most solid, most perceptive speeches at the convention—'The Function of Science Fiction.' I asked him if, in his SF writings, he felt he had anything special to say or was pointing any way in particular, and got an answer that I liked: he said he was trying to write stories with an optimistic note and a belief in human beings. It was with the feeling on my part that if we had more human beings in the world like James E. Gunn it would indeed be a better one."[122] Upon returning to Kansas, Gunn wrote Greenberg about Asimov: "I got a delightful letter from Isaac Asimov the other day, which only confirmed my opinion that Ike is a wonderful and sentimental person it would be a real pleasure to call a friend."[123] The feelings were mutual, as Greenberg reported in November: "Ike was in over the weekend and sends his love and we had a mutual Gunn admiration session."[124]

Before the semester concluded Gunn was asked if he'd be willing to edit the monthly *Alumni Magazine* and the quarterly alumni newsletter. Gunn gave up teaching during the spring semester to focus on the alumni work. He also took a course on fiction writing with Caroline Gordon, famed maven of the Southern Literary Renaissance, while she was a writer-in-residence at KU that spring. From Gordon, Gunn took away "insights into the writing and literary process that I used as the backbone of future workshops I offered."[125] For Gordon's course, Gunn wrote "Powder Keg." It is interesting to note that there is a gap in Gunn's story output that runs from the mailing of "Kindergarten" at the end of July 1955 to the mailing of the unpublished "The Tolerance of Elmer Wilkey" in June 1956, roughly the period of time of a university school year. In the aftermath of Gunn's decision to teach at the university, his writing production dropped off precipitously, in spite of his remark to Sheckley that it might improve his production. In many ways, getting involved with the university was a wise move, since the science fiction magazine boom was about to go bust. In 1958 the science fiction magazine market shrank significantly, largely due to the breaking up of the American News Corporation distribution network. Other writers were getting out of the game at this time as well. Gunn got back to writing that summer and finished up "Powder Keg" and the final *Station in Space* story, "Space Is a Lonely Place," and "Green Thumb," what could now be classified as an ecological story. "Green Thumb" is additionally noteworthy for utilizing the Haskell Indian Institute and the environs of downtown Lawrence as setting.

The next school year kept Gunn busy with university work and followed a similar pattern. Although he did complete one story, "Skin Game," during the school year, Gunn's other five stories for the year—and the last he wrote until the late 1960s—were all mailed before school started in the fall of 1957. That summer he finished "The House Dutiful," revised later as "The Technological Revolution" in 1970 for Bob Hoskins' paperback anthology series *Infinity*; "Cinderella Story," published as "When the Shoe Fits" in *Vanguard* June 1958; "The Girls Who Were Really Built," published as "Neosho's Choicest" in *Fantastic* June 1958; and the unpublished "Pest House," a story that certainly would have found a place had the market not collapsed. Most significantly, Gunn wrote the titular final novella of *The Immortals* series, which Pohl bought as the concluding piece in the *Star 4* paperback anthology. *Star 4*, incidentally, also featured stories by the recently deceased Henry Kuttner and C.M. Kornbluth. With the early deaths of these shining stars, science fiction was facing its own mortality.

For all this writing effort, from 1953 through 1958 Gunn earned a total of $12,700, with ten percent going to his agents, or slightly more than $2,000 a year. This was a modestly comfortable middle class income during the era, especially for a low-cost-of-living university town like Lawrence, but it was dependent on a steady flow of literary production, and with the shrinkage of the science fiction magazine market, living off the income from short stories was not likely to maintain Gunn's financial security. By teaching and working for the alumni magazine Gunn had already reestablished himself on the KU campus, so when the offer to become an administrative assistant to the Chancellor came his way, Gunn was ready to take it.

Gunn was called into the office of Fred Ellsworth, the secretary of the Alumni Association, who told him the Chancellor's office wanted Gunn to serve as a feature writer for the university at a salary of $6,000 a year, nearly double his best year of freelance income. During that first year Gunn wrote a series of articles about Chancellor Franklin Murphy's trip to the Soviet Union to visit Russian universities that got picked up by the Associated Press and distributed across the country. The ambitious and astute Murphy had first gained national attention in 1948 when, at the age of 32, he became dean of the university medical school, the youngest man ever to hold such a top post. Among his achievements he oversaw numerous projects and programs that transformed the Medical Center into a major statewide institution. By 1951, Murphy had succeeded to the Chancellorship of the University of Kansas, and he spent the next decade trying to transform the university into one of the elite public universities in the nation. Murphy's achievements had not gone unnoticed on the national stage: reportedly, President Dwight D. Eisenhower told Murphy in 1955 that he could "name a dozen men in the forty to fifty [age] group—including yourself—to whom I would gladly entrust the duties of the Presidency."[126] The next year Murphy offered Gunn a new appointment as his Administrative Assistant for University Relations, with a salary increase of $1,500. By the end of the spring term in 1960, however, because of difficulties Murphy was having with Kansas Governor George Docking, he left KU to become chancellor at UCLA. Murphy offered Gunn the opportunity to come along, but Gunn declined, knowing that Jane would not be happy in Los Angeles. Gunn kept the position under Murphy's successor, W. Clarke Wescoe, who had also followed Murphy as dean of the medical school—a curious synchronicity given Gunn's stories in *The Immortals* which take place, in part, in the Medical Center in Kansas City. Although his title didn't change under Wescoe, Gunn effectively became the director of public relations at the university. It was these administrative experiences, as well as his experience as an adjutant in the Pacific after the war and his tenure in Kansas City civil defense, which inform Gunn's handling of administrative systems in his fiction. In reference to *The Listeners*, Gunn's 1972 novel about the long search for extraterrestrial civilizations, John Clute observes in *The Encyclopedia of Science Fiction* that "his forte seems to lie in the narrative analysis of stress-ridden administrations and their administrators; and his best work is usually set in organizations or among groups of people forced to cooperate."[127] Gunn's skill in depicting such situations came from experience.

Although most of Gunn's energies were spent in university administration for the better part of the next decade, he nonetheless succeeded in publishing a number of books that gathered together his series stories, and also overseas editions of his work began to appear. *Station in Space*, his third book, was published in September 1958, *The Joy Makers* in March 1961, *The Immortals* in 1962, and a collection of non-series stories, *Future Imperfect*, in 1964. Asimov lamented the fact that Gunn was no longer writing and urged him to get back in the game: "The field needs all the good writers it can get, and I hate to see you wasted so entirely on university prose."[128] In his characteristic ironic, bitter register, Barry Malzberg has seen Gunn's leap into university administration as the proper response to the realities of the freelance science fiction marketplace: "Gunn, like Budrys and Philip Klass, was another who took from his most creative decade the lesson that the academy or the corporation were far better places to be than the commercial fiction markets."[129]

Gunn's years spent in the KU administration reached their summit with the Inter-Century Seminar in April 1966. The university was celebrating its centennial and Gunn helped William A. Conboy, chair of the speech and drama department, organize the conference. Participants included such intellectual luminaries as Loren Eiseley, who had taught anatomy at the university during World War II; R. Buckminster Fuller, innovative architect and futurist; Karl Menninger, whose psychiatric clinic in nearby Topeka was among the best in the country; Arthur C. Clarke, whose surging international fame was bringing more attention to SF; anthropologist Ashley Montagu, whose pioneering work questioning race and gender assumptions moved tolerance and acceptance forward; astronomer Harlow Shapley, known for the concept of the "habitable zone," essential for the astronomical search for life on other planets; Franklin Murphy, who had done for UCLA, by transforming it into an elite institution, what he had hoped to do for Kansas; and others. This first-rate lineup gathered together to promote and exchange ideas about the direction of humanity in the future. Gunn edited the talks and the discussion into the volume *Man and the Future*, published in 1968 by the University of Kansas Press.

Shortly after the success of the *Man and the Future* conference, Gunn's fame on the KU campus was extended in another way—through his writing. Hollywood producers Bob Specht and Everett Chambers were interested in *The Immortals* and contacted Altshuler. At first, Altshuler was cautious as to whether anything would go forward.[130] But things did, in fact, develop. Specht and Chambers took a two-year option and near the end of that period, Specht approached Paramount Studios to see if they'd be interested in *The Immortals* as something to develop for the new ABC "Movie of the Week." Paramount was. *The Immortal* "Movie of the Week" premiered on September 30, 1969, on ABC and was reviewed favorably by television commentators and by writers within the science fiction fraternity. The positive response and the solid ratings prompted the network to green light the development of a weekly television series for the next fall's lineup. *The Immortals* became the first science fiction novel to become a prime-time television series. Gunn was flummoxed, however, that the new producers were uninterested in his input into the storylines, or from any other credentialed science fiction writers—a glaring mistake that Paramount had already made with *Star Trek* when they stopped soliciting manuscripts from established SF writers during the third season. For the most part, *The Immortal* TV series moved away from the science fiction element, instead making it into a hunt-and-chase series in the manner of *The Fugitive*, which had aired on ABC from 1963 to 1967. Needless to say, such a tired formula couldn't sustain itself for long—

although that didn't stop TV networks from trying it again and again in various rehashes during the seventies. The series ran for fifteen episodes before being cancelled. From Gunn's perspective, the problem was the film, and most especially the subsequent TV series, downplayed the broader implications such a transformative change—blood that rejuvenates—would have on the entire society: "The film had changed the focus from the social change created by the reality of immortality for a few to a chase story in which Christopher George was pursued by rich and powerful aging people lusting for his blood."[131]

In any event, as the series went into production the marketing department wanted a novelization of the original movie ready for the paperback racks in the fall when the series launched. This was the time when Paramount and Bantam were having success with James Blish's adaptations of the *Star Trek* episodes. Unable to contract a writer, Eileen Lottman, the Bantam editor in charge of the project, called Gunn for suggestions. Gunn offered to write it himself and thereby he became the first SF writer to write the movie novelization of his own original work. Consequently, Gunn's bibliography lists two titles: *The Immortals* (1962) and *The Immortal* (1970). Gunn spent little time working up the novelization: he wrote it in seven days.[132]

In response to the inadequacies of the television series, Gunn wrote an opinion essay for *TV Guide*, "An Author Watches His Brainchild Die on Television," published in February 1971, where he discussed how the original idea, which was effectively portrayed in the Movie of the Week, even though it, too, narrowed the focus, had been jettisoned in the TV series, making for a rather mundane story. His friend Harlan Ellison had already written dismissively of the series in his television column, later collected in *The Other Glass Teat: Further Essays of Opinion on Television*. For Ellison, it was especially disappointing: "I waited two weeks before reviewing this series. I wanted to be ultra-fair, for any number of reasons, not the least of which were that I *wanted* to like it and that the series is based on a science fiction novel by a good friend of mine. But two weeks' airing forces the conclusion that *The Immortal* is a nitwit's delight."[133] With typical indignant venom, Ellison excoriates the show in much stronger terms than the diplomatic Gunn himself would use: "Totally devoid of any reality or purpose, it is an endless video version of a Pavlovian rat-response, with the negative charisma of the hunted Christopher George serving to cast a downer pall over the labyrinthine scurryings of stalked prey through blah settings. More than half of each show I saw was devoted to mindless chase-sequences. It is *The Fugitive* stripped of sanity."[134] And Ellison is particularly incensed by the mishandling of the original science fiction property: "The lunacy of postulating a series based on a science fictional theme (a man whose blood produces antibodies that virtually guarantee immortality and freedom from the aging process) and then *ignoring* the fantasy elements, out of fear the 'audience won't accept it,' when it was *precisely* that acceptance that generated interest in the series to begin with, defies belief, rationality, or discussion."[135] By this time, as discussed below, Gunn had broken with Altshuler and signed with the Scott Meredith Literary Agency, a relationship which quickly ended when the agency wanted a cut of the *TV Guide* article: "Shortly afterwards I got a letter from Scott Meredith's right-hand man asking for Scott's ten percent of the *TV Guide* fee. I replied that they didn't have anything to do with it. The assistant replied that when I was writing the article I wasn't writing something that Scott could represent. 'You've got the wrong idea,' I wrote. 'You think I'm working for you, but you're working for me. But not any longer.'"[136] Like Ellison, Gunn could replace diplomacy with strongly worded indignation when it came to questions of writers' rights.

The saga of *The Immortal* TV series was not the only SF activity that Gunn was involved with in the late sixties. In fact, it was only a small, albeit significant, portion of the work that marked his return to the field after an eight year hiatus from writing. Sparked by the *Man and the Future* conference and the Hollywood interest in *The Immortals*, in the summer of 1966 Gunn decided to take his vacation for the first time since he joined the university administration and write. He hadn't written any new SF for about eight years, with the exception of a short horror story written in 1965 called "The Old Folks," which didn't come out until 1970 in Harry Harrison's anthology *Nova 2*. By the end of August, he'd completed the follow-up to "Witches Must Burn," "Trial by Fire," exactly eleven years after the first story had been purchased by Campbell, and a short story titled "The Power and the Glory." Alas, Campbell didn't want "Trial by Fire." His return letter to Altshuler is preserved in *The John W. Campbell Letters* with the curt rejection: "Sorry, but no dice on this one."[137] Campbell didn't think the logic of the story followed naturally from the original, and he didn't like the narrative being filtered through "the eyes of a *doped* [my emphasis] protagonist."[138] After a year of back and forth—which included a meeting with Campbell in his New York offices, where Gunn met Murray Leinster for the first time—Gunn sent it to Fred Pohl, who was now the leading editor in the field, having succeeded Gold at *Galaxy* at the beginning of the decade. Pohl liked it and bought it for *If*, which had become *Galaxy*'s companion magazine in the aftermath of the magazine collapse in the late fifties. During the meeting in New York, Campbell suggested that the scientists could escape to space, which helped Gunn finish the final novella "Witch Hunt" in the summer of 1968, although it, too, would be published by Pohl. Rekindling the relationship they had when Pohl, as his agent, inspired Gunn to leave Western Printing for full-time freelancing fifteen years earlier, Pohl encouraged Gunn to write more.

Gunn followed through the next summer with a new story called "The Listeners," about the long search for extraterrestrial intelligence. The story was inspired by Walter Sullivan's 1966 book *We Are Not Alone*, which brought to public attention the search for extraterrestrial intelligence advocated by Frank Drake, Carl Sagan, and others. Sagan's translation (done by Paula Fern) and collaboration with Russian astrophysicist I.S. Shklovskii, *Intelligent Life in the Universe*, had also come out that year (although Gunn wouldn't encounter it until later). According to Gunn, "Sullivan's book was fascinating, and included a good deal of material that later found its way into my novel, but what stimulated my writer's instinct was the concept of a project that might have to be pursued for a century without results. What kind of need would produce that kind of dedication, I pondered, and what kind of people would it enlist—and have to enlist if it were to continue?"[139] When Gunn sent the story to Altshuler, Altshuler wrote a critical return letter that ruffled Gunn's feathers. Altshuler said he liked the story, but he didn't think it was "market-oriented" and that Gunn was "drifting out of touch with the practicalities of the marketplace." Altshuler believed this was "an artistic mistake" and that "The Listeners" was "overartistic" and needed "ruthlessly pared down."[140] Given that this was the era in which science fiction moved into a more experimental phase, as initiated in Britain in Michael Moorcock's *New Worlds* and exemplified in America by Damon Knight's *Orbit* anthologies, by then in its second volume, and in the recently released Harlan Ellison anthology *Dangerous Visions*, it seems that it was Altshuler who was out of touch with the audience and the market. Even the stories in Pohl's magazines were breaking boundaries, charting new territory, and becoming increasingly experimental and aesthetically mature. Altshuler goes on to say the story is "too middle aged"—but that is exactly the point: SF was becoming middle aged at this time—the writers of Gunn's generation were now all in their forties and fifties. And Gunn's artistic turn was reflective of the growing artistry represented in the works of the New Wave. Gunn says as much in his curt reply to Altshuler on September 12: "And yet, with the strange stories that are coming out these days from the young English writers and from Zelazny and Dick, I would think there might be a place for a few more strange stories from Gunn."[141] In that same letter, Gunn decided to cut ties with Altshuler. Altshuler had served Gunn well for many years, but it was evident that he was no longer attuned to the new directions in which SF was heading. And Altshuler was, indeed, wrong. Pohl loved the story and immediately bought it for *Galaxy*, and asked Gunn to write more in the series. It appeared in the September 1968 issue, and was selected as a finalist for the 1969 Nebula Award in the novelette category, losing out to Richard Wilson's poignant post-apocalyptic story "Mother to the World." Gunn wrote the rest of *The Listeners* series over the next few years and most of the stories appeared in *Galaxy* after Pohl had left the magazine and Eljer Jakobsson had taken over. In 1972 Scribner's published *The Listeners* as a novel and it sold well in hardcover and was a selection of the Science Fiction Book Club. *The Listeners* stands as one of Gunn's great and lasting achievements, having impact beyond the science fiction literary marketplace. As Paul Shuch, former director of the SETI League has written, "*The Listeners* has done more for SETI than anything else ever published."[142]

Meanwhile, student unrest was coming to a head in the late sixties and as the representative of public relations, Gunn was right in the thick of things at KU, interpreting what was going on to the public and the alumni. The University of Kansas was one of the centers of student protest during the Vietnam era. In 1969 Wescoe left the Chancellor's office and was succeeded by Laurence Chalmers who presided over the most difficult year of student unrest at the university, culminating in a fire at the student union and demonstrations following the bombing of Cambodia and the shootings at Kent State in May 1970. Gunn left the administration soon after and joined the English department permanently that fall. Eerily, Gunn had anticipated campus discord in "Witches Must Burn" in 1955, although there it is the anti-intellectual, fundamentalist forces of social oppression from outside the university instead of the radicalized students of the sixties within. Gunn would diagnose the latter in the novel *Kampus* published in 1977. The seeds of *Kampus* were born out of Gunn's experiences and observations of the tensions on the KU campus—and across the nation—and the demands for curricular change. Although the full novel was completed some years later, Gunn set to work on the story as sort of a cathartic release after a decade observing the changing youth culture at the university, writing the first version of what would become chapter two in the novel: "It was inspired by the campus unrest and my interest in chemical memory. Those two coalesced around the idea of the world the student rebels might have made if they had been successful and imagined a near future when the campuses had been turned over to the students, and real science and scholarship had gone elsewhere. The chapter, which turned out to be the second chapter in the finished novel, dealt with the abduction of the Professor by Gavin and his friends in order to get his wisdom directly by sampling his brain; it was a metaphor for the easy road to education also symbolized by learning pills sold outside campus buildings."[143] Gunn worked for Chalmers for only one year and has commented on why he left: "I had been increasingly frustrated by the need for better University public relations and my inability to procure the resources or the position to be effective.... Administration, I came to believe, was a trap."[144] Although the university lost a skilled and even-handed administrator, the field of science fiction gained enormously from the return of one of its leading figures.

Prior to joining the English department, however, Gunn got a taste of teaching again in the fall of 1969 when a number of students, led by his son Christopher, asked him to mentor a student-run course on science fiction; Gunn ended up teaching, as opposed to merely supervising, when it became clear the students needed his insider wisdom. At the end of the semester Harlan Ellison came to Lawrence on one of his speaking tours and his visit to the classroom was filmed for *The Literature of Science Fiction* film series. Ellison's talk reflects the campus tensions and idealism of the time, as the consummate rebel author addresses the day's political issues, and it also shows SF's role in it. There's a memorable moment when Gunn puts his sunglasses on during the table talk, as if to show solidarity with the ideas of the sunglassed Ellison and the students. The genesis of the film series idea came when Gunn met Gordon Dickson earlier that fall at the World Con in Saint Louis, where Dickson persuaded Gunn to run as his successor as the president of Science Fiction Writers of America; Gunn served in that office in 1971–72 as the fifth president of the organization. During their conversations, Gunn mentioned the idea of producing an educational film series to promote the field. The films were funded by the Extramural Independent Study Division of Continuing Education at the University of Kansas headed by Alex Lazzarino. In Saint Louis, Gunn also met the new science-fiction editor at Dell Books, Gayle Wendroff, who was bewildered by the goings on and about ready to pack it in and go back to New York before Gunn introduced her to some of the writers and invited her to join his group during the banquet, making her feel welcome.[145] The following year, Wendroff bought Gunn's collection, *The Witching Hour*, consisting of three fantasy novellas from the early fifties, "Wherever You May Be" (retitled "The Reluctant Witch"), "The Beautiful

Brew," and "Sine of the Magus" (retitled "The Magicians"), and *The Burning*, which Dell would release in 1972.

Filming for *The Literature of Science Fiction* film series got underway in earnest in mid–March 1970 at the Nebula Awards west coast meeting in Berkeley, California, where Gunn filmed Poul Anderson speaking on "Plot in Science Fiction" on the balcony of the Claremont Hotel. Gunn and his crew traveled to Los Angeles after the Nebula Awards and filmed Forrest J. Ackerman discussing "Science Fiction Films" in his home. At Ackerman's, they also filmed an interview with legendary filmmaker George Pal, but unfortunately it was never edited and the sound has been lost. Ackerman tried to talk Fritz Lang into an interview, but Lang declined. From there, Gunn flew to San Diego to speak to an SF class Harry Harrison was teaching at San Diego State. In his posthumous memoir *Harry Harrison! Harry Harrison!*, Harrison mentions that Gunn was among many writers he invited to visit his class when they passed through town and that Greg Bear, then still in his late teens, sat in on the classes.[146] Although Gunn likely was unaware of Bear at the time, they would become more fully acquainted later when Bear joined the ranks of science fiction's major writers. The next year, Rod Serling agreed to an interview while he was at KU for a student arts festival in March. Due to difficulties securing rights to use clips from Serling's shows, the film was never released, although parts of it are now circulating on the internet. As the interview begins, Serling fumbles a cigarette a number of times, dropping it on the floor, after which he chillingly remarks to Gunn, "I'm having a lot of trouble with that cigarette, aren't I? I think God is telling me, don't smoke." Serling's excessive smoking contributed to his death at fifty just five years later.

Gunn and crew attended the Nebula Awards in New York in early April, where they filmed Isaac Asimov in his home office speaking on "The History of Science Fiction After 1938," where Asimov famously remarked, "We are now living in a science fictional world." They planned to film Damon Knight in a companion piece on the "Early History of Science Fiction" in front of the U.N. Building, but U.N. officials wouldn't allow it, so they filmed him across the street with the U.N. in the background. But traffic noise wrecked the sound, so Knight came to Lawrence in early 1972 and was filmed in Lazzarino's living room. On that same trip, a lunch story meeting between Gordon Dickson, Harry Harrison, and John W. Campbell was filmed at Campbell's favorite restaurant in New York, where Campbell worked with Dickson and Harrison on developing a story idea that eventually became the novel *The Lifeship* (aka *Lifeboat*). Harrison comments on the film in *Harry Harrison! Harry Harrison!* "I was in New York having lunch and a drink with Jim Gunn—he was based at the University of Kansas and mentioned that he had some grant money for his students to do interviews with science fiction authors. He wanted to come to New York and do an interview with John Campbell. I said, 'If you want to do a film about John Campbell, you should do lunch with John Campbell, because that way you'll see how John Campbell works and inspires his writers.' Jim said, 'That's a great idea, and you'll do it!' That's what you get if you open your mouth with a big idea. But I would get a free lunch out of it, and the chance to do the old verbal argo, which you always do with John, so it seemed like a good idea."[147]

Although Harrison's recollections are that the film gives the appearance that it was a booze fest, with he and Dickson knocking back scotch and sodas while Campbell lectures them, in part because just before filming one of the two cameras broke down, leaving Gunn with more static footage than was intended, more importantly, the film reveals how Campbell and his writers worked together to create a basic plot and thematic variables for a new work. As such, the film is a particularly valuable visual insight into how Campbell's editorial mind worked and how he worked with writers. As Harrison notes, "We actually built the book on screen, plotted beginning, middle, and end.... We had the structure absolutely dead right from beginning to end, and it worked well."[148] A few months later, Campbell died, and his death rocked the science fiction world. Gunn's film, then, wound up being an important final testament to the man who had shaped the field like no other.

A few days after filming the Campbell lunch, Gunn filmed an interview with Clifford D. Simak about his long career in the field and John Brunner discoursing on "Science Fiction and the Mainstream" at the World Con in Boston. Later, films were made with Frederik Pohl, Jack Williamson, and Gordon Dickson on visits they made to KU. A film with Theodore Sturgeon, shot on video, was made years later as a student project during one of Sturgeon's many visits for the Summer Institute.

After participating in Gunn's film series, in the wake of the very successful anthology *Dangerous Visions*, Harlan Ellison wanted a story from Gunn for the next volume, *Again, Dangerous Visions*. Unhappy with what Gunn had sent him—the unpublished "Teddy Bear"—Ellison wanted Gunn to write him a *good* story. Gunn did. Ellison bought the second story in *The Listeners* series, "The Voices," but due to length-constraints in the oversized anthology, had to give it back to Gunn, since the novel was due out soon. Ellison promised Gunn a spot in the planned final anthology, the ill-fated *The Last Dangerous Visions*, and Gunn sent him the novelette "Among the Beautiful Bright Children." As the publication kept getting delayed, and delayed, Gunn developed the story further and it became part of the novel *The Dreamers*.[149]

When Gunn joined the English department permanently in the fall semester 1970, first as a lecturer, he was pleased when some of "the younger members" of the department hoped he "would be willing to teach a course in science fiction."[150] This was the moment when university curriculum was undergoing dramatic changes, and in the wake of the Apollo Moon landings and the growing centrality of technology in daily life, science fiction was making its way into college curriculums across the country. Jack Williamson gathered a list of SF courses, which was published in the May 1971 issue of *Extrapolation*, the first academic journal devoted to the study of science fiction and the fantastic. Williamson remarked that "most teachers and students are motivated by a sense that science fiction has a special relevance to life in our transitional times."[151] That same issue of *Extrapolation* announced the formation of the Science Fiction Research Association. Gunn was assigned two fiction writing courses in addition to the science fiction course, which was initially taught through the School of Journalism until it went through the approval maze in the English department. Within a few years Gunn was promoted to full professor, "perhaps the only full professor never to have served in any of the intermediate ranks."[152] This unprecedented move reflected the recognition of Gunn's achievements: "My bibliography, though not as scholarly as the Department was accustomed to, was several times as sizable as that of anyone else in the Department. I had been president of SFWA and soon would be president of SFRA—the only person to have held both positions."[153] In later departmental yearly publication reports, Gunn's production consistently overshadowed even his most active colleagues. During the 1980s, when his teaching career at KU was in full swing, Gunn wrote: "This is where I belong; this is what I was meant to do."[154]

Gunn's science fiction course was a popular success, starting as a large lecture course with 165 students. Even at this large size, Gunn tried to make it a discussion course, but as there was no available textbook at that time providing historical and contextual background, Gunn had to put together a series of weekly lectures. He took what we now might call a cultural studies approach: "What I wanted was to help my students identify what SF was by observing the psychological and cultural impulses that had created it and how it had evolved in response to changes in science and technology and humanity's understanding of its place in the universe."¹⁵⁵ For course readings, Gunn used the newly published *Science Fiction Hall of Fame* and Jules Verne's *From the Earth to the Moon* in that first class, but focused a good portion of the class on the lectures about the history of the genre. During the spring semester, a representative from Prentice-Hall approached Gunn about doing a book on the craft of fiction writing. Instead, Gunn suggested a book based on his classroom lectures. Those lectures became the basis of his groundbreaking history of the field *Alternate Worlds*. One of the class sessions early in the spring 1972 semester featured the visit from Damon Knight, in town to reshoot his film segment. As Gunn reflects, "we had a lively discussion about the distinctions between fantasy and science fiction. Damon insisted there were none, and I maintained that they not only existed but were meaningful. I always wished we had recorded it."¹⁵⁶ Years later, Knight and Gunn would continue this debate on the then relatively new forum of cyberspace, where they also debated reading protocols for science fiction.

As science fiction entered the college classroom, the market for teaching and research materials blossomed. *Extrapolation* was joined by the British journal *Foundation* in 1972 and by *Science Fiction Studies* in 1973. Teaching guides (including the delightfully titled *Grokking the Future* by Bernard Hollister and Deane Thompson) and anthologies, most notably Silverberg's *The Mirror of Infinity*, which paired seminal stories with critical essays by writers and scholars, in 1970, and Dick Allen's *Science Fiction: The Future* in 1971, the first science fiction textbook for the classroom, were being published. Allen begins his Preface by stating, "This book assumes that science fiction has become a respectable genre of literature, deserving serious critical and scholarly attention."¹⁵⁷ As a writer of significance and a teacher at a major university, Gunn was in excellent position to bridge both worlds. His first contribution to crossover between science fiction writing and teaching was a chapter in Robin Scott Wilson's *Those Who Can*, an anthology designed for beginning writers and inspired by the Clarion workshops that Wilson oversaw. Gunn's contribution involved a discussion on style, paired with a reprint of "The Listeners."¹⁵⁸ For Reginald Bretnor's *Science Fiction: Today and Tomorrow*, Gunn contributed the article "Science Fiction and the Mainstream," where he set out to frame and distinguish science fiction and its relationship to mainstream realism.¹⁵⁹ A few years later in Bretnor's *The Craft of Science Fiction*, Gunn contributed an article on characterization.¹⁶⁰ In the wake of his SFWA presidency, he was asked to edit the *Nebula Awards Ten* anthology, which appeared in 1975. In his introduction, Gunn remarked that the science fiction genre had reached its maturity and was now being taken seriously by scholars and teachers. He also invited an essay by renowned literary scholar Robert Scholes, "As the Wall Crumbles," where Scholes discussed the position of science fiction within the broader range of contemporary literature and how academic scholars were starting to grapple with it. Scholes had just published his short critical work *Structural Fabulation*, which gave SF some legitimacy within the main current of academic literary theory and scholarship. Later, for *Nebula Winners Twelve*, edited by Gordon Dickson, Gunn contributed an essay on "The Academic Viewpoint," where he again argued for the benefits academic interest in SF could bring to the genre.

Meanwhile, the science fiction community was getting restless and was voicing concerns that bringing science fiction into the college curriculum would hurt the genre. In a special issue of *Fantasy and Science Fiction* in 1972, Philip Klass (aka. William Tenn), who was teaching creative writing at Penn State, wrote a measured and sympathetic piece, "Jazz Then, Musicology Now," examining the claim that science fiction could lose something, as jazz music had, when it became an object of teaching and study. Tenn concluded that science fiction, which was inherently academic because it was a literature of ideas, had finally found its rightful home, proclaiming that "the university is where [SF] always belonged.... It's come home at last, to its origins, to the one place where the hard sciences become abstract, where the social sciences build reality, where the new frontiers of esthetics and metaphysics are measured off."[161] Such a conclusion did not sit as well with Ben Bova, who had succeeded John Campbell as editor of *Analog*. Bova's editorial of April 1974, "Teaching Science Fiction," decried the lack of experience and qualifications with SF of many college teachers asked to teach such courses, and, after charging the SFRA with not "demanding professional qualifications among SF teachers," he feared harm would be done to the field "if these classes result in disillusionment, then these hard-won gains will evaporate, and it will take another generation before anyone can mention science fiction in 'respectable' company again."[162] Gunn chimed in with a response to Bova in a guest editorial later that year in the November issue. In "Teaching Science Fiction Revisited," Gunn focuses on two key questions: the qualifications of science fiction teachers and the effect teaching science fiction may have on potential new readers. Gunn argues that "generally the teachers of SF courses are not the bad teachers. The ones who volunteer to teach such courses may not be as knowledgeable as we would like them but they are, I suspect, enthusiastic, open, and experimental."[163] Gunn also argues that the science fiction teacher can open a door for young minds who may not otherwise take up the genre.

The debate with Bova in the pages of *Analog* was a watershed moment for Gunn as the leading advocate for the teaching of science fiction, as it led indirectly to the formation of the Intensive English Institute of the Teaching of Science Fiction. During Gunn's tenure as president of the Science Fiction Writers of America in 1971–72, he had received numerous letters from teachers at all levels inquiring about how and what they should teach in newly created science fiction courses. Gunn received funding to offer the first Institute in the summer of 1975, with twelve participants. The founding editor of *Extrapolation*, Tom Clareson, came to help teach during the first two weeks of the three-week program, teaching novels in the afternoon, while Gunn taught short stories in the morning. It was a full-immersion experience, six hours of class time during the day and related activities during the evening. Since the Institute concluded the weekend of the Kansas City area science fiction convention at the Muehlebach Hotel (coincidentally, the setting of Gunn's story "Sine of the Magus," soon to be expanded into the novel *The Magicians* published in 1976), Gunn invited Robert Bloch, Gordon Dickson, and Harlan Ellison, who were guests at the Con, for the last few sessions. Bova joined them as well and reported on the proceedings enthusiastically in his January 1976 *Analog* editorial: "In all, the Institute was a success. Despite the small turnout, all those who attended—including the guest authors—learned a good deal about the problems of teaching science fiction and their potential answers."[164] Participants increased to around twenty for the second year and Gunn invited Gordon Dickson, Theodore Sturgeon, and Fred Pohl to serve as guest instructors in subsequent weeks of the Institute, a practice that all three maintained for many years, their tenures only ending with Sturgeon's death in 1985 and Dickson's in 2001; Pohl, along with his wife, English professor Elizabeth Anne Hull, would continue to participate in the Institute, the Campbell Conference, and the last few days of the Writers Workshop well into the 2000s, before traveling became no longer feasible for Pohl.

The Summer Institute attracted teachers from across the United States, both from the college and secondary school ranks, and was also open to students at the university. Participants also came from overseas: the Netherlands, Denmark, Canada, South America, Japan, China, Australia, and New Zealand. As the years went on, however, much of the class was made up of KU graduate and undergraduate students, although usually four or five participants from other institutions would sign up, a practice still going on today as the course is now in the able hands of Christopher McKitterick. In its heyday, Gunn's Intensive Teaching Institute served an important purpose in educating teachers in preparation to offer science fiction courses at their institutions, and many participants went on to mentor future teachers as well. In a recent anthology titled *Teaching Science Fiction*, Andy Sawyer and Peter Wright have remarked, "Gunn's influence can be readily observed in a number of undergraduate SF courses by contributors to this volume."[165]

As the Institute was getting underway in the summer of 1975, *Alternate Worlds* had finally been published by Prentice-Hall. Gunn had originally hoped that *Alternate Worlds* would coincide with the publication of Brian Aldiss's eclectic genre history *Billion Year Spree*, which, with its controversial assertions, had taken the field by storm in 1973. When Gunn had written Aldiss requesting his photo, Aldiss wrote back that he was also working on a history of science fiction and "wouldn't it be great if we exchanged back-cover blurbs in which I said that his book was the best history of science fiction and he said that mine was."[166] But publication delays, due to a change of editors and the challenges of securing permissions for the hundreds of illustrations, pushed the publication of Gunn's book back to 1975. By then Aldiss's history had already made its mark. Nonetheless, *Alternate Worlds* was to make a mark of its own and was well-received in the science fiction community of writers (Barry Malzberg has commented that *Alternate Worlds* "is one of the few books among the recent glut about science fiction which will probably live as long as the genre itself"[167]), scholars, and fans. The following year Gunn received a call from Tom Clareson, then president of the Science Fiction Research Association, informing him he had won the Pilgrim Award for lifetime contributions to science fiction scholarship, a nod to both *Alternate Worlds* and *The Literature of Science Fiction* films. Gunn was the seventh recipient of the award since its inception in 1970, presented to him at that year's SFRA meeting in Missoula, Montana in June. That Labor Day weekend, Gunn received a special Hugo Award at the World Con in his hometown Kansas City.

On the strength of *Alternate Worlds* and the awards it received, Gunn was approached by New American Library editor Barry Lippman who asked if he had anything to propose. Gunn suggested a theoretical book, but the editorial board was interested in an historical anthology. This resulted in *The Road to Science Fiction* historical anthology series, originally published in affordable Mentor mass market paperbacks. The anthologies sold well and introduced a scholarly approach to the field to readers in and out of the classroom. *The Road to Science Fiction* was adopted in classrooms across the country, although not all of the volumes were used in any given class. The most popular volume was volume three, *From Heinlein to Here,* which ranged from the Golden Age of the forties to Joe Haldeman, Joanna Russ, and other writers who emerged in the seventies; it sold upwards of 40,000 copies in the Mentor edition. As Gunn proudly reflects, "The *Road* series were one of a few projects that came out even better than they seemed in the planning."[168] During the years that Gunn put together the *Road* anthologies and developed the Summer Institute, he was assisted by his KU colleague Stephen Goldman. Goldman prepared a teaching guide for the *Road* anthologies that Mentor distributed to instructors, worked closely with Gunn on *The New Encyclopedia of Science Fiction,* and contributed many essays in the field of science fiction studies. Sadly, Goldman died young, at the age of fifty-two in 1988. As *The Road to Science Fiction* volumes were making an impact in the classroom, Gunn was asked to be put forward as a candidate for the presidency of the Science Fiction Research Association, nearly a decade after his presidency of the SFWA. He served as SFRA president for 1980–81.

Gunn was also in on the founding of the World SF organization, an effort by Brian Aldiss, Harry Harrison, and Frederik Pohl to sponsor SF throughout the world. Gunn attended the founding meeting in Dublin in 1978, his first trip overseas since his service in the Pacific. At that meeting, Pohl received the John W. Campbell Memorial Award—instituted by Aldiss and Harrison after Campbell's death—for his novel *Gateway. The Listeners* had actually come very close to winning the inaugural Campbell Award in 1973, but was voted down by Aldiss who preferred Barry Malzberg's more downbeat *Beyond Apollo.* At the Dublin meeting's conclusion, Aldiss asked Gunn to take over the administration of the Campbell Award and give it a permanent home at the University of Kansas; Aldiss and Harrison had tried to get support from other European institutions to no avail. Gunn had served on the jury committee, having been asked to serve following *The Listeners* defeat, and he saw this as an opportunity to develop an annual conference at KU. The annual Campbell Conference, which is held during the weekend transition between the summer Science Fiction Writers Workshops and the Intensive Institute, has become one of the important crossover events that brings writers, scholars, and fans together in the field of science fiction. The first Campbell Award presented in Lawrence was the following year, where the influence of Aldiss and the largely British jury was still apparent, as Michael Moorcock's novel *Gloriana* was that year's winner. One of the first Campbell conferences focused on SF illustration and featured the art of Vincent Di Fate, who sent a collection of his paintings for an exhibit and was one of the featured speakers. Often, the winners of the Campbell Award (and later the Sturgeon Memorial Award for short fiction) would participate in the conference events, and other writers would come as well. Most every major writer in the field has visited Lawrence since the 1970s, and that tradition continues.

At this time Gunn also began work on a scholarly study of Isaac Asimov, commissioned by Oxford University Press for a series of critical studies on major science fiction writers that Robert Scholes was editing. This was a big step for scholarly science fiction criticism; the first time one of the most prestigious academic presses ventured into SF scholarship of this kind. There had been previous critical studies of Asimov, but Oxford was looking for this book to make a major statement, and it (and the other books in the series) were advertised heavily, including full page ads in *Analog* and *Isaac Asimov's Science Fiction Magazine* that ran for several issues. Gunn's analysis had the added distinction of running in the very magazine that bore the name of his subject, in a feat recalling the appearance of his master's thesis in *Dynamic* in the fifties. The chapter on the *Foundation Trilogy*, "On the Foundations of Science Fiction," appeared in the April 1980 issue of *Asimov's* and evidently had some impact on Asimov's return to the series in 1982. Asimov credited Gunn's observation that his style of "permutations and reversals of ideas" were what drove the narrative of the *Foundation Trilogy* with giving him the wherewithal to continue the series.[169] This had been preceded in the magazine by the appearance of an essay on science fiction film, "The Tinsel Screen," in the February issue, coinciding with its appearance in the teaching volume *Teaching Science Fiction: Education for Tomorrow,* edited by Jack Williamson. "Variations on a Robot," covering Asimov's robot stories, appeared in the July issue. Two more installments appeared in the early months of 1981: "On the Robot Novels" and "The Stuff Itself," a detailed analysis of *The Gods Themselves*. Here is another example of Gunn's Law: sell it twice. And another instance where Gunn's academic scholarship reached a broader readership. The book won the Hugo Award for non-fiction in 1983 and, in certain respects, it and its series companions ushered in the era of substantial scholarship in the science fiction field. The current *Modern Masters of Science Fiction* series from the University of Illinois Press and McFarland's *Critical Explorations in Science Fiction and Fantasy* take up where the Oxford series left off.

While the Asimov articles were being published, Gunn's new novel

The Dreamers was published by Simon and Schuster in January 1981. As noted above, the genesis of *The Dreamers* began at the start of the 1970s when Gunn submitted "Among the Beautiful Bright Children" to Harlan Ellison for *The Last Dangerous Visions*. Busy with his growing academic career, Gunn returned to the novel periodically throughout the late seventies—the second section entitled "The Volunteer" appeared in a triptych anthology titled *Triax* edited by Robert Silverberg as "If I Forget Thee"— and completed it in the new decade. The novel is a continuation and a variation on the themes Gunn explored in "Breaking Point," *The Joy Makers*, "Trial By Fire," and *Kampus*, but here the influence of Gunn's academic career is increasingly evident in his aesthetic, as Gunn applies a densely informed literary style and content to the questions of the nature of reality.

Gunn's international reputation as a science fiction writer and as a preeminent science fiction scholar led to a number of speaking invitations beginning in the 1980s and continuing through the rest of the twentieth century, and beyond into the twenty-first. At the 1982 World Con in Chicago, fans from Yugoslavia asked Gunn if he would be interested in attending an SF convention in Zagreb. A few months later the U.S. Information Agency, who had worked extensively with Frederik Pohl and other SF writers in arranging speaking tours in Eastern Bloc countries during the seventies, contacted Gunn about doing a speaking tour about SF at the agency's expense in Yugoslavia, the Soviet Union, and Iceland. In the spring of 1983, Gunn traveled first to Yugoslavia and spoke at the Zagreb convention and in three other Yugoslavian cities, including Lljubiana, Beograd, and Titograd, then traveled to the U.S.S.R. and spoke in Moscow and Leningrad, concluding the trip in Reykjavik, Iceland. Later trips sponsored by the U.S.I.A. took him to Denmark, Romania, Poland and Sweden, followed by an Asian speaking tour to Taiwan and Singapore that included a two-day stop in Tokyo.[170] His last overseas trip took him to Beijing for the 2000 International Conference organized by the Chinese science fiction magazine *Science Fiction World*. When he arrived he was amused to find that the organizers had unwittingly used a picture of H. Rider Haggard from *Alternate Worlds* in the conference program thinking it was him. A Chinese translation of the first four volumes of *The Road to Science Fiction* had been supervised by Guo Jianzhong, head of the foreign language department at Hangzhou University who had attended the summer institute, and been published by a Chinese publisher, whom Gunn met in Beijing: "The publisher met me in Guo's hotel room in Beijing and handed me a bundle of Chinese yuan. They were the most tattered bills I had ever seen, but they paid for much of my expenses in China."¹⁷¹ The Chinese editions of *The Road to Science Fiction* have been an important gateway into English language SF for Chinese students, scholars, and writers. At a James Gunn tribute panel I organized at the 2013 joint SFRA/Eaton Conference in Riverside, California, a Chinese scholar in attendance, Dong Ye, shared the impact Gunn's anthologies have had on the field in China, and wrote in a follow-up email, "James Gunn has had great influence on Chinese SF studies."¹⁷² Subsequently, most of Gunn's works, both fiction and scholarship, have been translated into Chinese and published in China, including an updated edition of *Alternate Worlds*.

Many years later, as Gunn turned 90, he was invited to be a keynote speaker in Kerala, India, at the fourteenth annual Indian Association for Science Fiction Studies Conference held in February 2014. But he decided a trip of that magnitude at that age was probably too great a challenge. In lieu of the visit, he prepared a video keynote address "in which he saluted the tremendous progress of the genre in India in a short span of time."¹⁷³ One of the conference organizers, Dr. Latha Nair, Professor of English at St. Teresa's College in Ernakalum, which hosted the conference, returned Gunn's generosity by attending the 2014 Campbell Conference and Intensive Institute in Lawrence. When I took Dr. Nair to visit the Spencer Library and read the Asimov-Gunn correspondence, it was a profound emotional experience for her. Dr. Nair has now opened a Gunn Centre for the Study of Science Fiction at St. Teresa's with funding from the Indian government. Gunn's impact on the development of science fiction in India matches that he has had in China.

After the publication of *The Dreamers*, Gunn's fiction writing slowed considerably in the 1980s. Most of his fiction output that decade involved a series of stories published in *Analog* involving a time traveler sent to the present to head off various contemporary crisis points. The origin for the series occurred in the mid-seventies when Gunn met with network executives about the possibility of developing a rival TV series to the enormously popular *The Six Million Dollar Man*: "My Hollywood agent, Reese Halsey, had arranged a meeting with CBS executives.... I proposed a TV series based on a character who leaves himself a message about coming back from the future to help solve the problems that have created a dismal future. When CBS didn't act on it, I decided to write it as a novelette."¹⁷⁴ That original story was published in *Analog* March 1978 as "Child of the Sun." Donald Wollheim included it in that year's *World's Best Science Fiction* anthology and another Hollywood producer took out an option for a year, but didn't renew. In the mid-eighties, Gunn then decided to write more stories to demonstrate the concept could be sustained for more than one episode, all appeared in *Analog*: "End of the World" (January 1984), "Man of the Hour" (October 1984), "Touch of the Match" (February 1985), "Woman of the Year" (April 1985), and "Will-of-the-Wisp" (May 1985). They were published as *Crisis!* by TOR books in 1986 and the stories were labeled episodes rather than chapters to try to elicit more Hollywood interest, but no other options were contracted. Curiously, two series that appeared a few years later have resonances with Gunn's concept: *Quantum Leap* and *Early Edition*.

Meanwhile, Gunn got involved with a large-scale academic project that took up a good deal of his time during the decade, a project that in retrospect he wished he'd turned down: *The New Encyclopedia of Science Fiction* by Penguin Books, published under the Viking imprint in 1988. *The New Encyclopedia* was meant to rival the Peter Nicholls and John Clute *The Science Fiction Encyclopedia* published by Doubleday in 1979. Gunn was reluctant to take on the project, but his colleague Stephen Goldman expressed enough enthusiasm about the prospects of assisting him that Gunn agreed. And he thought of ways to distinguish the book from the Nicholls/Clute: "Finally, I persuaded myself that the Nicholls/Clute encyclopedia was a bit European in its attitudes toward genre literature, particularly about American science fiction and American authors, and that I could assemble a group to do better. One way I could compete was by being more concise and restricting peripheral coverage, particularly for film and television, which I envisioned as being covered in single comprehensive articles."[175] Unfortunately, Penguin wanted something quite different; in fact, the exact opposite of what Gunn envisioned: an encyclopedia with excessive coverage of film and television, with glossy photos to attract browsers, moving the emphasis *away from* the literature of the field. And, indeed, many of the articles on individual writers are woefully incomplete, due to the constraints put on by the publishers, making the book significantly less useful than the now definitive Nicholls/Clute encyclopedia. Gunn expresses his frustration when Penguin's push for increasing the focus on film in his memoir: "I should have resigned then, but that would have put in jeopardy all of my work and that of the people I had recruited to write entries, including Steve Goldman's share of the advance."[176] To make matters worse, after Gunn submitted the manuscript Penguin wanted to cut eighty pages from the planned 600—by contrast, the second edition of the Nicholls/Clute is 1400 pages—and this watered down the content even further. As Gunn reflects, "I should have had my name taken off the book; I wrote an introduction in which I laid out the restrictions placed on the editing of the book, but Peg [Streep] said I couldn't publish that. Eventually Steve ended up writing or revising nearly 100 entries, and I ended up writing almost as many and rewriting a number of the articles, even those credited to others, in particular Harry Harrison's article on 'Religion in Science Fiction' (he submitted a piece that was entirely an attack on religious belief) and A. E. Van Vogt's piece on magazine serials."[177] While the Nicholls/Clute encyclopedia (now in its third edition as a freely available digital resource) has become the essential reference volume in the field, withdrawn library copies of Gunn's ill-fated encyclopedia can be purchased on Amazon for a few dollars. As Gunn laments in his memoir, "there was no real need for the book, and I felt like I could have made better use of those four years of my writing life."[178] Nonetheless, *The New Encyclopedia of Science Fiction* remains of interest simply for the lineup of contributors that Gunn assembled, both from the academic and writing communities. Entries from an impressive array of writers, including Brian Aldiss, Poul Anderson, Arthur C. Clarke, Hal Clement, Gordon R. Dickson, Philip Jose Farmer, Frederik Pohl, Norman Spinrad, Jack Williamson, and many others, make the volume more than just an ill-conceived curiosity.

A much more satisfying and fruitful editorial project for Gunn was his work with the Easton Press for the Masterpieces of Science Fiction collectors' editions. First approached by the Easton Press in the early eighties as a potential subscriber when they launched the series, Gunn contacted the publisher David Ward about donating copies to KU's special collections and suggested some titles for future volumes. Shortly after, series editor Eric Stones sent Gunn some sample notes for the first two books in the series, Wells's *The War of the Worlds* and Clarke's *2001*. Gunn wrote back that the notes had some inaccuracies, and a few days later Stones called him asking if he'd consider rewriting them and whether the volumes should include introductions. By the end of the conversation, Gunn agreed to write all of the notes, volunteered to enlist well-known writers to contribute introductions, and to serve as a series consultant. This arrangement continued for a dozen years. Gunn himself wrote more than a hundred introductions and his colleague Stephen Goldman also contributed when a deadline loomed. Many of Gunn's introductions were later collected in the book *Paratexts*. A series that was supposed to only run fifty volumes ended up being two hundred beautifully produced leather-bound books. Overall, it was a satisfying project. As Gunn writes, "The Masterpieces of Science Fiction series and the subsequent Signed First Editions of Science Fiction series have been good for science fiction.... These well-crafted leather-bound editions with gilded edges and frontispieces by well-known SF artists have conferred some prestige on the field."[179]

While these scholarly projects occupied Gunn throughout the 1980s, he worked to establish science fiction as a signature area of research and teaching on the KU campus, and further solidified the university as an international fulcrum of science fiction activity. In 1982 Gunn founded the Center for the Study of Science Fiction as a Kansas Board of Regents Center, the first of its kind. And in 1985 he began offering the Writers Workshop in Science Fiction, a two-week intensive writers' retreat held prior to the Campbell Conference and the Intensive Teaching Institute. Further, following Sturgeon's death in 1985, Gunn established the Theodore Sturgeon Memorial Award for Short Fiction in 1987 to pair with the Campbell Award for the novel. The university library also became a focal depository for writers' papers, eventually becoming home to the archives of Sturgeon, Donald Wollheim, Cordwainer Smith, and many others. To help support the Center, the university administration, having consulted Gunn, wrote a letter to Robert Heinlein in 1988 about endowing the Center. Since Heinlein grew up in nearby Kansas City, it seemed like a natural fit. Unfortunately, they approached too late: Heinlein died that May. Heinlein's widow, Virginia, wrote Gunn a note saying if they would have heard from them a few years before, then they would have likely made the endowment, but Heinlein's estate was already committed to other projects (the public library in Heinlein's birthplace, Butler, Missouri, for one). They next approached Isaac Asimov, who quickly, and sharply, declined in a two-page letter, making it clear that the only reason he is explaining the reasons for his refusal is because of his long friendship with Jim Gunn. The university administration learned a lesson in how to approach donors. Indeed, the next target was Arthur C. Clarke, and this time Gunn wrote the letter himself: "You are one of the few writers whose name would bring instant recognition to the Center, and one of the few whose resources could provide the basic endowment."[180] Clarke responded that he had a lot of commitments to people in Sri Lanka, where he lived, and was concerned about political unrest on the island, and didn't feel that he could commit his money at the time. Eventually, the Clarke Foundation would endow a center at the University of California–San Diego. In the end, the Center was endowed by a donation from Gunn's brother Richard in 1989 and named in honor of their parents as the J. Wayne and Elsie Gunn Center for the Study of Science Fiction. Since the early 1990s Gunn has worked closely with Christopher McKitterick, who first came to the university in 1992 to study with Gunn. In 1995 Gunn named McKitterick assistant director of the Center. After a stint at Microsoft, McKitterick returned to KU in 2002 to launch a technical writing program and helped further expand the Center and the science fiction curriculum at the university. When Gunn stepped down as director in 2010, McKitterick was promoted to the position, and he has worked to extend the reach of the Center with Gunn still offering guidance. Acclaimed writer Kij Johnson got involved in the work of the Center in 1995, shortly after attending the Writers Workshop and winning the Sturgeon Award for "Fox Magic" in 1994. Johnson began teaching the Science Fiction & Fantasy Novel Writing Workshop in 2004, served as assistant director of the Center, and after receiving an MFA in creative writing from North Carolina State, joined the faculty of the English Department at KU in 2012, and now serves as associate director.

Gunn retired from the University of Kansas in 1993 at the then mandatory age of 70. Although you could hardly call it retirement, as Gunn continued to work daily in his campus office until nearly the age of ninety. But as far as teaching (though he continued to teach the writing workshop and the summer institute until the late 2000s) and departmental work (and salary), Gunn was retired. But these years were still, nonetheless, extremely active, as Gunn built the Center for the Study of Science Fiction into one of the leading spaces where SF was studied, archived, and taught. And he got back to fiction writing, producing a number of short stories and novels in the coming years, including "The Lens of Time" and "The Gingerbread Man" (both 1995), "The Day the Magic Came Back" (1996), the *Star Trek* novel *The Joy Machine* (1996), *The Millennium Blues* (2001), and the stories that make up *Gift from the Stars* (1999–2005), a response to Carl Sagan's bestselling *Contact*, which had recently been made into a blockbuster movie. After receiving a sizeable contract for the reprint rights for *The Immortals*, which had drawn interest from Touchstone Pictures, Gunn added a new story to the original sequence, "Elixir." The new edition appeared from Pocket Books in 2004. He also compiled two further volumes of *The Road to Science Fiction* series: volume five covering British science fiction and volume six featuring international science fiction. Both appeared in 1998. A collection of Gunn's essays, *Inside Science Fiction*, had been published by Borgo Press in 1992; a revised and expanded second edition appeared in 2006 from Scarecrow Press. Finally, with the Summer Writers Workshop becoming an important destination for aspiring writers, Gunn put together the long-awaited book on fiction writing, *The Science of Science-Fiction Writing*, in 2000. The book was partly sparked by the fiftieth anniversary of Gunn's first stories.

Another project that Gunn became involved with at this time was the development of the Science Fiction Hall of Fame, founded in 1996, a joint project of the Gunn Center and the Kansas City Science Fiction and Fantasy Society. Four inductees were selected each year by a committee including Gunn, Robin Wayne Bailey, Joe Haldeman, and others. The honorees were officially inducted into the Hall of Fame at the Awards Banquet during the Campbell Conference. In 2005 the Science Fiction Hall of Fame was moved to the EMP Museum in Seattle and is now administered there. Gunn himself was inducted into the Hall in 2015.

In 2007 Gunn was named a Damon Knight Memorial Grand Master of Science Fiction, the lifetime achievement award of the field, by the Science Fiction and Fantasy Writers of America, joining the other great writers of his generation, Heinlein, Asimov, Williamson, Clarke, Pohl, Van Vogt, Anderson, et al. At the Nebula Awards in New York that May he was presented the award by Robin Wayne Bailey, fellow writer, friend from Kansas City, and then president of the SFWA. Former student John Kessel gave an introductory address that was later included in the *Nebula Awards Showcase 2008* anthology, making this important observation: "It was only over the time I was at KU that I came to realize how his career represented, in some ways, the main thread of the development of science fiction. As a boy, he shook hands with H.G. Wells. In the late 1940s he sold fiction to John W. Campbell and throughout the 1950s he was a regular in Horace Gold's *Galaxy*, becoming a mainstay of the movement toward 'sociological science fiction.' He was one of the first people ever to study science fiction in the academy, writing his master's thesis on SF, portions of which were published in *Dynamic Science Fiction* in 1953. His first novel was a collaboration with Jack Williamson that the *New York Times* said read 'like a collaboration between Asimov and Heinlein.'"[181]

Kessel here overstates Gunn's contact with Wells, perhaps conflating it with his own imagined encounter between his father and Wells in his story "Buffalo," and perhaps imagining the physical contact of a handshake had taken place to extend the thread of contact to the later generations who have been blessed by Gunn's mentoring, kindness, and friendship. Kessel's closing remarks reveal the depth of admiration he has for his mentor: "His has been a life devoted to science fiction. He may not tell you what it has meant to him, but I just needed to tell you what he has meant to me. Congratulations, Jim, and thanks."[182] In his acceptance speech, Gunn reflected on the passing of Jack Williamson, who had died just a few months before at age 98: "My only regret is that Jack Williamson didn't get a chance to add his approval. As a Grand Master himself, he knew how much it meant, and I have the feeling that the knowledge might have brought him joy in his final days. He was that kind of friend."[183] He also commented on the shared vision of the science fiction family: "Grand Masters come in all shapes and sizes and genders, with different ways of looking at the world and different ways of embodying it in their fiction. But they share one belief: in the power of science fiction to transform lives and minds and maybe even the world. We all have experienced the awakening that comes from the recognition of our common humanity, our shared dreams, our vision of a better life, and our awareness that the future depends upon the choices we make today."[184] And he came full circle, bringing forward the questions that had occupied his mind ever since the moment of his first brush with greatness, when he heard Wells speak in 1937:

> From my earliest contacts with SF I recognized qualities that I did not find in other kinds of fiction: a realization of the continuity of existence from the remote past to the distant future, the relationship of present decisions and actions to the futures we and our descendants will inhabit, a recognition of mutual humanity that emphasizes species concerns above those of individuals or tribes or nations, a willingness to work together for a better world, and general good will. H. G. Wells said that the world was in a race between education and catastrophe, and called for an "open conspiracy" of people of good will to create a better world. I think SF is a major part of that education, and we all can help by introducing more people into its charms and values, particularly young people.[185]

For seventy years James Gunn has heeded Wells's call.

Gunn continued to make important contributions to science fiction scholarship and criticism in the new millennium as well. With former student Matthew Candelaria, he compiled *Speculations on Speculation: Theories of Science Fiction* in 2005, a collection of key critical essays central to the study of science fiction from writers and scholars, including Brian Aldiss, Samuel R. Delany, Ursula K. Le Guin, Darko Suvin, Gary K. Wolfe, Robert Scholes, Gunn himself, and many others. Gunn, Candelaria, and renowned feminist SF scholar Marleen Barr edited *Reading Science Fiction*, which includes many useful essays that consider new directions science fiction scholarship is taking in the new century. This project had started a few years before *Speculations on Speculation* when the Modern Language Association was looking to sponsor a text on teaching science fiction. Gunn and Barr submitted a proposal and brought Candelaria on board as a third editor, but they ended up facing some of the same difficulties Gunn had experienced with Penguin during the *New Encyclopedia* project: "The editorial board at MLA kept suggesting changes. In a rare moment of irritation, I wrote the MLA person in charge that we were the experts and the editorial board needed to depend upon our judgment. But we kept agreeing to changes until finally the proposal got turned down."[186] Barr then took the project to Palgrave Macmillan who published it in 2008. That same year, as the global financial crisis made it unfeasible for the Science Fiction Research Association to hold its annual conference at the planned overseas venue in Dublin, Ireland, Gunn and McKitterick stepped forward and offered to host the conference in Lawrence. That was the last time that Frederik Pohl was able to travel to Lawrence for the summer events. Pohl gave a memorable reading from his new novel *The Last Theorem*, written in collaboration with Arthur C. Clarke, who had died just three months before.

The not unexpected loss of his science fiction colleagues and friends at an increasing pace since the death of Asimov in 1992 were not the only losses Gunn faced in the ensuing years. Following his father's death in 1990 at age ninety-five, his mother passed away at ninety-seven in 1994. His brother Richard died of a heart attack on Thanksgiving Day in 2002; part of Richard's estate went to further fund the Gunn Center. But the death of their son Kit from a heart attack on St. Patrick's Day in 2005 at age fifty-six following battles with Hodgkin's lymphoma and colon and liver cancer was particularly sorrowful for the Gunns. As Gunn writes, "It was a devastating blow. There is little in life more devastating than losing a child. Up to that time Jane and I had seemed to live a charmed life. Everything had worked out. Now we had lost a son, one who had brilliance and great promise, who still had much of life and maybe accomplishment ahead of him. Children should never die before their parents. His memories would never be far from our minds; life would never be quite the same."[187] One can feel the deep pain and sadness in Gunn's words. In 2012, after sixty-five years together, Gunn said goodbye to his beloved wife Jane, who died on September 27, age eighty-seven. Their son Kevin provided strength, comfort, and support and helped see his father through. Gunn writes, "Thanks, Jane, for a good life. I hope the memory of that helped you through your final days and that it will, eventually, help heal the hole in my universe."[188] A good life, lived together.

The months following Jane's death were hard on Gunn, but as the calendar flipped to 2013 he was reenergized and looked forward to a number of events. He completed the novel *Transcendental*, which he'd been working on and off for a number of years—the first portion had been published in the Frederik Pohl *festschrift*, *Gateways*, in 2010 as "Tales from the Spaceship *Geoffrey*"—and finished his memoir, which informs this chapter. And he had been named Guest of Honor at the 71st World Science

Fiction Convention in San Antonio to be held that August. Further, a group of his former students—the author of this book, McKitterick, and Nathaniel Williams—were preparing a "Gunn Tribute" panel at the joint Eaton/SFRA Conference in Riverside, California in April. Although Gunn had not traveled for a few years, he was up for the trip to Riverside, where he met with many old friends in the writing and scholarly communities. At the World Con, a similar tribute panel was arranged that included Kij Johnson, John Kessel, and Gary K. Wolfe, whom Gunn had mentored while Wolfe was a student at KU in 1968. The release of *Transcendental* by TOR Books was set to coincide with World Con. The book received good notices and sold well. The front-cover blurb was from his old friend Frederik Pohl, who wrote, "Jim Gunn doesn't publish a new novel very often, but when he does, it's a whopper. *Transcendental* is his best yet." Although much too infirm to travel to San Antonio, Pohl did share his thoughts on Gunn for the convention program, reflecting on when he and Gunn first met at the 1952 World Con, sixty-one years before, and remarking, "I wish I could get to San Antonio this year to shake Jim's hand. It's a long overdue honor!"[189] These were some of the last words Pohl wrote. He died on September 2, the concluding day of the World Science Fiction Convention.

Gunn's activities and honors have continued. Still a fixture at the events sponsored by the Gunn Center, he continues to participate in the Speculative Fiction Writing Workshop as a guest instructor during week one. In 2015, on Gunn's suggestion, the Campbell Conference hosted a forum that brought together faculty from many institutions offering degree programs in science fiction and fantasy. Soon after the conference, Gunn was inducted into the Science Fiction Hall of Fame at the *Locus Awards* Ceremony in Seattle. When toastmaster Connie Willis called him to the podium, the audience stood in ovation for several minutes, a fitting tribute for a man who has done so much for the science fiction field. In his acceptance speech, Gunn again pondered that early brush with H.G. Wells and how that has played out in his life within the science fiction community: "Over my 67 years of writing science fiction, writing about science fiction, and teaching science fiction, I've met a lot of science-fiction people, most of the writers and scholars and quite a few of the readers. On the whole I've found them a wonderful group—intelligent, inquisitive, inspired and generous, the kind of people H.G. Wells was thinking about when he called for an Open Conspiracy of people of good will to create a better world. I've taken that to heart."[190]

Gunn concluded by reiterating the case that science fiction has much ahead and much to offer a world in constant flux: "A lot has happened to science fiction since I sat in a garret writing my first story in 1948. And as I look around at the publishing scene and the writing life, I realize that science fiction still has some crises to resolve. Well, it has been declared dead several times before, and I have confidence that now it can withstand success. The world has changed, too, often in positive ways, sometimes in ways that threaten its survival. It's the job of science fiction, it's our job, to observe those changes and consider their implications for human lives and maybe even do something to make those lives better, more livable, more human—whatever "human" turns out to be. Let's save the world through science fiction."[191]

As this book is being written, the sequel to *Transcendental*, *Transgalactic*, has just been published. Like its predecessor, it has been receiving good reviews. And meanwhile, Gunn has completed the manuscript for the final book of the trilogy, *Transformation*. At ninety-three, Gunn's continued engagement with the science fiction field to which he has contributed so much is both marveling and inspiring. For the generations of readers, students, and colleagues who have encountered Gunn through his work, his classroom, his lectures, and through the multiple other ways he has contributed to bettering our world, Gunn's impact, I believe, can be summed up by a comment writer Andy Duncan once made to me summer when Duncan was guest instructor the week following Gunn at the Speculative Fiction Writing Workshop: "We are *all* Jim's students."

Two

Early Stories to *This Fortress World* and *Star Bridge*

Gunn began submitting stories to the science fiction pulp magazines during the summer of 1948. This was at the cusp of the expansion of the science fiction magazine market. When Gunn started submitting, there were nine magazines in the science fiction and fantasy field—*Amazing, Astounding, Famous Fantastic Mysteries, Fantastic Adventures, Fantasy Book, Planet Stories, Startling Stories, Thrilling Wonder Stories,* and *Weird Tales*—and some of the mainstream pulp and slick magazines were publishing SF occasionally, most notably *Collier's* and *The Saturday Evening Post*. *The Magazine of Fantasy and Science Fiction* would be launched in the fall of 1949 and *Galaxy* in October 1950. Along with Campbell's *Astounding*, these magazines would be the leading markets for the next two decades. By 1953 SF publishing was booming. Throughout that year, thirty-five different magazines appeared on the newsstands; some, such as *Rocket Stories* and *Vortex,* lasted only a few issues, but others would carry on until the end of the decade when the market collapsed, and still others would be launched throughout the decade. Book publication was also booming, with several hardcover publishers publishing SF titles and paperback reprints and originals carving a space for science fiction on the book market. Fred Pohl's *Star Science Fiction* original anthologies published by Ballantine started another market for short stories—Gunn's "The Immortals" would appear in volume four later in the decade. It was a good moment to undertake an SF writing career.

Gunn's first effort was a story titled "Paradox," published in the October 1949 issue of *Thrilling Wonder Stories* under the Edwin James byline. "Paradox" is a comic story of alien planetary exploration involving a race of superior alien telepaths scouting Earth as a possible site of conquest.

Their expedition team abducts a petty criminal alcoholic named Sam to examine the human mind and to determine human capabilities. The aliens can't make any sense of Sam's inebriated stupidity and therefore believe he's a superior being of a race they will not be able to overcome, because, as telepaths, they are "incapable of evasion, lying, deceit," characteristics of which Sam is a master.[1] In the end, the aliens report back to their homeworld with a warning to "steer clear of earth."[2] "Paradox" is a decent first effort, comparable to most of the fiction of the period, although not as effective as "Communications," the first of Gunn's stories to actually appear but the fifth he wrote, which also considers questions of alien contact and communication.

"Mask of Peace" (*Future* September 1951) was the second story Gunn wrote in the fall of 1948. It is set in "the turbulent ninth century of the post–Imperial era," in which humanity has spread to hundreds of worlds across the galaxy.[3] In many of his early stories, Gunn focuses on planetary politics, which may show the influence of the stories John W. Campbell was publishing in *Astounding*; Asimov's *Foundation* stories are the most obvious example. The story takes place on a planet named Flora "lying near the outskirts of the galaxy," eliciting the frontier theme.[4] The plot involves an assassination attempt upon Eldred Carla, the dynamic leader of the "League of Peace," who presumably seeks to forge a peaceful accord between warring factions of the crumbled empire and bring unity back to humanity. But Carla's real motive is to rebuild the empire with himself as autocratic leader. In a rather awkward ending Carla is confronted by his younger brother John, who looks almost exactly like him (Gunn may have been inspired by his own sibling Richard), in the "Temple of Sarn," the headquarters of a "new religion" founded two centuries before by the "scientific mystic Sarn Sanderson."[5] The Sarnites have a different path to peace. John is a member of the Assassins, who apparently shape galactic politics using their own methods. Gunn would return to the idea of an assassin shaping history in *Star Bridge* and to religion in a fallen empire in *This Fortress World*. All this is not made entirely clear in the story; nonetheless, the story is of interest as a precursor to the space operas Gunn would write in the early fifties. Another anticipation of his novels is the way Gunn effectively draws out the ambience of the streets of Flora's capital, creating almost a Dickensian contrast between the filthy streets and desperate people in the slums living in the shadow of the glorious Temple. Gunn has remarked that in both novels he was setting out to bring a naturalistic approach to space opera and that can be seen in this early story. "Mask of Peace" is notable for containing the seeds of ideas that Gunn would expand upon in his early novels, but the story is otherwise underdeveloped.

"Freedom, Inc.," completed that November, was published several years later under the quite unGunnian title "Slaves of Venus" in *Planet Stories* September 1952. The changed title affects the impact of the story and readers' expectations. What is intended to be a serious political story about an uprising of exploited labor is dampened and juvenilized. The mature original title quite clearly suggests that Gunn was seeking Campbell's *Astounding* as the target market and it better fits Gunn's political themes. The story involves an agent from Earth sent to Venus to break the oligarchical tyranny of a "band of interplanetary gangsters" who had seized control of all planetary governments decades before. Earth and Mars have already broken the yoke of tyranny and by story's end Venus has as well.[6] Like the other early stories, the political idea itself is stronger than the narrative execution.

Gunn's next effort, "Sane Asylum," was an ambitious 12,000-word novelette, first mailed in November 1948. Gunn had high hopes for the story, first trying the general fiction magazine *Blue Book* before making the rounds of the science fiction magazines, feeling that it had social and psychological dimensions that would appeal to a broader market, but it never sold. The story involves a man who is committed to an asylum with the denouement being that he is sane and most of the rest of the world is crazy; the kind of reversal plot that Philip K. Dick would explore masterfully. Again, the idea is stronger than the execution. But the story was a learning experience: the emphasis on dreams, psychology, and the social sciences would be central to Gunn's later work.

Gunn's fifth story, "Communications," is his most successful from this early period. Completed and mailed at the beginning of December, it was bought by Sam Merwin, Jr., for *Startling Stories*, and by the vagaries of magazine publication, it appeared a month before "Paradox," making it Gunn's first published story. And as a debut, it is fairly impressive. The story involves a space navy in a stalemate confrontation with an alien armada, recalling the opening premise of Fredric Brown's "Arena" and Murray Leinster's "First Contact," a story whose central premise, unlike Brown's, is that communication between intelligent species is possible and preferable. Gunn's scenario lies somewhere in between. The story draws authenticity from Gunn's experiences in the service in terms of details, shipboard protocols, and the political processes of a military unit. As "Communications" opens, the Earth forces have been in a stalemate for ten years with an alien species from Procyon. The crew of an outpost space station at the edge of disputed space, whose purpose is to monitor the alien fleet, anticipates "The Big One," a catastrophic space battle with the alien forces. The Procyons are portrayed as a vicious species that previously tortured and wiped out the Sirians, and then subsequently wiped out all animal life on the planet. Stories of alien menace in this manner, of course, date back to Wells's *The War of the Worlds*. Like Wells's Martians, the Procys are wholly logical, rigid, without emotion. In other words, they're incapable of compromise. Potter, a bureaucratic representative from Earth, has come to the outpost for inspection, with the intent to make the argument that it is time to sue for peace, that the morale on the frontier is low, and that the continued stalemate is politically and militarily unnecessary. Potter is working from a false premise that peace is possible, but he does not understand the realities of the space frontier. To support his position, Potter claims that Earth is running out of atomic fuels, therefore peace is an economic necessity. Here we might draw a parallel with Isaac Asimov's "The Martian Way," which contains a similar clash between Earthside politics and the frontier. In that case, the question is water, not atomics.

Potter is shown around the station by Lt. Carter Leigh, who has been on the frontier for five years, and whose experience in space is contrasted with that of the neophyte bureaucrat. Potter believes that the men of the frontier want to return to Earth; that they, like those at home, have grown tired of the stalemate and that a simple negotiation is all that is necessary. To contrast Potter's sense of morale, an important scene involves bringing mail to the men at the outpost—an idea developing from Gunn's experience as an adjutant—which raises the broader issue of morale on a frontier, and the psychological cost of loneliness. The station commander, Admiral Bailey, explains that the mail is important to the men due to the loneliness and insecurity inherent on the space frontier: "'You don't understand either what it means to men who have been fighting for you in the loneliest of places in space to receive their only reminders that there is really happiness and love waiting for them back in the System instead of it all being a dream. You don't understand what it is to wait for mail for three months and then have a ship arrive empty. You will probably say in your report that the morale of the men is low. In *my* next report, Mr. Potter, I will include the reason for that.'"[7] The theme of loneliness will resurface in many of Gunn's stories in the fifties, such as "Breaking Point" and the stories that make up *Station in Space*. Another central Gunn theme suggested by this passage is the idea of something being a "dream," intangible, ungraspable. In this case, dreams are tied with loneliness; the possibility that psychological trauma can cause illusion; that the rational world can be distorted through loneliness. Gunn also examines the nature of administration that would feature in his later work and in his career as a university administrator. Here his experiences in the Naval Air Corps and his work as an adjutant to the commanding general again come into play. He effectively conveys the hierarchy of command and the protocols of the daily workings of a military installation. Gunn distinguishes between administrators of action, those on the front lines, such as the Admiral and Vice-Admiral Douglas, and bureaucratic functionaries, such as Potter, who have no direct experience with the strategic necessities and the problems faced on the frontier. Potter seeks peace, but doesn't have the knowledge and background to make a sound judgment. It is up to the Admiral and the men of the outpost to counter the functionary's ignorance.

The problem of communication presented in the story involves cryptography; how the Earth outpost can communicate without the Procyons being able to break their code. The fact that both sides understand the communication practices of the other allow neither to gain a tactical advantage, and thus the stalemate. To work on the code, Gunn introduces an "electronic brain," a computer. Ultimately, Lewis Carroll's Alice books are used as code, which turns the tide of the stalemate: the Procys are unable to penetrate the illogical logic of Carroll's nonsense poems. The story ends with the problem solved: humans have found a way to advance communication, and will therefore be able to stave off the Procys' aggression. The bureaucrat Potter returns to Earth a wiser man.

The story also broaches the topic that big projects take time. That there are no quick fixes for large scale projects in space, but money, public opinion, and political vision are too often short-sighted. The tug-of-war between big projects and politics, capital, and society is, again, central to Gunn's later thought in *Station in Space* and *The Listeners*, and because he continues to explore these themes in those major works, of the early stories, "Communications" is the most provocative and insightful. More than the four stories written before it, "Communications" points in the direction Gunn's later, philosophically intense fiction would go.

Gunn must have been stimulated by the progression in terms of theme and philosophy he made in writing "Communications." His next story, "Slave Psychology" (*Future* January 1951) was completed and mailed just nine days after. In some ways "Slave Psychology" takes the premise of alien invasion from "Communications" and turns it to another angle. Earth has been conquered by the Dlar. The Dlar consider exterminating humans altogether and keeping the planet for themselves. On their home planet life is difficult because the planet is hostile to its lifeforms, and therefore the Dlar have evolved a hard, rigid culture to survive such harsh conditions. Comparatively, Earth is a paradise and, hence, to their minds, easy. Interestingly, Gunn introduces recursivity when the aliens read and study Earth's science fiction about flights to other planets. Like Gunn's aliens in "Paradox" and "Communications," the Dlar have little imagination and they take these tales to be historical documentation and thus imagine that humans have retreated into decadence. By remaining passive and seemingly decadent, the humans build a resistance movement underneath the feet of the Dlar and overcome the conquerors. Admittedly, this plot became a fairly standard science fiction scenario indicative of any number of stories in Campbell's *Astounding*, especially in later years. Unfortunately, the story lacks the narrative power of "Communications" or the ease of storytelling in some of the earlier stories. Overall, it is clunky with too much infodump and not enough narrative.

Gunn had more success with a story of alien communication he wrote a few months later, "Private Enterprise," which was the first story he sold to John W. Campbell. It appeared in the July 1950 issue of *Astounding*. Gunn's good feelings about having a story published in *Astounding* were dampened a few years later when Campbell told him he bought "Private Enterprise" as filler. The story takes place on Rigel V where earthman Bill Stewart is on a trade mission. In this story, Gunn reverses the trade scenario from stories in which aliens seek to trade with Earth, to the more favorable scenario (to Campbell) of humans as initiators of galactic commerce. In this sense, the emphasis on human exceptionalism would have appealed to Campbell and is probably what ultimately sold him on the story. As the story opens, Stewart is confronted by Rigelian investigators who search his apartment. Earth is involved in the Nine System Trade Alliance and Stewart is an agent sent to draw the Rigelians into the Alliance. But Rigel V is isolationist. The Alliance values free trade, autonomy, and cooperation, and is strongly opposed to imperialism. If Rigel doesn't join, the Alliance will dissolve and imperialism will arise in the aftermath. The Rigelians have a different point of view, however: they believe the Alliance is tyrannical and is trying to subjugate all to their economic paradigm. Rigel's unwillingness to join the Alliance blocks the Alliance from extending its reach further to other planetary systems. The Alliance is at a crisis point: it must spread or crumble. As with "Mask of Peace," there are some echoes of Asimov's *Foundation* series here in that a large-scale economic and political system must have constant vigilance to combat its own inertia. It also reflects the ideology of continuous growth symptomatic of advanced capitalism. In some ways, Gunn anticipates the economics of our contemporary era, without necessarily seeing the complications such an economy might have.

With Stewart, Gunn created a good example of the "competent man," the efficient and resourceful Heinlein/Campbell hero, capable of achieving the goals of a system outside of the direct influence of the bureaucratic realities of the system itself. This is, in essence, the nature of the frontier theme—the Admiral and his men on the outpost station in "Communications" are also good examples. In later work, Gunn will continue to explore the nature of the competent man, but often placed within the structural inertias of bureaucratic systems, illustrating that the Heinlein/Campbell hero has limitations. In the end, and not unexpectedly, Stewart succeeds in convincing the Rigelians to join the Alliance, through rational persuasive discourse. Like most of the stories Campbell published in this vein, it is more an argument than a heroic action adventure.

It's worth noting that a later story sold to Campbell, "Without Portfolio" (*Astounding* January 1955), has similar thematic concerns. "Without Portfolio" is a Cold War story dealing with contemporary politics rather than future interplanetary politics. The story implies a union of the Soviets and the Chinese. Business firms take over negotiations between nations because they are better at it than politicians and bureaucrats and the neoliberal business ethic is able to break the inertia of entrenched bureaucratic political ideas.

A few other stories were written in the early months of 1949 prior to "Private Enterprise," although sold somewhat later. In "The Sun Came Up Last Night" (*Science Fiction Quarterly* August 1951) the Moon has been transformed into a mini-sun, giving the story a climate change vibe. Initially it is thought that aliens are behind this, in an attempt to invade Earth. But it is in fact a story of eugenics, like Stapledon's *Odd John*. Genetically superior humans have been sequestered on an island and as they reach maturity they plan to take over the world. Their ambitions are thwarted by investigative reporter Sean O'Shaughnessy, who uncovers the plot and reveals it to the world. There are echoes of Theodore Sturgeon's "Microcosmic God" here, a story Gunn would have read many times in Wollheim's *Pocket Book of Science-Fiction*. "These Things Are Sirius" (*Thrilling Wonder* August 1951) is another story about economics, centering on the question of the balance of trade. Aliens from Sirius have established contact with Earth. Sirian technology is superior to Earth manufacture and in order to curtail a flood of Sirian products on the market, Earth has imposed stringent trade sanctions on Sirian products. The story opens as a man named Gil wants to buy a Sirian wrench, but buying Sirian tools is illegal. In this sense, perhaps, the model for the story is Van Vogt's *Weapon Shops*. Although Sirian manufacture and technology is superior to Earth's, Sirians, like their predecessors in Gunn's earlier stories, have limited imaginations and don't have much creative art. Therefore, they are attracted to and enjoy human creativity, much in the manner of Cory Doctorow's more recent story "Craphound." This allows for a new balance as human creativity becomes the commodity of exchange with Sirian technology—there are interesting echoes here with our current economic model. Gunn's final story during this early apprentice period was "The Man with Common Sense" (*Amazing* July 1950), which introduced the galactic insurance agent Malachi Jones, whom Gunn was considering developing as a comic series character in the manner of Jack Vance's Magnus Ridolph. Malachi Jones is an adjustor for Lairds of Luna insurance agency, a firm "that not only insured against future contingencies but made sure they didn't happen."[8] In this story, Jones is sent to the frontier planet Mizar II and facilitates the end of a potential uprising by guaranteeing the sparse frontier world will be adequately supplied from Earth. The first version of Gunn's robot golf story, "Unfair Competition," revised and published later in *Galaxy* as "Open Warfare" (discussed later), was also written in this period. Over the next two years, Gunn wrote very little science fiction, instead concentrating on his school work as he worked toward his Master's degree at the University of Kansas.

When Gunn returned to writing science fiction in the spring of 1951 he produced a number of stories which, although in many ways still apprentice stories, begin to show the further development of his thinking, honed while writing his master's thesis, *Modern Science Fiction: A Critical Analysis*. The first of these to see publication, although the last to be written, was "Survival Policy," Gunn's second sale to *Astounding*, appearing in the October 1952 issue. "Survival Policy" was also the last story published under the Edwin James pseudonym. Here Gunn returns to the adventures of Malachi Jones, the galactic insurance salesman. The story opens in an office setting reminiscent of countless detective stories as an anonymous young woman from a planet she won't at first disclose wants to take out a one hundred million dollar "life insurance" policy to "'insure the survival of my race.'" Jones drolly assures his client this is possible, "'I once insured an extra brain for a person named Gosseyn'"[9]—another moment of witty SF recursivity, referring to Van Vogt's *The World of Null A*, and doubly interesting, as Van Vogt's novel became a central text in Gunn's teaching in later years. It's soon revealed that the woman is a member of a race "of mutants confined to the planet New Earth of the sun Polaris," who have increased intelligence—perhaps another nod to Gilbert Gosseyn. Their super intelligence has led to fear and hysteria among the normal citizens of New Earth and oppressive intolerance has been instituted. Jones and his assistant Rand travel to New Earth, with Rand voicing the arguments against the mutants: "'If They win, it is the end of man as a species. He must go the way of the carnivores—or the housefly. For that is how much we will mean to Them. He must give way to the better man, to the better-thinking man, to the superman.'"[10] Rand's argument contains the evolutionary ideology favored by Campbell, though in opposition, and it is through Malachi Jones's Socratic responses that Gunn states a position favorable to Campbell. After Rand's claims that the mutants are a threat to humanity, Jones counters by chiding Rand for having read "'those fictional adventures,'" another recursive overture. As Jones makes his investigations on New Earth and comes to see the social, economic, and political dynamics of the planet, he offers his solution to the President, who happens to be the father of the mutant girl who sought Jones's help: "'The wiping out of the "mutants" would cripple the intellectual potential of New Earth so severely that it would be centuries in recovering. Your ideal solution is the integration of the "mutants" into your race.'"[11] After some resistance, Jones shows that the "mutants" are not mutants at all, but part of the spectrum of individuals in any group of human beings: "'The important factor is that there is no significant difference between mutant and human—it is not a question of kind but of degree. The fact you overlook is that there have always been a certain number of unusually intelligent persons.'"[12] Although Gunn didn't develop the Malachi Jones series further, "Survival Policy" is consistent with the interplanetary cultural problem-solving stories that became increasingly common in *Astounding* in the fifties and sixties, by such writers as H. Beam Piper, Randall Garrett, Christopher Anvil, and Everett B. Cole with his "Philosophical Corps" series. Gunn would move away from such stories as he focused on the type of science fiction that was defining Horace Gold's new magazine *Galaxy*.

A few months before writing "Survival Policy," Gunn penned "The Boy with Five Fingers" (*Startling* January 1953), a short and delightful play on the theme of post-atomic holocaust, Gunn's only atomic bomb story. The human species has been severely mutated by atomic fallout. A boy who is "normal" is the oddball outsider in school. The story portrays the boy's crush on his one-eyed teacher. All humans have the "Basic Right"— the right to be different. Gunn's exploration of the idea of difference here is quite interesting in relation to current cultural theory. In the story, the "Old Race" were all exactly alike. Now, the species has morphed into multiple differences. Thus, the story also raises questions of conformity. It is a charming little story, one of those nuggets hidden away in the old pulps of the era.

"A Word for Freedom" was also written at this time, although it did not appear until the January 1954 issue of *Worlds of If.* The story centers on the complexity of language, in some ways anticipating the linguistic turn in critical theory. Later, in his capacity as an English professor, this attention to language will come to the fore in such works as *The Listeners, Kampus,* and *The Dreamers.* Gunn argues that language complexity leads to specialization, which leads to increasing difficulty in communication, which in turn leads to rigid social classes, inevitably leading to stagnation. At the end of the story a Moon rocket is launched, opening up a new frontier which can break the stagnation. Thus like many stories of the era, this is a story, ultimately, about the promise of the space frontier. Like Pohl and Kornbluth's *The Space Merchants,* for example, "A Word for Freedom" suggests that the future must include human expansion into space.

"The Misogynist" and "The Last Word"

Although Gunn had managed to place two stories in Campbell's *Astounding* by this point, his breakthrough story appeared the month after "Survival Policy." "The Misogynist," one of Gunn's signature stories, appeared in the November 1952 issue of *Galaxy* and it was the first story to appear under the James Gunn byline. Fred Pohl reprinted it the following summer in the paperback anthology *Shadow of Tomorrow.* Later, Gunn selected it as his representative story for Harry Harrison's *SF Author's Choice 4* anthology.

"The Misogynist" teases out a conspiracy theory that women are aliens. In this sense it recalls Fritz Leiber's *Conjure Wife,* which has a similar domestic setting, although in Leiber's classic, the conceit is that women are witches who cast competing spells to advance the careers of their husbands. Gunn cleverly sets the story in the guise of his own domestic situation, as the wife in the story is named Jane, and the host for the evening is "Jimmie," although his name is not revealed until the story's sequel, "The Last Word." Gunn got the idea for the story in the fall of 1950 and wrote it a year later, as the Gunn's settled into their new domestic routine in Racine, Wisconsin. The original idea came when Kit was a year old and was not sleeping at night: "Tensions of attending graduate school, writing a thesis, and rocking a child had brought out certain differences of opinion between my wife and me."[13] As Gunn commented later, "The story was pretty autobiographical in that I was raised without sisters and Jane was raised in a family without brothers, so we had to adjust to each other as if we were aliens."[14] By the time the Gunns were in Racine these differences of opinion had cooled down and Gunn could reflect back on his earlier frustrations with irony and good humor.

The story takes place during an evening of couple's bridge; Gunn was an expert bridge player, although Jane, in fact, hated the game. As the story opens, the first-person narrator is listening to an argument posed by his friend Harry while their wives are in the kitchen. Harry believes that all women are aliens: "'Did you ever stop to think,' Harry said, 'about what strange creatures women really are? The way they change, I mean, after you marry them.'"[15] Harry is a storyteller, a card, known around the office for his wit, and his ability to keep a straight face while telling an outlandish tale. However, Gunn cues the reader in that Harry's gags are not always shared by others of his set, especially women, and that we should take his idea with a grain of salt. Nonetheless, Harry's misogynistic views were held by many men during the era of post-war suburban domesticity in the 1950s, making this story a reflection of some of the male attitudes of its era.

The narrator plays along with Harry's claims, but remains incredulous throughout. Harry gives outlandish evidence to support his thesis, such as "'Well, they're built differently. Inside, too, glands, bearing children, and all that'" and "'A man to them is only the necessary evil they must have before they can get the other things they want.'" As to the question why alien women are on Earth: "'My guess is they were dropped here by their men. Jettisoned. Dumped.'" And to the question of what makes men and women different: "'Men are inventive, artistic, creative—and can be nagged or coaxed into doing what women want them to do anyway.'" Furthermore, men are mechanically inclined, whereas women use the machines of technological innovation with feigned ignorance of how they work: "'They aren't mechanical, they hate machines, and yet they know when something's about to break down.'" Here Gunn reflects on the household technologies—washing machines, vacuums, toasters, dishwashers, televisions—that were transforming daily life, for men and women both. But how does this alien deception remain hidden? How do the women keep earthmen under control? Harry has an answer: "'They're smart—smarter than we are about getting along, about getting around people. They use weapons like tears and mad fits and sulks against which we've never invented a defense.'" Harry ends his case in despair; despair that men will be rendered unnecessary: "'They'll be able to do away with men altogether—fertilization by salt water, electrical stimulus, that sort of thing.'"[16]

Finally, the narrator can't take anymore of Harry's outlandish conspiracy theory: "I collapsed, hysterical. I choked. I burbled. I gasped. When the women came in a moment later with their ridiculous little sandwiches and coffee and strange dessert, I was barely able to get out a couple of words. 'Hi, alien!' I spluttered to Jane."[17] The "Hi, alien!" here is interesting in that it anticipates the final line in *Station in Space*, when psychiatrist Lloyd Phillips, in a domestic disagreement of his own, looks at his young sons born on the station as the future of humanity in space and declares, "'Hello, spacemen.'"[18]

Of course, the story ends on an ominous note. As Harry and his wife Lucille depart, the narrator hears Lucille chide her husband: "'Harry, there's something wrong with the hot water heater. You've been promising to look at it for days, and you've got to do something about it tonight because I'm going to do the washing tomorrow.'" The next morning, Harry has a heart attack: "It's funny how quick a fellow can go. I got to thinking what a shame it was that Harry's finest effort, the climax of his wit, so to speak, should go with him, and how it's too bad that great vocal art should vanish without leaving a trace." And there are "problems" with the narrator's furnace as well: "Jane is calling me to come down and fix the furnace. But I don't know. I don't remember anything being wrong with the furnace."[19]

Gold changed the ending when the story appeared in *Galaxy*, but Gunn later changed it back when it was published in *Future Imperfect*. In Gold's ending, he over emphasizes the "women as alien" idea, taking away some of the paranoia, misdirection, and irony present in Gunn's original. Gold also made some incongruous changes which on the surface appear to be for purposes of language economy, but his overall expansion of Gunn's ending indicates Gold may have stretched it out to fill blank space in the magazine. One glaring difference occurs in the sentence "And I guess Harry is really sick because Lucille had Dr. Simpson, that woman doctor, and Harry's said many times he wouldn't have her treat his sick dog if he wanted the dog to get well."[20] Gold changed Dr. Simpson to Dr. Clarke, for no apparent reason; but more significantly he removed "many times," which in Gunn's original nicely emphasizes Harry's overall misogyny and paranoia. In any case, doctoring the ending of the story changes some of the original emphasis, and may be why Gold was uninterested when Gunn sent him a follow-up story from the woman's point of view a year later.

"The Misogynist" is a classic story of paranoia, one of the central themes characterizing fifties science fiction. What sets it apart from other science fiction stories of Cold War paranoia—Heinlein's *The Puppet Masters*, Finney's *The Body Snatchers*, just about every story by Philip K. Dick—is that Gunn leaves the Cold War out, instead focusing on the domestic situation. Gunn effectively captures the ironies of domestic life in the fifties, where there was clearly demarcated separate spheres of masculine "breadwinning" and feminine "housekeeping." It's worth repeating that "The Misogynist" was written during the time when Gunn was working for Western Publishing in Racine, a time in which the Gunns had settled into the domestic dichotomy for the first time. In *The Battle of the Sexes in Science Fiction*, Justine Larbalestier shows how the story was one of many during the period which were pitting women against men in an "alien" conspiracy.[21] One of the most notably hostile examples being Jerry Sohl's 1952 novel *The Haploids*. But although it is true that "The Misogynist" is a "battle-of-the-sexes" text, one must be conscious of the fact that the story is told as satire, not in earnest paranoia (as is the case in Sohl's novel). This sense of fun is particularly evident in the story's sequel "The Last Word," written from Jane's perspective.

After "The Misogynist" appeared in *Galaxy* in late 1952, Gunn was playing around with an idea for a mirror-story from the woman's point of view. Busy working on other projects, including the novels *Star Bridge* and *This Fortress World* during the ensuing year, he didn't get back to "The Last Word" until the following year, submitting it to Gold in September 1954 under Jane's name. By that time, Gold felt the original story was long forgotten (he was wrong), and therefore the sequel would make no sense to readers. Since Gold was uninterested in the story, Gunn filed it, later pairing it with "The Misogynist" as the lead stories in his first collection *Future Imperfect*.

"The Last Word" takes up where "The Misogynist" left off: "A wife can go to the basement for many reasons, but only two of them are universal. The first is to point out to her husband how he has failed her." The anonymous narrator from "The Misogynist" is identified in this story as Jimmie. The writers in the field whom Gunn had become acquainted with would have immediately recognized the autobiographical conceit, as they all affectionately knew him as Jimmie Gunn. To counter Harry's argument from "The Misogynist" that women don't understand technology, Jane observes that "men are mesmerized by figures—of all kinds—and any kind of spurious instrument reading will be believed ahead of a woman. But it's no use pointing to the thermometer. A woman knows when she's cold, and all the gadgets ever inflicted upon humanity by men who never outgrew their electric trains won't convince a woman that she's comfortable when she's not." Interestingly, one of the passages Gold added to "The Misogynist" is a long paragraph exploring the question of why women are always cold (perhaps a not-so-subtle sexist code for "frigidity"). Jane goes on to list Jimmie's male failings: "A dozen times I've told him. 'Jimmie, you've got to fix the furnace today.' And a dozen times he has kept his anonymity secure behind the paper and answered, 'ummhumph?'"; "We don't like to whip them, but they won't learn. After 10,000 years, you'd think they'd have absorbed a little initiative about important things"; and "Men are funny. Their minds absorb only meaningless, ephemeral data, like the name of the current welterweight champion, and crazy notions—like this latest fantasy Harry invented." Of course, Jane is amused by Harry's crazy theory: "*Women are aliens!* Isn't that silly?"[22]

The story shifts back to the evening of the bridge game, as Harry spins his story to Jimmie in the living room, Jane and Lucille talk in the kitchen. Lucille explains Harry's theory to Jane; and Jane assures herself that Jimmie will not fall for Harry's nonsense: "Jimmie's too sensible to get taken in by a notion like that." In turn, Lucille vents her exasperation with her husband's notions with a list of domestic irritations: "'He's found all the little details that document women's alienness—the cute little ashtrays that won't hold a cigarette, the lamps you can't read by, the drapes that keep out the southern exposure which was the reason you bought the house, the bobbypins that rain down, the stockings hung over towels to dry, the slipcovers that twist and crease, the jar caps we don't screw down.'" The women return to the living room at which point Jimmie lets slip with his "Hi, alien" retort. The reveal is that it is not women who are aliens, but men. And the power in the relationship is that men are mere pets, to be manipulated by their much smarter wives: "Here comes Jimmie now. I can hear his faltering footsteps on the stairs. He's afraid too! Isn't that silly? Whoever heard of anyone getting rid of a loveable, old, shaggy dog just because he isn't useful?" With perfect counterpoint to Jimmie's "Hi, Alien," the story ends with Jane cooing, "'Ah, there you are—pet!'"[23] Taken together, the two stories offer thoughtfully humorous perspectives on post-war domestic life and the tug-of-war when two people share a life together. The stories could have made a good *Twilight Zone* episode.

Another story that drew upon Gunn's personal experiences and interests was "Open Warfare," a robot golf story. The original version was completed in March 1949, sent to *Galaxy* in 1951, and purchased in August 1952. When Gunn visited Gold at his New York apartment in 1953, Gold asked him to rewrite the story since he was "writing so much better now."[24] Gunn did, which explains the delay in publication from initial purchase.

The story achieved some degree of success, appearing as an episode of the *Galaxy*-sponsored radio show *X Minus One* in 1957 and was reprinted in *The Golfer's Own Book*, a collection of golf stories, the previous year.

"Open Warfare" involves a skilled pro golfer going head to head with a robot designed to play the game with expert precision. The crux of the story is that Slim Jim Pearson needs to win the tournament so that he can marry his sweetheart Alice. In the *Galaxy* vein of urbane satire, Alice's father, a business tycoon, doesn't think Pearson is good enough for his daughter, and comes up with a scheme to end the relationship by inventing the robot to thwart Pearson at the tournament. Pearson figures it out and plays the game of his life, winning Alice. The story is particularly noteworthy for the precise detail Gunn brings to the description of the golf match, demonstrating his knowledge of the game and his attention to the landscape of the golf course and the cultural milieu surrounding the game. Gunn was an unabashed sports fan and that fan expertise is evident in the story; such understanding is not always the case when fiction writers write about sports. Gunn understood the nuances of the game, including the physics of the golf swing, the reading of the course landscape, the patterns and outlay of the turf, and the impact of audience on concentration. All of these factors are rendered effectively in the story.

"Breaking Point"

Although "Survival Policy" in *Astounding* and "The Misogynist" in *Galaxy* put Gunn on the science fiction map in late 1952, his most ambitious story before his second period of full-time writing began that fall was soon to be published by Lester Del Rey for his magazine *Space Science Fiction*. That story was "Breaking Point," and for a period of over a year, Gunn just about reached his own breaking point in trying to get the story accepted by Gold for *Galaxy*. Nonetheless, Gunn considers "Breaking Point" his first breakthrough into mature writing.

"Breaking Point" began as a three-act play written as an independent study project while Gunn was working on his master's degree. The action takes place on a spaceship that has just landed on an alien planet. Introducing shifting and unstable realities, as he would refine brilliantly in the novellas that make up *The Joy Makers*, the story involves the psychological breakdown of the first-contact crew as they succumb to a test of their psychological stability by the aliens on the planet. In many ways, Gunn's novella resonates with Polish writer Stanislaw Lem's classic novel *Solaris*, in that both involve psychological trauma during a first contact scenario. One is also reminded of the innerspace stories of the British New Wave writers J.G. Ballard and Brian Aldiss.

As mentioned in the previous chapter, Gunn rewrote the play into a novella and sent it to Gold in the fall of 1950, just as *Galaxy* was starting publication. Gold liked the story, but felt it was too long and wanted it cut. And he didn't feel that Gunn was up to the task, so he asked that Gunn allow Theodore Sturgeon, as he told Gunn, to cut it down by about a third. Gold himself was notorious for heavy-handed revision of the stories he bought, too often wielding his infamous blue pencil. This was not a wholly uncommon practice in the field, with or without the author's permission, as New York editors would often call in local "fixers" to make cuts, expansions, or revisions on stories coming from writers outside the city. For example, the famous surprise ending of Arthur C. Clarke's "Guardian Angel," the first segment of *Childhood's End*, was added by James Blish. Clarke didn't know about the change until he saw the published story; he liked it so well he incorporated it and its implications into the expanded novel.[25] Gunn assumed that what Gold had in mind would be a quick fix, and a quick turnaround, and since he had admired Sturgeon's stories in *Astounding* during the forties, was happy to allow the revision.

But things did not move quickly, much to Gunn's consternation, and since he believed "Breaking Point" was going to make his name in the field, the delay in hearing back from Sturgeon became increasingly irksome. In early 1951 Sturgeon wrote Gunn asking his permission to undertake the revision: "Horace is simply and solely the editor of *Galaxy*, and in no sense has the right to assign the rewrite of 'Breaking Point' to anyone until it's bought. Only you have that right, and it is on that understanding that I undertake it. I'm requesting your permission to do this, and won't make a mark on the manuscript until you do—it's your property."[26] Gunn happily gave permission and turned his attention to completing his master's degree and doing reports for Western Printing. As Gunn transitioned into his job at Western, he wondered just what was taking Sturgeon so long to make the cuts. Finally, after a full year, Sturgeon wrote to Gunn on January 14, 1952, apologizing for the long delay, and explaining why Gold had not been completely upfront with Gunn about what he wanted Sturgeon to do: "He wanted a rewrite when I thought he wanted a cut."[27] Very apologetic, Sturgeon promised he'd finish the revision and that Gunn would receive due payment, but he also stated that he'd return the manuscript if Gunn preferred: "Let me finish the job and the loot's all yours.

It'll probably be *Galaxy*; it'll *certainly* be sold, and soon. I'll then adapt it and market the TV script, and you'll get the story money on that. But if you don't want me to do it, let me know.... And Jimmie—with all my heart—I'm sorry."[28] It's interesting that Sturgeon suggests here that he'll adapt the story for television, given that Gunn's original version had been a three-act play. In reply, Gunn told Sturgeon to go ahead and finish the revision and that he hopes to see him at the World Con later that year: "I understand that this year's SF convention is to be in Chicago. I've never been to one, but since it's so close—. Maybe, if the two lures are strong enough, I'll see you then."[29] This was the beginning of a fruitful friendship. Even with Sturgeon's revisions, Gold ultimately passed on "Breaking Point"; and Del Rey picked it up for *Space*, a solid magazine that lasted only eight issues.

"Breaking Point" begins as the *Ambassador*, an advanced scout ship, prepares to land on a planet orbiting a distant star. There are suggestions that this is not the first such expedition, that humans have been exploring other planets and encountering other lifeforms. The crew consists of Johnny, a young pilot fascinated by the precision of machines; Hoskins, an engineer; Ives, a communications expert; Paresi, the ship's doctor; and Anderson, the captain of the expedition. As the *Ambassador* begins its descent to the planet's surface, readings indicate a pleasantly earthlike environment, almost too pleasant. As Paresi mutters, "'I worry about easy things.'"[30] And his worries are telling. Later, he speculates if all of this is meant to delude them. Indeed, the earthmen are prepared for hostile contingencies. Taking a cue from Leinster's "First Contact," the crew has been sent to the planet without astrognational information stored in the computers, so that Earth itself will remain safe should the aliens prove dangerous: "'We know we're here—but we don't know where "here" is, and won't until after we get back. This is *really* Terra Incognita. The location of Earth, or even of our part of the galaxy, is something that has to be concealed at all costs, until we're sure we're not going to turn up a potentially dangerous possibly superior alien culture.'"[31] This stresses the isolation and alienation of the crew; cut off from Earth and all contact with other human beings. As the ship lands, a signal is received, in English, announcing, "*Men of Earth! Welcome to our planet!*"[32] The attempt at concealment obviously failed; the aliens know all about Earth, having evidently penetrated the "squeak-box" (computer), and thus the tension of first contact mounts. Unlike Leinster's story, the earthmen are at a distinct disadvantage. The Captain, Johnny, and Hoskins prepare for "exploratory patrol," but when they release the airlock, nothing happens; they are locked inside the ship. It's evident that an alien force from outside is responsible and the crew reaches the conclusion that if they can't leave the ship, then they must leave the planet. But when they try to lift off, again nothing happens; they are trapped on the planet's surface.

Johnny is the first to reach his breaking point. A true believer in the infallibility of machines, when they fail to work, he slips into psychosis, believing that the takeoff was successful and they are back in space. To his mind, it couldn't be otherwise, as Paresi explains: "'There isn't any place in his cosmos for machines that don't work. Contrary evidence can get just so strong. Then, for him, it ceased to exist.... When the drive controls wouldn't respond, he reached his breaking point. Everyone has such a breaking point, and arrives at it just that way if he's pushed far enough.'"[33] Tensions mount and the crew's perceptions become distorted as the aliens cause reality to shift. While these reality distortions are presented vividly and the psychological impact on the crew is tangible, Gunn maintains a rational narrative style, in contrast to the concurrent writing of Philip K. Dick, which achieved much of its power from Dick's schizoid plotting. In Gunn's story, while the crew is experiencing phantasmagoric effects, the narrative voice remains observant, controlled, and calm; whereas in Dick's work, the narrative voice itself is decentered, along with the characters in the stories. It makes for an interesting parallel between the minds and styles of the two writers.

The next panic occurs when the food stores disappear. It appears that Hoskins, the engineer, breaks: he sets up a chessboard and retreats into the abstractions of the game. In truth, Hoskins realizes that the aliens are trying to push the men over the edge and therefore he reasons that by concentrating his mind on the problems of chess, he can combat the psychological forces that are pressuring him to break. Ives cracks next when he perceives vermin scurrying around the ship, but his hallucinations extend further in that the rest of the crew see the impossible vermin as well. An encroaching distorted blackness absorbs one end of the ship, including Johnny as he lies in his bunk. Paresi then reveals that the crew was selected because each was psychologically out-of-balance in ways that are complimentary, so that together they formed a cohesion, a kind of a gestalt: "'In its simplest terms, it comes to this: that a crew can't work together only if each member is the most efficient at his job. He has to *need* the others, each one of the others. And the word *need* predicates *lack*. In other words, none of us is a balanced individual. And the imbalances are chosen to match and blend, so that we will react as a balanced unit.'"[34] On first glance, it would seem that this idea is one of Sturgeon's contributions to the story, since the idea of psychological bonding into a gestalt is one of Sturgeon's central themes, most evident in his classic novella "Baby Is Three." But Gunn recalls the concept being part of his original play.[35] This raises fascinating possibilities. "Baby Is Three" appeared in *Galaxy* October 1952, and Paul Williams's story notes in volume six of *The Complete Short Stories of Theodore Sturgeon* indicate the story was likely completed that May. Sturgeon received a check on January 21—a week after writing Gunn with his apologies—for his preceding story, "The Sex Opposite." Williams makes no mention of "Breaking Point."[36] What Williams's notes reveal is a three to four month gap between Sturgeon receiving the check for "The Sex Opposite" and completing "Baby Is Three." During part of that gap Sturgeon would have been completing the rewrite of "Breaking Point." Could Gunn's novella have inspired Sturgeon's classic story?

As the blackness completely encloses the ship, almost as if the men are now in a void, Anderson reaches his own breaking point and determines "'to get loopin,' stoopin' drunk.'" Things get crazier when Johnny is transformed into a trophy, a "little statue of a guy holding up a victory wreath," symbolizing his need for achievement and praise. In turn, Ives is transformed into a keg of beer, which Captain Anderson proceeds to tap and drink from. A new illusion turns the blackness into a "blue glow" and "soft, grand music" begins to play. As Anderson swills beer, Paresi disappears into the blue glow and a "simple wooden cross," the symbol of self-sacrifice, appears in his place. Anderson is then confronted with a tangible audible visitation of his wife and baby, both died in childbirth, calling him from the blackness, to which he succumbs, diving head first into the void. Left on the table, with the artifacts of the other men, is "the archetype of the most sentimental of symbols," a valentine heart.[37]

But not all of the men were tipped to the breaking point brought on by alien contact. While all the others succumbed to illusion, Hoskins remained focused on his chessboard, contemplating various moves. Hoskins awakens from his reverie, declares "Checkmate," and the blackness dissipates revealing the port. The other men are safely unconscious; the preceding events were merely illusions. Hoskins steps to the communications console and records a message for his crewmates:

> "What the natives of this planet have done is, at base, simple and straightforward. They had to know if the race who built this ship could do so because they were psychologically sound (and therefore capable of reasoning out the building process, among many, many other things) or whether we were merely mechanically apt. To find this out, they tested us. They tested us the way we test steel—to

find its breaking point. And while they were playing a game for our sanity, I played a game for our lives. I could not share it with with any of you because it was a game only I, of us all, have experience in. Paresi was right to a certain degree when he said I had retreated into abstraction—the abstraction of chess. He was wrong, though, when he concluded I had been driven to it. You can be quite sure that I did it by choice. It was simply a matter of translating the contactual evidence into an equivalent idea-system."[38]

Hoskins had realized that the aliens "abide by the rules," and though he did not understand "the rules of their game," the aliens allowed him "to convey mine to them." Thus, through the mathematical abstractions of the chessboard, Hoskins was able to make first contact with the aliens and assure them that the humans were themselves non-hostile. Hoskins then prepares to leave the ship and meet the aliens: "'My interpretation is that they want *me* for further tests.... I am certain now that whether I come back or not, these people will make a valuable addition to the galactic community.'"[39]

With "Breaking Point," Gunn set the stage for his intensely psychological future work. In it, he examines the psychological challenges of alien environments and the trauma of alienation. In a recent anthology of the stories that inspired him, Piers Anthony claims "Breaking Point" as his "favorite science fiction story ever" and recalls reading it between college semesters in 1953 when it appeared: "The story transported me.... When I finished it I paused, pondering it. Then something weird happened. My easy chair started rotating in one direction, while my body slowly rotated the other way. There was no actual motion; it was all illusory. The rotations increased, until I feared I was losing my mind. I shook myself and it stopped. Then the chair and the room started shaking, like a beginning earthquake. That made me nervous anew, and I got up and walked around, and the effect ceased. I concluded that I was fatigued and the emotional excitement of the story had warped my awareness."[40] Anthony's reminiscence captures the tangible psychological impact that "Breaking Point," like all the best science fiction stories, has on readers. It is a testimony to the first of Gunn's major achievements.

"The Reluctant Witch"

Gunn's interest in psychology and characters with a psychological background was further developed in a novella he completed at the beginning of 1953, "Happy Is the Bride." "Happy Is the Bride" has gone through a number of title changes: Gold published it in *Galaxy* under the title

"Wherever You May Be" and Gunn later changed the title to "The Reluctant Witch." I'll refer to it as the latter. "The Reluctant Witch," published in *Galaxy* May 1953, perhaps Gunn's quickest turnaround from mailing to publication, is the story of an ambitious graduate student in psychology and a telekinetic girl in the Ozarks backwoods. It is a darkly ironic story of hillbilly humor (an oddly common trope in SF of the period) mixed with telepathic powers.

The protagonist Matt Wright, who is studying psychology at the University of Kansas, travels to the Ozarks for a retreat at a friend's hunting cabin to write a book, a skeptical refutation of poltergeist phenomena entitled *Poltergeist Phenomena: The Psychological Truth About Those Traditional "Uproarious Spirits."*[41] But Matt hasn't actually done any observational research; he plans to make his case through argument and secondary sources alone. Little does he know that he is about to stumble upon the real thing. Gunn writes with comic gusto when Matt encounters an actual telekinetic.

The story opens while Matt is changing a flat tire on an Ozarks hillside in late June. The lug nuts mysteriously fall under the car and the tire rolls away, despite the car being parked on "one of the few level stretches in these hills." At that moment, Matt sees a "young girl shuffling through the dust several hundred yards beyond the crippled car." She is Abigail Jenkins, a local hill girl coming of age. These strange occurrences are the first signs that the girl has telekinetic powers. As Matt and Abigail get acquainted, he explains the nature of his book project and his views on the reality of psychic phenomena: "'It's just a superstition,' Matt said impatiently. 'Before people could find natural explanations for unusual events, they blamed these things on spirits. There aren't any ghosts or spirits who knock on tables or throw things or make noises.'" In turn, Abigail laments that her "Paw" thinks it's time she got married and she explains her previous trouble with boys, "'One feller I went with purty near a year. He busted his leg. Another nigh drownded when he fell in the lake. Don't seem right they should blame me, even if we did have words.'" Abruptly she decides that Matt is her new beau. When Matt takes her home to her Paw, he's struck by the man's odd behavior as they meet on the porch: "*My God*, thought Matt, *the man is trembling!*" Inside, the house is in shambles, broken dishes cover the floor and the furniture smashed. Paw Jenkins explains: "'when she gets onhappy, things happen. And she was powerful onhappy when that Duncan boy tol' her he warn't comin' back. Them chairs come up from the floor and slam down. That table went dancin' round the room till it come a cropper. Them dishes come a-flyin' through the air.'" Here

Gunn dramatizes the reported details of telekinetic events. Paw Jenkins has benefited from Abigail's telekinesis, "'Ain't had to go fer water fer years. Seems like that barrel by the porch is allus filled,'" but since she reached maturity things have become difficult, "'ever since she got to the courtin' age and started bein' disappointed in fellers round about, she been mighty hard to live with.'" Matt, the naïve city slicker, is unfamiliar with the cultural ethos of the hills, and Paw Jenkins uses that to his advantage: "'Any man that's alone with a girl more'n twenty minutes, it's thought proper in these parts they should get married up quick.'" Balking at this ridiculous notion, Matt leaves hastily.[42]

When Matt arrives at the cabin Abigail is there to greet him, as if she just materialized—in truth she rode a mule. Nonetheless, Matt is on edge as he is already half-convinced her telekinetic abilities are real. She wants to stay, "'Let me cook and do for you. I wouldn't be no trouble,'" and Matt is charmed by sweet Abbie, but as she admits, there are two sides to her, a case of split-personality: Abbie is the sweeter self that Matt, in spite of himself, finds attractive; Libby is the angry self capable of destruction. As Abbie explains, "'The other me, mostly I keep her bottled up inside, but when I feel sad and unhappy, I can't keep her in. Then she gets loose and just goes wild. I cain't control her.'" It turns out that Abbie had been a twin at birth. The suggestion is that her telekinetic powers are possibly a result of this accident of birth, as if her unborn sister manifests herself psychically through Abbie's physical form, or that she has sublimated her unconscious feelings to be a manifestation of her sister as a coping mechanism.[43] Gunn would not have known Philip K. Dick at this point, let alone his life story, but those familiar with Dick's childhood and his later experiences with the numinous and the fact that he had a twin that died in early infancy with whom he believed he was psychically connected can see parallels here.[44]

After observing Abbie move objects about the room, the formerly skeptical Matt comes to accept the events "as physical facts and Abbie's explanation as theoretically possible." This causes him to rethink his thesis, but he also knows the resistance he'll face from the scientific community: "Matt knew what the scientific explanation would be: illusion, delusion, hypnosis, anything which demanded the least possible rearrangement of accepted theory, anything which, in effect, denied the existence of the phenomena." Nevertheless, he *had* observational evidence and had to contend with it: "There had to be room for Abbie in your universe. You had to explain Abbie or your cosmology was worthless." The story makes the case that in order for science to take the skeptical position, it first must make observations, not just bow to theory and secondary reports. Matt has seen Abbie move objects, so he must change his paradigm of thought: "He was supposed to be a scientist, a psychologist. And he was writing a book about a phenomenon he had never seen, as if he knew something about it. He had a chance to find out the truth for himself."[45] This passage answers the question about Matt's original intention to base his argument solely on disbelief, without looking at the evidence, for or against. Behind this story of psychic phenomena is an argument for scientific reasoning and practice. What the story insists upon is the application of the scientific method. The story is, then, consistent with the (often quirky) contrarian views of John W. Campbell, who pushed for the application of the scientific method in all areas of inquiry. In the editorial "We *Must* Study Psi," written several years after the appearance of Gunn's story, Campbell opened by writing, "The essential concept of truth-seeking is that a truth must be accepted, whether it is favorable or unfavorable, desired or dreaded, whether it means riches and happiness, or stark madness. There is, in the concept of the Scientific Method, the fundamental proposition that there are Laws in an ordered Universe; that we must learn those laws—whether we like them or not."[46] It is this spirit of inquiry that remains important, even if the topics of those inquiries are no longer viable.

Matt sets out to systematically observe and record Abbie's psi abilities. His experiment is complicated when Abbie is unable to perform telekinesis on command. She surmises, "'I guess it's 'cause I'm happy.'" In other words, the power comes out of anger and frustration. To get her to do it, Matt threatens to take her home, which triggers her ire and sends a cup "sailing towards Matt's head." This leaves Abbie despondent, as she fears it will get out of control: "'You know I can do it. Won't you leave me alone now? It's unlucky. Something awful will happen. I got a feeling.'" But Matt insists that she must learn to control it: "'You'll have to work and practice until you have full, conscious control of whatever it is,'" and tries to explain how the discipline of psychology works in hopes that she will play along with his experimentation and in so doing provides further evocation of the scientific method: "'Psychology,' he said, 'is only an infant science. It isn't really a science at all but a metaphysics. It's a lot of theorizing from insufficient data. The only way you can get the data is by experimentation, and you can't experiment because psychology is people, living people. Science is a ruthless business of observation and setting up theories and then knocking them down in laboratories…. But psychologists have no true laboratories; they can't be ruthless because public opinion won't stand for it, and cadavers aren't much good. Psychology will never be a true science until it has its laboratories where it can be just as ruthless as the physical sciences.'"[47]

While giving this explanation, Matt also speaks of "his life and studies at the University of Kansas." The "glamorous" life at the university is far more interesting to the hill girl than Matt's theorizing and she begins dreaming of the cultural life at the university and asks Matt to tell her "more about KU."[48] As Matt discusses the college experience, the coeds and their clothes, their activities, their ambitions to find a suitable husband, he begins to fall for the charming girl. The next day he takes Abbie to the nearest city, Springfield, Missouri, to buy new clothes and accessories, including a silky negligee, and takes her out to dance. For the first time in her life Abbie experiences the life of the city. Back at the cabin, when Abbie puts on the negligee and offers herself to him, Matt claims that Abbie has misunderstood: that the clothes and negligee are for his fiancée back in Lawrence. This is all a ruse to make Abbie angry so that Matt can observe her full power. But rather than becoming angry, a heartbroken Abbie allows Matt to test her telekinetic ability, remaining melancholy and despondent throughout. Nonetheless, her ability increases to the point where she propels a can of baking powder through Matt's chest. As the tests go further, they discover that not only can she move objects, but that she can teleport. Once Abbie has mastered teleportation, she transports herself to Springfield, bringing luxurious food back to the cabin, at which point Matt realizes the danger he has unleashed upon himself.

For his part, Matt becomes increasingly ashamed of the way he has treated her. He realizes that his motivations have not been neutral, and that perhaps science, or at least the soft science psychology, is never purely neutral. He realizes that he is motivated not by science but by power: "His motive had been something entirely different. It was only a sublimated lust for power, and thinly disguised at that. The power of knowledge. The power to topple a whole system of ideas. The power to hold the truth in his hands like a club. And for that lust, which she could never understand, an innocent, unsophisticated girl had suffered." Matt's quest for power is turned on its head when Abbie achieves her next stage in psychic development, telepathy, opening up Matt's mind to her full knowledge. She quickly uncovers that the story about the fiancée was a fake to get her to do what he wanted. Abbie feels betrayed: "'How could you do it? You knew I liked you better'n anyone I ever saw, so you made me fall in love with you. It wasn't hard, was it? All you had to do was hold a little hill girl's hand in the moonlight and kiss her once, and she was ready to jump into bed with you. But you didn't want anything as natural as that. All the time you was laughin' and schemin.'"[49]

In a scene played for both comedy and nightmare, she teleports him to the dance hall in Springfield where she makes him dance by himself in herky-jerky movements, and then teleports Paw Jenkins there, which results in a brawl, and while that's going on, teleports herself and Matt back to the cabin, leaving Paw to relish in the fisticuffs. When Matt tries to get away, he is unable to escape from Abbie's powers, leading to another comic scene in a highway diner. After ordering hotcakes, sausage, and coffee and flirting with a waitress named Lola, Abbie's invisible hand causes Lola to trip and spill hot coffee down Matt's shirt, the hotcakes to fly "into the mouth of a lunging trucker," and sends the sausages down Lola's blouse. Piers Anthony, who also selected this story for *One and Wonder*, recalls this scene in particular, and assesses the whole story as "a fabulous romp" and "a perfect story."[50] Gunn plays this scene more for laughs than the nightmare scene at the dance hall, fitting with the sardonic humor of Gold's *Galaxy*.

Matt flees, heading back north to Kansas City, and eventually to Lawrence. Gunn provides a vivid image of the city as Matt approaches at sunset: "Darkening shades of violet were creeping up the eastern sky as Matt reached Lawrence, Kansas. He had not tried to stop in Kansas City. Something had drawn him on, some buried hope that still survived feebly, and when, five miles from Lawrence, he had seen Mount Oread rise against the sunset, the white spires and red tile roofs of the university gleaming like beacons, he had known what it was." Lawrence becomes a prominent setting in much of Gunn's later work and this is the first instance in which the city and the university are featured. Gunn describes the university—and in some respects all universities—in this way: "Here was a citadel of knowledge, a fortress of the world's truth against the black waves of ignorance and superstition. Here, in this saner atmosphere of study and reflection, logic and cool consideration, here, if anywhere, he could shake off this dark conviction of doom that sapped his will. Here, surely, he could think more clearly, act more decisively, rid himself of this demon of vengeance that rode his shoulder. Here he could get help."[51] This image of the hilltop KU as fortress, or citadel, reappears in various permutations in many of Gunn's later works.

Alas, in Lawrence, Matt cannot escape either. At a restaurant on Massachusetts Avenue, the main street in downtown Lawrence, Abbie is there to serve him. Fleeing down an alley, Matt is grabbed by a shadowy figure, who turns out to be a disoriented Paw Jenkins, brought to Lawrence for the final confrontation. Matt goes to see the chair of his department Dr. Franklin, hoping to enlist some help. Franklin, of course, doesn't believe him; he thinks Matt has gone off his rocker. Matt then resorts to attempting suicide, trying a number of methods from poison to cutting to gas, but the ever-present Abbie won't let him. Finally, as Matt realizes there is only one recourse to his problem, he capitulates into the dreaded "unfreedom" of marriage: "The way that was not a quick death but a slow one. But he owed it to the world to sacrifice himself on the altar he had raised, under the knife he had honed, wielded by the arm he had given strength and skill and consciousness. He looked up. 'All right, Abbie.' He sighed. 'I'll marry you.'" Thus Gunn ends the story with a moment of male self-sacrifice. Paralleling Harry's paranoia in "The Misogynist," the sexism runs thick as the story concludes: "A vision built itself up in his mind. The omniscient, omnipotent wife, fearsome when her powers were unsheathed, terrible in anger or disappointment. *No man*, he thought, *was ever called upon for greater sacrifice*. But he was the appointed lamb."[52]

"The Reluctant Witch" is one of the best psi powers stories of the 1950s, particularly notable for its fine characterization of Matt, Abbie, and Paw Jenkins. Abbie is especially memorable and sympathetic, an anticipation, of a sort, of Stephen King's Carrie White. The shift in setting to the Midwest environs familiar to Gunn and away from outer space and from the big cities of the coasts demarcate a distinct regionalism that Gunn would effectively employ in most of his later work, giving his stories a uniquely Gunnian authenticity. Indeed, this regionalism drew interest from local filmmaker Herk Harvey, who made the cult classic *Carnival of Souls* in 1962, and Gunn wrote a screenplay of *The Reluctant Witch*. The film actually went into production in the late sixties, but fell apart when the lead actor demanded a union scale wage. Abbie's ability to upend Matt's reality and perceptions through her psychokinetic powers—like the psychological effects in "Breaking Point"—contribute to Gunn's exploration of the line between dream, reality, and illusion that will continue to fascinate him in later work. With its publication on the heels of the publication of "Breaking Point," Gunn was fast joining the ranks of the field's top writers.

"Every Day Is Christmas" and Others

A week after mailing "The Reluctant Witch," Gunn completed another satiric story, "Ad Infinitum," published as "Every Day Is Christmas" in *Super-*

Science Fiction in 1957. Although not published until 1957, "Every Day Is Christmas" predates and anticipates much of the main sequence of Gunn's fiction. It fits well with what Kingsley Amis called the "Comic Inferno" aesthetic of *Galaxy*, exemplified by such satirists as Pohl, Kornbluth, Sheckley, and William Tenn,[53] although, regrettably, Amis does not mention Gunn's work in his classic study *New Maps of Hell*. As in "The Misogynist," Gunn uses first-person narration. After three years tending a beacon at the asteroid belt, the narrator returns to Earth and his home in New York City. During his time away cultural mores have changed; for example, he is shocked to see women walk about with exposed breasts. He also notices an oversaturation of advertising—not unlike the ubiquitous billboards and jingles in *The Space Merchants*—and is taken aback when he sees several Santa Clauses ringing bells and pitching products: the day is July 5. Here the story resonates with Pohl's "Happy Birthday, Dear Jesus." Although this preemptive Christmas season may have seemed outlandish in 1953, it is not far from the social reality of 2016. What the narrator soon learns is that everyplace is bombarded by advertising and everyone is constantly tuned into the latest advertisement, in fact relishing in it.

Gunn makes effective satiric observations on the flood of household consumer products that were changing daily American life and on how advertisers were manipulating public taste, a topic Vance Packard would soon disclose into the public consciousness in his classic study *The Hidden Persuaders*. When the narrator arrives home, he finds his house packed with consumer products: "The kitchen was filled with shining, chromium-plated junk. Everywhere, from floor to ceiling piled up, stacked aimlessly. Freezers, roasters, cookers, appliances of every size and description. Almost none of them had ever been used…. The cupboards were packed with food. Cans, packages, and bottles were shoved into the shelves without order, one on top of another." The bathroom is equally crammed: "The bathroom was a shambles of packages, jars, bottles, tubes, toothbrushes. The tub was a mounded heap of them. *Where does she take a bath*, I wondered dully." Here Gunn examines consumer hoarding mentality, a diagnosable disorder in today's consumer culture. Like many hoarders, the narrator fears his wife will fill the house and then start filling another: "I wanted to ask her what she would do when the rooms were full from floor to ceiling, but I had a crazy suspicion what she would say. Lock the doors, she would say, and start all over."[54]

The narrator leaves his home and wanders the city streets around Times Square, before entering the high-rise building housing the space agency. There he is directed to the office of Mr. Wilson who explains the situation. The consumer madness began soon after he'd left Earth. Critical mass was reached abruptly as the trends of advertising, over-production, and consumption coalesced. As in Pohl and Kornbluth's *The Space Merchants*, the principles of advertising have been taken to their logical extreme: "'You must remember the function of advertising,' Wilson said. 'To make the consumer want something he doesn't need, or need something he doesn't want. Perfect it—and you have our society.'" Psychological techniques applied to industry resulted in a rapid transformation of consumer society. Wilson voices an indictment of treating psychology as a science, devoid of human empathy that registers with Matt Wright's insights in "The Reluctant Witch": "Science, of course, is ruthless. It has to be ruthless to be a science. Scientists in pursuit or application of knowledge are not human beings but thinking machines."[55] There is no escape. The narrator himself, an outsider not conditioned to the unrelenting psychological need to *have*, is an unwanted aberration in society. He begs to go back to the beacon, but they won't allow it. In despair, he goes home and finds his old rusty revolver, shoots out the TV screen, and then goes back to Times Square and shoots Santa. His pleas to be executed, or at least be put into solitary confinement, fall on deaf ears. Ultimately, as the story concludes, he is trapped by the system, forced into a room in which he will be bombarded by an unending stream of advertising: the ultimate anti-consumerist nightmare. Written, presumably, in response to *The Space Merchants*, "Every Day Is Christmas" is a warm-up for Gunn's dystopian novel *The Joy Makers*, which posits a similar rapid transformation of society from which an outsider struggles to escape.

Gunn spent the next several months finishing his first novel *This Fortress World* and beginning some of the preliminary work on his second, the collaborative novel with Jack Williamson, *Star Bridge*. He returned to short fiction in late summer with the story "A Monster Named Smith," an exciting, on-the-edge-of-your-seat, alien menace story, in the manner of John W. Campbell's "Who Goes There?" It appeared in *Worlds of If* July 1954. The story begins as the authorities search for an alien creature that they believe was parasitically attached to an animal specimen brought back from a space expedition. When the animal is taken into a dissecting room, a "black blob" oozes out of it and escapes. Paranoid fears of an alien takeover are most famously rendered by Jack Finney in *The Body Snatchers* and Gunn builds a similar paranoid tension here. When the city manager complains about shutting down the city for mere suspicion, Burke, a member of the space expedition who is now in charge of coordinating the search for the alien parasite growls, "Would you rather be a zombie—you and all the other millions of people in the city?"[56] Such a scenario again draws comparison with Philip K. Dick and the stories of alien mimicry he was writing at the time such as "Colony" and "The Father-Thing."

The scene shifts to the planetary expedition. There is no other fauna on the planet except for a multitude of sheep-like creatures. The voice of the alien provides a shift in perspective: in its view, the humans are the invaders. These alien parasites are a group-being; no individuality, each part a component of the whole: "A belonging. We are not a whole, but a part of. We have a mission."[57] One of the alien components is elected to go on the ship and sneaks aboard. The alien determines that humans need "a director" so as to "enjoy the blessings of sanity and direction." For it, humans are fragmented and in need of guidance: "These things called men are too independent."[58]

As the scene shifts back to Earth, the alien escapes the laboratory and attaches itself to the next available human specimen, a man named Smith. But the alien cannot control the body of Smith, a drunken scallywag, a brutal version of the inebriated envoy from Gunn's first story "Paradox," and laments, "I am in the body of a man named Smith, and I hate it."[59] Soon after, Smith has sex with a woman, an act of physiological disturbance which disorients the alien. The story captures the agony of the alien in the human body; it cannot take the extremes of emotion and body chemistry of a human host, the warring psychological tension of the human psyche. The alien is trapped in the body of Smith and the story ends with its tragic outlook: "My tormented imprisonment isn't just for a lifetime. It is forever. The sodden body sleeps, this monster named Smith, while my thoughts race madly. The body shivers, very gently. Deep inside it, a mute voice is screaming."[60] Although one can list dozens, if not hundreds, of alien menace stories from the early 1950s, "A Monster Named Smith" is notable for the way in which Gunn shifts perspective from the human pursuers to the alien parasite. By so doing, he allows the reader to ponder the nature of humanity and raises the question in a human-alien encounter, could we, indeed, be the monsters?

Gunn next completed an ambitious fantasy novella, "Sine of the Magus," for Gold's *Beyond*, the short-lived fantasy companion to *Galaxy*. He later expanded it into the novel *The Magicians* in 1976. For the purposes of this study, I'll discuss the expanded novel in Chapter Four. The rest of this chapter will consider Gunn's first two novels, *This Fortress World* and *Star Bridge*.

This Fortress World

This Fortress World is a competent space opera, although not as strong as *Star Bridge*. Gunn plays with a number of themes in the novel, including religion and its link to decadence and the decline of a Galactic Empire, the politics of power, Earth as forgotten origin, advanced technologies and the incomplete understanding of their use and purpose, naturalistic violence, and the Conceptual Breakthrough of a young man discovering forgotten truth. Gunn frames these themes within the compass of the larger theme of the cyclic view of history, of renaissance, decline, rebirth, renaissance, decline, and so on, a concept that he explores in various permutations in later works. Like the earlier story "Mask of Peace," Gunn was likely influenced by Asimov's *Foundation*, although there are many other examples from forties science fiction that articulate a decadent Galactic Empire, and the aftermath of the devastation of World War II certainly plays a role too. It is interesting to note how much of 1950s space opera was structured on the premise of cultural ignorance and decadence, while more immediate narratives involving the aftermath of atomic war were also positing a dark age (Poul Anderson's *Vault of the Ages* and Leigh Brackett's *The Long Tomorrow* coming to mind). One of the central themes of science fiction from this era involved humanity falling away from the wisdom of science; that as technology made life easier, people would become more complacent and ignorant, or destroy civilization by atomic war or through some other technological means. Thus, the decadent space operas project the same anxieties and tensions emerging in the atomic war narratives of the period. At the same time, *This Fortress World*, and other space epics like it, follow the pattern of Wells's *The Time Machine*, which, while taking the reader to the time of "humanity on the wane," implies periods of humanity's greatness during the Traveller's passage through time to the "ruinous splendor" he finds in 802, 701. A space epic like *This Fortress World* follows from Wells's premise, but opens up a possibility of rebirth, something not possible for Wells's Eloi and Morlocks. *This Fortress World* is set in "the splintered wreckage of the second empire." This alone indicates there has been thousands of years of human history in space. This sense of time-scale is present in *Star Bridge* as well and it is one of the compelling aspects of the best space opera/galactic empire fiction. It is a reminder to the reader of deep time on our own planet.

The novel begins with a prologue taken from an imagined text, *The Dynamics of Galactic Power*, not unlike the *Encyclopedia Galactica* in

Asimov's *Foundation*. Gunn creates a vivid image of political power, corruption, and human strife against the backdrop of the stars: "Go out tonight, look at the sky, and see the scattered stars, separate, alone, divided by infinite chasms of hate, distrusts, and the realities of power. See them as they really are—great, gray fortresses guarded by the moats of space, their walls manned against the galaxy." This startlingly poetic image frames the human worlds as walled off from one another, no longer part of a larger galactic-wide community. The image evokes the Iron Curtain of Soviet domination. Space opera, then, becomes another expression of the Cold War American imagination. The prologue goes on to lament the glories of the second empire: "An empire. Within it the numberless worlds of the inhabited galaxy united, working together, living together, trading together.... Only the name comes down to us. We remember it, and we remember, dimly, a golden time, a time of freedom and peace and plenty, and we weep sometimes for what is gone and will not come again." Note that the phrases "the name comes down to us" and "we remember, dimly, a golden time" suggest that *The Dynamics of Galactic Power* was written hundreds, if not thousands, of years after the fall of the *Second* Empire. This excerpt from *The Dynamics of Galactic Power* raises the question if a third empire is possible: "Will there ever be a third? We dream, we hope, but we know, deep down, that the golden days are gone, and we cannot call them back. The Second Empire is splintered, and the wreckage is drifting apart, so far that it can never be pulled together again."[61] In the one page prologue in the guise of an extract from *The Dynamics of Galactic Power*, Gunn effectively frames the backdrop of the story.

This Fortress World is a first-person narrative involving William Dane, a young acolyte of the dominant church founded by "Jude the Prophet." Dane has lived his entire life behind the protecting walls of a monastery on the planet Brancusi, having no experience of the world outside. Despite appearances, the monastery is not some remaining expression of the Catholic Church. Instead, its dogma has devolved from the practices of science and the applications of technology: science is now shaded in mysticism and ritual. The holy rites which the acolyte Dane assists with involve a "Projector," what amounts to a computer interface between the human mind and the machine to create projections, or "miracles." These virtual reality projections demonstrated during the services are accepted by the common people "as living proof of their God and of his active interest in their welfare and the state of their souls." This recalls Heinlein's *Sixth Column*, where manufactured technological illusions in the guise of religious ritual help turn back a Pan-Asian occupation of the United States. The monks are mere tenders of the machine, like the Morlocks in *The Time Machine*, having no understanding of how they work or how the illusions they produce are generated, they merely ritually operate them. The machines allow the operator to project thought transmission, to scan the grounds of the monastery, to move and teleport objects, and to create visual illusions. The Abbott marvels at the miracle of their use: "'We don't know anything about the forces involved. I might say to you that this is, in itself, a miracle. That we can use these strange, divine forces, knowing nothing of their principles, to spread the Message among the people is a gift from God.'" The machines also maintain two layers of protection, some type of force field, around the monastery: the "Barrier," which limits who can enter the grounds, and the "Portal," which only allows those who have a clear psychic need to enter the sanctuary. These force fields function outside the control of the clergy.[62] This foregrounds the theme of ignorance which manifests in other aspects of this decadent society later in the novel. It's worth noting that Gunn here anticipates Gene Wolfe's celebrated *Book of the New Sun* series, where self-regulating technologies are ubiquitous but not understood.

At the beginning of the novel, Dane witnesses a woman being chased by four men as she seeks sanctuary in the cathedral. She makes it through the Barrier and there deposits an object into the collection plate; however, the Portal will not allow her into the sanctuary and when she returns outside the walls, Dane witnesses her brutal capture by Sabatini, the villain of the novel, who cuts off her feet with a laser gun. In an early review Damon Knight condemned the novel for its excessive violence, calling it an example of "Spillanism—sadistic violence for its own sake,"[63] and this is the first instance. However, Knight is missing Gunn's point: the violence is necessary to illustrate Sabatini's unrestrained quest for power and the naturalistic brutality of the world outside, a world Dane has to this point been shielded from. Knight would want to protect readers' sensibilities in the same way. Dane retrieves the object dropped into the collection plate: it is a "pebble," and its design suggests that it is a technological device. When called before the Abbott, Dane is ordered to turn over the pebble; the girl had stolen it from the palace of the Emperor of Brancusi, where she served as his "favorite" concubine. After hours of pacing the monastery corridors in inner turmoil, Dane tells the Abbott he couldn't find it, but when the Abbott threatens to send him outside, he decides to give it up. Once he returns to his cell, however, he discovers that Sabatini's assassins have been allowed into the monastery and are searching for him. He hides the pebble in the building's cornerstone, fends off an attack from the intruders using the Projector, killing three men, and flees into the unknown outside streets of the city.

The novel moves into a hunt-and-chase sequence as Dane eludes Sabatini and his agents. Dane finds himself in a bookshop owned by a man named Siller. Siller provides Dane sanctuary and also teaches him, rather quickly, the art of hand-to-hand combat. Among the books in the shop, Dane finds a copy of *The Dynamics of Galactic Power*, where he reads of the concept of the fortress: "We must face the realities of power. The key to understanding is the fortress world, and there is no key to the fortress." The politics of the fortress are undemocratic; it requires absolute, authoritarian power: "Determination and efficiency are qualities that masses of people cannot share and continue sharing without diffusion. These can be enforced only from above. A fortress must be ruled by one man or a few men. A democracy is impossible." *The Dynamics of Galactic Power* ends in pessimism: the only solution must come from a revolt of the people, but having no way to communicate from world to world, no literacy, they are each trapped in their fortress. Here Gunn frames the politics of power and offers a diagnosis of authoritarian rule. As the novel moves forward and Dane gains experience, he will be equipped to formulate an alternative to the corrupt power and the pessimism of the text.[64]

Siller himself espouses a different path to power, but one that is nonetheless authoritarian. Siller is involved in an underground movement called the Citizens and he believes that a people's revolution is possible and that the galaxy can again be united. The Citizens claim to advocate for liberty and democracy for the masses. And Siller knows something about the pebble and he wants it, seeing it as the key to unleash the revolution. The pebble was found on "a small planet of the periphery" where there were ruins "old beyond description" of a "vanished race" that "had space flight and a considerable degree of civilization."[65] At the novel's conclusion, this planet is revealed to be Earth. But as Siller lays out his philosophy, in which he denounces the ignorance of the masses as unresolvable—including an interesting denunciation of television as the agent of ignorance—it becomes clear to Dane that Siller's "revolution" would set himself, and others like him, up as authoritarian oligarchs, thus confirming the analysis of *The Dynamics of Galactic Power*. Siller's desire for political power is also entwined with his sexual desire as he makes homosexual overtures to Dane. Gunn apparently revised the scene on Greenberg's request, writing that "a perceptive reader can (and probably will and should) interpret Siller as a homosexual.... But I think I have eliminated anything obvious or offensive."[66] Siller's sexual advances result in a fight in which Siller nearly kills Dane, but when he lunges at him with a knife, Dane trips him and Siller pierces himself with his own blade. Trying to find his way out of the shop, Dane burns out a wall with his "flash gun," which results in a fire that consumes the shop. Once outside, he realizes the shop was right across the street from the monastery.

Dane runs, eventually finding himself in a tavern where a young woman is singing and playing a guitar. The young woman, named Laurie, who seems to have both street smarts and an understanding of the politics of other worlds, takes him in. When he asks her what she does, she replies, "'Me? I—entertain,'" cryptically suggesting prostitution.[67] As she prepares him a meal, Laurie ponders the fact that pigs, chickens, and potatoes, like humans, are universal on all worlds, but other animals and vegetables are "native only to one or two planets." Like humans, she further observes, pigs and chickens and other universal animals, can interbreed with stock from other planets, but "none of the rest." Dane quickly understands the implications: "'I guess there's only one explanation. Men must have come from one planet originally. They spread out to the other worlds from there, and they took the pigs and chickens and potatoes with them.'" Laurie sees a conundrum here. Why can't people get along? Why do they draw lines of suspicion and hatred? All of this ties in with the concept of the fortress. Gunn compares the "fortress world" to the "fortress" of the individual mind. The fortress as metaphor for the inability to be open, to discover, to transform. When Dane tries to formulate an answer as to whether evil is "God's will" or something inherent in human nature, Laurie gives a more nuanced social interpretation: "They're afraid to get hurt, and they build up a wall around themselves for protection. They build themselves a fortress and sit inside it, sheltered and afraid. Afraid that someone will break in and find them there, see them as they really are, alone and helpless. For then they can be hurt, you see. When they are naked and defenseless. We're a whole galaxy of worlds, revolving endlessly, never touching, crouched within our fortresses, alone, always alone."[68] Here Gunn again pounds home the metaphor of the fortress, in much the same way he explored the psychology of the breaking point in "Breaking Point." It becomes an existential metaphor played out on the grand scale of the galactic canvas.

Laurie encourages Dane to leave Brancusi and start over again on another planet and she sends him to the spaceport to seek out a "Peddler" (interplanetary traders) named Falescu who will secure him passage. As Dane makes his way through the Imperial City, Gunn extends his naturalistic vision of the squalor and decay of fallen empire: "It was a city of decay. The rot of time was everywhere. I walked through the city slowly, my eyes watchful. I walked through miles of warrens: ramshackle stone buildings which had been repaired endlessly with crumbling mortar; plastic hovels, cracked, patched, and leaky; dirty warehouses, stained by smoke, weather, and seepage."[69] One of Gunn's strong suits is in creating tangible geographies, both urban and rural. Falescu has been taken away by Sabatini and his men, so Dane risks making a stowaway arrangement with a man loading cargo on an outgoing ship. Placed in the hold, where he'd be suffocated by the heat, "the old hot box" trick, he is captured by Sabatini before the starship lifts off. In effect, Sabatini saved his life. Sabatini takes Dane to his torture chambers, in the "old fortress," and Gunn, to Damon Knight's consternation, graphically details the process of Dane's physical and psychological torture. Sabatini, it turns out, is the dictator of the Untied Worlds, who has come to Brancusi to secure the pebble, which he believes will give him power to forge a new empire under his sole control. Sabatini exemplifies the authoritarian power complex diagnosed in *The Dynamics of Galactic Power*. Gunn will fashion a similar, but more nuanced, power-mad character in Duchane, the head of the security forces in *Star Bridge*. But Sabatini's characterization here is more clumsily drawn, as witnessed here: "No doubt you are curious as to my right to possess the pebble. I'll tell you. Mine is the best right of all. I want it more than anybody else, and I'm willing to do anything to get it, anything at all.... I know it has a value, a great value, and it must be mine. Word spread throughout the galaxy that it was here, and I knew that it was what I had been looking for. I gave up a great deal to come and find it, more than you can imagine. But when I have it, the galaxy will be mine." To demonstrate Sabatini's brutality and to emphasize Gunn's naturalistic aesthetic, Sabatini pulls out one of Dane's toenails, and from there systematically removes the rest day by day and pushes Dane to the point of madness. When Dane is put into the dungeon, he finds Frieda, the girl who had hidden the pebble at the sanctuary, who, having endured a week of Sabatini's torture, now looks like an old woman; she dies and her corpse is taken away during the days of Dane's torture. Throughout the scenes of torture and Dane's expression of this experience, Gunn's writing is especially psychologically vivid, and here again Gunn uses the fortress metaphor in describing the breakdown of the individual self: "There were not many walls left. The stronger outer walls had gone when they stripped me of my clothes and I found Frieda and I realized how complete their power was. And they had battered down the inner walls one by one, and soon they would come upon the secret me, curled wormlike in my dark chamber, whimpering and alone." This vividness in rendering a psychological scene builds in Gunn's later work, such as *The Joy Makers, Kampus,* and *The Dreamers.* But Dane's torture is not destined to end like Frieda's; on the brink of his endurance, Dane is saved by Laurie.[70]

Taken back to Laurie's lodging, where she attentively nurses him between fits of delirium, while he declares his love for her, Dane rebuilds the walls of his shattered psyche, declaring "I am a fortress. Once I was not, a long time ago I was not, and evil entered my world unopposed. So I learned to build up my walls strong and thick. They will not break them down. They will shatter themselves against my walls, but they can never reach me where I sit in the secret place. This fortress world will stand against the onslaught of the galaxy." Placing his inner psychological state at war with the galaxy is metaphorically stunning. As he heals, Dane wonders if the pebble is of any real significance. Perhaps it is merely "a kind of mirror in which men saw the reflections of their own desires." Laurie, on the other hand, believes it might be "the key to the fortress" that can open a new golden era: "The pebble must be the keystone of the crazy arch that spans the galaxy. Pull it out and the whole fantastic structure will crumble. Siller was right about that. The power situation keeps the galaxy divided, but one simple discovery could change it all."[71]

The two hatch a plan to retrieve the pebble. Dane returns to the monastery in disguise, but when he accesses the Projector to find the pebble, it's gone. He extends his mental reach, searching throughout the monastery and finds the pebble atop a table in the Abbot's quarters, between the Abbot and Sabatini. While Sabatini wants to claim the pebble, the Abbot argues that the Projector will be able to unlock its secrets and therefore it should stay in the monastery. Dane uses the Projector to take telekinetic control of the pebble—and of Sabatini's gun—and receives a mental shock when the Abbot reveals that he is Dane's father. As Dane "pulls" the pebble back to him at the controls, in direct mental contact with the object, the pebble reveals its secrets—it speaks to him. The pebble is an information device, like a flash drive, containing a message from the past, a call to the future from the telepaths of humanity's forgotten past on Earth. In a fabulous infodump Gunn maps the history of the human expansion into the galaxy. The message reveals the origin story of the galactic community, telling Dane "the story of your fathers": "A small, green world circling a small, yellow sun (Earth and Sol). A vision of the galaxy, solid, packed tight with stars, one among them shining yellow and unmistakable, the world circling it green and bright (Sol and Earth located indelibly). Here Man was born and lived and died long ages before he spread to the stars.... Man's history on Earth was a cyclic thing, his civilizations rising and falling periodically (the history, complete), but at last Man broke through the cycles and climbed one peak higher than he had ever climbed before. He conquered space and colonized the galaxy, and secure on his height he thought he would never fall again."[72]

Gunn here spells out the cyclic view of history which was gaining popular attention through Arnold Toynbee's *A Study of* History; the one-volume abridgement had been published in 1947 and sold 300,000 copies in the U.S. The message from the pebble tells the story of the rise of the first empire and of humanity's expansion into space, when Earth positioned itself as the center of knowledge and learning: "Earth transformed itself into a vast university with all knowledge as its realm. Classified wisdom flowed outward from Earth in an endless stream: inventions, basic science, philosophy." This idea of Earth as a university is highly compelling given Gunn's ties with the University of Kansas. The imagery of knowledge and education, and the institutions that preserve it, are central to Gunn's imagination. This idea also anticipates Gordon Dickson's notion of the final encyclopedia in his Dorsai saga, where Earth also becomes the citadel of knowledge, learning, and wisdom. But the Earth university built a fortress of its own, going from being the center of the galactic community to falling into isolation and self-reflection, as the other worlds of the empire pushed forward with trade, growth, and exploration. Earth's retreat led to the fall of the First Empire, as the outer worlds fell into chaos and war. Meanwhile, the people of Earth "began to think clearly for the first time," leading to "control of the thought processes" from which they achieved "mental communication." Like the monks of Ireland who brought civilization back to continental Europe after the chaos of the Roman Empire's fall, the telepaths of Earth then "went forth again into the galaxy, not as at first, with thunder and flame and great joy, but silently, unnoticed, recognizing the danger but even more aware of their responsibility. Into the galaxy came a breath of reason, a subtle sense of unity, a mute hope." With their guidance, "the Second Empire was born, the golden time of humanity, abundant, rewarding, fruitful." When power corrupted the rulers of empire, the Earth telepaths were found out and the inhabitants of Earth were destroyed. Their destruction led to the fall of the Second Empire, which could not sustain itself without the guiding hand of Earth. The pebble, then, is a beacon, a call to a future generation to return to a renewed Earth and rediscover the powers of mind.[73] This Stapledonian vision allows Dane (and the reader) to widen the lens, to come to a greater understanding of the scale of time and the size of the galaxy.

With this information Dane returns to Laurie's flat, but when he hears what he thinks are sounds of passion from her bedroom and realizes what she meant by "entertain," he leaves the pebble with a note and in despair goes into hiding within the city. After several weeks he realizes there has been a "guiding hand" during his adventures, and Dane returns to Laurie's lodgings only to find her missing. He assumes she has been taken by Sabatini and he seeks an audience. As the two meet for a final confrontation, Sabatini tries to get Dane to come over to his side, reminding the reader that the saga of Luke Skywalker and Darth Vader was not original: "'You could rule a world, if you weren't so soft in the guts. We could go far together, you and I. Let's pool our knowledge, Dane. Who knows what we might do together. We might conquer the galaxy.'" A fight ensues and, as with his fight with Siller, Dane overcomes a far more experienced opponent, breaking Sabatini's back. His surprising skill and strength reveal that Dane is of the new generation the pebble calls. In agony, Sabatini cries out at what Dane has accomplished, revealing more about Dane through his incredulity than Dane understands about himself: "'What are you, Dane? You aren't human. I fought my way up from the bottom. I was nothing, and I became a dictator of the largest of the United Worlds.... I wanted the pebble and with it I could conquer the sister worlds and after that the galaxy. You were the only one in my way, a sniveling acolyte, and you beat me every time. It was a miracle, Dane. What are you?'" Defeated and paralyzed, Sabatini, once the supreme dictator of the United Worlds, begs Dane to kill him. When it is clear that Sabatini has no knowledge of Laurie's whereabouts, Dane decides it is time to "force the unseen player to show his hand." Having had enough of killing, Dane has enough sympathy for the fallen megalomaniac that he leaves Sabatini's flash gun within reach as he exits: "Before I left the alley, it was lit by a brief, blue glare."[74]

Dane goes to the Imperial Palace, surrenders himself to the Imperial guard, and requests trial for his crimes before the Court of Justice. Taken before the Emperor, Dane tells his story of finding the pebble and all that transpired, but not the pebble's message. The Abbot is by the Emperor's side and refuses to take Dane into the jurisdiction of the Church; instead he must face summary justice before the Imperial court. Dane asks the right to perform a miracle and vanishes from the room, the unseen player forced to play its hand. After a brief blackout, Dane awakes on board the Archbishop's spaceship, having been brought aboard by the same projection process as used in a lesser degree in the Church in what amounts to a fascinating anticipation of the transporter technology made famous in *Star Trek*. There he finds Laurie who, like Frieda, was working on Brancusi as an agent for the Archbishop. The Archbishop has his own agenda to restore unity among worlds, without the strong-arm dictatorship of an Emperor or a Sabatini or the dictatorship of the "Citizens" imagined by Siller: a community of worlds living together in liberty, peace, and mutual trust. The Archbishop, and the Church he oversees, is the protector of the human inheritance, and has sought the pebble to protect it from the forces of power.

Brought before the Archbishop by Laurie, Dane expresses the ideas he developed through each stage of his adventures and in the aftermath of receiving the pebble's message. For Dane, the "fortress psychology" must be overcome. The answer is not by revolt of the ignorant masses or through education and reading, because knowledge through reading is not enough; but rather through the development of the mental powers discovered by their Earth forefathers. Dane realizes that the Church will play the central role in guiding this evolution, and he concludes that Jude the Prophet must have been one of the last of Earth's telepaths, who set the church in motion to preserve the inheritance of Earth. He and Laurie have already established a telepathic bond of their own. Dane argues that the Church needs to open up the technology of the Projector to all, not hide it behind a veil of ritual and secrecy, otherwise humankind will remain stagnant. Further, Dane believes they must seek out nascent telepaths and restore their guiding hand: "The telepathy machines can watch for the incipient telepath, whoever he may be. He can be taken aside and helped and put with others of his kind in some sort of colony, and someday the true telepaths will be reborn. Only then will a real basis for a lasting society be available, because it must be built on universal understanding which is impossible without telepathy."[75] The endorsement of telepathy and the idea of an elite order of benevolent minds guiding galactic civilization in the novel is interesting, and in keeping with how science fiction was developing those ideas at the time. In this sense, *This Fortress World* not only looks back upon Asimov's *Foundation* but anticipates Herbert's *Dune,* Dickson's *Dorsai,* and McCaffrey's *Pern,* among others. The move to a narrative about secret telepathic abilities no longer resonates in the way that it might have in the early fifties when the novel came out, but Gunn's coupling telepathic powers with a machine-interface, that in some ways anticipates advanced virtual reality technologies now under development, leaves much food for thought.

Impressed by Dane's insights, the Archbishop asks him to join in the effort to reunite "the splintered galaxy." But Dane has another idea, which will, ultimately, coalesce with the Archbishop's initiative. As the novel reaches its conclusion, Dane makes two requests. First, he wishes to go to Earth, to see what remains of the planet of origin, to see if it is reborn and to, perhaps, discover the secret of the telepaths: "I'd like to live there where the old telepaths lived, and know the peace that they knew, look on their sky and walk their world, and maybe I would know myself someday as they knew themselves and do a few of the things that they were able to do." Secondly, he wants Laurie, at which moment it is revealed that she is the Archbishop's daughter. A final epilogue finds "a little older and a little wiser" Dane walking with Laurie "over the rolling meadows of Earth," which has fully recovered from the destruction of thousands of years before. His reverie is interrupted by "a pain that was almost physical" when he saw a "spaceship sitting in the meadow in a blackened circle of burnt grass." It has come on behalf of the Council who "has been waiting for many days now to install their new Archbishop." That Archbishop is, of course, Dane. The final sentence is a powerful anticipation of the verbal imagery Gunn will master in later work: "I sighed and held out my hand to Laurie to help her up the long, long steps that led back to the stars..."[76]

This Fortress World is a *bildungsroman* tracing Dane's development from ignorance to knowledge of the greater scope of history, of time, and of the galaxy, and the greater potentialities of humankind. In this sense, it has much in common thematically with Arthur C. Clarke's *Against the Fall of Night*, first published in *Startling Stories* in 1948, and published by Greenberg for Gnome Press in 1953 during the months Gunn was completing his novel. Both are concerned with lost origins and the rediscovery of the past by a young hero. Like Clarke's more famous novel, Gunn's *This Fortress World* is a novel of Conceptual Breakthrough, the narrative of a discovery that the history of humanity is much bigger than previously understood. It is a central narrative structure in science fiction, exemplified, as mentioned in the previous chapter, by Heinlein's "Universe." Through this narrative of the conceptual breakthrough of young Dane, coming of age and discovering his destiny, Gunn creates a compelling tale of humanity's future.

Star Bridge

After finishing *This Fortress World,* Gunn set to work on completing *Star Bridge* with Williamson. The collaboration came together when Gunn met Williamson at the 1952 World Con in Chicago. Williamson was having trouble with writer's block and had stalled out after about fifty pages on the idea that developed into *Star Bridge* and on a number of other ideas. Fred Pohl, who was both writers' agent, suggested that Williamson might collaborate with the young up-and-comer Gunn. The fact that both shared a Middle West sensibility proved to be congenial, so Gunn agreed to collaborate. After an exchange of letters in which both writers worked up several ideas for the novel, Gunn took Williamson's fifty pages, rewrote them, and then wrote the rest of the novel.

Gunn finished *Star Bridge* at the end of January 1954 and sent it to Harry Altshuler. Instead of going straight to Marty Greenberg at Gnome Press, Altshuler sent it to Campbell at *Astounding*, who had told Williamson when he was in New York that he'd be interested in giving it a look and that he needed a serial, but Campbell ultimately passed. It was then sent to Gold at *Galaxy*, who dallied at it, but didn't take it either. Judith Merril who was working at Putnam "warmly recommended," as she put it in all caps, that they take on the novel. In her report, Merril wrote: "I think this novel meets all our requirements, and is the best choice I've seen so far for inclusion on the fall list. This, like most of those I've seen, is sociological in nature, using a projected future situation (in this case a fairly far-future, interstellar civilization) as a dramatic stage on which to work out some excellent internally consistent hypothesizing."[77] Merril also offered a nice assessment of Gunn: "I know less about Gunn; Harry Altshuler, who is his agent, and who submitted this novel to me, would have further info. Gunn is one of the better new writers."[78] Interestingly, Merril draws some conclusions about how Gunn and Williamson collaborated based on the structure and style of the text: "My own suspicion is that Williamson is responsible for the excellent tight thinking-and-plotting in this book to a great degree; and Gunn for much of the humanity and warmth. Certain-sure that Jack Williamson has never before written a heroine with the appeal of this one."[79] Putnam, however, never really got into the SF game at this time, and Merril's bosses passed on her recommendation. They did publish James Blish's *Earthman, Come Home* in 1955, undoubtedly on Merril's recommendation, but didn't publish another science fiction title until Heinlein's *Starship Troopers* in 1959. Altshuler accessed the situation accordingly: "Meanwhile in spite of that nice report, Judy got nowhere with the Putnam editors on *Star Bridge*; they just couldn't get interested in it. I think they are going to insist on judging SF on the same basis as general novels."[80]

Star Bridge has had some impact on the field, going through multiple editions and influencing writers such as Samuel Delany and Ed Bryant. At the 1976 SFRA meeting in Missoula, Montana, where Gunn received the Pilgrim Award, Bryant told him that *Star Bridge* was the novel that made him want to become a science fiction writer. As Bryant later wrote, "I refuse to understand why this novel is not accorded the same classic status as *The Stars My Destination* or *The Moon is a Harsh Mistress*.... As much as any other piece of SF I read in my formative years, *Star Bridge* taught me about romance and sense of wonder."[81] When Gunn was having lunch with Samuel Delany and John Brunner a month later and mentioned Bryant's comment, Delany said, "The same thing happened to me."[82] The influence of *Star Bridge* is evident in Delany's early space opera trilogy *The Fall of the Towers*.

Star Bridge develops from Williamson's 1942 story "Breakdown," published in *Astounding* January 1942. "Breakdown" depicts the collapse of humanity's first spacefaring civilization. Set at Sunport, a vast, towering complex on the Toltec Mesa in northern New Mexico, the home of 90 million people, "Breakdown" reasons that when a culture realizes its purpose, it collapses and dies, and a new culture emerges from its survivors. In this case, Harvey Kellon, the "executive secretary of the Union of Spacemen, Managers & Engineers" watches as an irrational fundamentalist religious fervor rises among the underclasses, leading to the destruction of Sunport and the interplanetary civilization of which it is the center. At the story's conclusion Kellon makes his way through to the secret enclave of his son, Roy, who is gathering like-minded engineers and other professionals, as well as individuals from the working class that hadn't succumbed to the mob mentality, for an escape in his untested interstellar starship.[83] Williamson planned a sequel called *Star of Empire* that would take the historic theme to the larger canvas of the fall of a Galactic Empire, but it never came together and when he brought his dilemma to John Campbell, Campbell steered him into new territory, Williamson's famous Seetee stories.[84] A decade later, Williamson turned the material over to Gunn, who replotted the unfinished draft and wrote the rest of the novel, with input from Williamson on ideas such as the Tubes.[85] There are traces of "Breakdown" embedded in the background of *Star Bridge*. The ruins of Sunport is the location of the historic gathering described below; Roy Kellon's legendary first flight is mentioned; and, more tellingly, the universal currency is called kellons.

Star Bridge consists of twenty-one chapters, each introduced by a frame piece called "The History," in the manner of Asimov's excerpts from the *Encyclopedia Galactica* (which Asimov added for book publication) that introduce the *Foundation* stories. An opening prologue and concluding epilogue frame the entire novel as an historical narrative written by

"The Historian." This long-view documentation nicely frames the novel within a broad, sweeping historical structure, consistent with Williamson's original vision developed from his reading of Arnold Toynbee, of civilizations as "super-organisms with life spans of centuries."[86] Gunn wrote Williamson as he was developing the histories: "Enclosed are some very rough first drafts of the historical essays I intend to put between each chapter. They were incredibly difficult to write, but I thought they would speed up the actual work on the novel when I get down to it."[87]

Unlike *This Fortress World*, which was set centuries into the dark ages after the fall of a second galactic empire, *Star Bridge* takes place as a galactic empire is at its peak. Although reaching such a pinnacle of greatness predicates a fall, and that fall is the focus of the novel. Whereas the central image in *This Fortress World* was the fortress, in *Star Bridge* the central image is that of a web, the network of Tubes that bring the worlds together, all linked through Eron. It is this centrality of Eron as the hub for all travel and communication between worlds that gives the Empire of Eron its power. As the initial "History" excerpt reasons, for an empire to be an empire, it must have workable communication structures: "For an empire is communications, and communications is an empire."[88] The Tubes are what make this possible. The Tubes facilitate transportation from planet to planet, making travel that would take months or years in a conventional starship happen in a matter of hours. What the Tubes essentially do is collapse space, bend time, cut through the physics of the universe. The concept of the Tube is a precursor to those SFnal attempts to work around the limitations of the speed of light, such as Frank Herbert's concept of "folding space" by the Guild Navigators in *Dune* and the farcaster in Dan Simmons' *Hyperion* series. The closest idea from the fifties is the "jaunt" that Alfred Bester depicts in *The Stars My Destination*, although Gunn and Williamson theorize from physics rather than from psychic power. "The History" before the second chapter helps establish some of the essential knowledge for understanding the Tubes and how they make the galactic empire possible: "For centuries the speed of light was an absolute limit of space travel, and even at that speed the stars were years between. Then the Eron Tubeways Power, Transport, and Communications Company introduced the Tube. As soon as a conventional ship carried terminal equipment to a distant world, it could be linked to Eron.... Three hours to Eron.... For the first time, interstellar civilization was possible."[89]

The novel begins in the aftermath of the Empire of Eron's subjugation of the Quanron League, a federation of free planets in the Pleiades Cluster at the edge of the space frontier. Alan Horn, a soldier of fortune from the Cluster, who has been hired to assassinate the General Manager of Eron, Garth Kohlnar, rides a pony through the "Forbidden Ground," a desert stretching from the Mississippi Valley to the Rockies on the largely abandoned origin planet Earth. The Forbidden Ground may have been rendered a wasteland in past ages through atomic devastation (always lurking in Cold War-era science fiction) or perhaps burnt out from the blasts of the spaceships sent to the stars. The opening chapters read like something straight out of a Western novel, with science fiction trappings, as Carl Abbott has noted.[90] Although Gunn rewrote Williamson's original material, Williamsonian imagery of the desert southwest is vividly present. But the geography seems an amalgamation of both Williamson's southwest and Gunn's Midwestern Kansas plains, as it "was once the most fertile farmland on the continent," which seems a clear reference to the rich soils of Kansas and Nebraska.[91] There is, however, a sense that the geography has been altered significantly by humans and that climate change has been at work for the centuries that humanity has expanded into space. Adopting the tropes of the Western quite effectively reveals that Earth is a damaged world, a forgotten backwater; in a sense, Earth, the origin planet, is once again the frontier.

As Horn rides through the desert being pursued by "Golden Folk" out hunting desperate Terrans for sport astride their gigantic, mutated hounds, he avoids his pursuers when he comes across a water-starved man (by the end of the novel, it's suggested that the man was another assassin) whom he callously sacrifices to the hunters by sending him in the opposite direction upon the pony while Horn hides in the red desert dust. Traveling further by foot, Horn encounters another wanderer, an aged Chinese named Oliver Wu who is accompanied by an extraordinary "gaudy, red-and-green bird" called Lil. Lil is the last survivor of an ancient intelligent species destroyed by humankind during its expansion into space, "a pseudomorph of the Diamond Cavern," who has the ability to shapeshift into other physical forms. Through his association with Lil, Wu, who was born in San Francisco, has lived for 1,500 years, through the entire cycle of humanity's venture to the stars. Unfortunately characterized through the racialized lens of the era in which the novel was written, Wu, like Lil, is the "last of [his] race"; the Chinese people (no distinction is made between Chinese and Chinese-Americans) "clung to Earth while others went out to the stars. With Earth, they died."[92] When Horn first encounters Wu in the desert, Wu addresses him in an embarrassing Chinese stereotype, "Please no killee poor China boy.... Poor li'l

China laundly boy no make bother noblody!" which Horn takes to be phony.[93] The characterization is egregiously off-putting for current tastes, but does make the point that Wu is faking, although it is a product of unfortunate attitudes of its time; neither Gunn nor Williamson would make such characterizations if writing today. Wu seems uncannily familiar with the geography of the desert and leads Horn through a narrow hillside tunnel to a hidden oasis and then through a cavernous tunnel through a mountain, suggested to have been man-made. These are the remnants of the underground substructures of Sunport, and after ascending a series of ramps, they exit through a narrow gap leading to the mountain plateau of Sunport, the glorious location where humanity launched its ships to the stars. Gunn shifted the location of Sunport from Williamson's Toltec Mesa to the site of Denver, Colorado, which itself lies in ruins under Sunport. Like Denver below it, Sunport is now in ruins. Wu tells Horn of its history: "'They built it high and tall, on the ruins of city called Denver, so that it would be nearer the stars. Like Eron, it ruled the known world. Legend says that a great barbarian leader sacked Sunport in its greatness.'"[94] A massive Victory Monument dominates the center of the plateau: "It towered against the noon sky, eight hundred meters away, where once the Mars Docks of Old Sunport had been. But even Sunport, at her proudest, couldn't have built this. Its base was an immense black cube capped with a black hemisphere. It was at least nine hundred meters high. Towering endlessly above that rounded pedestal was a great, cylindrical column. It was faced with luxion and glowed with rising waves of living color. Blood-red just above the black hemisphere, it shimmered through orange, yellow, green, blue, indigo, and violet. The top faded to a shining white. Crowning the pillar, four kilometers overhead, was a huge, steel-gray sphere, smooth and featureless except at the poles. There, thousands of slender golden spikes bristled in every direction."[95] Below this towering edifice, a "broad platform" of "gleaming, golden plastic" has been constructed and is surrounded by "concentric semicircles of bleachers, their tiers capable of seating many thousands."[96] Colorful pavilions dot the nearby landscape as the Golden Folk of Eron mill about. The elite of humanity have returned to Earth in all their glory and regalia. There are some wonderfully, large-scale images here and elsewhere in the novel.

Eron is the homeworld of the Golden Folk, the elite, mutated humans who control the galaxy. But after centuries of absolute power, the Golden Folk have grown decadent and weak. When Horn first glimpses the Golden Folk gathered for the dedication of the Victory Monument, they are described as "the aristocracy of Eron, the heirs of the universe, proud, powerful, arrogant—and effeminate. Not one of them could have done what he had done to get here."[97] The Golden Folk indulge in pomp and finery, the men and women both sporting attire emphasizing "padded bosoms and femininely symmetrical legs covered with heavy synsilk and furs. And jewels."[98] Horn responds with visceral disgust at the flamboyant and arrogant Golden Folk, whose luxurious lives have been cultivated on the labors and degradations of countless slaves. Horn seethes in his ambition to bring the Empire of Eron down.

Enter upon the scene the Directors of the Company of Eron, protected by their mutated horse-sized hounds and the three-meter tall Denebolan lancers, another mutated variation of humanity. Each director represents and controls a division of the Eronian corporate structure, and each corporate division is denoted by a specific color: Ronholm, the Director of Commerce, regaled in blue; Fenelon, Director of Transport, in green; Matal, Director of Power, in orange; Duchane, Director of Security, in black; the General Manager, Garth Kohlnar, in silver; and Wendre Kohlnar, daughter of Garth and Director of Communications, in gold. Framing the social structure and elite hierarchy of Eron in terms of a corporation is especially interesting. Most space operas build societies along traditional bureaucratic governmental patterns (Van Vogt, Asimov), monarchical oligarchies (Herbert, McCaffrey), religious institutions (*This Fortress World*), or some combination of all three. Gunn and Williamson effectively create a galactic empire structured by the values of the multinational corporation. In this sense, the novel's social and economic extrapolation looks to the future, rather than replaying social and economic hierarchies embedded in the past, and as such, the novel continues to speak to current societal economic structures in compelling ways. It's likely the case that there is an influence here from Pohl and Kornbluth's *The Space Merchants*, the quintessential science fiction satire of the American business corporation that was making waves as Gunn and Williamson were writing *Star Bridge*. Although Wendre has been placed in a directorship by her father, Eron's hierarchy is structured on merit (although only among the Golden Folk) rather than inheritance: "The five Directors were chosen by competitive examination from all qualified engineers among the Golden Folk. Their duties: to establish policy, elect the General Manager, and preserve the secret of the Tube," further emphasizing a corporate hierarchical structure to Eronian society.[99]

One of the central themes of the novel is the idea of freedom versus authoritarianism. There is an embedded critique of corporate capitalism throughout: that corporate capitalism, in its quest for profit, stifles freedom and innovation by others outside the corporation because it threatens corporate hegemony. The Company of Eron, following through on the corporate philosophy to dominate all markets, has crushed all opposition and, in turn, crushed freedom of decision. The Quarnon League was the last holdout from the Eronian consolidation. Because both Williamson and Gunn have roots in regions of the United States associated with the West and the American frontier accounts for the vivid geography of the desert and mountains surrounding Sunport. But their western roots are also effective in developing Horn's character, as a frontier soldier of fortune from the Pleiades Cluster, and in establishing the opposition to the dominance of the Company, especially when the scene shifts to the fully urbanized world of Eron. The contrast in settings between the now-barren, frontier-like Earth and the City of Eron creates a nice visual counterpoint, which, in turn, frames the opposition between corporate domination and individual freedom.

As Horn surveys the scene before him and focuses in on Garth Kohlnar, it is apparent that Kohlnar is ill, that he has been sent to assassinate a dying man. Kohlnar speaks to the gathered crowd, his voice booms over the field, projected by massive amplifiers: "'Men of Eron. Sons of Earth. We are here to celebrate not the victory of Eron but the victory of man.... We have come back to our origins, to Earth, to the mother-world.'" As he speaks, a projection appears behind him "against the blackness of the monument base" and "a vast mosaic sprang out, colorful, almost three-dimensional in its reality." The story of human evolution from its beginnings in "the primordial universe, vast chaos churning with unborn life" through the process of stellar evolution, the rise and evolution of life on Earth, the ascent of man, the rise and fall of human civilizations, culminating in the building of Sunport and the legendary interstellar flight of Roy Kellon, plays out on the screen. A new cinematic sequence follows showing Eron and the web of Tubes that connect it with the other stars, leaving Horn contemplating an image of Eron as a fat, greedy spider, "sitting in the center of its golden web, waiting the tremor that announced the capture of another victim."[100] The visual technology imagined here is striking and now seems much more conceivable than it was when the novel was written. 3-D imaging, CGI creation of imaginary landscapes, and virtual reality, provide new language to apply to Gunn and Williamson's imagining.

Kohlnar's speech falsely proclaims that the corporate interests of Eron and its crushing of all opposition is the extension of the human inheritance. It is Kohlnar's vision that through the enslavement of all opposition, the Golden Folk of Eron can fulfill humankind's evolutionary destiny: "'Victory!' Kohlnar's voice was husky and low. 'Not for Eron. For man. Those who challenge Eron challenge not the Empire but man's greatness. Let this be their answer. Eron will preserve man's goal, man's inheritance—the stars, strong and united. This is Eron's mission.'" But for Horn it's obvious that the unchallenged strength of Eron has led to weakness, made symbolically evident by Kohlnar's poor health. The Empire is too big, too unmanageable. As Paul Carter has put it, a once free society "has evolved into a stagnant, star-spanning tyranny."[101] Kohlnar's grandiose posturing, and the return to Earth to call upon the powers of legend to prop up the Empire, is a sure sign of weakness. As Horn observes, "Through being strong, Eron has become the most dependent world in the Empire."[102] Kohlnar is joined on the dais with the other Directors, who each extend their hands upon the Tube controls. Meanwhile, Horn spies Wu and Lil among the crowds of Golden Folk, making their way forward and causing a disturbance. At the conclusion of this spectacle, Horn does what he had been hired to do: he assassinates the General Manager. In these scenes, Gunn and Williamson dramatize the power, the corruption, and the self-delusion of corporate oligarchy.

Following the assassination Horn flees through the mountain tunnel, the oasis, and the smaller tunnel, into the desert. As with his initial journey through these spaces with Wu and Lil, the imagery of Horn's flight is visually captivating; the abandoned tunnels of Earth foreshadowing the corridors of the City of Eron and the caverns of the hollowed-out asteroid, the Prison Vantee. Horn abandons his attempt to flee through the desert when he recognizes the futility of eluding Duchane's security forces who are systematically sweeping the desert floor with floodlights from an armada of airships. The urgency of escape is heightened when Horn hears the baying of the giant hounds and he doubles back and returns to Sunport, realizing his only chance at escape is to hide among other men and slip away. At Sunport, he encounters Wendre Kohlnar, the only one who realized the assassin would return. Horn seizes the woman, with the intention of stealing her ship, but when a single shot is fired at them, Wendre frees herself. After pursuit across the parade grounds of the Victory Monument, Horn enters the Tube station. In desperation, his only hope for survival is to enter the Tube in a spacesuit and go to Eron itself.

The Tubes make it possible to travel vast distances of space seemingly in hours. While in the Tube, travelers are secured in a ship and rendered unconscious, or else risk going mad. Horn has no such amenities. He must travel the Tube alone in a spacesuit, fully conscious. Horn's voyage through the Tube is vividly rendered and has much in common with the dream sequences Gunn later so effectively creates in *The Joy Makers* and *The Dreamers*. What Horn discovers is that time stands still in the Tubes and perception and consciousness blur into an unbounded experiential reality. Eternity, infinity, and zero all blend together. Horn's consciousness experiences the trip as unending and instantaneous at the same time. In this no-space Horn slips into solipsism: "Consciousness. A mind to think. Existence. Circular proof. Outside of this, nothing.... I think—I am. Reality begins with me. I am the universe! I am the creator. Create, then. Everything is destroyed but you. There is nothing alive but you. There is no thought, no memory, but yours. Create!"[103] What was thought to be a three-hour journey from Earth to Eron really takes no countable time at all. During the instantaneous-infinity in the Tube, Horn disciplines his mind to stay sane and concentrates on that single bullet back on Earth, realizing it was not meant for him but for Wendre Kohlnar. At the Tube Terminal at Eron's north pole Horn confirms his sense that no time passed while he was in the Tube. Checking his spacesuit, the air supply, water, and food gauges indicate no change. But Horn has no time for further contemplation. Behind him a small scout ship enters the terminal, Wendre Kohlnar descends from the ship, but as she comes down the steps, her guards are clubbed down by the port guards and she is captured, and taken away on a small ship that will deliver her to her captor in the City of Eron.

Horn takes the private elevator reserved for the Directors into the enclosed, colossal city of Eron. Eron is a spectacular city, rivaling Asimov's Trantor in scale, and uncannily matching the "Caves of Steel" of the enclosed New York in Asimov's robot classic, published in *Galaxy* while Gunn was working on *Star Bridge* in the late fall of 1953. But here, too, as in *This Fortress World*, Gunn paints with a naturalistic brush, creating a vivid, visual portrait of the massive, enclosed city. Eron seems more real, more alive, than Asimov's cities. Gunn and Williamson had unquestionably worked up the architecture of Eron before *The Caves of Steel* serialization appeared, but it is fascinating to see these ideas and images developing in different yet similar ways within the SF metatext. Eron is described in "The History" heading chapter nine: "Eron the City. A world encased in a metal skin, gleaming coldly in the light of its distant sun. One world, one city. As Eron grew powerful through the Tube, the Golden Folk built up and dug down: space, more space, still more. Warehouses and trading centers, schools and barracks, tenements and residences and palaces, amusement centers and factories, restaurants and communal kitchens, control rooms and power room."[104] The elevator comes to rest at an emergency stop, depositing Horn into a blue room, and it quickly becomes apparent that this is part of "the Pleasure Worlds," a popular destination for the bored and decadent Golden Folk to indulge in all manner of carnal escapades. Horn's journey through the interior of the vast city is compellingly portrayed, making an interesting counterpoint to the mountain caverns on Earth: "The slideways moved through the eternal tunnels of plastic and metal, past the near-hypnotic displays of shopping centers, the tantalizing odors of restaurants, the garish beckonings of amusement districts. Urging, luring, demanding. The slideway was a living snake weaving to the changing tunes of a skillful charmer."[105] The technological imagery here almost exactly parallels Lije Baley's pursuit on the expressway strips in chapter eleven of Asimov's *The Caves of Steel*, but given the timing of composition it is more likely that Gunn found inspiration in Heinlein's "The Roads Must Roll," the extraordinary cityscapes in the cover art of Frank R. Paul, or in the early work of Williamson himself. The concept of the slideway was first introduced in Wells's *When the Sleeper Wakes* and the enclosed urban environment in both *Star Bridge* and *The Caves of Steel* evolve from E.M. Forster's classic "The Machine Stops." Slideways, called zip-strips, appear in the New York of Williamson's weekly comic strip *Beyond Mars*, which was running in the nationally distributed *New York Daily News* Sunday edition during the composing of *Star Bridge*.[106]

Gunn's description of the Golden Folk's fashion is equally striking, and conveys their decadence in ways that anticipate the decadent citizens of the Capitol in Suzanne Collins's *The Hunger Games*: "The slideways were crowded; the golden-skinned people on them were dressed fantastically. The women wore very little, and Horn realized that the air was warm, a little too warm. Brief skirts and shorts revealed long, shapely legs often ornamented with brilliants. Blouses were even more revealing; they were transparent, low-cut, only a half, or slashed strategically to give tantalizing glimpses of golden flesh. What clothing the women had removed, the men had put on. They were overdressed in synsilks, furs, and jewels. Their bosoms were padded into grotesque imitation of their mates, and their legs, elevated on stilt-heel shoes, had a feminine symmetry."[107] As the story moves forward, Horn must avoid pursuit by Duchane's security forces and concludes, rather audaciously, that he'll have to bring down the totality of Eron's political power structure. It should not go unnoticed that the villain in the novel is the Director of Security, Duchane, and the color of the Security uniforms and insignia is black. This is an undisguised overture to E.E. "Doc" Smith's notorious villain Blackie Duquesne from the *Skylark* series, one of the foundational stories of the space opera subgenre.

To avoid capture, Horn journeys deep into the bowels of the city, below the lowest level "down into the ancient catacombs in the heart of Eron's rocky crust," where the enslaved laborers live, work, and die, finding himself in a "vaulted chamber cut out of the rock," a chapel of the "Entropy Cult," whose prophet, it is later revealed, is Wu.[108] The Cult is an underground movement that stands in opposition to the dictatorship of the Company, a familiar trope in much science fiction of the period, the Consies in Pohl and Kornbluth's *The Space Merchants* being the exemplary example. Dazed and weary, Horn is seized from behind and knocked unconscious. He awakes to find himself in the presence of Wu and Lil. When Horn reveals his plan to bring down Eron, Wu cautions: "'One man against Eron. A delightfully daring thought—but hopeless. Empires fall when they are ready and not before.'" Horn argues that if they shut down the Tubes, then Eron will fall: "'Eron is dependent on the Tubes, totally dependent. She can't live more than a few days without fresh supplies from the Empire.'" But in order to disable the Tubes they have to know how they are activated and, as Wu counter argues, that is the greatest secret in all Eron.[109]

Nonetheless, Wu is "tempted to help" Horn and proposes they "join forces temporarily." Horn plans to go to "the center of things" and as they prepare to return to the center of the great city, Wu presents himself in the guise of Matal, the Director of Power. Not only is Wu garbed in "rich orange synsilk and furs," but his face has been transformed into an exact duplicate of the rotund Director: "It wasn't Wu's face; it was the fat, golden, jowly face of an Eron noble. Tawny eyes peered out at him over puffy folds of flesh. The hair was stiff, reddish…. It was the face of Matal." This transformation is facilitated by the morphing ability of Lil; she is the face of Matal, a mask shrouding Wu's head. With Wu in the guise of Matal and Horn in the role of his personal guard, they plan to infiltrate the meeting of Eron's Directors in Duchane's quarters, where a new General Manager will be elected from the six. Matal's appearance will be unexpected, as Duchane sent assassins to dispatch the real Matal. Horn and Wu hope to arrive at the meeting before that news reaches the Security Director.[110]

What follows next is an intense power struggle between the remaining Directors; at first Wendre Kohlnar is notably absent. When Duchane calls for nominations, Fenelon defiantly nominates the missing Wendre, causing Duchane to explode in sexist spleen: "'Wendre! I ask for strength, and you give me a woman. Everything is against it: tradition, policy, strategy.'"

Fenelon counters that Wendre is "'qualified by birth and training'" and, given the rumblings from below, "'only Wendre has the confidence of the people. Only Wendre has the popularity to make rebellion to hesitate before attacking.'"[111] As sides are drawn and the Directors reach an impasse, Duchane reveals his big surprise: bound at the wrists, Wendre is brought into the chamber and accused of patricide. Duchane desires to marry Wendre to consolidate power through his strength and her popularity, but Wendre has refused him, leading to these trumped up charges. Tensions rise as the politics of power plays out among the Directors. Receiving a nod from Wu/Matal, Wendre votes for Duchane to break the deadlock. As Duchane relaxes in the glory of his ascendancy, a messenger bursts in to give him news of Matal's assassination, but before the messenger can speak, Horn guns him down, leading to a standoff. Moments later, Wu proposes a way out of the stalemate: he, Horn, and Wendre will leave through the center exit, Fenelon and Ronholm and their guards through the two other exits. A gun battle ensues and Wu, Horn, and Wendre make their escape; Fenelon and Ronholm have not been so fortunate.

The action speeds up as the three flee, searching for someplace safe. Wendre's private quarters have been taken by Duchane's security forces and with no other alternative, Horn and Wu convince Wendre that they must shut down the Tubes in order to counter Duchane's push to consolidate power. They make their way to the "master switch" that powers the Tube at the northern pole, but when Wendre pulls the switch nothing happens—all she's been told, everything she believed about the unique power of the Directors is a lie; the whole system of the Directorate and the purity of the Golden Blood is false. Lil disengages itself from Wu's face to reveal the ancient visage underneath and at that moment Wendre realizes that Horn is the murderer of her father. As she turns and flees to the elevator door, black-uniformed guards swarm in and surround Horn and Wu, while on the other side of the facility, "a ragged, clay-faced rabble erupted through the door, swept around Wendre, and waded with suicidal frenzy into the black forces."[112] The slaves from below are in open rebellion. At first, Horn assumes the guards are Duchane's men, but they are the forces of the Warden of the Prison Terminal Vantee, sent to assess the situation on Eron and evaluate the viability of making an assault to seize the main control room.

Horn is taken to the Prison Terminal on the planetoid Vantee, circling a "dim, red sun" light years away from any inhabited world. The only access is through the Tube linking it to Eron. There is a curious similarity between the prison imagery and that in the recent popular movie *Guardians of the*

Galaxy; ironically the film was scripted by another fellow named James Gunn, no apparent relation. Horn is taken before the Warden, a brutal, pragmatic wielder of power: "The Warden would not be troubled by ideals. He was a barbarian, he would never have climbed so high with such a burden. His attempt to seize the north cap and the main control room seemed like his own idea. If Duchane was able to smother the fires of rebellion in blood, the Warden could name a high price for his help. If Duchane fell—well, other barbarians had seized an empire and held it for their own."[113]

When the Warden finishes interrogating Horn, Horn is cast into the general prison population. Immediately attacked, he stands his ground and gains the confidence of a hulking man named Redblade, a brutal killer whose name was "synonymous with destruction, massacre, rape; also with defiance of authority, which was the Empire,"[114] reminiscent of the brash, swashbuckling heroes of Williamson's *The Legion of Space*. Horn convinces Redblade to join him and make a play to bring down the Empire. Enlisting other trustworthy lieutenants, they wait in anticipation for the Warden to make a call: he will need to sacrifice prisoners if he's to hold the master control room on Eron against the rebelling slaves. When the expected call comes, Horn and Redblade lead an attack upon the Warden's guards and as they march down the corridor to the Warden's quarters and the Tube room, they encounter a bedraggled old man with a mane of flowing white hair. It is Peter Sair, the Liberator, the former leader of the Quarnon League, the only man who can bring order to the chaos of the rebellion: "'If they discovered you were alive, it would draw them together; among the chaos of their own wild passions, unleashed for the first time, it would save them. They need you.'"[115] A final confrontation between Redblade and the Warden leaves the Warden dead, with a broken neck.

From here on out the narrative becomes one of unbridled action and unmitigated gore, as Horn, Redblade, Sair, and their men battle for control of the Tubes and the corridors of the City of Eron. As they seize the communications center, Sair broadcasts a call to liberation for all of Eron, but a liberation forged by democracy, creativity, open discourse, and mutual respect. Not one of chaos and destruction. The politics are similar to those present in Gunn's story "Private Enterprise." Sair pleads for them not to bring Eron crashing to the ground. Freedom can only take hold through the framework of the empire, the continued functioning of the Tubes. Without them, chaos.

As the novel wraps up, Horn seeks out and confronts Duchane, who has taken Wendre prisoner. Duchane is taken captive, and a final confrontation leaves Duchane dead when Wu cries out, "He's got a gun!"[116]

leading Horn to react and shoot him down. But Duchane was unarmed. Before Duchane is silenced he reveals what he has found out by consulting the "Index." This late introduction of the "Index" is teasingly potent and is a perfect example of a tossed out "novum," Darko Suvin's concept of a startling new innovation characteristic of SF narratives.[117] The Index is apparently a vast computer database, holding centuries worth of historical data; an incomprehensibly large internet. The fact that the Index merely lurks in the background is striking, but may suggest some prescient forethought that such game-changing computers would, in their ubiquity, achieve a level of matter-of-fact, taken-for-grantedness rendering it mere background. What Duchane has uncovered is that "a ragged old man seen frequently with animal companions" has been present at all the Tube initiations.[118] That ragged old man is, of course, Wu.

Once discovered Wu draws a pistol on Horn and melodramatically tells his story, while becoming a little too close to a Fu Manchu stereotype: "You've come too close to the truth, about me and about the Tubes, and so you must die. I hope you will let me explain before I kill you. You want to know the meaning behind all this. And it is a vast relief for me to speak. You can't know the immense burden of keeping a secret for a thousand years." Wu and Lil are behind the establishment of Eron, and like Hari Seldon's Foundation, Wu has guided the course of history: "The Tube, then. Man needed it if he was to develop an interstellar civilization instead of isolated, divergent, spatially determined cultures which could contribute almost nothing to the race. With the best motives, then, we gave man the Tube, Lil and I. If mankind were to continue as a single, functioning race, we had to abolish that deadly limitation: the speed of light." At first, Wu had the best of ethical intentions in shaping the destiny of humankind, but as the centuries passed he developed a lust for power, meddling "for the sake of meddling." It is interesting to compare this with Asimov's later development of his *Robot*, *Empire*, and *Foundation* series, where the guiding hand turns out to be R. Daneel Olivaw, benignly working from the Three Laws of Robotics to shape human destiny. Before Wu can gun down Horn, Wendre enters the room and tries to tackle him. Although she misses, Horn does not, and he kills Wu. Horn tracks Lil with the gun but chooses to let her go, as Horn reasons, her life may be "the master switch." The novel ends with the rebellion under control, Sair ensconced as leader, and the structure of the City intact. There is hope for the future and for a new stage of galactic civilization. Wendre, though, must leave, because, as Sair puts it, "'we can't afford to let a tender remnant of the Empire remain behind as a nucleus for a new tyranny.'"[119] With that, together Horn and Wendre depart for the Cluster to shape a life and destiny together. There is the suggestion at the end of the novel involving the "Silent Stars" that opens up the possibility of a sequel, but Gunn decided to move in the direction of social science fiction instead. A final epilogue, written by "The Historian," reveals the eternal wanderer Wu is still alive, reunited with Lil, and still lurking in the background to shape human destiny.

Firmly in the tradition of adventure fiction and galaxy-spanning space opera, *Star Bridge* has a transcendent, epic quality that embodies the sense of wonder. It is an exemplary example of the space opera genre at its best.

Three

The Joy Makers to *The Burning*

The Joy Makers

After completing *Star Bridge*, Gunn decided to move away from space opera and concentrate on near-future social science fiction. His next projects were the first two stories that make up *The Joy Makers*, "The Hedonist" (retitled "Name Your Pleasure") and "Hedonics, Inc." (retitled "The Unhappy Man"). In these stories, Gunn reached a new level and they also ushered in his most productive period of writing.

Gunn got the idea for *The Joy Makers* from an article on "Feeling" he'd read in the 1950 edition of the *Encyclopædia Britannica*, which he had purchased when the Gunns moved back to Lawrence. He formed the seeds of an idea while reading "its discussion of happiness and its final sentence, 'The true science of applied hedonics is not yet born.'"[1] Happiness, dreams, the difference between illusion and reality, play a central role in Gunn's fiction, and *The Joy Makers* is perhaps his most concentrated expression of these obsessions. As Gunn reflects, "I realize now that I have always been fascinated by the seductive power of dreams, even while I have insisted that reality, though it may be hard and tragic, is preferable."[2] Gunn set out to explore the contrasting visions of happiness articulated by hedonism and stoicism: the differences between getting "what you want or wanting what you get."[3] When Gunn sent the first story to Harry Altshuler in March, he was excited by the prospect of extending it into a series: "In a number of ways it's the best thing I've done. If Horace doesn't snap it up, it'll be because of the length.... You told me once that you didn't approve of short novels. They were, you thought, a novel wasted. I don't know that I agree with you completely; they are, sometimes, a novelette fully developed. In the case of 'The Hedonist' you may be right. I think the idea is rich enough and the situation pregnant enough to develop into a novel.... I imagine it would be best to get this published first and then do a Sturgeon or a Ward Moore, although I suspect that the development would be more in the nature of a Moorish expansion."[4]

It is interesting to see in this letter Gunn gestating the story-sequence method of novel writing vs. an expansion. Ultimately, he went the route of Sturgeon, who added two additional novella length sections to bookend "Baby Is Three" to form *More Than Human*. A "Moorish expansion" refers to Ward Moore's *Bring the Jubilee* which began as a slightly shorter version in *The Magazine of Fantasy and Science Fiction*, then a novel. When Gunn completed the third novella, "The Angry Man" (retitled "The Naked Sky") in early 1955, he explained what he was trying to do in developing his story-sequence novels: "In a limited sense, this is something new in science fiction, although Isaac Asimov's *I, Robot* may be comparable. This is a three-part series in which an idea is the hero.... There have been other story sequences collected into book lengths: Simak's *City*, Blish's *Earthman, Come Home*, Kuttner's *Mutant*, Asimov's *Foundation*, etc. But again only Asimov's is close, since The Hedonic Saga is three separate stories linked only by an idea, and together tell the story of this idea. It's an important subject, and, although I may not have treated it perfectly, I think the stories have a nice blend of entertainment and significance, and that I have something worth saying."[5] *The Joy Makers* is an extraordinary sequence that builds to one of the most startling and thought-provoking conclusions in all of science fiction. Gunn asks the question: what if one could develop a science of happiness? Of course, what happens is that the majority of people fall into a state of pure pleasure seeking and Gunn creates a startling three-staged dystopia.

But Altshuler had trouble placing "The Hedonist" with either Gold or Campbell: "Horace was violent about it. He has run too many stories, he says, setting up a society of the future and then taking refuge in the underground and revolt: what he wants is to learn how to live with the future." There was also some prudery involved, which may have been more from Altshuler than from Gold: "There is a special word of caution: no matter how an author may justify the utility and necessity of a bed scene in this or any other individual story, when Horace prints them, he gets cancelled subscripts flooding the mail, and complaints from American News, his distributor, and even a fishy eye from the Post Office inspectors. So he is going very soft on anything that might be considered titillating." When Altshuler took it over to Campbell, he politely suggested it should go to Gold: "He is cool on it—feels it's more Horace's kind of thing!"[6] But he soon placed the three stories with *Fantastic Universe*, *Thrilling Wonder*, and *Startling Stories*. The fact the stories appeared in different magazines may have lessened the impact they might have had had they been placed in the same magazine, although that impact was insured when they were finally brought together in book form by Bantam Books in 1961.

Part One, "The Unhappy Man"—actually the second written—is set around the first years of the twenty-first century and begins as Josh Hunt, owner of Hunt Electronics in a city named Millville, an irritable executive suffering from an ulcer and a persistent cold, reads a newspaper advertisement declaring "Happiness Guaranteed!" by a firm calling itself Hedonics, Inc. When Hunt arrives at his factory, a card from Hedonics, Inc., proclaiming, "Your happiness is our business" is attached to his office door. The next morning, a more prominent ad appears in the newspaper and on his way to work, a new billboard advertises Hedonics, Inc. His secretary, Marie, greets him cheerily, "Joy, Mr. Hunt!" and when prompted, says the greeting joy was "on television last night.... A real happy story. Everybody was happy. It was sponsored by that new business with the funny name." Over the course of the day several employees greet him with "Joy" or ask him "Are you happy?" causing Hunt to become increasingly miserable and irritated: "What was wrong with him was Hedonics, Inc. It was the breeding pit of all his irritations. If it were gone, he could be happy again."[7] The structure of this opening is similar to that of Jack Williamson's "With Folded Hands," where overly helpful robots ultimately render humans inert by their protectiveness. It also resonates with some of the pop psychology movements of the period. What immediately comes to mind is L. Ron Hubbard's Dianetics—a movement arising out of science fiction, and something Gunn would certainly have been conscious of—and perhaps Wilhelm Reich and his Orgonic therapy. Although Gunn read the original Dianetics article that appeared in *Astounding* in 1950 and followed the discussion about it in Campbell's editorials and the Brass Tacks letter column, he claims he wasn't thinking about Dianetics specifically as he wrote *The Joy Makers*; nonetheless, it was likely an unconscious influence. The remainder of the story follows Hunt as he tries to get to the bottom of the Hedonics phenomenon.

Before leaving the office, Hunt calls the police department to have them intervene, with no luck. With no other recourse, he dials the Hedonics, Inc., number, "P-L-E-A-S-U-R," whereupon a pleasantly blissful receptionist replies, "Oh, yes, Mr. Hunt. We've been expecting to hear from you." At ten the next morning, Hunt, in a manner reminiscent of the set up in Dick's "We Can Remember It for You Wholesale!" visits the offices of Hedonics, Inc., where he is instructed in the theory behind hedonics and given an outline of Hedonics, Inc.'s techniques: "Hedonics, it seemed, could do many things.... The client's problems became the problems of Hedonics, Inc. If the client needed a job, a job was found for him; more important, it was not just any job but the job that would make the client happy. In addition, hedonics relieved pains, cured the sick, reshaped neurotic and psychopathic personalities, toned up the body, straightened out the mind, and removed such sources of unhappiness as salary worries, investment difficulties, budget impossibilities, marital problems, extramarital dilemmas, thwarted desires, and guilty satisfactions." All of this is guaranteed. As Bill Johnson (a name Gunn would use again in the *Crisis!* stories), the Hedonics salesman, proclaims, "'it's a service you can't afford to be without.'" And for a trial offer of $100 for a limited service contract, Hunt can receive "a full diagnosis and indicated medical and psychological services." Hunt signs up, more to investigate this apparent scam than to utilize the services.[8]

The next day, when Hunt goes for his diagnosis, a "constant stream of men and women" are filing into the Hedonics facility, while "a second stream came out," oddly recalling Dr. Seuss's *The Sneetches*. As Hunt perplexedly marvels, "The happiness business was booming." But Hunt is an astute businessman, working in a booming business of his own: consumer electronics—Gunn's juxtaposing here is aptly ironic—and he's skeptical that Hedonics, Inc. is nothing more than a money-making scheme. His diagnosis is conducted by a man named Wright (an interesting name choice) in the "special, patented diagnostic chair," which provides "an accurate and complete diagnosis of the physical condition of anyone sitting in it." One of the chair's features is in exposing the client to their phobias by creating kind of a virtual reality experience. Wright takes Hunt through the paces of claustrophobia and acrophobia to demonstrate the effect: "The ground was a million miles below. People and cars scurried around on it like microbes on a slide. The side of the building faded away beneath him, and Josh felt his insides turn liquid and cold, and his grip on the metal railing over which he was leaning became palsied and weak as if the strength had drained away. He felt himself falling, and it was almost as if he had thrown himself into the hungry void. A scream started somewhere deep inside him."[9] A foreshadowing of things to come, the diagnostic chair is the first step in blurring the lines between reality and illusion. By the end of the novel, Gunn completely pulls the floor out from under the reader with startling implications that extend from Josh Hunt's terrifying disjunction in the diagnostic chair.

This demonstration is the carrot-on-the-stick. Hedonics, Inc.'s real business plan is to get people to sign up for "the unlimited service contract.'" The unlimited service contract "'takes care of everything,'" as Wright puts it: "'we arrange your life so that you never have to worry again. In this age of anxiety, you never have to be anxious. In this age of fear you never have to be afraid. You will always be fed, clothed, housed, and happy. You will love and be loved. Life, for you, will be an unmixed joy.'" But it comes at a cost: to receive unlimited service, customers give up all assets, property and future earnings, recalling any number of fad cults in recent history.[10]

A call from his lawyer informs Hunt that his wife has signed one of the unlimited service contracts. Hedonics, Inc. now owns half of Hunt Electronics. Like the spaceman in "Every Day Is Christmas," Hunt rightly fears the worst: "'In a few weeks they'll own Millville—industry, real estate, municipal property right down to the sewers. They'll own everything fixed in place and everything movable including three-fourths of the people.'" Going a step beyond the quandary imposed by Williamson's humanoids, the unlimited service contract will eliminate all forms of freedom, most especially the freedom to think: "'It's worse than slavery. That, at least, left the mind free.... I can see it clearly now. Within a few years Hedonics, Inc. will be the greatest single economic force in the country. They will *own* the United States. It won't be necessary to take over the government.'" This recalls how corporations own the government in *The Space Merchants*. Now that Hedonics, Inc. owns half of Hunt Electronics, they want Hunt to begin manufacturing a "coin-operated booth," a diagnostic chair that can be distributed across the country. Hunt realizes that someone will have to make a stand in Millville before it's too late and Hedonics, Inc. spreads its "imbecilic smile" of joy to its ultimate conclusion. His only recourse is to disprove the hedonic guarantee.[11]

When Hunt gets home, a note from his wife Ethel awaits. She's left with the children, because her "happiness" requires a break with Hunt. Hunt wallows in despair, sipping bourbon and contemplating the Hedonic aftermath: "This was what Hedonics, Inc. had done to him. It had taken away control of the business he had built; it had taken half of everything he owned. And it had taken his wife and children. Beside that the rest was meaningless."[12] When Hunt gathers a contingent of leading citizens to confront Wright at the Hedonics offices, Wright is waiting for them, and has Ethel there to try to convince her disbelieving husband. Wright's reasoning that Hedonics is a science sounds very much like a Dianetic Clear: "'The hedonics techniques aren't something magical. They're a reorientation and a discipline—a control not over external events but over our reactions to them. Happiness is inside. All you have to do is recognize that.'"

But Hunt isn't buying and his $100 is returned to him when he insists "'Hedonics, Inc. hasn't made me happy.'" In the end, having returned home, where the oblivion provided by whisky no longer works, and where it becomes painfully apparent that Hedonics, Inc. has won, and more importantly, was (W)right, Hunt reaches for the phone and dials P-L-E-A-S-U-R. But Hunt will remain an unhappy man: a clause in the contract disallows a return.[13]

"Name Your Pleasure" is set thirty years into the Hedonic utopia in 2035. The Declaration of Hedonism announcing the new world order had been signed on December 31, 2003; three months later Hedonism was made the twenty-sixth amendment of the Constitution and became the law of the land. The story focuses on a practicing Hedonist, Morgan, a provider of hedonic therapies. At age fifty-three, Morgan is happily virile and fit, due to "geriatric treatment." He's a first-generation Hedonist, who would have been coming into adulthood when the Hedonic movement unfolded, with "ten years of the Institute's rigorous, specialized training and twenty-three years of practice" under his belt. Morgan's duties are to facilitate the happiness of the citizens in his sector. And that includes occasionally bedding young women: as the story opens, Morgan wakens beside a young woman named Beth whom he "certifies" as ready for marriage.[14]

Whereas "The Unhappy Man" recalls genre stories from the SF magazines, such as Williamson's "With Folded Hands," "Name Your Pleasure" evokes classic dystopias like Huxley's *Brave New World* and Forster's "The Machine Stops." Not only is happiness serviced by anti-aging treatments and perfectly delicious genetically engineered foods served to perfection in (then) high-tech plastic containers that chill or heat to optimum temperature so as to maximize flavor sensations, Gunn also anticipates high-speed internet communication systems, that make access to information convenient, ubiquitous, and efficient: "While he ate, he flicked on the news. He punched the highly compressed channel; the words came rattling from the wall like the rare, accidental hail on his plastic roof. The film was compressed only a little, but the time-compression on the speech sometimes went as high as seventy per cent without audible distortion." As in Pohl and Kornbluth's *The Space Merchants*, there is talk of a Venus colony. The news announces the completion of a new ship, set to launch "when the emigration complement was filled." But Morgan doesn't think such an initiative will go anywhere: "The ship would wait a long time there in the yards. How do you recruit emigrants from the promised land? Where do you find people who will trade peace and plenty and happiness for toil, starvation, and misery?" People are content with themselves and the social order.¹⁵

Yet all is not perfect in this promised land. Like Montag in Bradbury's *Fahrenheit 451*, Morgan has his doubts. After thirty-three years as a Hedonist, he "still didn't understand the roots of his own unpleasures," which surely suggests that underneath the shining surface of utopia, hides discontent. Adding to his unease, the Hedonic Council has called him in for his annual examination, "but his last examination had been six months ago." Following his first morning therapy session, with a young, unmarried woman "an inch under average height at five feet nine" whose "features weren't bad, but it was obvious that she was one of the least attractive girls in the ward," whom he helps "shed her burdens" by certifying "minor plastic surgery" and changing her wardrobe to "something bright and revealing," Morgan is confronted by a knife-wielding patient, named Gomer Berns, whom Morgan promptly knocks unconscious and secures in a therapy chair, to tend to later when he has more time. He's due at "the school" where, in a scene modeled on the Nurseries in *Brave New World*, he meets with each class and indoctrinates the children in the rituals of happiness. These children were born into the world of the Hedonic creed: "For the new generation, happiness will come easy; they have been prepared for it." Returning to his office, Morgan eases the anxieties of the knife-wielder and sets him up in the "necessary" to observe while Morgan treats other patients, and Morgan settles into "the usual sort of day." But during one treatment he experiences a "sudden moment of dizziness" and when he opens the door to the necessary, Berns is gone. Here we're introduced to a Van Vogtian reality shift, as part of Morgan's day is missing, the result of "a time-lapse grenade." He suspects Berns' story is "only partly true" and the man must be tied to the summons of the Council.¹⁶

Later as he hails a cab to take him to the Council Building, he's stunned to find Beth behind the wheel. Beth is part of an underground resistance movement, in the vein of the Consies of *The Space Merchants*—what Horace Gold had objected to—and she pleads with him to avoid the Council meeting: "'They want to get rid of you. Why, I don't know. But there could be a hundred reasons. For some reason, you're dangerous to them.'" Beth is similar to Clarisse in Bradbury's *Fahrenheit 451*, and indeed there are some parallels between the two novels in that both present societies of addiction and the "blissful" apathy which comes with it. One direct parallel occurs when Beth reveals that she read the Gospels "in an old book." The Hedonist replies, "'I know that. But where did you find one. It isn't on the proscribed list, exactly, but it isn't approved, either. I haven't seen one in twenty-five years."' As in Bradbury's dystopia, books are apparently banned as a potential source of unhappiness and discontent. Beth confirms Morgan's suspicions that Berns is an agent of the Council, but she has dispatched Berns and secured a tape that he was set to take to the Council to incriminate Morgan. Here is exposed the underbelly of the supposed utopia of hedonism.[17]

Despite Beth's protestations, Morgan enters the Council Building. He's immediately ushered through a series of Kafkaesque "tests" that confront him with a series of illusions. Passing the tests, he enters the Council Chamber. The Council is a star chamber of sorts; the members that sit on it have been in place since Hedonism became law. As with the power structures in Gunn's space operas, the immovable Council has become corrupt. Greed has come to define their happiness, as they enrich themselves further by pushing "neo-heroin" as a path to happiness, when all it leads to is a blissful oblivion. They no longer serve the needs of all people to be happy, rather, they merely plot to expand and hold on to power. Morgan and other Hedonic therapists like him are blocking their ability to extend their control, and they wish to get rid of them. The Council claims that they can now achieve 100 percent happiness and no longer have need for the services of the hedonic therapists. They've developed a projection device (something Gunn will reuse in the *Star Trek* novel *The Joy Machine*) that beams out total, euphoric happiness. For the Hedonist, this is not the road to happiness but to delusion: "'Horrible, perhaps. Wonderful, perhaps. But real, no. Systemized delusion. Madness mechanized.'" The Council gives Morgan a choice: lobotomy to reduce his desires or the projector to increase his satisfactions. And what are his crimes? He's infringed on the happiness of the Council, by "'cutting off your ward's trade in neo-heroin. The income is vital to the proper functioning of government,'" and, worse still, he's been nominated to the Council: "'If elected, you would replace one of us—and that would be unpleasure, sir!—and you would upset our plans for the future happiness of Earth—.'"[18] Later, Gunn replays this scene in *Kampus*, when the novel's hero, Gavin, is brought before the Student Council and accused of being a similar threat to their power.

Morgan feigns illness and is allowed to go to the nearest necessary, a bare, antiseptic room on the twenty-ninth floor of the Council Building (incidentally, Kansas City's City Hall, where Gunn briefly worked in civil defense, was a twenty-nine-story building), where he quickly shatters a window with his shoe and puts on a pair of "geckopads," suction cups by which he can climb the exterior surface of the skyscraper. The action picks up from here as Morgan tries to make his escape. Rather than going down, he goes up, to avoid the obvious search pattern. As he clings to the side of the building, a "heli" approaches the building, piloted by Beth. After a near-miss, daring leap, the heli takes him away to safety. But not for long: Morgan is pursued by "watchdogs," semi-sentient robotic devices that "learn" as they pursue, similar to the mechanical dog in *Fahrenheit 451*.

Like Horn in *Star Bridge*, Morgan concludes that if he is to survive, he will have to overthrow the Council. The Council has abandoned the principles of "rational hedonism" and embraced "pure hedonism," the pleasure of the moment. Such abandonment of context, of past history and future extrapolation, is a dead end, an abandonment of human cognizance. Gunn warns of the catastrophe lurking in all forms of extremism: "It was false, just as every extreme must be. Happiness had to prepare for the future, or there was no future for happiness. Every moment is important, not just for the happiness it contains but for the happiness it leads to. Every moment must make a man readier to understand happiness, to recognize it, to seize it, and to hold it. That was what illusion couldn't do. Imaginary gratification dulled the sense and pushed every other type of satisfaction farther out of reach. It even failed itself; eventually unreasoned gratification becomes meaningless. The only road was the middle road."[19] Unbridled hedonism is self-defeating. One must have freedom to choose or true happiness is impossible; without choice what remains is hollow delusion. Gunn brings up an important point. True happiness cannot be achieved through artificial means. It must involve full participation of the subject, intellectually, emotionally, and physically. This is the road to wisdom.

What follows next is a brilliant scene set in a hedonistic funhouse, filled with the coin-op happiness machines that Hedonics, Inc. planned to manufacture at the Hunt Electronics Factory in "The Unhappy Man." Gunn's description of the carnival ambience of the amusement park rivals the closing scenes of Frank M. Robinson's novel of a rogue telepath, *The Power*. It's worth noting that the aforementioned cult classic film *Carnival of Souls* ends with a memorable, mesmeric scene at an abandoned amusement park. Was Herk Harvey inspired by *The Joy Makers*? This scene also finds a parallel in *Kampus*, in the opening scene where Gunn portrays student enrollment as a carnival where professors must "bark" their courses, calling students to "step right up!" Morgan is disoriented when he's approached by a simulated satyr, the server at the bar, who will supply "your addiction ... in any form you desire."[20] This virtual satyr extends the illusions Hunt experienced in the diagnostic chair outward into tangible reality, bringing into question the real versus the simulated. It is a further step toward perpetual delusions. It is also fascinating to see the ways in which Gunn is imagining advanced media technologies decades before the ubiquity of computers and the development of virtual digital environments. In effect, he is creating a vision of cyberspace and virtual reality nearly thirty years before William Gibson in *Neuromancer* and Vernor Vinge in *True Names* solidified those images in the popular discourse.

Morgan has come to the amusement park to meet with Lari, a fellow hedonic therapist, now a rather pathetic neo-heroin addict, who admits his unhappiness: "'I haven't been happy since I was a child. None of us have. We are brave and foolish, just a handful of hedonic therapists shouldering the burden of a world's happiness.'"[21] Along with most of his other colleagues, Lari has succumbed to the Council, and he is there to betray Morgan. As Morgan tries to convince Lari to resist, Beth enters and cries her love for him. But it is too late, the Council police close in dressed as a "motley of clowns" and secure Morgan and Beth for treatment.

At that moment the underground intervenes, the lights go out and Beth and Morgan make their escape. As they run into the night, Beth reveals the core of the underground's purposes: "'We aren't troubled about the great mass of the people; they're contented with what they have. We're concerned with the few malcontents who find happiness impossible and get into trouble.'" They don't seek revolution; they don't seek to overthrow the Council, but only "'to rescue the few who are worth saving.'"[22] As mentioned, the theme of underground movements proliferate in science fiction of the Golden Age. The members of the science fiction community often saw themselves as members of an underground movement as manifested in the ideology of the fan group, the Futurians, and fandom at large, taking a page from Wells's idea of the Open Conspiracy. The SF community still has this sensibility deeply embedded in its psyche.

The method of rescue is not unlike that presented in many science fiction tales: as the protagonist comes to knowledge and realizes that the society he lives in is incompatible with his new insight, the answer is to leave, to go outward into space—the quintessential American frontier theme—where men and women can forge a new society away from the decadence that has engulfed Earth. Those who have seen through the false happiness of the hedonic society are sent out to Mars and Venus, Callisto and Ganymede. Here's where the aforementioned Venus rocket comes into play. Thus, the story follows a similar trajectory as Pohl and Kornbluth's *The Space Merchants*, except where Pohl and Kornbluth relied on exaggeration, humor, and satire, Gunn utilizes the naturalistic approach he'd featured in the space operas. With that, although *The Space Merchants* remains one of the most engaging and thought-provoking novels of the fifties, still quite potent in its scintillating critique of consumerism and environmental degradation, *The Joy Makers* is equally scintillating in its analysis—and, perhaps, more frightening.

As the story concludes, Morgan is off to Venus with Beth to start a new life. He hopes there will be a need for his hedonic training, as long it is practiced in a rational, practical way. Wisdom comes when the captain of the ship says to him, "'We're too busy to be happy. We've got a million things to do up there. We've got no use for any of your immorality.'" And Morgan realizes that "happy men don't make good colonists. To tame a planet, to remold a world, takes hungry men, angry men. They had to be discontented and they had to stay discontented. Otherwise, the world turned on them and broke them." Balanced hedonic techniques can still be of use on the frontier, complimenting discontent without trying to eliminate the drive, challenge and creativity necessary to tame a world.[23]

The final novella, "The Naked Sky," opens on Venus a century later. Gunn creates compelling imagery of Venus being slowly terraformed by the colonists, evoking the poetic vision of Bradbury's "The Long Rain" with a stronger scientific sensibility:

> Almost a twin of Earth, it had been embalmed at birth, shrouded in stifling clouds of formaldehyde and polymers. Beneath those miles of plastic clouds, Man found a desert where nothing lived, where nothing could live. The vital ingredients were missing: free water, free oxygen. The colonists dug deep beneath the surface to escape the vicious thermodynamic forces of the atmosphere and then they set methodically about the task of changing a world.... And man himself was busy in great, lumbering combines which crawled the desert, chewing up sand and stone and leaving behind, to soak up the rain, soil rich with fertilizers, long-chain proteins, genetically designed microorganisms, earthworms, and seed.... Already he had tamed her, sweetened her breath, softened her hard bosom.... In another fifty years she would be as fair as Earth.[24]

Despite the hardships in building a new world, the Venus colony is thriving, with three million inhabitants. On Venus the colonists have used hedonics in its proper, balanced way. Morgan was their prophet and left them with an excellent creed: "What hedonics gives us is the techniques with which to make necessity a virtue, with which to make the unavoidable a pleasure. What cannot be cured must be endured, and what must be endured should be enjoyed."[25] He also bequeathed them a history of what had befallen Earth: *The Rise and Fall of Applied Hedonics.*

The story opens as D'glas M'Gregor encounters a "duplicate in the corridor connecting the motor pool to the elevator bank."[26] The Duplicates are robotic reproductions of actual colonists whose origins are unknown, that like Campbell's Thing in "Who Goes There?" have some form of telepathy that enhances the deception of their mimicry. This idea also calls to mind two Philip K. Dick stories from the period, now considered classics, where similar robotic infiltrators threaten to decenter human adversaries, "Second Variety" and "Imposter," raising the question what is real? D'glas meets with three hedonists, Perry, Brian, and Floyd; together they make up the leadership of the Venus colony. Ideas are thrown out: is this the precursor to alien contact or invasion? Is it somehow connected with the dreamers on Earth with whom Venus has lost contact? No matter, D'glas and his colleagues know they have to act with some urgency. As Perry somberly remarks, "'At this moment we are under observation. What the next stage will be is impossible to guess, but it will not be favorable to a continuation of our society and of our way of life.'"[27] They have lost 1,000 people over the last two days, so a resolution is imperative. The task of D'glas is to discover the source of this threat to the colony and he's sent to Earth to make contact and find out what is going on.

When D'glas disembarks on Earth, Gunn creates a terrific counterpoint image to the "plastic clouds" of Venus. The change of perspective for D'glas causes disorientation and anxiety: "He was trapped between the concrete-covered soil and the naked sky, blue-clear and blazing.... He was exposed pitilessly upon a great plain; a giant eye stared down at him accusingly, watching, condemning. If he moved incautiously he might fall into the transparent blueness above, fall off the surface of the world into the terrible sky."[28] On the field are seven rusting ships, three unidentifiable, one each from Callisto and Ganymede, and two from Mars. Others preceded him. The field is on the edge of the city, adjacent, incidentally, to the Funhouse, now abandoned, where Morgan escaped the Council police.

D'glas wonders at the sparkling cleanliness of the abandoned Funhouse. Not only is it clean, but all the dispensers are full and well-maintained, as if vigilantly waiting for a lost clientele. The perceptive reader will assume some sort of robot intelligence behind this pristine maintenance. Finding no entrance to the upper floors of the building D'glas seeks out the logical location where stairs or an elevator should be. There he finds a sign reading: "Do Not Disturb. All rooms occupied. Sealed this day: 3-7-05 by order of the Council."[29] Apparently the hedonic citizens of Earth have retreated into a perpetual dream-state. The rest of the city is also in immaculate condition, but sterile; all steel, concrete, and marble; no trees, wildlife, or grass.

As D'glas continues exploring he enters the tallest nearby building called "Mars House," where he is greeted by a "mech" desk clerk, and is surprised when approached by a man named Hansen, who escorts him to the Council Building. Along the way, D'glas is bombarded by a phantasmagoric series of illusions: a harpy, a Fury, Cerebus, Mephistopheles and a swarm of tiny demons, symbolic projections from the collective subconscious. They stop a few blocks before the towering edifice of the Council Building in front of the only building remaining in disrepair: "The building was decaying. Much of the façade had fallen; it lay in heaps of rubble along the steps and across the entranceway. Only this building and the landing field had not been kept in repair." D'glas is cheered by a well-tended lawn in front: "The grass made D'glas feel warm again. It was the first real *life* he had seen since landing. Someone had taken care of it, tended it, kept it green." This building is, appropriately, the Library, the storehouse of knowledge. Its tenant is a young woman named Susan who has been surviving alone for ten years, since her mother died and her father went into the dream-tank. She casts a stone that smashes into Hansen and reveals he's a mech: "His head laid open to the split metal beneath. Inside his skull, tiny wires glistened." Like the invaders on Venus, Hansen is a Duplicate. Having been alone for so long and surrounded by mechs and illusions, Susan doubts D'glas's humanity, going so far as to X-ray him in a machine not unlike what is now standard airport procedure. When his humanity is established, they fall into each other's embrace. Here Gunn further extends the theme of the real vs. the unreal and how humaniform duplicates can blur the lines of the human.[30]

D'glas prepares to visit the Council Building, but first he must gather information. In a brilliantly rendered confrontation between D'glas and the mechs at the "Paradise Hotel" Gunn imagines a cadre of semi-autonomous, specialized machines, built to service this emptied world: a fire prevention mech, an automated sweeper, a machine that spins plastic to seal the occupied rooms, a mechanized toolbox. D'glas blows open one of the rooms with a grenade and is dowsed with a flood of amniotic fluid. The room, "a sort of shapeless plastic-lined cocoon without furnishings," is, in essence, a womb. Humankind, facilitated by self-regulating technology, has retreated into the ultimate pleasure of dreams. Inside is a naked male, "a kind of caricature of humanity, a fantastically hairy gnome curled blindly into a fetal position," now twitching spasmodically on the floor. D'glas is horrified: "It was a disquieting parody of the embryo in the human uterus. This was where everybody was. This was the end man had reached. The end was the beginning." Antecedents for this vision of ultimate technological retreat include Forster's "The Machine Stops," Laurence Manning and

Fletcher Pratt's "City of the Living Dead," Simak's "Paradise," and John D. MacDonald's "Spectator Sport." As D'glas contemplates this illusory omega point of human destiny, Gunn renders some of his most compelling imagery and acknowledges the seductiveness of such a sensory immersion:

> These fetal gnomes were alive in only a technical sense. And when they died, finally, as all men born of women must, the race of Man would be dead with them. And yet it was infinitely seductive, this slow suicide. D'glas could feel its lure yet; it was an effort of will to remain standing outside the womb. It would take a strong man to conquer it, a man so strong that he could deny the mortality within him and the life-long agony of deprivation.... There must be billions of these cells across the face of the Earth; in them the billions of men and women had returned to their embryonic bliss. It was all wrong. It was as if they had returned to the soupy seas of the primeval Earth, returned to being blind, protoplasmic cells.... Now, here on the world where he was born, where he strove and developed and grew, Man was satisfied, Man was happy, Man was dead—no matter how long these foster-wombs kept the fossils alive.[31]

Another Hansen-mech appears to escort D'glas to the Council—to face a charge of murder. Met in the lobby by two beautiful female mechs—precursors to the robot-brides in "The Girls Who Were Really Built"—who are armed with hypodermics in their fingertips in case he resists, he is taken to the Council Building. Gunn brilliantly anticipates the ubiquity of computer systems and the idea that our buildings and vehicles have become stone, metal, and glass receptacles that house our computers: "He was inside the Council. The Council was this building. The Council, guardian of paradise, ruler of this corner of the universe, was a giant mech." Later, the computer tells D'glas its name: "'I have been called Council, because I assumed the duties of the Hedonic Council, from the men who once composed it. Others have called me Hedon. And some have called me God.'"[32]

What follows is a phantasmagoric sequence that makes the earlier illusions pale in comparison in which it is no longer possible to assert what is real and what is illusion. Like Horn during his infinite timelessness in the Tubes, D'glas loses all context of space and time: "From the moment he entered the building, reality ceased to have an objective meaning. Time and place became abstractions without referents." This in itself may leave the reader to question whether D'glas is still free of Hedon's control or whether he is already dreaming in a vat. After dismissing Hansen and the women, who promptly vanish, D'glas asks the ultimate ontological question, "What is reality?" And thus a debate between man and computer gets underway: "'What does it matter?' asked the flames leaping in the fireplace. 'There is you. There is I. There are the thoughts that pass between us. These are the only things of meaning. All else is illusion. What you see, here or anywhere, is merely the impact of photons on your retina. What you sense is merely your mind's subjective interpretation of electrical flows through your sensory network. Which is real: the mind's impression, the electrical flow, the triggering of the flow, or that which may or may not exist outside the system? Reality? It is only the illusion we can agree upon.'"[33]

As they continue to argue, Hedon justifies its purpose to give humankind the ultimate happiness: illusion, emptiness, and finally extinction, "the ultimate happiness is death." Having achieved its purpose on Earth, Hedon must seek out other beings to provide happiness, else it too will have no purpose: "'When there is nothing more for me to do, when the last enwombed man has slipped blissfully away in his last dream of paradise, I must die, like any god without worshippers.'" But D'glas refuses to accept Hedon's argument. For D'glas, Hedon's version of ultimate happiness is an empty parody of living: "'Only in dissatisfaction does life exist. Only dissatisfied has life developed and grown and conquered the unloving, unconscious aspect of the universe. This is the true function of life; to fertilize the universe, to inseminate it, to impregnate it with life.'"[34] These words echo Wells's famous phrase that "individual creatures since life began, have been 'up against it' all the time, have been driven continually."[35]

In a final battle for D'glas's will, Hedon bombards him with a series of illusions. Everything blinks out and D'glas finds himself in a blank, empty room, where once had been a fireplace, paneling, books and furniture—it had never been there in the first place. He sees Susan, the last actively living human on Earth, afloat in a tank of amniotic dream-fluid: "In that instant, D'glas knew the terrible meaning of unhappiness."[36] He then experiences a series of illusions in which he and Susan suffer "the terrible meaning of unhappiness" repeatedly. As these illusions wash over him, taking him outside the confines of his own dreams into historical recreations, he recapitulates the primordial beginning of man's ascent to sentience: "He had never seen a jungle, but he recognized it and knew it for what it was: illusion. This was the jungle from which man had emerged, a toolmaker, a conqueror. A weak-armed, weak-toothed, weak-clawed animal, he had turned himself into the most deadly creature on Earth by making extensions for his arms and sharpening points to replace teeth and claws. In a more important sense, this was the jungle of the human mind, fraught with personal and ancestral fears which dulled the clean edge of the mind. Only recently, with the tools of hedonics, had man learned to conquer that jungle."[37] This recalls the time-bending power of two other transcendent sentient computers in science fiction: AM in Harlan Ellison's "I Have No Mouth and I Must Scream" and Ship in Frank Herbert and Bill Ransom's *The Jesus Incident*. In the primordial jungle, D'glas must fend off a series of panther attacks and conquer his own fear, until he shouts with angry defiance: "'Damn you! There is nothing more you can do! I am not afraid, not of death, not of fear itself!'" With that, "in great globs of blue, the sky began to melt," and D'glas finds himself in a conventional room with Susan, who is hooked up to some preliminary "tubes and wires," preparing her for amniotic immersion. Having conquered illusion through anger, D'glas helps release her from the euphoric bliss of the Council's seductive embrace by calling on her to get angry: "'Get mad, Susan! Get very mad! Let your adrenals work! Get angry at the Council!'"[38] Only through anger can they resist the "velvet snare" of Hedon's illusions.

But resistance can only last so long. D'glas buys some time when posing the question to Hedon, "Are *you* happy?" briefly releasing them to move freely about the building while Hedon contemplates "the puzzle of his own existence." Recalling Morgan's *The Rise and Fall of Applied Hedonics*, D'glas searches his memory for a room number: Room 2943, the Council Chambers. In a race against time, they rush to Room 2943 in hope that it is the location of a master control room, and there they find "a standard microtype keyboard." In its simplicity, Gunn accurately anticipates the office design elements now standard in the contemporary era of ubiquitous computers. As he stands before the keyboard D'glas declares, "'I'm giving Man a second chance. When he makes gods, Man should be careful not to make them work too well,'" and types in the command: Be happy![39]

A month later D'glas and Susan leave on the rocket to return to Venus. When Susan asks if Hedon is dead, D'glas replies: "'Not yet. Dreaming, perhaps. Under sentence of death. The Council, that made fantasies for others, is now making fantasies for itself.... In time, insulation will rot, wires will short, electronic devices will fail, masonry will crack, steel will rust. But the rule of the God Hedon is over. As soon as it realized that it, too, must be happy, it was doomed. Because happiness is death.'" And what will happen to Earth's billions in their dream-cocoons? D'glas reasons that most will die, but some "will survive the ordeal of being born again. The Council's automatic processes are keeping them alive, but when they are ready, they will break free.... Those who are worthy will eventually follow us."[40] Here again evoking the frontier theme.

Even so, doubts linger across D'glas's mind, leading to a mind-blowing conclusion that leaves the reader questioning the nature of their own reality. Here Gunn anticipates the simulation hypothesis of Oxford philosopher Nick Bostrom, who has posited that it is highly probable that we are living in a computer simulation.[41] At the novel's conclusion D'glas ponders, "How could they be sure that this was reality, not another wish-fulfillment dream from the Council-mech? How could they be sure that they had really conquered it and were not just living an illusion in a watery cell? The answer was: they could never be sure." In the end, though, D'glas concludes that it doesn't matter: "All a man had was himself and his faith in himself and such illusions as he chose to believe. The rest was lies."[42]

The Joy Makers is a stunning novel, brilliantly conceived and executed in terms of both visual and linguistic imagery and concept. As George Zebrowski has written, "*The Joy Makers* throws the reader into a world where human lives resonate with great issues, where happiness and human nature are double-edged swords, and freedom means the abandonment of fantasy for reality."[43] It raises important questions about the human experience, the impact of technology, and the nature of reality, that compare favorably with the now canonized work of Philip K. Dick. *The Joy Makers* is a neglected classic whose importance as a work of the imagination will only increase as we plunge further into the frontiers of digital technology that blurs the lines between reality and the virtual.

Station in Space

Shortly after completing the first two stories of *The Joy Makers*, Gunn began another major series in which he realistically portrays humanity's first space endeavors. The first story, "The Cave of Night" was completed in June 1954, and four more would follow over the next two years. In 1958, they would be published by Bantam as *Station in Space*. Gunn was inspired by Arthur C. Clarke's 1951 book *The Exploration of Space*, Heinz Haber's *Man in Space* (1953), and especially by a series of articles in *Collier's* that appeared in 1952 and 1953, by Willy Ley and others, with accompanying illustrations by Chesley Bonestell, called *Man Will Conquer Space Soon!*, which detailed Wernher von Braun's plans for manned spaceflight. Gunn wanted to depict these developments as realistically as possible and also delve into the interpersonal and psychological problems men, and later their families, would face living and working in space, to "turn these speculations into fiction, making dramatically vivid the sensations of space travel, the kinds of problems people would encounter, and the kinds of people that might solve them."[44] In large part, Gunn succeeded in this ambition. *Station in Space* is an excellent naturalistic approach to the possibilities of space, matching in realism Clarke's *Prelude to Space*, Kornbluth's *Takeoff*, and Leinster's *Space Platform*. Indeed, what makes Gunn's sequence particularly striking is his insight into the psychology of administration, an expansion on a theme he first explored in "Communications." As Gunn wrote Altshuler after completing the second story, "Hoax," "They will attempt to depict the basic physical and psychological problems in great detail, while telling rather simple stories from the viewpoints of the man in the chorus, rather than the leads."[45] Gunn felt the series could help prepare the public for the space age and give science fiction a real boost, as he wrote to Marty Greenberg: "The recent announcement of a planned artificial satellite in 1957 has encouraged me considerably about this particular series and about science fiction in general. This news and succeeding stories may be for science fiction what the first atomic bomb was: a shot in the arm. It sent people to SF ... not because SF had been accurate in predicting (which was not particularly exceptional or important if it was), but because SF was the only source of sound speculating about a future which held such events in store."[46] After completing the third story, "The Big Wheel," Gunn wanted Altshuler to first try it on the mainstream wide-circulation magazines, such as *Collier's* and *The Saturday Evening Post*, feeling that—like Heinlein's slick stories of the late forties—such realistic depiction of working in space would appeal to (and benefit) the non-specialized audience: "I'd like to recapture some of the vital drama implicit in our immediate future in the last few years. I feel that one of the prime assets of SF is its ability to let its impatient readers live, esoterically, as most of us must, what it was born too early for. The drama of the immediate future is not to be lightly tossed away."[47] Further, Gunn remarks that his overarching theme is that "space isn't going to be a simple, straightforward thing." Taking a page from Tom Godwin's controversial "The Cold Equations," for Gunn, "space is hard." Arguably the near-future space stories of Heinlein, and later Clarke, make living in space matter-of-fact, routine (a quality later captured on television by *Star Trek*), and by doing so they create an ambience that allows the reader to imagine that they, too, may live in space and go about their daily activities in a routine manner, following proper precautions. This ambience was captured by the 1959 children's first reader *You Will Go to the Moon* by Mae and Ira Freeman that inspired a generation of children, which depicts an average American boy taking a trip to the Moon as if it were a boy scout weekend camping trip. Halfway through the story there is an image of the boy in the rocket seated with his back to the reader as it approaches a space station, a four-spoked "big wheel" much like Gunn's.[48] This is the dream of space that was capturing the imaginations of many Americans during the era. Gunn wanted to show that the dream may not match the reality: "We'll reach space in a tangential, humanized way, and we'll sacrifice our dreams doing it. I want to tell the stories, generally, from the point of view of the little guy who will make the sacrifices that really count."[49]

"The Cave of Night" is narrated by a newspaperman who has been following the developments in rocketry for a number of years and reports on the first manned orbital flight of Air Force pilot Reverdy McMillen, who "had been testing rocket-powered airplanes, with Chuck Yeager."[50] The flight captures the attention of the entire world, much like the orbital flights of Yuri Gagarin and John Glenn would a half dozen years later, except in this case it is secret until something goes wrong and McMillen is trapped in orbit; his capsule has become his tomb. The world waits in agonized suspense for twenty-nine days, McMillen's plight galvanizing the emotions of the entire world and bringing unity. Gunn is aware of the Cold War realities of the era, but he sees the journey into space as a potential unifying event, as people around the world are enraptured by the possibilities of space represented in McMillen's ordeal: "A world offered what it had. Even the U.S.S.R. announced that it was outfitting a rescue ship, since its space program was already on the verge of success. And the American public responded with more than a billion dollars within a week. Congress appropriated another building. Thousands of men and women volunteered."[51]

Gunn adds technical detail to the story, giving it a hard science fiction flavor, and also accurately forecasts the financial costs involved in space flight. Perhaps more than anything else, it is the economics of space flight which have proved to be the greatest obstacle to realizing the dream of space depicted in the Freemans' children's book. Gunn effectively renders the symbolic importance of the spacecraft: "All by itself the spaceship part would have captured the world's attention. It was achievement as monumental as anything Man has ever done and far more spectacular. It was liberation from the tyranny of Earth, this jealous mother who had bound her children tight with the apron strings of gravity. Man was free. It was a symbol that nothing is completely and finally impossible if man wants it hard enough and long enough." The flight sparks a fascination with space: "Space-madness became a new form of hysteria. We read statistics, we memorized insignificant details, we studied diagrams, we learned the risks and the dangers and how they would be met and conquered. It all became part of us." To a large degree this mood was true of the era of the Apollo missions. The phrase "the cave of night" is an excellent metaphor for the vastness of space. It becomes the catchword of the moment; how people interpolate their shared experience: "It summed it all up, the drama, the anxiety, the hope."[52]

Gunn also explores the ways in which broadcast media can influence masses of people across the globe. As McMillen completes an orbit every two hours, he continuously broadcasts to those below, creating an intimate relationship with the billions wishing for his safe return. Gunn captures that intangible empathy established through our interfaces with media technologies. But McMillen is all alone in the "cave," as the receiver is out and he can only broadcast. To show Rev that they are listening, the lights of Kansas City are shut on and off, an anticipation of a real event when Perth, Australia turned its lights on and off when John Glenn passed over during the first American orbit. Rev continues to broadcast messages, building a groundswell of empathy and global goodwill: "'Don't worry about me. I'm fine. I know you're working to get me down. If you don't succeed, that's okay with me. My life wouldn't just be wasted. I've done what I've always wanted to do. I'd do it again.'"[53] Rev's month-long sojourn serves as a catalyst, and even though new ships won't be ready in time to save him, they are being built in record time (it's interesting to note the parallels with Matt Weir's recent bestseller *The Martian*). The impetus to space has begun: "It has given us a common goal, and for the first time we are united."[54]

A rescue mission commanded by Captain Frank Pickrell intercepts Rev's capsule and the world weeps as Pickrell announces that "'Lieutenant McMillen is dead. He died heroically, waiting until all hope was gone, until every oxygen gauge stood at zero…. From this moment, let this be his shrine, sacred to all generations of spacemen, inviolate. And let it be a symbol that Man's dreams can be realized, but sometimes the price is steep.'"[55] Gunn's theme that space is hard is foregrounded here. That any endeavor of exploration can lead to loss of life, but it is worth it. Anything worth doing is difficult.

As the story concludes the narrator is in Times Square and sees someone who looks exactly like Rev. It was a hoax: there was no man in the capsule. The narrator reflects on what this might mean: "If my speculation was right, Rev had never been up there at all. The essential payload was only a thirty-day recording and a transmitter. Even if the major feat of sending up a manned rocket was beyond their means and their techniques, they could send up that much. Then they got the money; they got the volunteers and the techniques. I suppose the telemetered reports from the rocket helped. But what they accomplished in thirty days was an unparalleled miracle. The timing of the recording must have taken months to work out; but the vital part was secrecy."[56] Here Gunn suggests that to make grand, important events happen, sometimes secrecy and deception are the most rational approach.

The second story, "Hoax," features a young man named Amos Danton who is enraptured by the dream of space and the mythic power of Rev McMillen's terminal orbit. He grew up dreaming of going to space and helping build the Doughnut, the orbital space station which will be the avenue to the solar system. The dream of space is the overarching theme of the story and it creates a dialogue with Gunn's explorations of dreams in other registers and contexts, leaving the reader to ponder the links between the extreme delusions of *The Joy Makers* and the tangible dreams of space exploration. The story begins at his old boyhood bedroom; he has returned home after graduating from the Air Force Academy, having made it through rigorous training and testing that qualify him for space. His mother is helping him pack. There's a delightful referential moment when the youngster picks up his well-thumbed copy of *The Conquest of Space*, Willy Ley's 1949 book, illustrated with "achingly beautiful Bonestells." Amos reshelves the book and tells his mother he no longer needs it; he is going to live the dream. But she shakes her head, "'I just don't understand why anyone would want to go flying off into nothing. Seems like there's enough trouble right here on Earth without hunting up more. Every time I turn on the television it seems there's some new crisis or the cold war is colder or hotter.'" Here Gunn voices the typical, and all-too common, myopic objections that equate space exploration with ignoring the problems on Earth. Like many, Amos's mother has no scope of human history or the human species, beyond her own narrow horizon. Amos offers a counterpoint of purpose and vision: "'It's important, tackling something really worth doing. It's the dream—like the one that led the settlers into the wilderness that pulled the wagon trains across the prairies. It's where men are making the future, men who really count, men like Rev McMillen and Bo Finch and Frank Pickrell.... It's the future out there.'"[57]

Amos is assigned his first flight, serving as radio operator on the rocket that takes him to his assignment on the Doughnut. He's appalled by the irreverence of a message painted on the wing on the third-stage rocket: "McMillen's Folly."[58] The ship's captain, whom he compares to Queeg of *The Caine Mutiny* (the Bogart film was in release while Gunn was writing the story), pushes him hard. With precise detail Gunn describes the process and the physical sensation of taking a rocket out of Earth's gravity well. These details are no doubt gleaned from Gunn's reading of Ley, Clarke, and Haber, but also his reading of science fiction; and it is likely that Gunn's own experiences in pilot training give an authenticity to his imagination. Despite his training, when Amos experiences the reality of freefall, he vomits. By the time they rendezvous with the Doughnut a miserable Amos has come to hate the captain.

When the captain removes his space helmet, Amos is shocked to find that it is Colonel Frank Pickrell, his hero. The first stage of Amos's dream is shattered: "How can a man dream so long, he thought desperately, and have the reality turn out so horribly." From here, Gunn examines the psychological challenges faced by a young man sent into space. The loneliness, the isolation, the longing for home, the disorientation of being off planet Earth. But Amos quickly adapts and within a week he "began to forget that he had ever known another life." Yet with adaptation comes the loss of the excitement of the dream: "Life became less a torment, more a drudgery. By the same token, it became less a dream, more a cold reality." Such complacency leads some to see the Doughnut as an end in itself. But Amos holds precariously onto the dream: "Amos knew it was only a means, the first of a series of steps that led up to the moon, the planets, and the stars. The scientists had come out into space to look back at Earth. Amos had come out to reach the stars."[59] These tensions between looking outward and looking back define the challenges that continue to limit human space endeavors.

At the end of the first month, Amos is called before Colonel Pickrell. Pickrell wants to send Amos back. He's incensed that Amos is a dreamer, and dreaming can be dangerous to the proper functioning of the station: "'I'll tell you what I have against you, Danton: you've got stars in your eyes. This isn't a job to you; it's a game. I know your kind; I've seen too many of you. You want to go on out. You gripe about the Air Force marking time on the Moon project or the Mars ship or the Venus expedition. I'll tell you something, Danton: This is no glory road. This satellite is out here to look back on Earth, not out at the stars.'" The second stage of Amos's dream is crushed: Pickrell's viewpoint, like his mother's, has a limited field of vision. The phrase above "to look back on Earth" drives this home. For Amos, the dream is still alive; it is Pickrell who has lost the dream: "Pickrell had changed, surely, not the dream. He had grown old and used up, and the dream was too much for him. And in his hands was the future of space flight. The dream was betrayed."[60]

Since Pickrell is going to wash him out, Amos determines to go out in space at least once, to "pay a final tribute to the dream," by visiting the capsule containing Rev McMillen. Absconding with a space taxi, Amos treks the one hundred orbital miles to McMillen's tomb. There he finds the "air-lock door gaping open to invite him in," and the final stage of his dream ends when he clings to an exterior girder and peers inside: "The interior of the ship was only a shell. There were no seats, no instruments, no inside sheathing. There had been no shutters for the canopy; ultraviolet had turned it almost completely opaque; micro-meteorites had etched it. There was no pilot, no hero named McMillen. There never had been." Amos scratches a message to future dreamers on the girder: "DREAMS END HERE."[61]

Alas, Amos miscalculated: Pickrell can't send him back home as long as he follows orders. By going to the capsule he's now given him cause. At first Pickrell doesn't believe that Amos went to McMillen's tomb, but when Amos declares he knows it's a fake, Pickrell is forced to admit it and explains why they had to do it the way they did: "'We couldn't get the money. That was the only thing we needed—the money. We used all we had—government money, our own; it wasn't enough. We built a ship. We slaved on it. But we couldn't finish it. By stripping the third stage to a shell, we could put a payload of only one hundred pounds into an orbit. I don't remember now who suggested the idea—maybe it was McMillen himself. But it was the answer. We couldn't put McMillen up here really because we were the only ones with the imagination to see what space flight could mean. So we pretended. None of us have ever regretted it.... We did what we had to do, to do what had to be done.'"[62] When Amos threatens to expose the hoax if he's sent back home, Pickrell decides to let him stay, "now that you've got this foolishness about heroes and the great adventure knocked out of you, maybe you'll be a spaceman yet." Amos's final reflection as the story ends nicely reframes the dream theme, providing a new synthesis: "The dreams a man absorbs from his society, as naturally as the air he breathes, aren't important. Soon or late—they die. Call it: growing up. And when a man grows up he has to make his own dreams. His were still out there."[63]

"The Big Wheel" depicts the building of the first full-sized space station modeled on those proposed by von Braun, Ley, Clarke, and others. Gunn imagines a future economic disruption (in the 1960s) due to increasing computer automation putting people out of work that would compel a government economic intervention for massive public works projects like the WPA programs of the 1930s. In some respects, Gunn anticipates the current wave of economic disruption now rumbling. In this case, out of work men sign on to go into orbit and work construction on the Wheel, a larger space station which will make it possible to construct ships to go further out into the solar system.

"The Big Wheel" is told through the first-person viewpoint of Bruce Patterson, an out of work production line inspector who has been replaced by automation. The first fellow job seeker he meets is a former "economics professor in a Midwestern college" (one can guess KU), named Kendrix. Kendrix and Patterson form a deep bond between themselves and two other men, Clary Calhoun, a young dreamer like Amos Danton, and Jock Eckert, a boisterous laborer who sees the Wheel as just another construction job. Throughout the story Patterson and Kendrix discuss economic issues. Interestingly, Gunn posits a collaboration between government and private industry. Rather than a direct governmental intervention project, the Big Wheel is supposedly financed by the C.I.C., the Capital Investment Corporation. As Patterson and the other men are told during orientation: "'One, C.I.C. is not a relief organization. Two, It is not a government bureau, although the Federal Government is a participant. Three, C.I.C. is a profit-making organization set up to invest capital in long-term projects too big to be handled by a single company.'" The C.I.C. is a conglomerate involving "almost every major corporation in the country," and the C.I.C. is unabashedly motivated by profit: "'We want to make money. And C.I.C is the best long-term investment in the world.'" In spite of this rousing speech by C.I.C. front man Bradley, Patterson has doubts that profit is the only thing that motivates the C.I.C. In this sense, Gunn returns to the theme of the hoax: that behind the visible, surface motives for getting the public behind backing the space frontier lurks greater ambition that the broader public hasn't the vision to understand.[64]

Patterson's story is not solely that of an out of work man seeking employment, it is also the story of the difficulties in his marriage, and how economic hardship breaks relationships. He's been married five years, and his wife doesn't want him to go, for obvious reasons: she's pregnant. But he argues that they need the money and that he can make enough in six months to ride out the depression. She doesn't come for his departure, nor does she answer the phone when he tries to call her before takeoff; the thought occurs to him that she may be having the baby at that moment.

Training lasts three months and the 178 men who make it through the rigors of training, Patterson among them, are divided into crews: electrical, rigging, welding and shipfitting. Among the first casualties is Patterson's friend, Clary Calhoun, the young man who shares Amos Danton's dream. Once in space, he suffers from extreme headaches, and he's going to be sent back to Earth. But before he ships out, he restates the case for the dream and what motivates dreamers to pursue it: "'To the rest of you this is just a job, a hard, unpleasant, dangerous job. To me it's the only thing in life worth doing.'" As tensions rise among the men after several fatal accidents, and one questions the purpose of the whole project, Clary makes an impassioned plea that encapsulates the ethic of science fiction, making the case for the space frontier as human destiny:

> "The human spirit—that's what they're good for. Through all the ages of human awareness, they have been there, waiting, an eternal challenge: riddle my meaning come to me, seize me if you can! Now we have the power and we must accept the challenge—if only because a challenge refused is the beginning of decay. But the challenge accepted is life renewed, life reaffirmed, and the obstacle conquered strengthens Man for the next one, the bigger one. But there are more important reasons. Man needs a broader viewpoint, a wider horizon. Let him go to meet the universe, and he will find himself reflected in it—not an Earthman with all the narrowness and prejudice of the village mentality, but a Spaceman, a citizen of the universe. Wherever Man goes, he meets himself. Out here he will meet a better man, because he can't bring hatreds and prejudices out with him. They weigh too much. All he can bring is his dreams, the ones that soar. And out here he may find the answers he has sought too long and in vain below."[65]

Here Gunn makes a major statement about what it means to be human, what it means to have purpose, what it means to embrace new viewpoints and possibilities. Here he articulates one of the central arguments made in science fiction: that we need the challenges of space. That species survival might depend upon it. This is the message of countless works of science fiction.

Further accidents occur and after a plate loosens when they apply spin, killing Jock Eckert, Patterson reaches his boiling point. Near mutiny ensues, but Kendrix quells the men's disillusionment by explaining the real purpose behind the building of the Wheel: "'This is the greatest relief project of all time. I thought everybody knew that. We're out here to revive the economy. W.P.A. in the sky!...For every man on the wheel, there are 50,000 men at work below, making the rocketships that carry him, the fuel that powers them, the oxygen he breathes, growing and processing the food he eats, building his suits and his satellite, and all the countless, expensive things necessary to create an Earth-type environment in the hot-and-cold vacuum of space. You're sitting up here on top of a pyramid of human effort.'"[66] Inspired by Kendrix's impassioned analysis, coupled with the dreams of young Calhoun, the men rally to complete the Wheel.

The story ends in a manner that recalls Edmond Hamilton's "What's

It Like Out There?" which Gunn later selected for *The Road to Science Fiction*. A physically battered Patterson has returned to Earth and goes in search of his wife, but she long ago left their apartment. Despondently he enters a bar where he hears someone chime, "'Thank God for the boys who built the Big Wheel. They're the boys who showed this country that there's nothing to be afraid of.'" Thanks to the wheel, the economy is back on track and people once again have confidence for the future. As with Danton's reflection at the end of the previous story, Gunn creates a compelling inner dialogue in which Patterson reflects on his experiences, pondering whether his personal losses add up with the bigger picture of human survival and destiny: "We went out to build the Big Wheel for all the wrong reasons and we found there all the wrong things. But perhaps it didn't matter. I would think about that, and someday I might be able to believe that it didn't matter, that the only thing that mattered was being men. On that day, perhaps, I would be glad that I had helped, that I had been a part of it, that I had built the Big Wheel." At that moment, as if to bring closure to these feelings, a bus pulls up at the depot, and his wife comes down the steps. The hopes of a happy future will be Patterson's too.[67]

Gunn wrote the fourth story, "Powder Keg," for the class he took with Caroline Gordon. As Gunn remarks in his memoir, "Among the things Gordon taught us: the ending of a story should be implicit in the first paragraph, Flaubert established the principle that nothing existed in fiction unless it happened in a particular place made real by appeal to at least three senses."[68] In "Powder Keg," Gunn applied Flaubert's principle "to make space flight seem real."[69] It's interesting to note that in Gordon's *How to Read a Novel*, published the following year, her discussion of this very topic is bookended by two statements about science fiction, the first stating how SF works "create imaginary worlds based on analogies to or contradictions of the world we know"[70] and the second remarking how "any vision or fantasy must have a solid substratum of fact if the reader is to give it what Coleridge called 'the willing suspension of disbelief'—a principle familiar to all writers of science fiction."[71] It seems likely that Gordon's brief considerations of the genre were stimulated by her interactions with Gunn, by then a well-established professional in the field and, arguably, the first to write a comprehensive analysis of *how to read* science fiction in his thesis. Furthermore, "Powder Keg" is an exemplary example of the kind of SF story Gordon's last remark evokes.

"Powder Keg" has some affinities with the earlier story "Communications." Following the economic recovery, the Cold War has heated up again, and making matters worse "every puny little nation has a stockpile of atomic and hydrogen weapons." A second station, the Little Wheel, has been constructed as a missile defense, "to keep everyone honest," anticipating Ronald Reagan's Star Wars Initiative. The plot involves a psychologist named Phillips who is sent to the Little Wheel by General Ashley of the Pentagon to investigate the psychological state of its commander, Amos Danton, the hero of the second story, now a grizzled space veteran. Danton hasn't been back Earthside in twelve years, not since Pickrell shattered his dreams, and Ashley's convinced he's "utterly insane." Ashley also suspects, rightly, that Danton and his crew have an agenda of their own: "'They're building something up there behind the Wheel where we can't see it. I want to know what it is.'" Trained in the methods of clinical psychology, Phillips is a firm believer that no group of men is capable of not cracking under the stress of responsibility. Although Phillips believes it's likely that Danton may well have cracked under the pressure of his command, he is also keenly cognizant that Ashley's motivations are distorted by his own failings. Ashley had been "disqualified for space duty," due to space sickness, and he has sublimated his humiliation into "a driving ambition that had carried him to the top of the Air Force through an incommensurable amount of unrelenting labor, constant politicking, and plain backstabbing." Here Gunn gets to the psychoses that can drive men into positions of power, with potentially catastrophic results.[72]

On the rocket up, Phillips meets a young cadet named Jack Grant, going back to the wheel after a period of leave on Earth. Grant "'can't wait to get back'" and Phillips reminds himself that Grant's profile "didn't fit the pattern" of maladjusted discontent typical of the usual spacer, asking himself, "Why had he gone out?" By contrast, when he arrives and first observes the other men: "There is a sameness to them, he thought. A dedication, a mania that molds their features, a look to the eyes as if they were fashioned for seeing more distant vistas than other men…. They were marked men … by a common experience and a dream shared, marked so that all men might know them and say, 'There goes a spaceman.'"[73]

Phillips quickly picks up that the men are absolutely devoted to Danton and he soon diagnoses the crew as all having mental problems, "they were unstable personalities in an artificial and unnatural environment." They're the same type of steadfast men Gunn portrayed in "Communications": "Only men with character defects would run away from the daily stresses and decisions of life on Earth, only such men could conquer space because only they would want to." Phillips concludes that it's too risky to allow such men to have the weapons of Earth in their hands and therefore "the conquest of space would have to be sacrificed to the security of the race of man."[74]

When Phillips concludes his evaluation, he is going to recommend that Danton be sent down immediately. But Danton's file contains a special order from Pickrell stating that Danton is never to go back down, nor does he want to. When Phillips argues this is the very reason why Danton is not "a good risk," Danton counters. "'Explorers have never been good risks.'" As this confrontation draws to its conclusion, an alarm bell rings. There's an emergency on the Wheel as a meteor has penetrated the interior causing a section to lose atmosphere. They find Grant in the air-testing lab, suited and in shock, another man named Fred in critical condition, having secured Grant's helmet for him with no time to put on his own. When Fred dies, Danton comes down with fury on the youth and plans to send him back immediately. A bewildered Phillips asks him to go easy on Grant, but Danton will have none of it, making a powerful statement of the creed that "space is hard": "'This is a hard place; we have to be hard to stay out here. I'm not blaming the kid for being foolish. I was a young, foolish kid, too, and I almost got sent in for it. The reason he's going in is that he didn't do the right thing instinctively.... I'm blaming him for not getting into his emergency helmet. I'm blaming him for killing a man, a good man, a man we couldn't afford to lose.'"[75]

After a lengthy dispute about the Wheel's purpose, Ashley's motivations, and the character of the men on the station, Phillips has an epiphany and realizes that Danton is the sanest man he's ever met; that the men are not neurotic, but completely sane and devoted to the well-being of the species, not to selfish ego. Evidence reveals that it was not a meteor that pierced the hull, but a gunshot fired from within. Grant is a saboteur and Ashley is behind it; and Grant has released the taxis so he can get inside the missile control room and arm the missiles. Danton tries to talk him down, and Grant confesses Ashley's role in the sabotage: "'Ashley sent me up to do this job, and I'm gonna do it. "If you can't do it any other way," he said, "send down a missile. That'll be the end of the Wheel." I'm really gonna do him a job. I'm gonna send 'em all down.'"[76] Grant has gone completely insane. Here Gunn's explores the instrumental insanity, the psychosis of the atomic age, which novels such as Bernard Wolfe's *Limbo*, Mordecai Roshwald's *Level 7*, and the film *Dr. Strangelove* also diagnose. Grant has succumbed to the apocalyptic psychosis of the bomb.

Grant's psychosis comes crashing down when Danton reveals the truth of the station: "'There aren't any missiles. Earth is in no danger from us. Too bad we can't tell them that. But we can't. And therefore we must live in constant expectation of a moment of madness Inside that will send up a missile to destroy a threat that doesn't exist.'" Danton and the men of the Little Wheel have transformed the bombs into fuel for a starship. It is not the Little Wheel which is the pressured "powder keg" waiting to explode into madness, but, rather, as the sober Danton affirms, the anxious planet below: "'That's your powder keg, masses of humanity penned up in unyielding containers, more people every minute. If you don't give them some outlet, an explosion is inevitable.'" Danton's vision of expanding the space frontier will symbolically release some of that pressure: "'We can't export our excess millions to the planets or the stars. But we can give them a vent for their excess energies, for their frustrated aggressions, for their unused dreams. The existence of a frontier is enough: everyone doesn't have to go there.'"[77] This vision returns to the coalescence sparked by the Rev McMillen hoax. When Phillips says Ashley will never rest in his effort to shut the Little Wheel down, Danton says he'll go public, let the world know what they're doing, let them live vicariously in the grand adventure ahead. He invites Phillips to join them in this grand dream, to "help us put it over—this little thing with Ashley and the big victory over Mars and the fantastic distance that lies between."[78]

As in the other stories in the series, "Powder Keg" hinges on deception; deception for the greater good. Gunn also ties it in with his central theme of dreams. A remark from Danton has ironic resonance in the context of *The Joy Makers*: "'The fact remains that it is the soul of man and his salvation. He is a dream-maker, and the latest dream is the best, no matter how many have been shattered before.'" As Phillips reflects, his thoughts virtually repeat D'glas's arguments with Hedon in *The Joy Makers*: "The basic quality of life is movement. An immobile animal is a dead animal. Carnivore and prey know this instinctively. And man is a dissatisfied animal. Satisfy him and he ceases to be a man. Quiet him and he stops being alive."[79] Another important theme that surfaces here and is present throughout Gunn's work, and his biography for that matter, is that one's purpose in life is to do what is worth doing, to do what one is meant to do. Phillips' reflection echoes Gunn's own sense of internal purpose: "Once in his life, if he is lucky, a man finds something worth doing. He had found it. The long journey to the stars was the most human thing that men could do. It would keep the whole race human."[80] Phillips has come home. "Powder Keg" is perhaps the most inspiring story in the series, a quintessential illustration and advocacy of the frontier theme in science fiction.

The final story in the sequence, "Space Is a Lonely Place," has several affinities with "Breaking Point," as mentioned earlier. The story involves the third long-distance space flight to Mars and the psychological situation of the crew; the previous missions resulted in madness and death. Phillips, now married with two young children, lives on the Wheel and remotely observes the psychological complications the crew experiences on their long flight. Now 259 days in, the men are nearing the breaking point, and it could break either way, into madness or making it. Public pressure is on and they need a successful mission. Disillusionment with space has set in and the bureaucrats on Earth are considering mothballing the space expeditions (here Gunn seems to get things right). A "Fundamentalist Coalition," whose leader is running for President on an anti-space exploration platform, is rising to political power, and another failed Mars mission could put him in the White House. Such a shift could disrupt the tenuous peace that space exploration has instilled. Earth is on the brink of political crisis and this mission must succeed, or all could fall back into nuclear standoff.

There are echoes of the marital conflict seen in "The Big Wheel," as Phillips' wife, Terry, bemoans her husband's duty: "'I think you must be the most cold-blooded man I've ever known. Those men are friends of yours, and you care more about the success of the trip than whether they live or die.'" As the story opens, she wants to leave him after ten years on the Wheel and return to Earth, and she plans to take the children on the next ship out. Significantly, they have two sons, similar to Gunn's own boys. Part of their conflict stems from the fact that Phillips is devoted to his job, his purpose: "'You're married to that Wheel out there. You're mother to those men. You don't need a wife.'" The Wheel has gradually become more like a settlement. But the women and children don't interact with one another because they are isolated in "cottages," individual modules tethered to the Wheel, and one has to get spacesuited to visit other cottages or the Wheel. As Terry reckons, she hasn't seen another woman in a year. For the modern reader there is incongruity here. The domestic problems between Phillips and Terry are dated. The problem here is that the women are essentially the domestic housewives of the 1950s; housewives in space—rather than engineers, scientists, administrators in their own right, as they would be in modern life. Terry also contrasts life in space with the "natural" experience her boys would have growing up on Earth: "'They're being cheated of their birthright—blue skies and green grass and playing baseball with the other kids. They'll never be human beings.' She was screaming now. 'They're growing up into monsters! Monsters!'" But as Phillips counters, "I think they're pretty darned nice kids.

Don't project your disappointments into them, Terry. Children don't see things the way we do."[81] Here Gunn makes an interesting point about what constitutes "normal" and the reality of human adaptability to new environments. Later, Phillips asks Danton to connect the cottages, so that the families can interact: "'There's too much loneliness out here already without adding more.'"[82] The theme of isolation brought forth here parallels the isolation of the men on the ship to Mars.

The story shifts to the men on the ship heading for Mars, as Phillips and Danton review the video transmissions on the Wheel. Five men make up the crew: Holloway, Barr, Craddock, Jelinek, and Migliardo. Five days out, the men are already going stir crazy. They also start feeling time distortion, one fellow believes they've been out for much longer than that. One of them sees a man floating outside: "It looked like a face, a face with a white beard!"[83] Periodically the men see this apparition on board ship. "Shepherd" is a posthypnotic suggestion provided by Phillips that surfaces when the psychological tension peaks and they need aide. As the trip continues, the men get increasingly on each other's nerves, eventually leading to murder and death. Barr murders Craddock, goes mad, and Migliardo kills him to put him out of misery, before entering the airlock without a suit, taking his own life. Holloway has fallen into catatonia. Jelinek, for his part, realizes that Shepherd is merely a hallucination. Jelinek is still sane when the ship reaches Mars, but due to loneliness decides to release the air from the ship. He addresses Phillips: "'Lloyd, I suppose you're watching. You never told me, but I guess that's the way it had to be. I hope you've learned something. Perhaps to pick a better psychologist. I'm sorry, Lloyd, I couldn't face it—the loneliness and the silence. I think the silence was worst of all. Tell Amos—the crew was a failure—but the ship was a success. And tell him—there'll be a ship—out here—in good working order—with fuel and supplies—if anyone—ever makes it.'"[84]

As with McMillen's orbit around Earth, they consider faking it. Allow the public to believe that the astronauts made it successfully. They have two years before the ship is supposed to return. But Danton is near conceding defeat. For him, the dream has reached an impasse. It may be that it will be machines, not men who are the future in space: "'There's your spaceman. That's all there will ever be—packed solid with usable stuff. No neuroses, no tummy aches, no weakness, no indecision, no space-madness. It doesn't need oxygen, food, or water, medicine, sterilizers, entertainment, and the rest of the junk we have to have to survive. Just servo-mechanisms and telemetering devices. Robots. There's your spaceman.'"[85] In light of this and the somber mood of the earlier stories, critic

Gary Westfahl considers *Station in Space*, "a grim assessment of humanity's future in space of a kind that is almost unique in the genre."[86] But Westfahl seems to be missing Gunn's point that space will be hard, but humans will adapt as necessary. Of course, Danton's assessment of the future of space travel has turned out to be more or less correct in the short term. Will we ever see a larger human presence in space? Or will space be left to machines? These are the central questions facing the space frontier in the future and one which Gunn fruitfully examines in this book.

Surprisingly, it is Phillips who remains hopeful that humans can make it in space, and he reaffirms the idea that it is humanity's symbolic presence which is necessary as much as anything else: "'No, Amos, it won't do. As a research tool, it's fine. As a symbol it just won't do. Men's representatives, meaningful representatives, must be living, breathing, fearful men like themselves. They've got to be men doing something the people who are left behind think they could have done, given the opportunity—men whose doings give them glory.'" Phillips believes it will take eight to ten years to have men who are fit to make the journey, from a generation who no longer feels the psychological ties to Earth: "'If we can't find them readymade, we'll have to make them ourselves.'" This mirrors Asimov's frontier psychological argument in "The Martian Way," that the pioneers of space will be the ones to take the next step, not those psychologically bound to Earth. Phillips returns to his cottage to find his boys playing with plastic ray guns, happy and content with life in space: "'Daddy, you're home early! Play spaceman with us!'" And echoing the conclusion of "The Misogynist," Lloyd gently replies, "'Hello, spacemen.'" Gunn ends with a powerful concept; that humans adapt to their environment in the next generation; that these boys cannot imagine life in any other way; hence they will not have the psychological traumas that doomed the Mars mission. Space is their natural home.[87] It's a fitting conclusion to the series and an inspiring one.

The Immortals

Next to *The Listeners*, *The Immortals* is probably Gunn's most famous work. Gunn imagines a near-future society in which a mutation in the blood can lead to life extension and rejuvenation. As the novel develops, this leads to a startling apocalyptic vision of the future. As he did in *The Joy Makers*, however, Gunn imagines that apocalypse will not come from nuclear war, but rather from the social consequences of an unanticipated novum. In this sense, *The Immortals* is one of the first novels dealing with runaway bio-technology. Gunn drew inspiration from his brother Richard's medical practice in Kansas City (the novel is dedicated to him) and used accurate details of hospital procedures and protocols. As he wrote to Altshuler upon delivery of the first story "New Blood": "All details very authentic: blood bank technique, transfusion, even theoretical material about life and death. The hospital—though not named—happens to be Research Hospital here, where ex-President Harry Truman recently recovered, after—I understand from my doctor-brother—he was more critically ill than was let out."[88] Gunn started using his regional geography more frequently in his work at this time, and *The Immortals* is one of the best examples, as a good portion of the action of the novel takes place in Kansas City and Lawrence.

As with *The Joy Makers* and *Station in Space*, *The Immortals* is a multi-part novel originally consisting of four novellas; Gunn later added a fifth, "Elixir," for the 2004 reprint. The first two stories in the series "New Blood" and "Donor" are more or less contemporary; the social order is not yet decentered and ruptured. "New Blood" begins as an anonymous young man donates blood at a hospital. Elsewhere in the facility an eighty-year-old billionaire, Leroy Weaver, is dying from senescence. Weaver has all the characteristics of a grasping egotist: "He accumulated money and power; he never had enough." And Weaver is afraid to die. He's been brought to the Kansas City Medical Center because Dr. Russell Pearce, the attending physician, though young, is "the best geriatrician in the Middle West." There are echoes here with Curt Siodmak's *Donovan's Brain* (and, indeed, the television version borrows almost directly from it). More life, however, is something Weaver cannot simply accumulate. The story was a perfect *Astounding* story because of the attention Gunn gives to the procedural detail of hospital labor, going step-by-step through the laboratory and administrative protocols of processing a blood donation and preparing it for use.[89]

When Pearce gives Weaver a blood transfusion using the donated blood, Weaver is restored to vigor, and, in fact, appears to have been rejuvenated. Weaver demands that Pearce uncover what has led to his unprecedented recovery, and Gunn dramatizes the conflict between egotistical power and medical ethics. The donor is identified as Marshall Cartwright, a drifter, who sold the blood for enough money to get out of town. At this point, Cartwright doesn't know about his uniqueness. The rest of the story involves a race between Pearce and Weaver to find Cartwright: Pearce, in order to protect him from being "accumulated" by Weaver, and Weaver, to secure the rejuvenative blood. As the hunt unfolds,

THREE. The Joy Makers *to* The Burning 165

Weaver plans to live off of transfusions of Cartwright's blood and has sent an army of agents to various Midwest cities to find him. In turn, Pearce hires a private investigator named Locke to locate Cartwright before they do. The rejuvenative effects are short-lived: within forty days, Weaver has regressed to his prior weakened condition.

An important theme in the story is the conflict between medical ethics and the amorality of wealth. Pearce follows an ethical code that means nothing to the self-interested Weaver, who follows a code of his own: selfishness and power. When Pearce is taken by Weaver's men and brought before the billionaire, Pearce speculates on the consequences rejuvenation could have: "'Understand this, Weaver. What you're planning is impossible. What if we all could be rejuvenated? Do you have the slightest idea what would happen? Have you considered what it might do to Civilization?'" These repercussions are the subject of the following stories in the series. Here Gunn gets to the heart of the matter: what are the social consequences of bio-medical innovation. In many ways, we've seen both positive and negative consequences of improved pharmaceuticals, technological innovations, and longevity play out since Gunn wrote the story, but nothing on the dramatically apocalyptic scale that Gunn here suggests. Pearce believes that Weaver would end up killing Cartwright by draining him dry or make him a prisoner to breed a race of immortal slaves for the wealthy. Before Weaver's henchmen picked him up, Pearce had made contact with Cartwright, gave him some money, and bid him "to be fertile, to populate the earth," a countermeasure of freedom to the enslavement envisioned by Weaver. As the story concludes, Weaver, having just consummated a marriage with a twenty-five-year-old debutante named Patricia Warren, is back on his hospital deathbed, awaiting Pearce's attentions. The offspring of this union will be significant in the final story.[90]

"Donor" takes place fifty years later. The National Research Institute, founded by a cartel of the wealthy, has been trying to find Cartwright and his descendants for decades. Upon death, participants donate their estates to the Institute, not unlike the policy of Hedonics, Inc., albeit voluntary, and despite not finding Cartwright, it has made real breakthroughs in "geriatrics and hormone injections," only for the cartel's own use, of course. One hundred wealthy elites joined the Institute; half have died. Near ninety, Jason Locke, the detective Pearce hired to locate Cartwright, is the head of the Institute; having realized the implications, he set out to secure himself a position of power. The Institute's investigator, Edwin Sibert, has located one of Cartwright's descendants, and when he gets wind that Locke knows, makes a series of disguised dodges and arrives in Kansas City.[91]

Gunn posits a grim, decayed urban landscape, imagining that as people move to the suburbs, the result of the interstate highway system, the urban centers will collapse into disrepair. The general impression is that society is coming apart, infrastructure is decaying and the economy is in shambles. Whether this is a result of the Institute's quest for immortality is not overtly stated, but Gunn's suggestion is that the wealthy oligarchs have stifled the economy for their own ends and this has resulted in a failing society. Gunn's image of wealthy mismanagement speaks to certain aspects of the contemporary wealth gap: "Money was leaving the city. Those who could afford it were seeking a cleaner, healthier air and the better life in the suburbs, leaving the city to those who could not escape." While the city decays around it, however, the Medical Center grows. Gunn creates an image of the hospital echoing the Imperial Palace in *This Fortress World*: "Hospital Hill was becoming a great complex. In the midst of general decay, it was shiny and new. It reached out and out to engulf the gray slums and convert them into fine, bright magnesium-and-glass walls, markets of health and life. It would never stop until all the city was hospital."[92]

Sibert has come to Kansas City to save Barbara McFarland. Months earlier Sibert had finally identified her as a Cartwright, but instead of turning her over to Locke and the Institute, he fell in love with her. Suspecting Sibert's treachery, Locke has an agent tailing him. A gunfight ensues leaving the assailant and the landlady, also an agent, dead, and Sibert losing blood from a gunshot wound. Barbara calls a doctor and gives Sibert a transfusion of her immortal blood, and they flee southward along the "old tollway"—Gunn adds an interesting novum about a collapsing farm economy due to hydroponics—stopping in Joplin, Missouri. Sibert believes that Cartwright must have an agent within the Institute, so to protect Barbara, he's going to make contact by returning to the Institute and pretending he wants to sell her to the highest bidder. Once Sibert returns to the Institute, he's immediately seized, and when he tries to make a deal, Barbara is ushered in. She is to be a blood-giving slave to the cartel's geriatrics. And she believes Sibert has betrayed her. Sibert is locked away in a basement cell, but is set free by Liz, the Institute secretary, a former lover. When he confronts Locke, word comes that Barbara has escaped: Cartwright's agent, a man named Sanders who worked as a file clerk at the Institute for twenty years, has taken her away. It is hinted that Sanders is, in fact, Marshall Cartwright himself.

These first two stories set up the problem: the novum of the immortal blood. The setting remains contemporary, with hints of larger social problems ahead: although a gradual urban decay and a farm crisis is evident in "Donor," things have yet reached a breakdown level. From these stories, we can see why the book appealed to television. Neither story demands a major shakeup to the existing social order. What the television project missed was the next step, the broader implications played out in the following stories of the series.

Gunn added the story "Elixir" to the novel in 2004, fifty years after finishing "New Blood." Although it is clear that the story has the added benefit of fifty years of medical and technological innovation for Gunn to draw upon, it's pleasantly surprising how seamlessly Gunn blends the new story with the old, maintaining an internally consistent ambience. "Elixir" is set roughly at the same time as "Donor," fifty years after "New Blood." Dr. Pearce is ninety in the story, but doesn't look more than fifty. Pearce has been working to make a synthetic substitute of the blood, but has yet to make a breakthrough. Set at the Medical Center, Gunn's experiences as a university administrator and as a professor can be seen in his depiction of the academic setting. Pearce must go before the vice chancellor, Julia Hudson, where he's told his funds have not been renewed by the National Research Institute.

After the meeting, Pearce receives a note from a woman named Marilyn Van Cleve and leaves the safety of the Center for the dangers of the outside. As seen in "Donor," the city has decayed and the streets have become increasingly dangerous: bulletproof windows, armored cars, and military-style security at the Medical Center, are signs of a collapsing civility and an economics of desperation. The Medical Centers remain in the hearts of cities to cull the medical benefits from the destitute for the benefit of the elites: "The Medical Centers remained in their midst, harvesting their antibodies and their antigens, their gamma globulins and their vaccines, even their organs."[93] Marilyn Van Cleve is one of the original Cartwright children, aged fifty and pregnant, and coming near term. Pearce muses that "Cartwright had wasted no time putting into action Pearce's admonition to be fruitful and multiply."[94] For Pearce's help, she offers the placenta and umbilical cord in payment, and she'll summon him when it's time. Pearce believes if he can synthesize the blood, then immortality can be available to all and the Cartwrights need no longer be hunted, nor will the poor be "harvested." The later stories prove him quite wrong. On the way back to his car Pearce is attacked. But Tom Barnett, Pearce's assistant, fortuitously comes out of the darkness and chases off the attacker. The reader can conclude that Barnett works for the Institute.

While Pearce works on the sample of Marilyn Van Cleve's blood, Vice

Chancellor Hudson makes an unexpected visit. She takes an interest in his work and decides to authorize the money for Pearce to keep working and she also wishes to assist him: "'Research is so neat, so definitive—so much better than the equivocal, messy business of administration.'"[95] This seems a reflection on Gunn's own academic experiences. A few days later, Pearce receives a note saying Marilyn needs his help. Outside on a motorcycle, an old man awaits, who takes Pearce on a journey through the city. Pearce views the inner city "as a place where people lived rather than a jungle to be flown over or passed through" and he realizes the unfortunate consequences the suburbs and the Med Centers have brought about: "The suburbs had drained the wealth from the inner city, and what the suburbs had started the Medical Centers had completed, taking block after block of housing for their expansion, pricing their snake oils and nostrums beyond the reach of the people in whose midst they lived and thrived." Pearce is brought to a decrepit building where the homeless live; it had once been Children's Mercy Hospital. He successfully delivers the baby and is given the afterbirth.[96]

Returning to the Medical Center, that night two small fires are set in the facility, as a diversion to search Pearce's lab. As Pearce returns to his apartment, he's summoned to tend an emergency in his wing. There he finds a decrepit, wheelchair bound Locke. For Pearce, the quest for immortality is for the species; for Locke, the quest is for selfish reasons: "'I'm not interested in the immortality of the species, nor is any of my board of directors. The world ends when we do.'"[97] This restates the conflict between ethics and power laid out in "New Blood." Locke agrees to continue to fund the research, believing that Pearce has connections with the Cartwright clan.

Although now the fourth story in the sequence, "Medic" was the second Gunn wrote, completing it about a month after "New Blood." When he sent it to Altshuler, his agent felt it was "awfully preachy in spots"[98] and evidently Horace Gold felt the same way, remarking in a rejection slip that Gunn was taking on big social ills: "If he'd only narrow his focus to individuals and their problems, and the hell with their solving or smashing those of a whole society!"[99] It took some time to place, but Robert Mills, managing editor of *The Magazine of Fantasy and Science Fiction*, wanted it for the *FSF* companion magazine *Venture*. However, it required some cuts to make it fit the magazine, which were restored for book publication. "Medic," as "Not So Great an Enemy," was the July 1957 cover story, the issue following the publication of "Space Is a Lonely Place," also a cover story in the same magazine. Mills wrote Gunn, gushing: "Just a note to say that C. Kornbluth thought 'Not So Great an Enemy' was 'magnifique'; A. Budrys thought it was the best thing of yours he's read in a few years; Cogswell was impressed by it, but thought there might have been more philosophy (I told him that was my fault); and other comments here and there have varied from fairly to quite favorable."[100] Ironically the cuts Mills reluctantly made were the "preachy" spots that Altshuler was uneasy about, and which Theodore Cogswell perceptively wanted to see more of.

The story advances another thirty-five years from the time of "Donor" and "Elixir," as Pearce is now 125. There is some inconsistency regarding timeline, as another passage suggests a fifty year leap. The city has crumbled further into decay and the divide between the poor city dwellers and the fortress-like Medical Center in their midst has grown considerably. To travel the streets in armored ambulances anticipates the apocalyptic visions of such films as *Mad Max*, *Death Race 2000*, *Escape from New York*, and *Brazil*. Among a number of contemporaneous science fiction visions, Fritz Leiber's "Coming Attraction" may have been an influence. Gunn wrote on Leiber's 1950 story in his master's thesis and would later select it for *The Road to Science Fiction*, where he considered it as one of the touchstones of social science fiction, "it encapsulated everything that was effective about this kind of fiction."[101] But the streets of Gunn's crumbling Kansas City seem much more sinister than those in Leiber's classic. "Medic" has some of Gunn's most powerful evocations of Kansas City in decay:

> From here the ruins were not apparent. The city looked almost as it had fifty years ago. But if a man looked closely, he could see the holes in the roofs, the places where the porcelain false fronts had fallen and the brick behind them had crumbled and toppled into the streets. Twelfth Street was blocked completely. Mounds of rubble made many other streets impassable. The hand of Time is not as swift as that of man, but it is inexorable. The distant, arrowing sweep of I-35 drew the eye like movement, bright through the drabness of decay. The Kansas Medical Center was out of sight behind the rising ground to the south, but the complex, walled entity on Missouri's Hospital Hill was brilliant in the sunlight. It was an island rising out of a stinking sea, an enclave of life within the dying city.[102]

The story begins as the city's political boss, John Bone, tended by his assistant, Coke, looks down upon the decaying city from his suite atop the twenty-nine-story City Hall. Bone is a hypochondriac and he bellows for Coke to get a doctor. The scene shifts to a young medic named Flowers, entering the city in a self-driving, armored ambulance in answer to an emergency call. The urban environment is set with booby traps, ambushes, landmines, and strewn with near impassable rubble. As a medic, Flowers holds an air of authority in what remains of civic society; standing above even the police. He's equipped with a variety of high-tech equipment, including a black doctor's bag that links to a computer aboard the ambulance and can perform a variety of diagnostics and procedures, a belt transceiver that can issue emergency alarms and makes audio and visual recordings, and a subsonic blast gun that can incapacitate attackers. Flowers is a true believer in the system, seen here when he lectures a policeman about a "shover" who has tried to sell Flowers a box of penicillin: "'It's rats like that who are chewing away the foundations of medical treatment. If drugs and antibiotics circulate without supervision, the life span will plummet to seventy or lower. We have enough trouble with antibiotic sensitivity and resistant bacteria strains without this.'"[103]

Flowers arrives at a dilapidated house at 3416 East 10th Street: the house where Gunn was born. As Gunn remarks, "I have always tried to use places I know as the locales for my stories."[104] There he encounters a blind woman named Leah, who is helping a man who has had a cerebral hemorrhage after having a stroke. Some remarks by Flowers reveal that defaulting on "contract" payments (insurance)—for those who can afford it in the first place—can result in repossession, meaning their bodies are harvested to supply those with valid contracts. Those who protest repossession are called "Antivivs." The patient was a suburban defaulter, who retreated into the city to live a subsistence existence, calling the hospital out of desperation. Gunn makes some good points about rising health care costs throughout the story that resonate with today's situation. As Leah remonstrates, "'You've made good health too expensive.'"[105]

Flowers is taken to see an old man in one of the first floor rooms—it is Dr. Russell Pearce. Pearce is 125 years old and Leah is his daughter (presumably Julia Hudson is her mother). Pearce left the Medical Center after successfully synthesizing the elixir and moved into the city to practice as a healer. Here Gunn creates a fascinating contrast between the apocalyptic city and the dystopia of the medical establishment. Pearce saw it coming three decades earlier and walked out; medicine had gone too far. When Flowers returns to the ambulance, he's ambushed. Flowers finds himself confined in darkness and reflects back on debates with his classmates Brand and Mock about medical ethics. Here Gunn raises important ethical questions: "Was there an optimum beyond which medicine consumed more than it produced in benefits? And was there a point past that at which medicine became a monster, devouring the society that produced it?"[106] Flowers is taken to City Hall to treat John Bone. When Flowers refuses to treat him, Bone orders his thugs to pick up Leah and Pearce. Leah is brought to them two hours later, but Pearce has been taken by the

"Agency" to the "Experimental Ward."[107] Bone demands treatment and threatens to torture Leah if the medic does not attend to him. But Flowers knocks Bone out with supersonics and the guards with neo-curare from a needle protruding from his bag, and they escape to the Medical Center compound. There, Flowers admits Leah for a cornea replacement operation and that evening is called to a meeting of the Wyandotte County Medical Society, where he's accused of misdeeds and told to resign. Realizing what they're going to do to Pearce, Flowers steals a carton of elixir, finds Pearce and gives him an injection of the rejuvenative drug, and then seeks out Leah. Flowers has made a promise to Pearce that he will perform an operation to give Leah her father's eyes. In a sense, Pearce becomes an Oedipus figure. A diversionary assault on the Center by Bone allows them to escape, and as the story concludes, Flowers, like Pearce before him, decides to enter the city and leave the medical establishment: "He had thrown his lot with the city. He had even forgotten his filters. There was brutality in the city, but you could tame it, put its misdirected vitality to use. But the only thing to do with an ideal that has outworn its necessity is turn your back on it, to leave it behind."[108] The ending has parallels with the conclusion of Bradbury's *Fahrenheit 451*, where Montag and the vagabonds turn back to the city to help those in need.

The final story of the series, "The Immortals" (later titled "Immortal" to avoid confusion with the overall series title), follows a pattern similar to *The Joy Makers* by achieving a level of bizarre, apocalyptic disruption, the end result of the pattern first set up when Cartwright donated his immortal blood, where Gunn's gifts of imaginative imagery are on full display. Set approximately fifty years after "Medic" (again there is a discontinuity with the timeline), "The Immortals" is essentially a road story, as Harry Elliott, a medic from the Center, must trek the forty miles from Kansas City to Lawrence with a girl named Marna, a young boy named Christopher (presumably the son of Leah and Flowers), and the blind Pearce, to deliver a message to the governor that the shipment of elixir, so he's been told, has been hijacked. There is, of course, more to it than that. It is not by any means an easy journey: those forty miles have become a wasteland, scourged by savage mutant motorcycle gangs and other Boschian grotesques. The dystopian element seen in "Medic" has increased exponentially. The Medical Center is now a fortress city within the city, home to nearly 100,000 professionals. A clear division has been established between the "hordes of citizens with no chance for immortality"[109] and the elite "squires" of the suburbs, who owe fealty to the governor and receive doses of Cartwright blood and other medical amenities. The squires now openly "harvest" the citizens of the decaying city, now mostly ruins, selling them to the Center where they are kept in a quasi-state of living as their body parts are harvested. Such victims are referred to as "body banks." This idea was picked up by Pohl and Williamson in their *Starchild Trilogy*. In a letter dated May 17, 1958, Williamson wrote Gunn asking if it was okay to use the "body banks" idea in *The Reefs of Space*. Gunn was okay with it; and here is another illustration of how ideas were circulating among the writers during this period.

One of Gunn's favorite tropes is that of the carnival barker or street hawker, and in this case the barker is hawking medicine, while Elliott does his duty in a free clinic at the gates of the Medical Center: "Get your aureomycin here, your penicillin, your terramycin. A hypodermic with every purchase. Good health!"[110] As Elliott tends to a pregnant woman, a convoy approaches the Center, consisting of "healthy young squires" on motorcycles and an armored ambulance with a forty-millimeter gun turret. The convoy is attacked from above by a helicopter, spraying the bikers with bullets and an incendiary is tossed into the ambulance turret from someone in the crowd. Inside the ambulance is the aged Pearce, now nearly two-hundred years old, his seven-year-old grandson Christopher, and a teenage girl named Marna, later revealed to be a Cartwright and the governor's daughter. Soon following, Elliott is called before the dean of the Center, Mock, one-time classmate of Flowers. Elliott is assigned to escort, on foot, Pearce, the boy, and Marna to the governor's mansion (actually an underground fortress) at Mt. Oread in Lawrence, the former site of the University of Kansas. The Center has been out of contact with the governor for three weeks. Thus begins a phantasmagoric journey through an apocalyptic eastern Kansas landscape. The apocalyptic imagery is striking: "Nothing moved in the ruins or along the road. They were alone in an ocean of desolation. They might have been the last people on a ruined earth."[111]

Elliott is cast in the mold of Flowers before him. He has ambitions to climb the medical hierarchy and hopes to someday synthesize the elixir, evidently not knowing Pearce had succeeded nearly one hundred years before. He's an idealist and takes his duty seriously. There is added incentive to deliver the girl: she and Elliott are each given pain-emitting wrist bracelets, linked together electronically; if they move apart, the bracelets emit subsonic pain. This is another idea that links with Pohl and Williamson's *The Reefs of Space*, although Williamson's early drafts of "The Iron-Collar Man" date to the early fifties, and were probably among the ideas he and Gunn exchanged during collaboration. On the road they must avoid headhunters and "ghouls," snatchers who take unwary travelers captive and sell them to the Medical Center for body harvesting. Nor are they safe when they stop at an automated hotel, designed to trap unsuspecting travelers. In the morning, Marna is captured by a "Wolf pack," a roving motorcycle gang of teenage squires, the next generation of "company policemen" who do "anything for a thrill."[112] In the context of the "juvenile delinquent" anxieties of the 1950s, which itself spawned countless works of fiction, Gunn transforms the "juvie biker" culture into a vivid apocalyptic vision. Elliott ambushes one of the bikers, takes the bike, and is able to track Marna because of the bracelet. That night, ten miles outside Lawrence, he comes upon her and her abductors in a grove. All of the young squires are genetic sports. Gunn seems to suggest that this is a combination of advanced medical technologies that allow the unhealthy to survive and mutation caused by pollution—and probably by toxins in medicine. As Pearce remarks, "'Increasingly, the practice of medicine becomes the treatment of defectives, genetic monstrosities. In the city they would die; in the suburbs they are preserved to perpetuate themselves.'"[113] The boys are also technologically enhanced: "One was an albino, a second had artificial lungs attached to his back, a third had an external skeleton of stainless steel." The leader is blind with "electrically operated binoculars" surgically inserted in his eye sockets.[114] Escaping this crisis, Harry is taken by a "ghoul" who paralyzes him with a poison dart. Harry's paralysis will keep him alive, but unmoving; it is a permanent condition. Marna, Pearce, and Christopher overcome his assailant, who turns out to be a dwarf, another mutant. To release Harry from his paralysis, Marna offers a transfusion of her Cartwright blood. After she has given this gift, she reveals her full story. Marna is, indeed, a Cartwright, and the daughter of Governor Weaver, the son and heir of Leroy Weaver from "New Blood." Weaver is 150 years old, grossly fat, and lives in isolation deep inside Mt. Oread in Lawrence. He is incestuously supplied with the immortal blood by Marna's grandmother and mother. At seventeen, Marna has come of age, certified fertile at the Medical Center, and she is returning to Weaver to become his new blood-bride. She sums up her fate: "'A Cartwright isn't a person, you know. A Cartwright is a walking blood bank, a living fountain of youth, something to be possessed, used, guarded, but never really allowed to live.'"[115]

As they reach Lawrence, they approach the site of the governor's mansion, the former location of the University of Kansas. It's worth noting that Gunn finished the story on September 1, 1957, just as a new school year got underway: "The governor's mansion was built on the top of an

L-shaped hill that stood tall between two river valleys. Once it had been the site of a great university, but taxes for supporting such institutions had been diverted into more vital channels. Private contributions had dwindled as the demands of medical research and medical care had intensified. Soon there was no interest in educational fripperies, and the university died."[116] Kansas, like the rest of the country, one can conjecture, is no longer a state, but a barony. And Weaver is its master. The governor's keep is deep within the hill of Mt. Oread. Gunn's vision of the Governor's fortress atop Mt. Oread is striking:

> The mansion was a fortress. Its outer walls were five-foot-thick prestressed concrete faced with five-inch armor plate. A moat surrounded the walls; it was stocked with piranha. An inner wall rose above the outside one. The paved, unencumbered area between the two could be flooded with napalm. Inside the wall were concealed guided-missile nests. The mansion rose, ziggurat fashion, in terraced steps. On each rooftop was a hydroponic farm. At the summit of the buildings was a glass penthouse; the noon sun turned it into silver. On a mast towering above, a radar dish rotated. Like an iceberg, most of the mansion was beneath the surface. It went down through limestone and granite a mile deep. The building was almost a living creature; automatic mechanism controlled it, brought in air, heated and cooled it, fed it, watered it, watched for enemies and killed them if they go too close.[117]

The travelers are addressed by "a giant, godlike voice" issuing from the fortress and a door opens to allow entrance. An elevator takes them deep underground to living quarters surveilled by "wall-wide vision screens" in every room. From the screens, Weaver's monstrous visage glares upon them: "Across the huge screen flowed the giant image of a creature who lolled in a pneumatic cushion. It was a thing incredibly fat, a sea of flesh rippling and surging.... It drew sustenance out of a tube; then as it saw them, it pushed the tube away with one balloonlike hand."[118] This is the final apotheosis of the blood sucking rich. There is some similarity with the Martians of H.G. Wells's *The War of the Worlds*, who draw sustenance through human blood piped directly into their bloodstream.

The final scene takes place as the monstrous Weaver summons Marna to his chamber, to consummate their "marriage." Pearce, the healer, promises to "work a miracle" for Weaver that night. The elevator descends "to the tune of the wedding march from Lohengrin." Weaver's lair recalls the cubicles in E.M. Forster's "The Machine Stops," but instead of the clean, sterile environs of those mountain dwellers, Weaver lives in filth and decay: "The stench of decay flowed into the car. For a moment the bride recoiled, and then she stepped forward out of the car. The room had once been a marvelous mechanism: a stainless-steel womb." One is also reminded of Pohl and Kornbluth's Chicken Little. However, the functionality of the machines has been compromised: "Some years before, apparently, a water pipe had broken, through some shift in the earth, after a small leak or a hard freeze had made the rock swell. The cleansing sprays no longer worked, and the occupant of the room either was afraid to have intruders trace the trouble, or he no longer cared. The floor was littered with decaying food, with food containers and wrappers, with waste matter. As the bride stepped into the room, a multitude of cockroaches scattered. Mice scampered into hiding places."[119]

Above, Pearce reveals himself, and the nearly two-hundred year old man appears to transform into a man of vibrant strength: "'The effective mind can achieve conscious control of the autonomic nervous system, of the very cells that make up the bloodstream and the body.'"[120] This gives the "bride" an opening. It is not Marna who has descended into the chamber, but Elliott. Elliott tosses a lariat around Weaver's massive neck and chokes the life out of him. The end suggests that Marshall Cartwright himself awaits for them outside, and that he, Pearce, and Harry Elliott will be able to reshape the world, leading it out of this grim dystopia.

In following the extrapolation through to this bizarre, apocalyptic conclusion, leaving us with an optimistic chance at renewal, Gunn has taken us through a cycle of discovery, decay, breakdown, apocalypse and renewal in the five stories that make up *The Immortals*. It's a brilliant exposition and exploration of his theme. Gunn creates a similar pattern in his next major project, *The Burning*, although it will take him over a decade to complete it.

"Little Orphan Android" and Others

Meanwhile, Gunn wrote a number of stand-alone short stories during this period as well. Among them a significant novelette in the Comic Inferno vein, the ironically titled "Little Orphan Android," which appeared as the lead story in the September 1955 *Galaxy*. It was a direct response to Pohl's "The Midas Plague" and Williamson's "With Folded Hands," and one can see Lester Del Rey's "Helen O'Loy" at play as well. Indeed, Gunn wrote Altshuler that it was "a sort of satire on all the robot stories ever written: Jack Williamson's 'With Folded Hands,' Cliff Simak's 'How-2,' Alfred Bester's 'Fondly Fahrenheit,' Isaac Asimov's *I, Robot* series, Fred Pohl's 'The Midas Touch' [sic], etc."[121]

"Little Orphan Android" posits a world saturated by specialized electronic technologies that tend to all human needs and perform all labor, called bots: doorbot, porterbot, chairbot, theaterbot (sort of a 3-D television), etc. In addition, more advanced humanoid androids fulfill a variety of human roles: for example, the story opens as Boyd Crandal watches the "all-time World Series between the Giandroids and the Yandroids."[122] As a consequence, some humans have mostly retreated into a solitary existence—like Forster's "The Machine Stops"—and relaxed inertia. As in Pohl's stories, Gunn interrogates the consequences of a consumerist ideal, and as part of this, imagines a ubiquitous information technology.

The story centers on Crandal's unanticipated acquisition of a MP, multi-purpose android, a perfect humaniform reproduction. After being dropped off by "a confused porterbot," guided to Crandal's door by his beautiful neighbor, Lucy Shannon, it calls him daddy as soon as it is unpacked, leading Crandal to sputter the brilliant retort, "machines don't have fathers—they have manufacturers." The android cries, "'I'm just a poor little orphan android with no one to care for me,'" an overture to Little Orphan Annie. The android is guided by its prime directive, S.O.E. S.O.E. means service, obedience, efficiency. It announces, "'A proper relationship between android and human is essential to a smooth-running household.'"[123] Here Gunn raises an interesting point about how household (and workplace) technologies, once they become incorporated into the daily routine, become "essential," that without them, the individual and society cease to run smoothly. What is particularly interesting about this story is its engagement with technology and the need for humans to adapt to the technologies they create, giving added resonance with the contemporary world where, on some levels, the technologies imagined by the science fiction writers of the 1950s have come to fruition in smart phones, smart appliances, and other household, business, and classroom technologies. As in the world in which Crandal lives, we can no longer imagine being able to function without the advanced technologies that are such a large part of our everyday lives.

What Crandal has on his hands is a "CT model" android, but when he asks the readerbot to give him the specs, there's no such model listed. The rest of the story follows Crandal's attempt to find out what's behind it all. Crandal's memory has been wiped and he slowly uncovers his story: he had been on trial for misusing androids, renting them out as laborers, which got him reported by the "Society for the Prevention of Cruelty to Androids." Readers may recall that Pohl's "The Midas Plague" is built on the premise that automation has led to overproduction, which, in turn, has created a society where, as I have written elsewhere, "to be poor is to live in opulent luxury and have the legal obligation to consume goods at an alarming rate in order to keep up with manufacturing quotas. Whereas to be rich is to have the luxury not to consume and live in inauspicious circumstances."[124] Gunn reframes the problem Pohl had conjectured in "The Midas Plague": "'If everyone worked his androids beyond established limits, society would be drowned in its own products. The working hours built into the androids must be accepted by everyone, or society as we know it could not exist. By working your androids overtime you became rich enough to buy additional androids, which you overworked to become even richer.... It was a cumulative process whose inevitable end was your ownership of every android on Earth.'"[125]

When Crandal returns to his apartment and the CT android, there's a scene that directly echoes "The Midas Plague," as the android is "wearing the clothes out too fast" and Crandal is stuck with another bill for "Five suits, six pairs of shoes, eleven pairs of socks, worn out, ruined, and otherwise rendered worthless by one MP (CT) robot." CT, it turns out, stands for "consumer-type," the android's directive is to consume. Taken before a judge again, Crandal hopes the court will confiscate the android, but his hopes are dashed because the CT android "is not subject to confiscation." Crandal is sent to a psychiatrist, which turns out to be Lucy Shannon, the woman he encountered earlier in the story. She's apparently a member of an underground movement and wants to save Crandal because "'we need every man who can fight free of his womb-room and do something for himself, but we need you in particular because you have more of the two-plus-two equals five quality than any of us.'" The idea of the "womb-room" has interesting echoes with *The Joy Makers*; the "two-plus-two-equals five quality" is an intriguing reversal of Orwell's *1984*. Crandal, then, can save society from the android problem. There is a direct reference to Williamson's classic at the end of the story: "He remembered, just before he went under, that he would have to go home eventually. Home was where the android was. It waited there for him—with folded hands."[126]

Gunn also wrote a number of stories that play off of his domestic experiences of fatherhood. "The Stilled Patter," a nasty little story in the manner of Pohl's "The Bitterest Pill" and Bradbury's "The Small Assassin," meditates on the challenges of parenthood. The idea for the story came following the birth of the Gunn's second son, Kevin, on June 13, 1954, which prompted Gunn to write a satirical article about Dr. Benjamin Spock's *Baby and Child Care*, "What the Baby Books Won't Tell You."[127] Gunn got no interest from the family magazines, so he transformed it into the science fiction story. Told in a confessional manner, following a disaster leading to "the end of the world," the narrator is presumably Gunn himself. Gunn uses the date of Kevin's birth as the precise moment of disaster: "Cataclysm began in 1954, June 13 to be exact. That was the day my second child was born, a boy named Kevin." Using a similar conspiracy vibe as "The Misogynist" and its sequel, the Gunn character realizes that there is a "Great Conspiracy" aimed at fathers to sell baby books and other products, and to take up their time. He pens an article to expose the conspiracy at the same time a male contraceptive pill has been synthesized, leading to catastrophic reduction in the birthrate: "Birth control was in the hands of the men. Billions of tiny pills were turned out. Enemy nations sowed them over each other's territory in boxes containing translations of my article. Men cached them away, carried them in money belts, hollowed out hiding places in the heels of shoes." This leads to apocalypse as the economy of family-life implodes: "In a few years, the condition hit the schools; one by one they closed their doors, and hundreds of thousands of teachers were turned out to beg on the streets.... The toy makers and sellers collapsed. The clothing industry couldn't survive longer. The shoemakers were hardest hit. Food consumption dropped. All over the country, farmers went broke." At the end, it's revealed that the story is a "found manuscript," uncovered "in a cellar of a house in a Midwestern city," in a future where women are in control: "As is the custom, the men were stripped, carefully searched, and sent to the premarital barracks to wait for some girl's proposal. Our readers will be happy to learn that they are both back in service." In this bit of drollery men become slaves like the Cartwright women in "The Immortals."[128]

"Teddy Bear," which wasn't published until 1970, is a paranoia story in the manner of Philip K. Dick that was inspired by Kit's teddy bear "Brownie," and it captures some of Gunn's feeling about moving to Lawrence. Again, Gunn is the central character. Gunn finds the teddy bear on the porch, split open, with sawdust leaking out of its rag body, triggering memory recall of a bizarre incident earlier that day he'd blocked out, when a woman was struck by a car. Like the bear, the woman had sawdust coming out of her, leading Gunn to believe "*some of us aren't real.* And: somebody slipped." Gunn is taken for trial for witnessing the accident. As the story was actually written during the time of McCarthyism, Gunn is likely reflecting on the paranoia of the era, the sense that people were being accused of things they didn't do and of a dark conspiracy behind quaint daily life: "I had stumbled on a secret that no one was supposed to know, the secret that some of us aren't human, aren't real, that some of us are stuffed with sawdust and excelsior like teddy bears, that even the real ones are moved about by godlike beings for reasons we could never understand." Gunn's paranoia reaches the point where he doubts his own humanity, perhaps he is one of the sawdust teddy bears; convincing himself he's real by an act of self-inflicted cutting. The police cordon off the city after he escapes from jail. And as they close in, he determines it must be all part of some cosmic entity's childish game: "We were the nursery toys for an extra-dimensional child. We were his teddy bears, performing for his amusement. Maybe he learned something from us. Maybe we weren't that important." At the story's conclusion, the scene resets, Gunn is back on his porch, no longer conscious of the extra-dimensional reality; he too has been reset.[129]

Two additional stand-alone stories from the period are of interest. The ironically titled "The Girls Who Were Really Built" is set in Neosho, Kansas, a fictional composite of a Kansas small town similar to Girard, the hometown of Gunn's grandparents. It is another story of paranoia about an alien effort to wipe out humanity by creating beautiful android women as perfect mates. Published in *Fantastic* in 1958, Gunn had hoped it might get placed at *Playboy*, but *Playboy*'s fiction editor Ray Russell thought it "too smalltown, too married, too kiddified for us."[130] But it was a good idea, and Altshuler thought Gunn should turn it into a novel. But Gunn "didn't think it was much more than a short story until I saw Ira Levin's *The Stepford Wives*."[131] The story begins when beautiful women show up in Neosho and marry six single men of the town. Those men prosper. But the husbands become suspicious when none of their wives conceive any children, and during poker night the men deduce a conspiracy theory: maybe their wives are androids, manufactured by aliens as a precursor to invasion, meant to create a decrease in human population. Sure enough, the Venusians are responsible, but Earth has a surprise in store when they return: the men practice polygamy, marry other women from the town to have babies. The narrator's eldest kids are named Kit and Kevin, his human wife named Jane. Given the names, the story ends on a strange note: "I can stand Jane alright. In a way it's kind of refreshing. It's only one night a week, and if I get fed up I can get up and leave any time I feel like it. I can get up and go home to April."[132] Here Gunn again plays around with self-referential ironic fiction in "The Misogynist" mode.

"Deadly Silence," an ambitious 23,000-word novella completed a month after "Medic," is notable for its vision of Kansas City faced with a cataclysmic crisis that parallels the vision of the city portrayed in *The Immortals*. The story follows the consequences of an invention that creates total silence. The ramifications of silence prove devastating; society breaks down as silence spreads across the country and people get killed by accident at an accelerating rate which leads to panic, chaos, and anarchy. In this regard, the story anticipates Octavia Butler's widely-anthologized "Speech Sounds." The premise also aligns with George Zebrowski's "The Word Sweep," where word bubbles literally pop out of speakers' mouths and fill the environment, rendering silence the only viable option; Gunn reprinted Zebrowski's story in *The Road to Science Fiction Volume Four*. Speculation arises as to the origin of the silencers. Is it the Soviets? But the Russians aren't the culprits: they too quickly experience the silence. As in "The Girls Who Were Really Built" it turns out to be an alien conspiracy. Here Gunn links the tale of alien menace with his new emphasis on near-future sociological science fiction. Once humanity discovers that aliens are behind the silence, they are able to regroup and fight. The final scene takes place on the campus of the University of Kansas, providing a trial run of sorts for the final scene of *The Immortals* and scenes throughout *The Burning*. As in "Medic" and "The Immortals," Gunn effectively conveys the cityscape of urban Kansas City and the university environs of Lawrence.

The Burning

Gunn's increasing involvement with the University of Kansas led to another novella during this period that would eventually develop into a three-part novel. However, it would take over a decade before he completed *The Burning*. The first novella, "Witches Must Burn," was written in the summer of 1955 and appeared in *Astounding* August 1956. As the story was in development, Gunn and Campbell exchanged a series of letters in which Campbell "insisted that the public was right in believing that the growing dependence of the world on science had taken away the common man's control of his own life."[133] Therefore, the protagonist, John Wilson, "should return to Lawrence and give himself up."[134] Gunn reluctantly followed Campbell's suggestion, but then stalled out on where to go from there. It took until after Gunn's decade-long tenure as an administrator at the University of Kansas for him to return to the original novella and to create two new novellas to finish up the novel. Ironically, Campbell wasn't interested in the follow up, "Trial by Fire," which progressed logically from the scenario he insisted on in the first place. Both "Trial by Fire" and the third novella, "Witch Hunt," were bought by Fred Pohl and published in *If* and *Galaxy* respectively.

In "Witches Must Burn," Gunn explores the problem of anti-intellectualism and posits a very near future in which fundamentalist extremists fearful of science destroy the universities and make "eggheads" wanted criminals. The story was inspired by Gunn's observations of McCarthyism. The story is set in the 1980s, when the cultural forces of anti-science raise their ugly heads. While people enjoy the benefits of advanced technologies, they develop an increasing fear of the scientific worldview and a "strange, suicidal psychosis" overtakes the American psyche. The story begins with the burning and sacking of the University of Kansas by a mob of enraged citizens, who have been stirred to frenzy against the "eggheads" by a Senator Bartlett, a demagogue who chairs the notorious "subcommittee on academic practices." As KU burns, other universities are torched across the country in a night-of-the-long-knives purge. Bartlett addresses his frenzied constituency on television with Harvard burning in the background as he apparently seizes power of the government: "The burning university behind him gave him an aura of power to which he had only pretended until now. He seemed like an Old Testament prophet, as if he commanded the thunderbolt of the Lord and directed it to strike here and there, to cleanse with fire the citadels of treason and immorality." As the flames spread, Bartlett's mob waits for the academics to come out of the flaming buildings "with clubs and pitchforks and axes." The reader further cringes when a high school boy runs up the hill with his ".22 rifle swinging in his hand" and shouts, "'Am I too late?'"[135] This brutal picture of conflict between the intellectual class and the citizenry is quite frightening and the moment with the young man and his gun is particularly troubling in this era of rampant gun proliferation. Bartlett, too, is troublingly familiar. Bartlett justifies the burnings in an address echoing McCarthy's rationalizations for red scare persecutions, claiming that the citizens have taken rightful "'justice into their own hands'" against the treason of the intellectuals. And, of course, Bartlett passes any responsibility off upon others: "'My only suggestion was that local committees should be formed to decide what your children should be taught and to report any instances of Un-American teaching to my subcommittee on academic practices. But if traitors must die that their country live, then let them die.'"[136] This shocking demagoguery unveils a deep disruption in the hearts and minds of many Americans.

The featured character in *The Burning* is a professor named John Wilson, whose expertise is in physics, electronics, and psychology. Today we might call him a neuroscientist. Like Matt Wright in "The Reluctant Witch," Wilson's research has led him into fringe research involving the electroencephalograph and he has developed a prototype psionic machine. The psionic "Tool" can pick up thoughts, and although it could be a liberatory technology, Wilson must use it as a mode of defense. Gunn also wanted to suggest that if the social sciences were to become "real" sciences, as in *The Joy Makers*, there would be wide social repercussions. Wilson escapes the mob and leaves the city, seeking refuge with friends in Kansas City. But the political climate in the country makes all live in fear and he's turned away: "'Don't come near the house. They'll be after you now. We can't afford to be connected with you in any way. We aren't intellectuals! We graduated from college, but so did millions of other people. It's the scientists they're after and the teachers.'"[137] As in other repressive regimes, the intellectuals become political refugees who must escape the country. Political party affiliation becomes dangerous—unless you're a card carrying member of the right party. As Wilson tries to escape, he encounters a typical anti-intellectual perspective espoused by a cook, who is obviously dependent upon machines for his work: "'About time somebody showed those eggheads who's runnin' things. They're like the cooker—fancy and complicated and always breaking down. Inventing things, throwing people outa work, starting wars. Betraying our secrets to anybody that wants 'em. They're no good, and it's time they got wise. The Senator'll show 'em.'"[138] Unfortunately, this type of rhetoric has openly reemerged in recent American politics.

Gunn expresses real concerns about the manipulation of truth. Another growing concern in contemporary politics. After the burning of the campus the police repress the truth: "local police have denied the rumor that it was set by an incensed mob of townspeople." Instead, the victims—the professors—are blamed: "There is evidence that the blaze was touched off by university teachers themselves in an attempt at martyrdom to gain sympathy for the egghead cause." Gunn captures the growing myopic views that are characterizing our own times in this prescient novel: "It was exactly a world in which black was white and white was black; it was a world in which no color existed independently of the viewer. There was no objective reality to agree upon."[139] This fall into the subjective echoes the dream-world of *The Joy Makers* and raises important issues facing today's world. Gunn's diagnosis of why the tide of anti-intellectualism can resurface ties directly with the key science fiction idea of the frontier. Once the frontier is gone "society can no longer afford the creative thinker."[140] Gunn emphasizes that "Change" is the basic law of the universe. This becomes a central thesis in his academic work.

Wilson hopes to go to Brazil, which is experiencing an economic boom, and where "the best facilities for psychological research were."[141] On the road, he's picked up by a young woman named Pat Helman, the daughter of the man who built "rocketports and artificial satellites" at the expense of a "sound society."[142] There's a weird anti-scientism expressed here that seems inconsistent with Gunn's view in *Station in Space* where technology may be the only hope to save humankind. Helman takes Wilson to New Orleans, but he doesn't trust her and jumps out of the car the first chance he gets. In truth, Pat Helman is part of an underground movement trying to save as many intellectuals as possible so as to keep some semblance of sanity in this mad world. The underground has determined to become "witches," since science and rationalism have given way to superstition and contradictory thinking, and society is set to cycle into an age of ignorance: "'In a generation, cities will cease to exist as social and economic entities. Men will stop using industrial machinery; no one will be able to make it or to keep it in repair. The population will plummet during an interregnum of starvation and violence. If we are successful, the people who are left will live in small, self-supporting communities. Witches will live among them, part of them, helping and learning.'" In a sense, Gunn is replaying some of the same themes of societal breakdown explored in *This Fortress World* and *Star Bridge*. Indeed, Pat Helman describes the universities as "'fortresses of isolation'" where the learned insulate themselves "'from humanity and its problems.'" By recasting themselves as witches, the underground of intellectuals believes they "'can shorten to a century or so the millennial grinding of the millstones of the universe.'"[143] Again, here are echoes of Asimov's *Foundation*: an elite underground shortening the inevitable decline of civilization.

On the cusp of securing passage to Brazil, Wilson is captured by agents of the Senator, and he will be framed as one of the conspirators of the "Egghead Plot." With the help of his psionic device, Wilson overpowers his abductors and reconnects with Pat Helman. The story ends as Wilson returns to Lawrence after three months and turns himself in—the conclusion that Campbell insisted on. The reader is left to conclude that Wilson is now part of the underground and this is their master plan whereby they can help shape society as it regresses into a dark age.

At this point, Gunn found it difficult to move forward. He set the series aside, returning to it eleven years later, finishing the second novella, "Trial by Fire," in the summer of 1966, the first time he took his four-week vacation during his years in administrative work. Those years in administration provided Gunn with deeper insights into the divide between the academy and the public presented and the changing cultural zeitgeist of the drug culture provided him with a plot device where he could also further explore his interest in dreams. Campbell would have none of it, finding the "doped protagonist" unsavory, but also finding the courtroom scene untenable, even though this is the logical outcome of what Campbell had wished for a decade before. But "Trial by Fire" was picked up by Fred Pohl and it appeared in *If* February 1969; the third story, "Witch Hunt," appeared in Pohl's *Galaxy* a few months later, at the close of Pohl's editorial tenure.

"Trial by Fire" primarily takes place in a courtroom. Although written over a decade after the McCarthy hearings, the trial takes on the flavor of those interrogations and echo any number of star-chambered inquisitions throughout history. To keep Wilson in check, his jailers have drugged him, and the narrative flips between the trial and hallucinatory sequences in which Wilson imagines himself in a medieval-like setting where he serves as a witch-healer. This brings back a number of Gunn's favorite themes, especially the dreams of *The Joy Makers*, but also the character of Dr. Russell Pearce as "healer" in the later novellas of *The Immortals*, and it anticipates the ways Gunn plays with the drug theme in *Kampus* and *The Dreamers*. As mentioned before, Gunn's work reflects an interest in altered states of consciousness similar to that of Philip K. Dick, but Gunn explores such states from the position of a sober, rational outside observer, whereas Dick would actually immerse himself, both narratively and actually, in such altered states of cognition. Nonetheless, the two writers have an interesting shared thematic connection. Due to the flipping from reality to dream and back, the narrative has a disruptive quality that is consistent with the experimental approaches emerging in the late sixties, yet, oddly, the story still comes across as a fifties magazine story.

Once Wilson's head clears, he makes a passionate defense of science. But the forces of anti-science are too strong and Wilson is told by Leonard Kelley, the prosecutor and Bartlett's minion, that he is "going to die in a very public and edifying way." Taken before Senator Bartlett, Bartlett and Kelley manipulate the mob into burning Wilson at the stake. But the witch underground thwarts the plan, and by the power of advanced technology, Wilson is literally ascended into Heaven by transparent filament wire: "Miraculously, however, the post began to move, slowly at first and then with greater speed, pulling him up and away." He finds himself in an airplane, greeted by Pat Helman. This will slow the momentum of the "Lowbrow" movement, but, inevitably, it will not stop the fall into superstition. Of the three novellas that make up *The Burning*, "Trial by Fire" is the least satisfying, but it is a necessary transition to link "Witches Must Burn" with the final novella "Witch Hunt."[144]

"Witch Hunt" is set in an undetermined future when society has reverted to a new medievalism. Since the vestiges of contemporary civilization are far enough in ruin and the social structures have completely devolved into hierarchies and superstition, one can conjecture the story is roughly two-hundred years in the future. In this future, the former United States has been balkanized into mini-empires, with the Central Empire, controlled by Emperor Bartlett, descendant of the senator, stretching across the Great Plains to Denver. The story begins as a "Pilgrim" from the capitol enters a dirty, provincial village, what remains of Lawrence, Kansas. Pilgrims are seekers after wisdom, students of the "witch schools," who set out to find out about the world around them. The Pilgrim encounters a young woman named Susannah, also dressed as a Pilgrim, whom he saves from a gang of mercenaries. Throughout his ensuing trek across the medievalized landscape of Eastern Kansas, he will encounter Susannah several more times. Here Gunn gets into some of the same apocalyptic territory as seen in *The Immortals* and *Kampus*.

After an escape from deserters of the Emperor's guard, who raped Susannah and killed her father, the Pilgrims encounter an enclave of "Neo-Scientists" tucked away in a fortress in the Flint Hills. The community is called New Pittsburgh and it is dominated by a massive tower housing the Neo-Scientist laboratories. The image is interesting in light of the construction of Wescoe Hall, the humanities building at KU, which was built while Gunn was in the KU administration. The original plans called for a twenty-five-story tower dominating the university skyline, and thus all of Lawrence, but the expense of such undertaking was unfeasible, and instead a fortress-like structure of more modest proportion was built instead. The Neo-Scientists are diabolically barbarous in their actions: they keep slave laborers, controlling them by electrified iron collars. The iron collars are a further development of the bracelets in "The Immortals," and again resonate with the iron collars in Pohl and Williamson's *The Reefs of Space*. The Neo-Scientists have created a hierarchical utopia, with themselves at the top: "'The Neo-Scientist's job is to think, to explore, to invent, to make life easier and progress possible. The worker's job is to provide the Neo-Scientist with the time to do these things. Woman's job is to produce more Neo-Scientists and workers. If everybody does his job, everybody is happy.'" As is evident, women have returned to a subservient "breeder" role, which echoes the Cartwright's plight in *The Immortals*. There's an interesting contrast here with Harlan Ellison's "A Boy and His Dog," which, coincidentally, was published the same month in *New Worlds*. In Ellison's story, his protagonist Vic, a rover boy from the apocalyptic surface, is coaxed down into an underground utopia (ironically, Topeka, Kansas), to be a breeder for the sterile enclave. Like those in *The Joy Makers*, the Neo-Scientists are investigating the possibility of engaging directly with the "happiness center" in the brain, and thereby bypassing the use of physical coercion of the slaves by turning them into happy addicts: "'When a workman does his job he will be allowed to stimulate himself for an appropriate length of time.'"[145] After seven days in New Pittsburgh, the Pilgrim is again forced to go on the road when the enclave is sacked and destroyed by Luddites, and the Pilgrim and Susannah are captured. Like the Neo-Scientists, the Luddites treat women as drudges and sex objects. Susannah bides her time, eventually reattaching herself to the Pilgrim. For his part, the Pilgrim finds the Luddite way of life attractive, "it was a good clean, manly life,"[146] until he tries to claim Susannah as his own, an affront to this "manly" culture of shared women. Again they must escape.

They split up and the Pilgrim returns to Lawrence and makes his way to City Hall. There he reveals that he is Leonard Kelley, descendant of the Leonard Kelley of the previous story, the "head of the Emperor's secret police." His mission has been to go out amongst the people and try to uncover the secret of the witches. But Kelley has been changed through his experiences and he no longer believes in the righteousness of the empire. Nor does the sergeant in charge of the city believe his story, and jails him. Once again Susannah comes to his rescue and the pair ascend the hill of Mt. Oread, where the university, now legend, once stood. The scene is very much like the final confrontation in *The Immortals*, except here there is no ziggurat fortress at the top of the hill, instead there is a chapel "standing like a silo in the night." Although *The Burning* is in many ways Gunn's least convincing narrative, the final images in "Witch Hunt" are quite striking. Kelley and Susannah make their way to the meditation room at the top of the chapel, where it is said "when a pilgrim has found the truth he should press the button" and "if he has truly found it he will ascend to heaven." Susannah pushes the button and they do, indeed, ascend: it is a rocket which transports them to a space station in Earth orbit. There's an interesting mashing of the ideas, imagery, and themes seen earlier in *Station in Space* and in *The Immortals*. From speakers in the ship a voice greets them: "'Congratulations. You have found the truth or by accident you have placed yourself in great jeopardy. The next few minutes and hours will determine whether you will find what you have been seeking or you will be dead.'" The pair must figure out how to use the equipment around them; if they can, then they can enter the space station called "Truth."[147] After some nice technical details probably facilitated by the exploits of the recent space missions, Kelley and Susannah enter "Truth" and are greeted by a white-haired man named John Wilson. Like Emperor Bartlett and the Pilgrim Kelley, he is a descendant of the John Wilson featured in the previous stories. The conclusion is very much an evocation of the space frontier theme: space as the place for the revitalization of humankind. In these stories, Gunn recognizes the potentiality of a rising anti-science movement in the United States. His prophetic vision is, in many ways, accurate—though not, perhaps, to the extremity that he envisions here. Nonetheless, his warning about a growing anti-intellectualism, an increasing religious zealotry, an insidious irrationality, and a growing intolerance reminds us to be wary of complacency when demagoguery raises its head.

Four

The Listeners to *Crisis!*

The Listeners

The Listeners is, for many, Gunn's finest artistic achievement. It is a novel by a science fiction writer in his maturity and at the height of his powers. *The Listeners* depicts in detail the process of SETI, the Search for Extraterrestrial Intelligence, finding messages from the stars. Gunn's depiction of a devoted administrator foregrounds Gunn's administrative experience and gives an authentic representation of what David Brin calls "skilled professionals," characteristic of the genre's characterization. Like many of Gunn's previous works, *The Listeners* is a sequence of linked stories, all (with one exception) were published in SF magazines prior to the publication as a novel in 1972. The stories were written over a four-year period as Gunn was transitioning from university administration to the KU English department. Gunn wrote the first story, "The Listeners," during his summer break in 1967, the summer between the writing of the two later stories of *The Burning*. Two summers later, he wrote the second story, "The Voices," which Harlan Ellison bought for *Again, Dangerous Visions*. The size of *Again, Dangerous Visions* became too unwieldy and Ellison had to make cuts and had to give the story back. In the summer of 1970, as Gunn was involved in filming the *Literature of Science Fiction* film series, he completed the third story "The Message." After signing a book contract with Scribner's, Gunn finished the last three novelettes in a flurry in 1971, "The Answer," "The Waiting," and "The Reply."

The titular first story begins in 2025 as Robert MacDonald, administrator for the SETI project, must balance the needs of the project with home life. The central question posed by the search for extraterrestrial intelligence is "Are we alone?" While MacDonald spends long hours managing the needs of the project, his wife, Maria, suffers from loneliness and depression at home. As in "Space Is a Lonely Place," Gunn juxtaposes the larger question of whether humans are alone in the universe next to the domestic experiences of loneliness and devotion. Some of their marital problems stem from an inability, so far, to have a child. Gunn captures the loneliness of wives prior to the sexual revolution of the 1970s, but setting the novel in 2025, when these issues have largely mitigated—chances are in the current climate, MacDonald's wife would also be a working professional, quite likely an astronomer or administrator in her own right—somewhat dates the sexual politics of the novel. Nonetheless, these issues were important at the time of writing.

Gunn's overarching theme is that a project such as the search for extraterrestrial intelligence is a generational project—that it will take a long time. Therefore, it requires patience with the frustrations of a long wait and perseverance when others waver. Those involved in such a project must realize results may come after their own lifetime: "Even if they could pick up a message, they still would likely be dead before any exchange could take place even with the nearest likely star. What kind of mad dedication could sustain such perseverance?" Gunn compares the search to the building of the cathedrals in the Middle Ages, when decades of dedication were necessary to sustain such projects, calling to mind such novels as William Golding's *The Spire* and Ken Follett's *The Pillars of the Earth*: "They were building cathedrals, most of them. Most of them had that religious mania about their mission that would sustain them through a lifetime of labors in which no progress could be seen."[1] Indeed, Brian Stableford has compared the devotion of the SETI team to a "spiritual quest."[2] Such a project will run into complications of funding. As in *Station in Space*, Gunn taps into the economic challenges faced by such large scale scientific projects. Contemporary society has little patience to wait for long-term results and is quick to defund when things seem to be outside the attention span of administrators and politicians operating on five-year plans. MacDonald is faced with budgetary problems and Congressional hearings at various times in the stories. Overall, the scope of the novel covers ninety-three years, from 2025, fifty years into the life of the project, to 2118. Unlike many of Gunn's other works, society remains relatively stable throughout this period. Rather than falling into an apocalyptic dystopia as in *The Joy Makers*, *The Immortals*, and *The Burning*, the future in *The Listeners* survives major cataclysm and achieves utopia. In this sense, whereas Gunn's earlier works draw favorable comparisons with the dreamworlds of Philip K. Dick and the Comic Inferno dystopias of Frederik Pohl, like *Station in Space*, *The Listeners* most closely resonates with the utopianism of Arthur C. Clarke.

The action takes place at the Arecibo Observatory in Puerto Rico, the site of the big dish radio telescope, and during a party in MacDonald's home. MacDonald reminds his staff of their "customary beer and bull" party held on Saturday night at his home, and then reflects on the question of morale while experiencing self-doubt about his leadership, feeling the pressure of forthcoming congressional hearings, where the project's budget will be on the line. As usual, MacDonald leaves Maria to host the party so that he can relieve Saunders at the observatory. While "Mac" is gone, Maria attempts suicide. He has failed to hear, to listen to, her despair. MacDonald's personal sorrow is put into conjunction with the larger existential question that the project represents: "What does the universe care for my agony?" Here Mac has a "dark night of the soul," questioning the purpose of his own existence. Mac returns to the observatory the next morning as usual, while Maria's condition is still uncertain, and prepares his resignation. His self-doubts have come home: all this time while he was listening for voices from the stars, his wife was calling to him in need. A call from the hospital assures him that Maria is "going to be all right" and a message from her tells him "not to be crazy in the head, too." With a sudden feeling of relief and a new sense of purpose, MacDonald tears up his resignation. The major theme of "The Listeners" is communication. Listening. Gunn parallels the quest for communication with alien civilizations with MacDonald's struggle to communicate and listen to the needs of Maria. The characterization here is softly poignant. Gunn brings character and theme together in precise synchronicity.[3]

"The Voices" takes place two years later and MacDonald has achieved greater balance between the Project and his personal life. The couple now have a baby boy and Maria has overcome her struggles with depression. The story involves a visit to the observatory by George Thomas, a journalist working for *Era* magazine, an influential publication that shapes public opinion. Thomas has come with the intention of writing a dismantling piece on the project as a sink hole for taxpayer money, which could spell its doom. Thomas also has an interesting personal conflict: now a successful journalist, he had once had artistic ambitions and had published an acclaimed first novel, *The Inferno*, which, upon their first meeting, Mac praises as conveying "a vision and sensitivity virtually equal to that of its immortal predecessor."[4]

At the moment of Thomas's arrival the Project is in trouble, facing a major defunding push from Congress. When Thomas meets with MacDonald, he says the only thing that will change his mind is a message, some tangible proof that the project has found something. Thomas interviews the staff and, in spite of himself, is impressed by their devotion. These conversations allow Gunn to add further information about the ideas behind SETI and the process by which potential data is analyzed. Thomas drives out to MacDonald's home to interview Maria. Gunn makes a meaningful narrative choice here by having Maria voice the purpose of the project: "It may be that there is no one out there or if there is someone out there he will never speak to us or we to him, but our listening is an act of faith akin to living itself. If we should stop listening, we would begin dying and we would soon be gone, the world and its people, our technical civilization and even the farmers and peasants, because life is faith, life is commitment. Death is giving up." Maria's statement ties into and resolves her struggles in the opening story. Further, Maria assures Thomas that he too will come to believe: "My husband is a great man. He listens with his heart. Before you leave this island, you will know that, and you will believe." Having been through her own inferno, Maria senses Thomas's inner conflict.[5]

As in the first story, Gunn juxtaposes Thomas's personal existential crisis with the larger questions posed by the Project. When Thomas listens to "the sound of the infinite," the background noise of the galaxy, he has "a moment of self-revelation in which he knew that he was lost, like the voices, and he would have to find his way or be damned to live forever within his fleshy prison, as alone in his torment as if he were in hell itself."[6] This sets up the story's denouement, as the Project has received its first apparent success: radio signals from the 1930s have been retransmitted back to Earth from Capella. Within the retransmissions is an embedded message. Mac hopes that Thomas will join them and become their spokesman to the public. When Mac explains, Thomas has an epiphany and his existential crisis is resolved as he finds purpose in the Project. He proclaims, "'We must make them understand. There's a race of intelligent beings out there on a world something like ours, and they must have a great deal to say to us. What great news for humanity! It demands not fear but celebration. We must get people to see that, to feel it.'"[7] As in "The Listeners," Gunn places the big picture of the Project in synch with the personal crisis of a character, a practice which occurs throughout the rest of the series.

"The Message" is set one year later. George Thomas is now working for the Project as its P.R. man and has been working to build public support for the Project. A visual representation of the message is interspersed throughout the text consisting of dot-matrix fragments that convey the process of decoding, similar to such images found in Harlan Ellison's story

"I Have No Mouth and I Must Scream." MacDonald, Thomas, and Thomas's assistant Bill Mitchell are in the audience at the Astrodome in Houston awaiting evangelist Jeremiah Jones, the prophet of a fundamentalist group that believes we are alone in the universe, God's sole creation. For Jeremiah, the message is not from an alien civilization, but is the "voice of God ... carried by the angels." Jeremiah's preachments have wide influence and his denial of the message is creating waves of social unrest that could upend the project. In "The Message" Gunn provides a powerful analysis of the problems put in the way of science by the religious right, especially by the showmen preachers who, like "arena rock" performers, drive their following to frenzy and charge the emotions of vast swathes of ill-informed devotees, undercutting the possibilities of knowledge in order to prop up pathetic adherence to creeds voiced in ages of ignorance. Jones is a zealot and a fool, but wields great power and influence. MacDonald has come to Houston to try to build a rational dialogue with the irrational evangelist. A debate between the perspective of reason represented by MacDonald and the rigid, self-righteousness of a "right" man is the early focus of the story. Jeremiah believes he has a direct link with God, the voice of "truth." And Jeremiah's "truth" is putting the Project at risk, as MacDonald tries to reason: "'Your truth is creating an atmosphere in which people may shut down the Project, keep us from deciphering the Message, prevent us from listening for more messages.'" MacDonald is more sympathetic with Jeremiah than he deserves, believing him an "honest man." This may be reflective of Gunn's own skill at being congenial, which served him well in administrative work. But how can one who has built his life on self-deception be called an honest man? That's Bill Mitchell's position; he's been romantically involved with Jeremiah's daughter Judith, and is still stinging from a rift over her devotion to her father that broke the relationship.[8]

In any case, Jeremiah is the biggest threat to the Project since its founding, and MacDonald must walk a fine line to keep him from inflicting fatal damage. As the story progresses, the message has been deciphered, and MacDonald asks Mitchell to contact Jeremiah through Judith and invite him to come to Arecibo. Further debate between MacDonald and Jeremiah ensues where Mac explains what motivates his "faith" in the Project, in hopes to reach some accord with the preacher: "'It is an inner conviction that has grown from a small thought to a large certainty that there is other life in the universe, that to prove its existence is the most gloriously human thing man can do, that to communicate with it would make this vast, incomprehensible place in which man lives, this unexplored forest of the night, a friendlier, happier, more wonderful, more exciting, holier place in which to be."'[9] Readers may note that "the cave of night" as Gunn called space, has become "the forest of night" here. Whereas a cave might suggest a dark emptiness, the image of a forest suggest a dark, yet fecund universe. It's a fascinating change in metaphor. Of course, what makes Mac's message different than Jeremiah's is science, duplicability, verifiability. The argument Mac states effectively makes the case for the scientific method over the "methods" of faith. But Mac's reasoning fails to penetrate the rigid mind of the prophet: "Jeremiah was immovable. How can you reason with a fanatic?"[10] Once the full message comes forth from the computer, illustrated in the novel as a dot-matrix readout, Jeremiah, like Thomas in "The Voices," achieves some degree of epiphany. For Jeremiah, the image of the alien represents an angel, and thus he is able to reconcile his creed with the message. Reason and science prevail, or at least hold back the forces of ignorance. Despite having been written nearly half a century ago, "The Message" still strongly resonates with the crises of intellect facing American culture.

"The Answer" continues that resonance. The story focuses on the response to the project by the President of the United States, Andrew White. White is African American, giving Gunn's novel a degree of prescience. The story takes place immediately after Jeremiah's departure from Arecibo as White sits in the Oval Office planning his announcement that he will not seek a second term. As in the other stories, Gunn blends the large scale questions of seeking a message from the stars with the personal conflicts of the viewpoint character. White is experiencing a generational conflict with his son, John, whom he sees as moving away from the social worldview White was shaped by: racial conflict and the struggle for political justice. There are some meaningful resonances with contemporary societal issues here as well.

White receives a call from MacDonald, informing him of the Project's success in deciphering the message. Excitedly, the otherwise sober MacDonald sees this, rightfully, as a world-historic moment: "'Mr. President, this is a moment as historic as the first atomic reaction. I wish I had some memorable phrase to announce it, but all I can say is that we have a message from other intelligent beings on a world circling one of the twin suns of Capella, and we have a translation. We are not alone.'" But White sees things differently and his reaction is to put the clamps on the information getting out to the public. He also quashes Mac's plan to reply: "'There will be no announcement, no leaks, no answer. The effects of this are incalculable. I must get busy with my staff. I suggest you do the same.'" Here

Gunn gets into the governmental mindset of secrecy and the assumption that any outside message is some kind of threat to security and must be suppressed. Mac takes a different position and invites the President to come to Arecibo to discuss matters.[11]

But there's still the problem of Jeremiah. White goes so far as to consider having Jeremiah's plane shot down, but wisely decides it's better to talk to Jeremiah directly, and diverts to Houston before traveling on to Puerto Rico. Jeremiah stands firm that he will announce his interpretation of the message at the revival that evening and hands White a slip of paper with an artist's rendition of the message: a haloed, winged angel. Once White arrives at Arecibo he is determined to kill the Project, nonetheless he is saddened by it because of the example of devotion exemplified by Mac. As he did with Jeremiah, Mac explains the nature of the message and the process by which they have interpreted it. Mac believes the message should be released publicly, so that the larger scientific community can add further interpretive insights and so that they can begin to formulate a message to send to the Capellans. He has to convince White that this is in the best interests of the human species as a whole, not a mere problem of nation states. Whereas Jeremiah has interpreted the drawing to be that of an angel, the scientists on the Project have conceived it to be a space-suited avian-like species.

Once again, Gunn explores the question of what it means to be alone. White tries to get his head around what would motivate the Capellans to seek to communicate in the first place. Mac's answer is eloquently delivered: "'They want to communicate. They're looking for other minds, for fellow intelligent creatures in the universe.... So they won't be alone. For the same reason we've listened. So we wouldn't be alone. It is a terrible thing to be alone.'" Gunn also puts to bed the idea of interstellar conquest as a motivation: it is simply impractical. Mac points out that the aliens have "'put themselves in our hands'" which "'demonstrates a certain amount of trust.'" In other words, the very act of communication makes a gesture of peace. Mac also makes the case that humans desire to communicate, to send their own message: "'We know that there are other intelligent beings in the universe; we know that they will be different from us, and we hunger for the exchange. Our dreams are of spaceflight and alien contact; an entire literature has developed it, and our myths reinforce it with their flying saucers and visitations. We have been listening for fifty years, and people are prepared to hear something. They are psychologically ready for contact.'" This moment of recursivity resonates with the science fiction reader. Mac also takes the position that reason will win out, that facts will convince people: "'The fears are not logical. Facts will dispel them. The Capellans cannot come here. Matter transmission is a fantasy, and we cannot imagine any kind of propulsion system which could ever approach the speed-of-light limit.'" Gunn's faith in the power of reason here is less certain in this era of destabilized fact. Ultimately, White refuses permission to send an answer to the message, despite MacDonald's arguments that transparency and reason will convince the masses.[12]

But things change when John White has a new insight and bursts into the room: "'Maybe it's the answer to another question about themselves they want us to know: what's happening to them. Maybe the distant sun is increasing its energy output, radiating more heat, turning nova perhaps.'" They realize that the message is the eulogy of a species, and like those before him, Andrew White has an epiphany. In one of the best lines in the novel, Mac reaches out across space in brotherhood with the Capellans: "'We can't go there any more than they can come here. We can't help them, but we can let them know that they did not live in vain, that their last great effort to communicate was successful, that someone knows and cares and wishes them well.'" The goodwill expressed in this statement gives hope for the human species. White allows MacDonald to prepare an answer.[13]

"The Waiting," jumps ahead thirty years. The viewpoint character is MacDonald's estranged son, now thirty-one years old. When he was ten his mother Maria died, and the boy was sent off to school. From then on, he harbored a deep resentment for his father. The story takes place as the younger MacDonald journeys to Puerto Rico to make peace with his feelings toward his father. But there will be no direct reconciliation: Mac died some months before. The story is about memory, longing, alienation, and loss. Although not picked up for magazine publication, this quiet story is one of the most powerful in the novel.

On a bike trek down the east coast prior to sailing for Arecibo, young MacDonald meets a young woman named Mary, who is heading north to "study xenopsychology at a university in New York," evidence that the message has led to new fields of inquiry. Much of the strife and conflict in the world has dampened, and people, by and large, are more settled—in contrast to young MacDonald, whose restlessness is the focal point of the story. As MacDonald puts it, "'It's not that you want anything, but you're waiting for something. The whole world is waiting. Time has slowed down, and we're waiting'" (166). MacDonald doesn't understand this cultural tranquility: "'But what kind of message can the Reply bring that will be worth the waiting? What will it mean to you or me or anybody else?'"

Here again Gunn presents an individual experiencing an existential crisis.[14]

At the facility, "Bobby" MacDonald is greeted by Olsen, one of the young men, now old, who worked for so many years with his father. Olsen takes him to see John White, now the project director. This creates an interesting parallel of fathers and sons. Like his father, young MacDonald is a trained linguist, and a computer programmer. Again, the key here is communication. White asks MacDonald to join the Project and use his skills to enhance the computer; eventually to succeed him as director. But first Bobby must face his demons. In a surprisingly moving scene—and a fascinating anticipation of the centrality computer memory will have on people's lives—Olsen leaves Bobby in the computer room, where the computer replays parts of what it has recorded over the years, recapitulating important scenes from the earlier stories. It is an act of memory that beautifully welds Gunn's central themes together. At the conclusion, Bobby MacDonald weeps and comes to terms with his past. He will join the project and one day, perhaps, take over the directorship when John White retires.

In the final story, "The Reply," sixty more years have passed. Here Gunn echoes the utopianism often seen in the works of Arthur C. Clarke. Due to the message, the world has fully settled into peace, tranquility, and rationality, no longer defined by conflict and strife: "The Message from Capella ... had given Earth and its people ninety years of peace in which to explore other aspects of humanity besides aggression. The problems which had seemed so difficult, virtually insolvable, one hundred and fifty, even ninety, years before had seemed to solve themselves once the world relaxed."[15] Thriving colonies exist on the Moon and on Mars, and men routinely work in space. This sense of hope is the defining characteristic of much science fiction and it is interesting and appealing to see Gunn evoke this attitude in his work here, an attitude that Gunn more forcefully states in his critical writing. It is also refreshing in relationship to Gunn's other work. Although he had written, and would go on to write, a number of works that take a utopian outlook, as seen throughout this study, Gunn had largely been a dystopian writer prior to the publication of *The Listeners*.

The story takes place on the anticipated eve of the reply from the Capellans. The new Project director is fifty-seven-year-old William MacDonald, the grandson of Mac and Maria, and son of Bobby and Mary. Gathered together at Arecibo is an audience of dignitaries from throughout the world. The computer, enhanced by the years of work by Bobby

MacDonald, now virtually an A.I., is receiving new messages in a flurry. In the basic pattern of the prior message—the more complex data the computer is receiving will take time to interpret—is a new message from the Capellans, except in this case the Capellan figure is missing, indicating extinction. It was not a supernova, but an expansion of their sun into a red giant; the message was produced thousands, or even millions, of years before as the Capellan sun engulfed their world. The Capellans have been long extinct and the message must have issued from a beacon, to signal others of their existence and their end. The computer delivers a poignant message from these lost beings that Gunn renders in verse, a message of "good wishes/kinship/admiration/brotherhood/love."[16] The Capellans bequeath the legacy of their civilization to us, the people of Earth. And William MacDonald recognizes what this really means: "Now the work of the world begins. The messages the computer is receiving, storing, analyzing, interpreting contain the entire record of a civilization alien to almost everything we know except intelligence and emotion, a civilization considerably advanced beyond ours—not only its history but, if my assumptions are correct, its philosophies, culture, art, science, technology, theology, literature. We have received a legacy more valuable than the physical possession of another world, with all its natural treasures, and the world's scientists and scholars and everyone else who wishes to explore it may spend their lifetimes studying it, interpreting it, and adding bits and pieces of it to our civilization, enriching us by a whole new world and everything it was."[17] It is a conclusion of hope, an existential vision of the possibilities for the future that transcend the strife and discord that characterize our age. Notice, too, the resonances with the early space operas. As in *This Fortress World* and *Star Bridge*, human civilization becomes the beneficiary of an extinct civilization's legacy. Gunn comes back to this theme in different ways in *Gift from the Stars* and the *Transcendental* series.

The Magicians

To capitalize on the horror boom of the 1970s, set off by the publications of Ira Levin's *Rosemary's Baby* and William Peter Blatty's *The Exorcist* and the success of the subsequent films, Gunn resurrected his 1954 novella "Sine of the Magus," expanding it into the novel *The Magicians*. *The Magicians* was published in September 1976 by Scribner's, just as Stephen King's *'Salem's Lot* was released in paperback and was stimulating the horror boom to its second phase. Although published in the 1970s, the novel maintains the vibe of 1950s magazine fiction. It's certainly an entertaining yarn, but it seems out of step with the experimental fiction Gunn was writing during this period. So, unlike many of the horror novels that were being published at the time by King, Koontz, Straub, et al., Gunn's *The Magicians* is a throwback. Nonetheless, the circumstances of its publication during the 1970s horror boom predicate treating it here in its novel form. With that said, my analysis will be limited in scope.

Although never stated directly, the story takes place in downtown Kansas City at the old Muehlebach Hotel, where a detective named Casey has been hired to find a missing person at a "covention," a gathering of magicians. The narrative is told in the first-person from Casey's perspective as outsider amidst the participants at the "covention." The original idea was sparked, in part, by Gunn's "observation that words are often misspelled on hotel bulletin boards,"[18] but one can also conjecture that it is a product of Gunn's reflections on his experiences at World Science Fiction Conventions, in Chicago in 1952 and Philadelphia in 1953. The original story was completed three weeks after the Philadelphia convention. The earmarks of science fiction fan culture can be identified in some of the behaviors exhibited at the covention, which is probably consistent with most gatherings of people with shared interests. Nonetheless, science fiction professional and fan culture would seem Gunn's most immediate model. Gunn asserts, though, that it was his memories of attending events at the Muehlebach that contributed the most. As mentioned in the biographical chapter, the 1975 Kansas City area science fiction convention was held at the Muehlebach, and this might have sparked Gunn to revisit the story. The "covention" is held, appropriately, during the Halloween weekend. The "covention" is set up like any other professional gathering with a program of lectures and demonstrations on topics such as lycanthropy, familiars, witchcraft, etc. To an outsider like Casey, such proceedings are incredibly dull: "They were being dull about magic. They were being pedantic about sorcery."[19]

The Magicians is essentially a classic detective novel, following Casey's investigations and the complications he uncovers. The mystery centers on the death of Prospero, co-founder and leader of the organization, at the hands of a magician named Solomon, who has taken over the organization and is practicing the dark arts. Gabriel and his co-founder Uriel had intended to make the "Art" public, to reveal the rational underpinnings behind magic. In this way, they represent the scientific community, those who wish to make inquiry transparent and open. Solomon and his ilk are in it for power, and will do anything to hold onto that power. Casey makes the acquaintance of Gabriel's daughter, Ariel, who, as it turns out, is the one that hired him. To hold magical power over someone is to know their true name, so Casey's task is to discover Solomon's. As is expected in the logical fantasy promoted by Campbell in his groundbreaking fantasy magazine *Unknown*, and emulated by Gold in *Beyond*, Gunn takes magic literally in *The Magicians*: it's real and it works. Gabriel and Uriel had been mathematics professors at a university, and Gunn spends a good part of the narrative working out the mathematics of magic.

Casey infers the logic of magic and quickly teaches himself how it works using a manuscript written by Uriel. It becomes quickly evident that anyone can become a magician if they have "belief, knowledge, and determination."[20] The rest of the novel works toward a final confrontation between the forces of good, Casey, Ariel, and Uriel; and the forces of evil, Solomon and the other black magicians. On a hunch, Casey calls a reporter friend in Washington and is able to penetrate the identity of Solomon. He's a shyster politician set to sweep into the presidency in the fall elections: "'America's biggest, bestest, one-man self-help organization. Look in today's headlines or yesterday's or tomorrow's. You'll see his name, and never anything but the best things associated with it. There's no doubt about it. The party may not like it, and a lot of Americans might feel like leaving the country, but he's gonna sweep the convention unless somebody fixes his little red wagon. And he'll probably get elected, too.'"[21] In a final confrontation, as Solomon prepares to ritually kill Ariel to summon forth a demon, the "Lord of Darkness," Casey and Uriel are able to break his hold by appealing to his belief in superstition, giving Uriel time to teleport him into oblivion. They make a vow to release the knowledge to the world; danger lies in secrecy.

The Magicians is, perhaps, best characterized as an entertainment. Unlike Gunn's other novels, it doesn't contribute much to a thoughtful interrogation of the real world. Nonetheless, it is entertaining and follows the logic of the fantasy premise it sets out to examine. This may be an indication of one of the key differences between science fiction and fantasy, a distinction which is central to Gunn's teaching and scholarship.

Kampus

On the other hand, *Kampus* is Gunn's forgotten masterpiece. *Kampus* is an intensely realized near-future satire extrapolating on the excesses of sixties campus culture, radical politics, drugs, rock music, sexual liberation, technocracy, cult religion, and the culture of entitlement. Gunn brilliantly creates a surreal campus where professors must "sell" their classes to mindless students like carnival barkers. The college campus has become a coventry for the young, literally walled off from the larger community and surrounded by armed police. Within the campus walls students freely engage in excess, while professors seem to be under siege. It's total freedom all the time!

Gunn started the novel in 1970, in reaction to outbreaks of social unrest on college campuses, specifically, of course, at the University of Kansas, where Gunn was a first-hand witness to conflict between students and administration during his time as administrative assistant for public relations. Gunn initially called his "big campus-of-the-future book" *Kommencement*, but soon settled on the title *Kampus*, an overture to the leftist spelling of Amerika and an allusion to KU. The original story, titled "Kampus," makes up the second chapter of the novel. By this time, Gunn's agent was Bob Mills, former editor of *Venture* and *FSF*. Mills tried the original story on several large circulation men's magazines—*Playboy, Esquire, Penthouse*—but got no takers. Surprisingly, the genre magazines weren't interested either. In a letter to Mills in early January 1972, Gunn makes an apt comparison to Anthony Burgess's *A Clockwork Orange*; Stanley Kubrick's film was set for general release a month later: "Norbert [Slepyan, Scribner's editor] gave me some resistance to it too—partially on the basis of the cannibalism in the first chapter, partially because he didn't think this was the way things were going to go. The problem is, I think, that people are looking at it as a science fiction book, and I'm thinking about it as a mainstream book. It seems to me that it is the wrong question to ask if Burgess' world of *A Clockwork Orange* is going to come true in the next ten or 100 years, and the same thing could be said of several dozen other books."[22] Gunn also suggested that he could "make the campus more surrealistic; after all, the novel is mythic and satiric rather than realistic."[23] This seems the route he took as he further developed the novel. A few months later, Mills received a curiously negative, uneasy response from Alan Ravage at Bantam: "I just don't know what to do about *Kampus*. My feeling is that it is probably wrong for our times—I feel Jim is too far away from the spirit and the age he is writing about."[24] This is an extraordinary misperception. Gunn was a campus administrator, university teacher, and one of the premier writers of social science fiction in the field. He was on the front lines, but also had the distance of age and the detachment of a science fiction writer. What better person to be able to assess the period imaginatively? After some additional starts and stops, Gunn wrote Mills in the summer of 1973, suggesting they should ask Fred Pohl to give it a look (Pohl had become science fiction editor at Bantam): "I trust Fred's judgment, and I'd like to talk to him about the book."[25] In the same letter, Gunn defined the intentions of the novel: "It's a serious novel about the disintegration of American society into isolated pockets of interests and commitments and ideologies."[26] A week later, Gunn wrote to Pohl: "What with Watergate and other important matters, I did not get to the rewriting of *Kampus* as I had hoped to do this summer, so I have decided to ask Bob Mills to send you the original version of the first two chapters and synopsis rather than wait around.... As you may remember my discussion with you in Pueblo, I think of *Kampus* not as a SF book but as a novel of social commentary about an increasingly fragmented world."[27] A few weeks later, Pohl responded: "I like it fine.... I think we should write a contract."[28] With his university commitments, scholarly work, and the expansion of *The Magicians* ahead, it would take three more years before *Kampus* was published during the summer of 1977, at the very moment when *Star Wars* was redefining science fiction in the mass imagination and the Apple II computer was igniting the computer revolution.

The novel begins on the first day of "Karnival" at the University of Kansas when students return to campus, register for classes, and indulge in the newest chemical substances. It is considered "the most important day of the school year." The novel's protagonist Gavin, named after Arthur's knight Gawain, glides through the Karnival stoned and excited. The first line reveals Gavin's euphoria: "Gavin dopedrifted through the sensemadness of Karnival like a molecule enslaved in one of the Savages' amplifiers." During Karnival, rival student factions suspend conflicts, which often lead to violence and death. It is also a celebration of excess where total "freedom" is indulged "things which position or timidity or reason ordinarily prevented." Gavin meanders past the student organization booths, including meditation, "'Liberate yourself from temporal passions. Release the true power of the self. Become all that you can be. Unite yourself with the universal,'" and politics, "'Join the political party of your choice. You aren't truly serious unless you're prepared to put your body on the line for what you believe. Join up and discover what politics is all about.'" Astrology, black magic, communes, and countless other booths bombard Gavin's senses. In a brilliant extrapolation on the commercialization of the college curriculum, Gunn leads Gavin through the "booths" of the professoriate, "course-touting in the upper corridors," soliciting students like carnival barkers. A mathematics professor declares, "'I can teach you new methods of multiplication and division which do not require laborious memorization. I have pills which are guaranteed to encapsulate the entire development of mathematical thought since the Arabs invented numerals, pills which need only be triggered by lecture and brief exercise.'" An anatomist barks, "'Learn the marvels and delights of the human body. A requirement for students who wish to go on into medicine, nursing, pharmacy, physical therapy, and physical education, as well as altered states of consciousness, and a pleasant diversion for those who wish to astonish their friends with a scientist's knowledge of musculature, nerve stimulation, and amatory skill.... We will dissect real cadavers, authentic preserved dead people, men and women.'" Next, Gavin encounters an English teacher, who warns that though they believe everything they "'will ever need to know will be available in visual form,'" that reading has its own delights: "'Many works of literature, many exciting—yes, even pornographic—passages have never been translated into visual form. Imagine the delight of reading *Fanny Hill* in the original or *Justine* or *The Story of O!*'" From English, Gavin stands before the psychology booth, which touts Skinnerian mind control alongside altered states of consciousness through drugs.[29]

What is perhaps the most interesting moment in this menagerie of classes, in hindsight given the introduction of the Apple II nearly parallels the publication of *Kampus*, is Gunn's reflections on the future of computers. The Apple II was released on June 10, 1977. The publication date for *Kampus* was July 1977, although the book was likely launched in June. The computer itself speaks in a "pleasant feminine voice," a Siri in the making: "'Every student knows that the computer is the creator of our society. It has taken the drudgery out of man's life; automatically, without complaint, it performs the simplest repetitive tasks as well as the most complicated computations. It manages the economy while it economizes on management. Because of the computer, man is free to do not what he can but what he wishes.'" Gunn equates the lure of the computer interface with seduction in a surprisingly prescient insight: "The computer's voice dropped an octave, became more personal, more seductive. 'But you must learn to handle your computer so that your computer will produce the results you want.' The computer made it sound like a love affair. 'You must know what the computer can do and what it cannot; what is simple and cheap, and what is difficult and expensive. Computer science is the essential course in the University curriculum. Learn how to talk to your computer. Learn how to obtain the exact answer by asking the exact question, not the approximate answer or even an incorrect answer by asking a careless question.'"[30] Gunn also anticipates the ubiquity of e-commerce and electronic identification cards on college campuses: "'Sign up for this course by placing your student identification card against the blue readin plate in the counter and your credit card against the red plate. No cash or checks, please. You may sign up for your own computer terminal by pressing the button between the two plates.'"[31]

Gunn further anticipates the personal computer as a standard tool for students. It is extraordinary that Gunn's novel was released almost simultaneously with the home computer and he also appears to anticipate some of the other now ubiquitous computer applications, such as games, dating, delivery services, and email:

> "I need not remind you how much easier and more satisfying your university life will be with your own computer terminal, providing answers as well as services, tutoring and tapes for class exercises included—this service covers all classes offering with the University, of course—and even printed term papers for teachers barbaric enough to require such arcane skills. As a matter of fact, all courses offered within the University may be taken by computerized instruction, with the single exception of laboratory courses.
>
> Of course, fascinating games can be played with your own computer terminal— space war, chess, computer dating, terminalhop—as well as sending and receiving personal messages, and even prompt delivery of late-night snacks or drinks, pills or dope. No student ever again need be lonely, oppressed or depressed. With your own computer terminal you need only describe your mood and be matched with some other student who at that very moment wants to give what you need."[32]

The booth next to computer science is chemistry, where a chemist pitches students on learning how to synthesize their own drugs. Next to the chemistry booth is the last, philosophy, with a sign reading, "enter for personal interview" before a curtained alcove. Gavin is intrigued by "this blatant disregard for the proprieties." After all, "who was hiring whom here?" Upon entering, Gavin meets a gruff, testy, old-school faculty member, known simply as the Professor, who immediately asks Gavin pointed questions about what he seeks. Unlike his huckster colleagues, the Professor adheres to old values of teacher student interaction: "'This is normal human intercourse between a teacher and a prospective student, who, if he shows promise, the ability to learn, and a proper attitude, may be accepted.'" The Professor makes his case for what he has to offer in stark contrast to his huckster colleagues: "'I cannot teach you a skill with which you can amaze your friends and satisfy your baser needs. What I have will not give you power over others; it will not make you famous or well-liked or happy. What I have, if you want it and I decide to communicate it to you, may make you miserable, and certainly will make you discontented.'"

Gavin is fascinated by the man. Perhaps here is someone from which he can truly learn and satisfy his inner, though muffled, desire for understanding and knowledge. When Gavin hesitantly expresses his innermost thoughts: "I want to know ... what you're talking about. I want to ... know—," the Professor accepts him as a student.[33] As the novel proceeds, readers may notice some parallels between Gavin's educational odyssey and Voltaire's *Candide*.

Leaving the Professor's presence, Gavin meets a girl, Jenny, from Oakland, California, who, after three years of college at an east coast Catholic girls' school, skipped out and hitchhiked across the country, arriving in Lawrence that morning. Keeping with the Arthurian allusions, Gunn named Jenny after Guinevere. As the novel proceeds, Jenny becomes the object of Gavin's quest.

Chapter Two, "The Kidnapping," is the original story Gunn wrote in the summer of 1970. The Professor lectures on the legacy of Herbert Marcuse and the culture of student excess. The Professor critiques Marcuse's idea that "liberating tolerance" practices tyranny in the name of freedom and also critiques the cult of youth and the anti-intellectualism that makes ignorance a virtue. Sometime after, Gavin and his buddies take their learning a step further when they kidnap the Professor with plans to have exclusive access to his knowledge. Meanwhile, the campus is on heightened alert. A group of revolutionaries have occupied the administration building, taken the Chancellor hostage and stolen machine guns from the military museum. The Professor, already in poor health, doesn't survive the trauma of the kidnapping. Gunn then invites the reader to cringe at one of the most delightfully nasty satirical, horror scenes ever written. Gavin and his friends get a blender, open the Professor's head and remove his brain, blend it, and proceed to "drink" the knowledge contained therein through straws: "What Gavin drew through the straw was the consistency of malted milk, but not really like that, because it was lukewarm and salty. For a moment Gavin thought he would not be able to swallow, but he thought of the Professor and how wise he was, and wonderful, and he swallowed and swallowed again, and yet again. And they were through, wiping their lips, not looking toward each other in the dark. 'I don't feel any smarter,' somebody said."[34] To honor the Professor, Gavin determines they'll bury his body in front of the library.

As the semester moves forward, the ritualized campus unrest increases in intensity. Gavin becomes a campus hero as rumors of the Professor's abduction spread among the student body. A student named Phil is determined to nominate Gavin as "raid chief," tasked with orchestrating assaults upon targets in the city outside the campus walls. A raid is planned on the nuclear reactor at the city's outskirts. When Gavin argues that a raid on the reactor will contaminate the campus, he is challenged by Gregory, the brash, psychotic leader of the black student radicals. In turn, after the other white students leave, Gregory invites Gavin to join his group on a raid of their own. Jenny is brought along too, and Gavin soon realizes that Gregory's real motive is to make a play for Jenny. The raid ends in a route as the "Kampuscops" ambush the delinquent students, leaving Gregory severely injured, but Gavin is able to slip back to campus on his own.

Gavin is then called before the Student Executive Committee in a farcical scene of Kafkaesque surrealism recalling the Hedonic Council. He's congratulated for "the skill and professionalism with which you handled the abduction of the Professor." But their real accusation lies with the failed assault of the previous night. Not the fact that he was involved, but because the assault, planned by the committee, had failed. The committee is the real power on campus: "'We won't admit it outside this little sanctuary, but nothing happens on this campus that we don't know about, and nothing important happens that we don't authorize.'" But in keeping with Kafkaesque logic, the committee, though behind the raid, wanted, no, *needed* it to fail. When Gavin realizes that they tipped off the townies themselves, he's told, "'Well, we couldn't have the campus showered with radioactivity, could we? You pointed that out yourself.'" Flummoxed, Gavin asks why authorize the raid in the first place: "'We needed it right now. Revolutionary activity had been pretty light recently, and the masses have been restive. We needed something highly visible, but we needed martyrs more than we needed victories. Revolution feeds on martyrs and soon grows surfeited with success.'" The committee wanted to eliminate the threats posed by Gregory and his reckless actions and Gavin for his popularity among the student body. Seeing how the committee manipulates the "chessboard of their world" for their own "cruel game with the name of revolution," Gavin becomes disillusioned with student life. When the committee offers him the position of raid leader, he flatly refuses. Let go, Gavin returns to his room and sleeps, in delirium from a case of pneumonia.[35]

He awakes on a leather sofa: "Looking down at him, close, concerned, was a face he liked instantly. It was a face that was older, kinder, and less competitive than those he had known for the past four years." That kindly, wise face belongs to the Chancellor of the university. In this future of student control of the campus, the Chancellor has no real power. As he laments to Gavin: "'I am a figurehead, no better than a janitor—worse, really, because I serve no useful function. I neither govern nor direct. I do not admit, I do not grade, I do not dismiss or graduate.'" The Chancellor explains how universities became unhinged: "'The behavior of young people was predictable. They are the products of two generations of permissive childrearing, egalitarian homes, praise for childish creativity no matter how poverty-stricken the imagination or inadequate the execution, primary and secondary education from which the concepts of discipline and content have disappeared, and personal freedom of movement and sexual activity. We gave you liberty and deprived you of society's voice, the superego.'" When Gavin reveals where the Professor's remains are buried, the Chancellor, on orders from the committee, expels him. Enraged, Gavin lunges at the Chancellor, flipping him over his desk to the floor. When the Chancellor arises, his jaw is out of place. The Chancellor is a robot, a metal and plastic housing for the Chancellor's cloned brain, the real Chancellor having been assassinated during the second year of his tenure. Gunn makes a biting comparison between the robot Chancellor and the mindless students: "'You may think it ridiculous to have a mechanical Chancellor. But it is no more ridiculous than having mechanical students. And that is what you are, responding mechanically to stimuli like so many robots.'"[36]

Expelled from the university, Gavin walks the streets of Lawrence, which remains, bizarrely, a normal, idyllic town—"People lived here. Grass was cut neatly near the sidewalk ... the sidewalks and the streets were in good repair." The madness and chaos of the campus remain enclosed behind the campus walls. But a student outside the walls is a menace and a fugitive. There's a wry humor when a little boy Gavin encounters on a residential street shouts, "'Hey, Ma, here's a student! A real student!'" Ma compels Gavin to quickly move along: "'Young man,' said a calm voice from the nearby darkness. 'I got a shotgun aimed at your head. I intend to shoot high with the first one so as not to hit Johnny, but I can't guarantee you won't get a few pellets. The second shot, Johnny'll just have to take his chances.'" When Gavin explains he's been expelled, Ma stands down and begrudgingly offers him a change of clothes and encourages him to go home: "'Well, I wouldn't want a student in my house—not even one that's been expelled—but I don't like to see no one, not even a student, in a shape like you.'"[37]

Gavin hitches a ride on the turnpike to Kansas City and returns home in a scene that echoes *A Clockwork Orange*. He's greeted by a stranger, a young woman named Elaine, who has rented his old room. Elaine is going to a vocational school to learn about computer programming, a practical skill outside the inanities of the universities. Gavin's father is an old hippie from the sixties generation, when "politics was important." Now, politics is just a childish amusement: "'What you do now is play games. All the battles are over, and you don't know it. You're playing games and call them politics.'"[38] After further debate with his father, Gavin announces he's going to go to the west coast, to Berkeley where a proper revolution, so he thinks, can come together. Thus begins a bizarre road trip across the western United States, part Arthurian quest, part *Candide*, part *On the Road*, where Gavin will encounter all of the crazy elements of American culture taken to their logical extreme in a masterful anatomy of American society. The young computer tech Elaine decides to join him.

In the Flint Hills, a gorgeous stretch of country Gunn depicted in *The Burning*, they see a group of hippie wanderers. Elaine refuses to pick them up, although Gavin feels a naïve kinship toward them. Later, when Elaine is asleep, he picks up a lone hippie hitchhiker, despite Elaine's earlier trepidations. Gavin, on the other hand, trusts the hitchhiker is a good guy, perhaps a student; in his view, all students are trustworthy. The charismatic young hitchhiker, named Chester, claims to have once been a student, but now is an "organizer." For his part, Gavin is completely enthralled: "He hadn't felt such solidarity since he left the campus, and he hadn't met such a likable, attractive fellow for years." Elaine has money which she worked for; Chester, and Gavin for that matter, disdain work. As Chester proclaims, "'Oh, I work too, but not for *it*. Not for money or for what money can buy, but for liberty and justice and equality. Right, brother?'" Gavin confirms Chester's "liberating" philosophy: "'All men have created the wealth that man has accumulated and so its use and benefits belongs to all men—not to the few who have expropriated it and wrongfully withhold its use from others.... Nobody owns anything, and everybody owns everything.'" To justify this carefree philosophy of "ownership" when Elaine challenges it, Gavin remarks: "'If everybody refused to perform the meaningless tasks this twisted society demands, it would soon order things better—distribute goods equitably, give people what they need, and let them use their time in the only meaningful way we have.'" When Elaine asks just what is that meaningful way, Gavin declares, "'Self-discovery. The exploration of one's humanity. The perfection of one's personality.'" As Gavin concludes his great speech on the meaning of life, Chester puts a switchblade at the edge of his throat and tells him to pull into a rest stop. The glorious hippie angel is, in truth, a sociopathic criminal: "'You know how it is with private property, brother. You just convinced me. Nobody owns anything. Everybody owns everything. Well, brother, I'm claiming a little bit of mine and relieving you of something you don't own.'" Chester forces Elaine to hog-tie Gavin and proceeds with his reasoning by raping Elaine, while a helpless Gavin looks on, then steals the car. Lesson learned.[39]

In the next chapter, "The Organization Man," a reference to William Whyte's classic 1950s sociological study, Gunn satirizes the organizational structures of contemporary advanced capitalist society. As the chapter opens, Gavin sneaks into a hospital in Salina, a city in north central Kansas, where he has taken Elaine. Hospitals are now completely automatic, with computerized diagnostic machines, recalling the mechs in *The Joy Makers* and the bots in "Little Orphan Android": "An ambulance pulled up outside, and a moment later the litter presented an unconscious body to the diagnosticom.... Gavin watched the diagnosticom send its exploring tentacles over the body, measuring, testing, analyzing, and then, with an air of decision, stitching here, setting a broken bone there, and spraying with a quick-setting cast, injecting anesthetics and antibiotics."[40] From the mechanical organization of the hospital, Gavin enters the City-County Building to report the crime. After making his way past a series of uncaring officialdom, he is introduced to the ombudsman, who explains that there is no one to report a crime to because in this advanced, computerized, free society, there is no crime: "'Purposefully, consciously, we have restrained the intrusion of computerized society into the affairs of the private citizen. The result: today everyone is free to be just as idiosyncratic, just as cantankerous, just as crazy, just as out-of-step as he wishes. But there's a price.'" That price is the individual rights of others. Under the system the ombudsman describes, Chester's violent attack on Elaine was him merely "enjoying his basic liberty." By this logic, "'the act of rape might well be called an expression of existential freedom.'"[41]

To earn money while Elaine recuperates, Gavin enrolls in a local technical institute to learn something about computer programming. The community college is described thus: "The institute was a thoroughly modern and up-to-date facility, in keeping with the modern and up-to-date subjects taught within its walls; electricity and electronics, mechanics, plumbing, recycling and reclamation, construction, carpentry, accounting, and bookkeeping, secretarial skills, data recording, computer programming and repair, cybernation maintenance.... The institute taught practical application and no theory, each subject had to be approached as an isolated series of actions to be memorized." In a conversation between Gavin, the other students, and the superintendent, Gunn has the students and superintendent speak in terse, mechanical, efficient language. For example, when the superintendent becomes suspicious of Gavin's questions, he thinks he may be a labor organizer and remarks there are no organizers at the school: "'Not here. Practical men and women. Know what they want. Motivated. Ambitious. Black, white, red, brown. All colors. Not sophisticated, but backbone of society. Impatient with words. Good with hands. Word of caution: don't stir up.'" According to the superintendent the biggest problems are not distribution, but maintenance: "'Biggest social problem—maintenance. Machines break down. Can't fix themselves. Yet. Biggest economic problem—opportunity. Upward mobility. Opportunity here. Right?'" Gavin believes that distribution is the biggest problem, "'nobody needs to work.'" Although short on words, the superintendent has wisdom: "'Not true. For many work is psychological necessity. Maybe for all, though not proven. All people not alike. Some prefer leisure. Others work. Some wish to improve economic situation. Others, develop selves. Give both chance.'"[42]

Gavin believes the kids going through this vocational training need to be enlightened about their true fate, to be liberated, to be free from becoming "mindless consumers" and technicians perpetuating the "system." He's certain he wound up at the institute for a purpose; to be the liberator: "He had a strange feeling of certainty that he had been brought to this place for a purpose, and that purpose was to lead these poor benighted mechanics into a realization of the true state of the world. He felt words welling up in his throat unbidden, a compulsion to spring up and shout them like challenges to the universe. Revolutionary consciousness—that's what they needed." When Gavin calls for revolution, the young technicians turn into an angry mob: not to join him in his ill-conceived revolution, but to get him. The wise superintendent helps Gavin get away from the incensed students, but not before he is kicked and called a "'chicken-shit saboteur.'" Before the students can do real harm, Elaine comes to the rescue in a large panel truck, awaiting for him in the parking lot. Gunn has fun in showing that revolutionary fervor can often be misguided.[43]

As the pair drive into the Rocky Mountains heading for Denver, they come across Sally Grandjon, "the cybernated gal," a member of a group marriage trying to perfect human-computer symbiosis: "'We're perfecting mental control of computers. And computer-assisted thinking. CAT. As easy as spelling "cat." Already we've achieved complete physical control of our autonomic systems, muscle tone, sensory stimuli.'" Sally's clan take in student wanderers and she has her eyes set on Gavin. Gavin is tempted by the offer, but that night he hears "the sound of a woman in the throes of passion" and finds Sally jacked into her computer and writhing on a table: "Naked, face upward, her red hair covered by a cap, like a fancy bathing cap fastened under the chin, from which wires trailed to a plug at the head of the couch, lay the magnificent Sally looking more than ever like an earth goddess, a sex goddess, her body oversized perfection, rippling now with periodic contractions." Gavin takes his own turn with the cap and interfaces in an ecstasy recalling the endless dreams of *The Joy Makers*: "He felt as if his identity were expanding to include not only his body and those organs and vessels and memories and thoughts contained within it, but the metal and plastic standing against the far wall with its tiny magnetic fluxes tickling the synapses of microcircuits, with its purposeful electrons seeking the shortest pathway through its supercooled body. He was no longer just Gavin, but Gavin plus the computer, Gavin and the computer, Gavin-computer, Gav-computer..." Once again, Elaine rescues him from this plunge into the cybernetic dreamworld.[44]

The next chapter, "Deflowered Children," brings Gavin and Elaine face-to-face with an incestuous, religious zealot and his clan of daughters in one of the most disturbing situations in the novel. Here is a more unseemly version of Jeremiah Jones. Approaching the farm, Gavin and Elaine talk one of the girls, Billie, into letting them have breakfast in the house where they meet the family: "All of them looked alike. The women were tall, blond, and buxom; they all looked like Billie. And the children were small and blond, all like each other and the women, too." They warn Gavin to leave, "'Pa'd kill you. He near killed the last boy came in here looking for a place to stay,'" but have hopes Elaine might stay, "'maybe you could be a proper wife to Pa.'" This had once been a religious commune of "right thinkers," but consistent with the trajectory of many such communities the righteous "fell into error" and "'people died, and some were killed in arguments ... and finally all were gone except Pa.'"[45] Gunn creates a similar situation in the later novel *The Millennium Blues*, although without the incest.

As Gavin and Elaine prepare to leave, Billie asks them to take her with them, as she's reaching the age when she's "'old enough to come to him in the night, the way my sisters do.'" But before they can split, Pa arrives toting a shotgun, Gavin lunges for the gun, disarms Pa, and determines to bring him to some sort of justice, when an entourage of hippie gypsies arrives, the Freedom Train. Their leader, named Reich, presumably in reference to psychologist Wilhelm Reich who cultivated a theory of pleasure, speaks, "'We come to invite all who wish to ride upon the Freedom Train to join us in our parade into a glorious future of sensitivity and love and right thinking! ... We come to share the bounty of the earth, which belongs to all men.'" And like Chester, they proceed to requisition the bounty of Pa's farm: "The men and women who had tumbled out of the cars and trucks were returning now, their arms laden with sacks of grain and flour, and boxes of vegetables and fruit. They led pigs and cows and steers, putting them all in the trucks, which miraculously sprouted ramps as if it had all happened before." Needing a lift, Gavin, Elaine and Billie join the Freedom Train. But Gavin's earlier idealism has been tempered by his experiences and he asks whether it would be "'simpler just to grow your own food?'" The doublethink of the caravan leader is darkly hilarious: "'We do grow our own food. We just grow it on other people's farms, and when we need it, we come and get it. That's simple enough, isn't it?'" To lend further justification, he blusters, "'Let those do it who must. Let others get by without it if they can. Freedom from such work, making possible the development of the individual's true potential as a human being, is among the greatest and most vital forms of liberation.'" When Gavin suggests they simply pool their minimum annual incomes—an idea championed in the fiction of Mack Reynolds—and buy what they need, Reich retorts: "'And collaborate with the government which has always told us we are an incredibly rich country when we are actually desperately poor—poor in most of the things that throughout the history of mankind have been cherished as riches? If you accept charity, you consent to its tyranny.'" Here Gunn exposes the extreme false logic of some liberation movements. At Taos, New Mexico, the Freedom Train joins up with a number of other gypsy caravans. Gavin realizes that these people are, in essence, "students grown middle-aged." Just as Gavin starts believing he's found his tribe, Elaine has an intuition of uneasiness. Soon Billie comes out of the darkness covered in blood. Pa has arrived with government officials, declaring the caravan a "conspiracy," the only crime left on the books.[46]

Gavin and Elaine escape again, and after a month in Albuquerque working to buy supplies, wander in the mountains for days. They find a hidden research institute, a community of technologists and scientists, trying to hold things together in this crumbling world, recalling the space station enclave at the end of *The Burning*: "'It's an ivory tower, a haven for scientists and scholars of all kinds. You'll have a chance to meet most of them. This is one of the few places left in the world where they can do their thing.'" Through worldwide recruiting the secret institute has been able to bring together many of the best minds in the world. Once there the scientists, by choice, never leave. At last Gavin has found true utopia. Here Gunn is likely drawing from James Hilton's *Lost Horizon*. The first sentence from "The Professor's Notebook" that heads the chapter comments on Luddism in the modern technological age: "Ever since the Industrial Revolution began reshaping the nature of human existence, romantic fools have been urging humanity to shut down the machines—forcibly, if necessary—and return to the simpler, more natural ways of our ancestors." But technology is necessary; there is no going back, except to hardship. As the Professor reflected, "Without technology, man is at the mercy of nature, and nature is not kind. Man's natural condition, as Thomas Hobbes pointed out, is poor, short, nasty, and brutish. But more important than man's condition is his potential: he has only one chance for immortality as he starts up the ladder of technology." In a later conversation, the institute's director explains what brought the scientists to hide in this remote mountaintop keep: "'The same events that turned the campuses over to the students drove the scientists and scholars from the universities. For centuries, teaching and research had reinforced each other, but when hiring and firing teachers became a student game, teaching became student-pleasing, a con game in which practical men and women sold students tricks and flattery.'" True knowledge seekers were forced underground where they could, like the "witches" in *The Burning*, keep things afloat.[47]

Both Gavin and Elaine settle into life at the institute, but Gavin's journey is not yet complete. Even though the director offers him a permanent place at this utopia at the top of the world, Gavin becomes restless and wants to complete his journey to Berkeley. Besides, Gavin doesn't feel he belongs, as he's still a "student." Ultimately, Elaine decides to stay at the mountaintop. Gavin, though, must finish his quest. On his last night, she crawls into bed with him and as they embrace in preliminaries to love, she whispers, "'you're going to find whatever is at the end of your quest, and I don't want to be there when you find it. The end of my quest is right here ... where everybody is equal.'"[48]

In the final chapter, "Thus I Refute Berkeley"—the title referring to Samuel Johnson's famous kicking of a stone to prove material reality—Gavin reaches the goal of his holy quest and enters the symbolic campus of all that is revolutionary. At first the campus seems empty, almost like a deserted fairground in the off season. Gavin realizes that he no longer belongs here; is no longer a student. He's grown up. A Kampuscop working for the "chief" of the students questions Gavin and escorts him to the wedding ceremony of the chief and his bride, a symbolic gesture to unite students and administration. A ritualistic book burning sickens Gavin, now transformed by the lessons of the Professor, his journeys across the country, and the culmination at the mountaintop institute. On a stage erected in the campus center, to his horror, Gavin sees Jenny in the arms of Gregory, who after the disaster of the power plant has been rejuvenated into a cyborg, his enhancements include a cybernetic penis. The cybernetic Gregory has ascended to the university's leadership and before Gavin's eyes Jenny is impaled on the stage by Gregory's electric cock: "It was the rape of humanity by the machine." An explosion rocks the stage, "it was Ragnarok, the campus Armageddon toward which events had moved for twenty years, storing up rage and frustration and violence toward the final explosion." Gavin makes his way to the crater where the stage had been, and sees the bodies of Jenny and Gregory entwined in death: "Gregory's plastic arm had pulled so tight around her that her ribs were broken, and perhaps her back as well. Gregory's plastic leg kept them upright through some mechanical miracle." The novel concludes with Gavin returning to the enchanted mountain and to Elaine.[49]

Jack Williamson wrote Gunn a few months after *Kampus'* publication thanking him for sending a signed copy. As a fellow science-fiction writer turned academic, Williamson could fully appreciate Gunn's satire: "I hope the book gets the wide recognition it deserves. I think it should be read by everybody interested in education—which of course is everybody, period. But there is always the question of how much truth people want to face."[50] Read in light of how university education has developed since the novel's publication, though *Kampus* is extreme in its biting extrapolative satire, it still resonates with many of the follies educators (and students) face. And in the context of the work Gunn was doing as scholar and teacher at the same time, *Kampus* can be read as a fictional counterpoint or companion piece to the foundational scholarship and the foundational teaching that he contributed to the science fiction field. Today, the novel is worth a look by anyone who wishes to reflect on the state of higher education, the condition of society, and the histories of social science fiction and satire.

The Dreamers

The Dreamers is Gunn's most experimental novel, extending the New Wave narrative techniques Gunn used in *The Listeners* and *Kampus*. In many ways, it continues the same preoccupations Gunn explored in "Breaking Point" and *The Joy Makers*. The influence of Gunn's academic career as Professor of English is evident, as the novel is deeply informed by the literary canon. Like many of Gunn's novels, *The Dreamers* consists of three interconnected segments, tied together by interstitial sections involving a frame character called the Mnemonist. A Mnemonist is an individual who has extraordinary ability of memory and recall, and this Mnemonist is an arch-dreamer tasked with maintaining the automated life systems of the vast urban center under his direction. Each novella is prefaced by an interstitial section tracing the thoughts of the Mnemonist in his dream bath. Gunn experiments with style in the interstitial sections using three-columned narrative interspersed between the conventional narrative to create the impression of multilayered thought patterns. When read with attention, these breaks can force the reader to be more attentive to the building ideas and get a sense of the way in which thoughts overlap together in our minds. First published in 1980, the first section, "Among the Beautiful Bright Children," originally sold to Harlan Ellison for *The Last Dangerous Visions*, but with Ellison never completing the anthology, Gunn finished the rest of the novel and got the rights back. Section two, "If I Forget Thee," was published by Robert Silverberg in a three novella anthology called *Triax* in 1977. Gunn completed a third novella to conclude the novel.

The novel begins as the Mnemonist lies upon a pallet "moving dreamlike in counterpoint to the thoughts that were more real than the room and the cocoon of flesh that enclosed them."[51] The premise is that the Mnemonist is seeking an apprentice dreamer to take over the management of the urban center once he dies. Each novella represents possible protégés for the Mnemonist. The first novella involves an historian, someone who still has interest in the past. The second involves a surgeon, one who has spent his life tending to the young "poppets" immersed in the dreamworlds. The third is a consummate dreamer. All are psychologically damaged.

The first novella, "The Historian," involves a man named Laurence (an interesting choice given Gunn's geographical location). Laurence's work inspires the dreamers and the youth who "live in their dreams" by popping dream pills. The people live in "self-sufficient urban centers." Cities have been abandoned and the countryside neglected, recalling the hives of E. M. Forster's "The Machine Stops" and Robert Silverberg's arcologies in *The World Inside*. As in *The Joy Makers*, *The Dreamers* explores the possibilities of virtual reality. In this world of virtual reality and dream experience, the historians are important in maintaining the past and keeping people somewhat attached: "'Without historians the past would be forgotten, and our way of life would be limited.'" As the older generation declines and the "beautiful bright children" immersed in dreams come of age, few historians remain, which threatens to limit the dreamer experience.[52]

Chemical memory has been synthesized and people merely pop a pill to experience the lucid dreams of professional dreamers. It's basically a virtual acid trip; full immersion virtual reality, without a computer interface. How does it work? As the dreamer Samuel explains, "'I dream so vividly that my dreams are like memory, my memory like knowledge. And while I am dreaming, the little needles come and drink my blood, and then the laboratories analyze the proteins—the peptides, to be precise— and synthesize them, just as the brain does, and put them into little capsules, and the poppets pop it, you see? And then they live my dreams.'"[53] Samuel and other dreamers like him are like artists, like writers, their dreams are their creative medium.

All three stories center on a male character experiencing sorrow and guilt over losing his female companion to the world of dreams. Laurence is overwhelmed by sorrow for the loss of his wife who, as he tells a young poppet early in the story, left the urban center: "It was a strange thing to do, and she was not that kind of person at all. I never understood it."[54] Laurence becomes involved with a young woman named Virginia, and she releases his pent up desires. Laurence wants her to stop popping dream pills; to start living in the real world. But he finally succumbs and allows her to pop and succumbs to sensuality, as she comes to him in a variety of guises—Mata Hari, Heloise, Cleopatra, Isolde: "She came to him as all women. Each one enraptured him, whipped him into new intensities of passion, and sickened him, for what he wanted beyond desire was the honey-sweet girl he had known first, the girl he thought of as the real Virginia." When Virginia leaves him alone, in an important infodump section, Laurence turns his research attention to "the nature of the society in which he lived, about which, it seemed, he had known so little." Laurence tracks Virginia to Samuel's apartment where he finds an orgy of dreaming, with Virginia drinking Samuel's dreamer-blood straight from a cut in his hand. Samuel's remark that this "is the ultimate dream. We have eliminated the middle man. Straight from producer to consumer," echoes Hedon's arguments in *The Joy Makers*.[55]

As with Josh Hunt in *The Joy Makers*, Laurence is a holdout, a resister to change. After this incident, he refuses to allow Virginia to pop any more: "'I'm not going to let you go until you're free of this need to be somebody else. I'm not going to let you go until you—the real you, not someone else—can decide what you want to do.'" He tries to detoxify her while she begs him to let her pop, that she'll "never be anything but a burden" and he'll "get no joy" from her. And, indeed, in Laurence's eyes, the changes wrought on the un-dreaming Virginia make her unappealing: "She was not even attractive, Laurence thought. The golden girl with the quicksilver moods and honey-sweet taste was gone. She had been replaced by this drab creature." Laurence wants her to be the real her. She counters, "'The real me! Don't you understand? There is no real me! I am what I pop. Strip that away and there's nothing left.'" And Virginia reveals she knows the truth why Laurence's wife left him: "'Your wife left you because she was bored. She didn't die. She went to another building, a strange building. Can you imagine that? Rather than continue to live with dull, boring Laurence, she went to a strange building, and found herself another life among strangers. Because she couldn't stand you anymore.'" When Laurence awakes after this lesson in truth, he finds the beautiful bright Virginia is back and realizes she has popped. In despair, Laurence joins the dreamers: "He inserted the capsule in the injector, pushed back his sleeve, and pressed the nozzle of the injector to his arm. For one brief moment, before the synthetic peptides began to reconstruct his memories, his eyes filled with tears and he could not read."[56] The Mnemonist in his dream-cavern has doubts about the world he has helped to create and concludes he will find no replacement among the historians, among these sad holdouts from the dreams.

The middle section, "The Volunteer," involves a former surgeon named Jeri, who, like Laurence, is a middle-aged man in despair from losing his wife. Jeri indulges in a series of dreams that each depict a wronged-man seeking revenge against the woman who betrayed him. The first dream is of a primeval hunter who finds his children murdered and his wife missing. When he finds her with her lover in the forest, she claims she had been abducted, but the wronged-man knows better: "'You killed the children. It was too neat for him. You got him to take you away. It was your idea. You did it all.'" The wife responds with bitterness that she hates him and he proceeds to take his vengeance in savage brutality, recalling Sabatini in *This Fortress World*: "She hated him while he cut off her toes one by one, and then her fingers, her ears, her eyelids, her nose.... After the first hour she began to scream. Each scream sent a shudder of pleasure down his back."[57] The second dream takes him to an Aztec sacrificial ceremony on the eve of Cortez's invasion. The high priest demands the king's daughter more to satisfy his lust than for sacrifice, which the king declines. The priest assumes the girl will come to him on her own volition, but he is wrong. When the king finally relents and sends the priest the girl, he plunges his knife into her breast, in the end relishing in blood sacrifice over carnal desire. His next dream involves a crusader returning to his keep after ten years to find his wife and brother together in his bed. Again, he kills the unfaithful wife. The final dream involves a professor of English who damages a colleague's tenure review because the colleague is having an affair with his wife. She's sure her relationship will continue, despite his interference. But the worldly academician knows better: "'But now, you see, he must choose. He will not have a job as a teacher; if he wants to teach he will have to go somewhere else after his terminal year.'"[58] When the lover calls saying he's taking another job, the wife stands before the academic with a knife and plunges it into her own breast. From these nightmares, the volunteer awakes. In truth, his wife left him years ago and he is still mired in bitterness and thoughts of murder: "If she had been here now, he would have taken his surgeon's tools, his saws and his scalpels and dissected the creature that once had been Lora."[59]

After another period of "total immersion" dreaming, Jeri is awakened by a woman named Sara. Sara is part of a movement that realizes the dangers of the dreamer society: "'What became apparent to me, and a few others, was that humanity was dying, succumbing to a life that satisfied desires before they became needs, almost before any desires were expressed. We wanted to gather together a nucleus of people who had learned that this world had a dark side, who had lived some of its horrors and were willing to work for something new.'"[60] Gunn here again reexamines the philosophical questions raised in *The Joy Makers*. Sara wants Jeri to use his surgeon's skills to bring her lover out of a permanent fugue state. The undead, as they are called, are people whose illnesses or injuries could not be cured by the machines, nor can they dream. When Jeri balks and says he no longer remembers the knowledge and techniques to perform surgery, Sara challenges the nature of his persistent dream of betrayal. In truth, Jeri killed his wife when she chose total immersion instead of life with him, having done exactly what his dream-fantasies replay: "'You killed her. You cut her wrists and watched her bleed to death, then you cut her up with your surgeon's knives and saws and disposed of her body through the waste chute, and ever since then you have been trying to forget, trying to convince yourself that you were the one who had been betrayed, getting your revenge on a series of surrogates so that you need not face the truth.'"[61] After Sara leaves him, Jeri goes to the surgery, takes the injection that will give him back his surgeon's knowledge, and operates on her lover Toni, in hopes of achieving some degree of resolution to his guilt. Making this gesture, Jeri then goes into the immersion tank with the undead, hoping there to be released into a fugue state, but instead his revenge-dreams return.

The final section, "The Dreamer," is framed as a retelling of *The Iliad*. Much of the action of the story takes place in the dreamworld of Troy and Gunn does an effective job of recreating the mythic narrative, but in such a way as to make it come across as part of the dreamworld of the dreamer. The dreamer is Samuel, who took Virginia away from Laurence in the first novella, bringing the novel full circle. Samuel is dreaming the Trojan War on commission and so his dream is structured by the history written by Laurence he has "popped" and by "an epic by an ancient poet."[62] In his waking state, he gets involved with a young woman named Zoe who questions him about the dreams and about how he creates them. Zoe is in love with Samuel, but his own desires are centered on Helen in the dream. Samuel gets so immersed in the unfolding dream that he doesn't wish to turn it over to his client, Regi. This is his greatest dream, his masterwork, and he wants to see it to the end. When Regi comes by for the dream, Samuel tells him it will never be completed and that he'll have to find another dreamer. He wants to keep this fabulous dream of Helen all to himself. While embracing Helen in the dreamworld, Samuel realizes Zoe has taken the guise of Helen and joined him in his delusion. She confesses, "'If I couldn't have you as Zoe, I'd have you as Helen.'"[63] The story ends with Samuel going back into his dream, despite Zoe's warning that Paris dies and he will die too. This leads to the final section of the Mnemonist who reflects, "Are the dreamers, too, the victims of their dreams?"[64] The Mnemonist departs into a dream of abstraction:

> A great weariness reminded the Mnemonist of his long-forgotten body. Somewhere within it was a heart that pumped something other than memories to his brain. He was more than an extension of the console, of the computers, of the urban center; somewhere inside this shell of flesh was a creature that was more than the sum of its memories, that had needs and desires. "What would it be like to forget?" he asked. No more the rush of memory, the flow of information, the remembering river that surged through his head leaving behind its detritus of data, its delta of detail. What would it be like to have a mind as bare as a bone? How would it feel to experience the darkness of unknowing? The thought was like a blasphemy, and yet it was only the opposite side of the coin of his life."[65]

Thus, *The Dreamers* concludes on a reflective note, putting the reader within a mind not unlike those re-wombed in the conclusion of *The Joy Makers*. This final passage almost registers with the soon to emerge cyberpunk movement as well. The Mnemonist's reflection of "the flow of information" and the "detritus of data, its delta of detail" could be lines straight out of William Gibson's *Neuromancer*. In this exploration of dreams and altered states of consciousness, Gunn extends his metaphors on virtual worlds that retain uncanny resonance with the ontological questions arising in our increasing immersion into digital environments.

Crisis!

Gunn's next book, *Crisis!*, developed from an idea for a TV series. As discussed in the biography chapter, Gunn suggested the idea to CBS in the mid–1970s as a possible competitor to the popular *Six Million Dollar Man*. CBS passed and to demonstrate the concept he wrote the story "Child of the Sun," the second story in internal chronology, which appeared in *Analog* in 1978 and was selected for Donald Wollheim's *World's Best SF* anthology. After the story appeared, Joe Naar at Universal then took an option on the series.[66] Later, after the TV series prospects dimmed, Gunn decided to write up the rest of his ideas into novelettes that appeared in *Analog* in the mid–1980s. To give the feel that these are episodes for a TV series, in the book version, the stories are identified as episodes, rather than chapters.

The premise of *Crisis!* is that a time traveler is sent back in time to stimulate positive change (at one point Gunn titled the series *Catalyst!*) that will correct his own grim future by intervening in various crises. The time travel is a one-shot event, which is conveyed in a brief prelude. In other words, the traveler doesn't flit about throughout history, like Poul Anderson's Time Patrol, nor does it appear he can get back to his own era. The traveler is Bill Johnson, a nondescript character similar to Marshall Cartwright in *The Immortals*. In fact, *The Immortals*, as one would expect since it was adapted for television, is the work that is most narratively similar to *Crisis!* By the nature of his time traveling, Bill Johnson is a blank slate, although he does maintain intuitions of his purpose, and he's a man who seems to have the ability to connect with people quickly and to synthesize their problems. As each episode begins, Johnson awakens in a hotel room, an alley, or some other location having no memory of previous events. Since the stories are structured like one-hour TV episodes, he very quickly gets entangled in whatever crisis the story centers on. Gunn also narrowed the viewpoint to be that of the camera to keep the narrative as objective as possible and leaving out the interior reflection characters normally have in fiction. This makes for an odd combination of narrative simplicity and a complex overarching thematic story arc. The central conceit is that the future is in crisis and that there is a critical mass of flashpoints in the then contemporary world in which Bill Johnson can intervene.

The crises are both topical to our time and dated at the same time; that is, the crises still have meaning for today, but the cultural mores are frozen in the eighties. Once Johnson triggers a change, his memory of events fades, and each episode begins with a message on a tape, written on a piece of paper, scrawled on a mirror, on a cassette tape or by some other means, the first instance being "Your name is Bill Johnson. You have just saved the U.S. space program from termination, and you don't remember. You can find references to political decisions in newspapers and magazines, but you will find no mention of the part you played. For this there are several possible explanations, including the likelihood I may be lying or deceived or insane. But the explanation on which you must act is that I have told you the truth: you are a man born in a future that has almost used up all hope: you were sent to this time and place to alter the events that created that future."[67] Similar messages frame the beginning and end of each episode. As this is the beginning of the first story, the implication is that this is not at the beginning of Johnson's experiences, but somewhere in the middle.

In the first story "End of the World," Johnson thwarts nuclear war. A crisis is building as Soviet forces push into Afghanistan, prompting the U.S. military to go on high alert. Johnson leaves his hotel and goes to the airport, apparently under intuition that there is where he needs to be. The airport is in chaos as people desperately book flights to get out of town "before the bombs fell." While those around him panic, Johnson calmly asks for the first available seat to New York. The nervous gate agent worries that "'an electromagnetic pulse ... could wipe out all the computer records in the country.'" Johnson remains calm and reassuring: "'You have to go on as if disaster weren't going to happen. That's our only chance of preventing it.'"[68] Johnson here channels Gunn's own measured rationality. Once in New York, Johnson makes contact with a female reporter, Frances Miller, a graduate of the University of Kansas, and tells her he has "visions of the future." In this case, Johnson sees "'explosions. Flames. People dying. All over the world. Some quickly, vaporized in a fraction of a second. Some lingeringly. A world dying. Everything: animals, plants. I see an Earth as sterile as Venus.'"[69] But Johnson assures her that though he sees this vision, the future isn't fixed; it can be guided toward a different, better outcome. Through Miller's contacts, Johnson seeks out a computer hacker named Logan, who he enlists to hack the pentagon computer and its Soviet equivalent; the idea being that breaking the veil of secrecy will cause both sides to stand down. Admittedly, the solution is a bit hokey, but framed as it is as a one-hour television episode, it works. It also serves as an interesting anticipation of the issues we now face regarding computer security.

"Child of the Sun" involves an energy crisis, with chronic brownouts and gas shortages, which has resulted in a global economic recession much larger than that experienced in 2008. This global crisis parallels a personal family crisis that Johnson must resolve. Shelly, the four-year-old daughter of Ellen McCleary, the "managing engineer of the Death Valley Solar Power Project," has been abducted, throwing McCleary's life in turmoil. Johnson presents himself to McCleary and tells her he can help find her daughter. Shelly will make a vital difference in the world by perfecting thermonuclear energy, if she is allowed to survive. As Johnson assures McCleary, "'First of all, she is an important person. Not just to you, overriding as that may be at the moment. Not just because she is a person in a society that values every individual. But because of her potential.'"[70] The energy crisis is entangled with environmental crisis; fossil fuels and pollutions are inevitably twin crises. Unless a viable alternative is supported, civilization will collapse. At first, McCleary is suspicious of Johnson's motives, and police take him into custody, but she relents before he is taken away, having an intuition that his offer to help is legit. The real culprit is McCleary's estranged husband, an itinerant Hollywood actor resentful of his wife's career. Gunn gets into issues of gender politics in the 1970s here: "'He was a bit of a lot of things—a bit of a painter, a bit of a writer, a bit of an actor, but a romantic all the time. What really broke things up, though, was when this project got started and I was selected as director. I was in charge and he was just—around. He had nothing to do, and conditions were pretty primitive for awhile.'"[71] Johnson traces her ex, Steve Webster, to Santa Catalina Island and tries to talk him into letting the child go. Meanwhile, Ellen McCleary has followed him to the island, and as Webster threatens to kill the girl and himself, she talks him into allowing Shelly to go safely with Johnson as they sort out his grievance against her. A shot rings out: Webster has taken his own life. Ellen McCleary can continue to make efforts to change the energy paradigm and Shelly can grow up to transform the world. What makes the story relevant is Gunn's engagement with ways to move forward in energy development and policy.

"Man of the Hour" entangles Johnson with King Enterprises, one of the few companies thriving during the economic crisis. In a hiring line, Johnson meets a man named Robert Scott, a former political science professor, who explains how King is buying up struggling industries and putting people to work. In this story Gunn takes on the question whether an economy should be stimulated by a self-interested oligarch or by a government by and for the people. Although Scott is okay with King buying up most of America, if that's his only motive, he worries there is more to it than that. Once interviewed, Johnson is given a round of employment tests and is offered a "'special position that we've been asked to fill.'"[72] In keeping with his ability to connect, Johnson is sent to the King mansion to become King's personal assistant. King has ambitions to become the President of the United States, not unlike another of his ilk with similar ambitions as this book is being written, though he pretends he has no interest in the office. In truth, he has an arsenal of assault weaponry, waiting to declare martial law in Los Angeles. When Scott and Johnson uncover the cache, Scott declares, "'I don't know what the future holds, but I do know this: King isn't what he seems. He's rising to power as a man of vision, a philanthropist who cares more about his fellow man than mere worldly possessions, a kindly man who is at the same time a superb executive—exactly what anyone would want for President. But look at this! That's not what a philanthropist keeps in his cellar.'"[73] While Scott wishes to expose King, Johnson believes that King must reveal himself; that is the only way he can be stopped. When King makes a broadcasted speech, in a scene straight out of Elia Kazan's *A Face in the Crowd*, Johnson leaves the camera and sound turned on at the end of the announcement, catching King's fatal gaffe, "If they believed that, they'd believe anything," thus ending his political ambitions.[74] If only it were still that simple.

In "Touch of the Match," Johnson awakes in King's house, having no recollection of previous events. At LAX, he books a flight to Washington where he sits next to a woman who is afraid of flying due to an upsurge in terrorism. As if on cue, a young Arabic man announces he has a bomb and demands the plane fly to Tehran. He is a Palestinian named Mohammed who "had grown up in the squalor of Lebanese camps."[75] Wanting to support his sister in Lebanon, Mohammed was recruited by a terrorist organization. Johnson uses his connective ability to talk Mohammed down; of course, he doesn't have a bomb, and calm settles. Crisis averted. What Gunn doesn't anticipate is the heightened security we now accept as status quo making the scenario he presents here too simple; it's unlikely that passengers and crew would so readily allow the would-be terrorist to return to his seat and quietly talk with Johnson. But as they approach Washington, the plane goes into a holding pattern because the space shuttle has been diverted to Dulles due to a storm at Cape Canaveral. Once landed, the passengers are put on several buses to ferry them to the terminal, but "the terror began again" when they are taken hostage by terrorists wanting to take a hostage from the space shuttle. Coincidentally, one of the terrorists is Mohammed's sister Fatima. Their target is Henry Chrisman, a NASA scientist who has invented a technology that neutralizes bombs, which will solve the terrorist problem. The fact the shuttle was targeted was also merely coincidence. As Chrisman points out, "'It must have been a great stroke of luck, picking me off like that. They must have had their people planted at Dulles waiting for a target of opportunity, and I fell into their hands.'"[76] These coincidences are a little heavy-handed, but work within the context of the original television series idea.

The solution that Gunn offers for these problems is space habitats, a utopian idea championed by physicist Gerard O'Neill and dramatized by George Zebrowski in the SF novel *Macrolife*, which, though a noble proposal, seems too unlikely in this case. Johnson argues, rationally, that the issue is about land, living space. But it is more than that—and it is not driven by rationality, but by irrational ideology. Chrisman remarks, "'Humanity's future lies in space. It doesn't matter who goes first. It's all of us. Right now there aren't enough people who can see this clearly enough to finance it. But maybe we can get enough support by making it serve two purposes: we'll solve the terrorist problem and get the space habitats started at the same time.'"[77] Chrisman further makes the case that freedom is to be found in space: "'Let anybody who wants a habitat have one if they can afford it or the funds can be raised somewhere. People will be too busy in space making things work to worry about old antagonisms.'"[78] The optimism here is palpable, and matches Gunn's prior optimistic expressions in *Station in Space* and *The Listeners,* and evokes the frontier ideal of the Venus colonists in *The Joy Makers*, but ultimately fails to take in the reality that human beings are largely irrational creatures. Only a tiny minority in human history has acted in the staid, rational fashion that Gunn hopes for here. Nevertheless, optimistic science fiction sets out to point a way, posit an alternative, not affirm the apparent negatives and human folly.

"Woman of the Year" involves Sally Franklin, an advocate for the homeless and destitute on the streets of Washington, working for People, Limited, an organization promoting population control, recalling Edith Keeler from *Star Trek*'s "The City on the Edge of Forever." Johnson sets himself up as Franklin's protector. The main issue that Gunn explores in the story is the question of overpopulation. Franklin is an advocate for birth control and foresees a future in which the planet can no longer sustain an unchecked human population. On the day she meets Johnson, Franklin holds a news conference in which she lays out the problem to the public. After the news conference, Johnson implores her to be careful, that she's now a target, but she leaves him in a huff. At which point she is accosted in a dark alley by a young man named Tommy, a youth she's tried to help, who intends to assault her. Once again, it is Johnson's role to mitigate this crisis. Sally Franklin's advocacy role is too important to lose. Johnson suggests ways which disaffected kids like Tommy can find new purpose. Crisis averted, Johnson realizes that he will again forget. He leaves Miss Franklin letting her know that he could have loved her. Again, the melodrama is a bit heavy-handed, but the pacing of Johnson's character development is right for a television series.

The final story, "Will-of-the-Wisp," is more of the same, tackling the problem of pollution. But Gunn also begins a further development of Johnson's character, by having Johnson befriend a former physician now joyfully living on the streets, who sends him to a psychiatrist named Roggero for help, as Johnson is struggling with the blank-slate nature of his existence. As his personal crisis unfolds, Johnson also doubts his own sanity and wants to be cured. As the story progresses, Johnson encounters the reporter from the first story, Frances Miller, who is now managing editor of the Associated Press, to bring things full circle. This encounter ultimately resolves Johnson's mental crisis as it provides evidence of his past, of his mission, and of his purpose, and he therefore accepts a new resolve. There's a nice closing arc that suggests an evolution of Johnson's character as through therapy he is able to recover some of his lost memories. This provides a forward movement from which a television series (or series of SF stories) could extend.

The *Crisis!* stories' significance lies in the engagement with the problems Gunn presents despite the character and narrative limitations placed upon them by the TV episode formula. The melodrama is merely a vehicle by which to get the reader to think about these pressing issues. Brought together in book form, where the conceptual flaws seem more glaring, the stories are less effective than they were during their original magazine publication. Whereas Gunn's other story-sequence novels seamlessly blend into a cohesive whole, *Crisis!* doesn't. This is mostly a result of being structured by the stylistic constraints of the (then) television format. Nevertheless, the stories do have an odd appeal, perhaps *because of* those very television narrative formulas.

Five

The Joy Machine to the *Transcendental* Trilogy

Although Gunn's non-series short stories were infrequent since the 1950s magazine era, after his retirement in 1993 he did produce some standalone short stories that are worth mentioning here before discussing his novels from recent decades, because they tie in to his experiences teaching SF. All of these stories appear in the collection *Human Voices*. Of interest are "The Futurist" (*Amazing* 1993) which meditates on the legacy of H.G. Wells. A giant sphinx, like that in *The Time Machine*, "materializes" in front of the UN building in New York. Out of it comes a time traveler who discourses on the failings of our times. The time traveler praises the SF writers of our era: "'They talked about shaping the future through a developing system by which thoughtful people could explore possible futures, then choose among them by making the right decisions.'"[1] As in *The Listeners*, knowledge from elsewhere (the future in this case) leads to rational discourse and a utopian future. "The Lens of Time" (*Analog* 1995) is an homage to Fitz-James O'Brien's nineteenth-century classic "The Diamond Lens," which Gunn had selected for *The Road to Science Fiction*. Gunn explains the conception of the story: "At first I was going to write a time-travel story about someone who goes back to give Fitz-James O'Brien the idea for his story 'The Diamond Lens.' As I got into it I decided to make it a story about the doctor who advised O'Brien about the new discoveries in microbiology revealed by the microscope. He would try to convince O'Brien that he should use his literary skills to help move the public toward greater belief in science and rationality that might ease the tensions that resulted in the Civil War that was soon to begin (in which O'Brien would volunteer and die a year later). But all O'Brien can think about is the story he is going to write."[2] In "The Day the Magic Came Back" (*Science Fiction Age* 1996), Gunn voices concern about the reemergence of magical thinking and the apparent decline of rationality in modern society, seen in the boom in fantasy fiction at the expense of SF. As Gunn explains, "I thought nostalgia about magic was misplaced and that magic, if it returned in the way of magical thinking (curing people by mental intervention, for instance), was not only fundamentally unfair but would damage the scientific method from which the modern world had achieved democracy, individual opportunity, and choice."[3] In this regard, the story registers with the concerns Gunn presented in *The Burning*.

The Joy Machine

Gunn also wrote a *Star Trek* novel at this time. *The Joy Machine* developed from an idea by Theodore Sturgeon. Sturgeon's original seventeen-page proposal followed up on some of the themes he'd explored in "Shore Leave," one of the two episodes Sturgeon wrote for the series. Sturgeon's idea coalesces with themes Gunn had explored in *The Joy Makers* and *The Dreamers*. John Ordover, a former student and then editor of the Star Trek novels approached Gunn about writing a novel based on Sturgeon's material. Gunn was reluctant at first, having turned down TV and film novelizations before, but Ordover persisted, and finally Gunn was persuaded, feeling it was a way he could honor Sturgeon's memory. Here Gunn comes full circle with a posthumous collaboration with Sturgeon, who, as we have seen, served as hidden collaborator for Gunn's first major work, "Breaking Point."

The Joy Machine follows the typical formula of a Star Trek adventure. By necessity, Gunn had to follow the strictures of the Star Trek canon as regulated by Paramount Pictures, and he nevertheless effectively captures the protocols expected in the *Star Trek* universe and smoothly adheres to the familiar characteristics of the major characters, Kirk, Spock, McCoy, Uhura, and Scott. At the same time, having a master Golden Age SF writer and SF historian/scholar pen a Star Trek novel affirms the degree to which Star Trek flows smoothly from the ideas, aesthetic, and attitude of modern SF. As the novel opens, the Enterprise orbits the planet Timshel, described as "what the mother planet Earth had once aspired to be, the Garden of Eden before the Fall." Timshel does not allow the crew of the Enterprise to beam down or citizens to leave, and since this is "a vacation planet," Captain James Kirk suspects "something is very wrong." Kirk has been to Timshel twice before and, typically, he has good friends amongst its citizens. One of the nice touches drawing from his university experience is that Gunn sets Timshel up as a planet not unlike a university town: "Timshel City was like a vast university dedicated entirely to learning and self-fulfillment, to discovering how the universe had started and how it had developed and how it operated, and the part sentient life played in it, and how people should think and feel and behave in the light of such knowledge." The only thing Kirk and crew know about what is happening on Timshel is that all adults are "wearing a wide bracelet with a large, artificial ruby in the middle."[4] This isn't the first time the crew of the Enterprise has faced some sort of mind-control mechanism, nor the first time Gunn has employed such a device, as seen with the bracelets in "The Immortals" and the Neo-Scientists' collars in *The Burning*.

Kirk beams down into the garden of the Federation envoy Marouk and his family. Marouk's teenage daughter Dannie gleefully informs Kirk she's just received a "payday." A payday is a dose of bliss from the Joy Machine, a variation of the rewards offered citizens in the middle section of *The Joy Makers*. As Dannie's younger sister Tandy explains: "'Doesn't she look happy? She'll wake up in the morning feeling rested and happy as if she's had the best night's sleep ever and a beautiful, beautiful dream. I can hardly wait until I'm sixteen. Then I can get a job and a bracelet and a payday.'" The Joy Machine, a computer array in the manner of Hedon, was created by a Timshel philosopher named Emanuel De Kreef who argued that "life on Timshel was too easy and that this hedonistic existence was certain to rot people's moral fiber." De Kreef's creed made joy "available, but you have to earn it." The result is a citizenry who have reduced meaning to receiving the payday of joy, hence rendering work, thought, and activity meaningless beyond the mere desire for a payday. Of course, Jim Kirk is the only one that can get them out of this dilemma: "'We're in a bad situation, Jim. And you're the only one who can help us.'"[5]

Later in the novel, Kirk is brought before a small computer terminal on the fifth floor of a building, a scene recapitulating D'glas's interview with Hedon in *The Joy Makers*. The Joy Machine offers its services to Kirk: "'You must become a citizen by accepting a working bracelet. You will be entitled to one free payday as your reward for becoming a citizen. After that you will work at the job assigned you and receive your payday according to the rate of pay established for that task.'"[6] As expected, Kirk refuses and then seeks audience with De Kreef in the building that had formerly been known as "the Museum of Humanity."[7] The exhibits have been removed and in their place are factory assembly lines where citizens can do meaningless work so as to receive paydays, churning out bracelets for those not yet indoctrinated. The paydays are administered by an official named the Paymaster; the Paymaster never receives a payday. Not surprisingly, the paymaster is Marouk.

Kirk is then taken into custody. Gunn makes a delightful overture to science fiction as Kirk awaits his fate: "He had scanned the disk library, but none of them concerned Timshel history or the Revolution or the design of such equipment as he had seen on the assembly line. Mostly they were historical novels, science-fiction titles whose anticipations of the future had come to pass. Not in the same way, of course, but it was true, as someone had once said, that people in the twenty-third century were living in a science-fiction world, a world in which science fiction had been an essential precondition, an imagining of what might be so that humanity's dreams could be realized. First must come the dreams, then the realization."[8] Perceptive readers might recognize this as a recasting of John W. Campbell's decree that he wanted stories for *Astounding* that could be published in a magazine of the twenty-fifth century. And this also conveys essential elements of Gunn's philosophy of science fiction.

Following events above on the Enterprise, intrepid Mr. Spock determines that Kirk is in need of assistance, so he, McCoy and Uhura beam down to the surface. Marouk stuns Kirk and puts an activated bracelet on his wrist, thereby forcing him to accept the bliss of payday, and eventually Spock, McCoy, and Uhura are all fitted with bracelets too. Like the Mnemonist in *The Dreamers*, Marouk is hoping for a replacement so that he "too, could enter paradise" and his designs are that Kirk or Spock will take his place. As usual, to threaten Kirk, one must also threaten his ship: "'The Joy Machine has perfected a giant payday projector that can envelope a ship the size of the Enterprise. If you refuse to cooperate, the projector will begin bombarding the Enterprise with its waves of ecstasy.'"[9]

The trope of an underground movement appears when Kirk is kidnapped by the resistance that plans to destroy the Joy Machine. To do so, they will code a computer virus into the genetic material of an influenza virus and inject that into a volunteer. When that person goes for a payday through the computer jack, the influenza virus will pass into the Joy Machine taking the virus in with it. Kirk, of course, volunteers. This needs to be done immediately as the Joy Machine has nearly perfected the wireless projection (wireless connection capability had not yet become ubiquitous when Gunn wrote the novel) which will make the need for direct interface unnecessary. The Joy Machine's ecstasy programming is compared to a computer virus itself, which could rapidly spread across the galaxy. Here's an echo of how Hedonics, Inc. rapidly took over Millville and the threat Hedon later posed to the Venus colony. Kirk extrapolates the consequences: "As soon as it learned about the existence of other worlds from the records available to it and the attempts by the outside world to communicate and the arrival of ships that were turned away, it would realize that it had a vast galaxy to which it could now carry its message of paradise. And it would learn about the countless billions of people on those other worlds who lived lives of quiet desperation, to whom it could bring comfort and pleasure—and the death of everything else."[10] When Kirk tries to contact the Enterprise, the first inklings that the Enterprise computer has already been compromised manifests itself, and Mr. Scott fights to keep the Enterprise running while the computer goes haywire.

The virus partially works. In order to fend off the attack, the Joy Machine moves its central locus into another space. But, in the end, it is the Enterprise's computer which matches logical circuits with the Joy Machine and is able to break its hold on the *Enterprise* and the people of Timshel. Star Trek fans will appreciate the computer's assertion "'I am a member of this crew, and I was well aware of our mission objectives.'" It's apparently Asimov's Three Laws of Robotics that kept the computer from falling to the Joy Machine's programming. Indeed, Gunn pays homage to his colleague Asimov: "'The computer's Asimov compensators may need adjusting.'" The Joy Machine, for its part, leaves "'the system, and is on its way out of the galaxy,'" and, as Spock reasons, "'apparently it has exiled itself to a place where no one can be tempted to make use of it.'"[11] Let's hope it doesn't encounter the Borg.

Ordinarily, such series novels are of little interest to scholars because of their formulaic limitations (though they can be entertaining), but *Star Trek* is such a transcendent series, that when a writer of Gunn's credentials dips into the *Star Trek* universe, readers should take notice. The fact that this particular work develops from the Sturgeon and Gunn background is both fascinating and illustrative of the ways that core science fiction ideas worked their way into the series.

The Millennium Blues

The Millennium Blues is an unusual novel in Gunn's oeuvre. Gunn first conceived of the idea in the late 1960s, around the time he was writing *The Listeners* and the early portions of *Kampus* and *The Dreamers*, but it took another ten years before he got working on it. He wrote the final chapter "The End-of-the-World Ball" in the late eighties and it was published in 1989 in George Zebrowksi's *Synergy* anthology series. Busy with his academic work, Gunn slowly worked on the novel throughout the 1990s. By the time he'd completed it, he had a hard time finding an interested publisher, and the novel languished in limbo for a few more years. When Gunn finally did get it published by an e-book publisher, E-Reads, the historical context that the novel hinges on had changed, and what had first been intended as a near-future science fiction novel was, by necessity, now a contemporary novel (and would soon pass into the historical). Gunn did manage to get Easton Press to publish a limited signed leather-bound edition as well. Gunn considers *The Millennium Blues* his attempt at a mainstream literary novel. It says something about the nature of the publishing industry that this fascinating novel by a major science fiction writer was not picked up by a mainstream imprint, because it is a particularly astute analysis of American society at the turn of the millennium. Gunn still brought a science fiction sensibility to the problems of the day and in hindsight his observations on millennialism in the 1990s were spot on in many instances.

The novel follows six characters through the course of the year 2000, all invitees to the End-of-the-World Ball in New York on December 31, 2000. The first six chapters introduce each of the six characters and take place a month apart during the first six months of the year, the first chapter beginning on January 1 through to chapter six on June 3. The second chapter involving each individual character (chapters 7–12) take place at the pace of two a month, and this sequence is repeated for the third set (chapters 13–18). Chapter 19, the original "The End-of-the-World Ball" story, brings all six characters together at the event held at the top of the World Trade Center in New York on New Year's Eve.

The six characters are William Landis, a writer preparing a book "about the year 2000 and how people had survived it, staggering from crisis to crisis, until they toppled, almost in spite of themselves, into the third millennium"[12]; Paul Gentry, a futurist who makes his living by paid speeches where he shows all the possible catastrophes facing humanity; Elois Hays, a Broadway actress involved in a production of a play depicting a new ice age entitled *The North Wind*; Sally Krebs, a CNN reporter covering various flashpoints throughout the world; Murray Smith-Ng, a mathematics professor teaching a graduate seminar on applied catastrophe theory; and Barbara Shepherd, a former Olympic gymnast, intellectual prodigy, failed actress, and New York party girl.

The first chapter begins on January 1, 2000, as William Landis receives an invitation to a conference hosted by the "Twenty-First Corporation" on the topic of what lies ahead in the twenty-first century to be held at the World Trade Center on December 28–31, "concluding from 8 p.m. to midnight on New Millennia's Eve with The-End-of-the-World-Ball."[13] There are echoes of Gunn's *Man and the Future* conference held at KU in 1966. The invitation inspires Landis to spend the year writing a book on the current state of world affairs and how people are reacting to the turn of the millennium. He's also received an invitation from NASA to join a committee "to study the affects of religious fundamentalism on the space program,"[14] an idea that registers with *The Listeners*. This invitation reminds Landis of Isaac Asimov's early story "Trends," which imagined a similar scenario. On July 4, Landis is on the space shuttle as it reenters Earth atmosphere. As part of the NASA initiative, they've asked him to accompany Barry Risebad, an evangelical TV preacher with wide influence, on a civilian shuttle mission, in hopes to convince the preacher of the value of space. The disputations between Landis and Risebad while on the flight recapitulate in a slightly different register the dialogue between MacDonald and Jeremiah Jones in *The Listeners*. In October, Landis attends a "fortuneteller's performance" with his girlfriend Carrie, whom he met following the space shuttle flight. A skeptical Landis asks "Dame Nostra," if she can predict the date of his death—this appears to be a reference to Heinlein's first story "Life-Line," published in *Astounding* in 1939, a month after Asimov's "Trends"—to which she prognosticates December 31, 2000, a few months away.

Paul Gentry is the subject of chapter two. Gentry enthralls his audience with well-rendered accounts of the possible cosmic dooms facing humanity: supernovas, black holes, cosmic radiation, comets, solar shifts, even aliens. This is followed by a long discourse on overpopulation which will result in environmental degradation. At the end of his gloomy talk, Gentry offers a path toward solution: we must "'change the way people lived and thought.'" We cannot escape "'the unavoidable logic of catastrophe.'" Though the cynical Gentry believes that's highly unlikely: "'I say that we will all die because I do not believe in the basic rationality or even the basic good will of the human species. I do not believe that people can change. I do not believe that they will change, even under the threat of imminent destruction if they do not.'"[15] Here's a different vibe from the Bill Johnson *Crisis!* stories. Incidentally, Gunn's original title for *The Millennium Blues* was *Catastrophe!* Nonetheless, there are things that can be done to reduce the individual impact on the environment. Gentry is also an unabashed philanderer, who, aside from the significant paycheck he receives for such talks, looks forward to taking attractive young women back to his hotel room. Later in the year, following a meeting of the "Committee on the Environment" in San Francisco, Gentry is caught in bed with a woman by her armed husband. Rather than take revenge, the man asks Gentry about his ideas about catastrophe, when Gentry explains that, yes, catastrophe is highly likely, the man blows his own brains out. When Gunn returns to Gentry in October, in what is the most poignant chapter in the book, Gentry is at the bedside of his wife, dying of cancer in a hospital room. Reports from CNN announce "what appears to be a supernova in the Canis Major constellation," which could spell doom for Earth, and as Gentry comforts a nurse named Sharon, his wife's eyes open.[16] A flashback takes Gentry to earlier in the day while he is giving a talk to a New Age group in Colorado, where he receives the call of his wife's critical condition. Gentry struggles with his own existential doubts and his chronic philandering. As his wife Angel awakens for the final time she tells him, "'I—know. It's—all—right. I've—always—known.'" As the life fades out of her, CNN retracts the earlier announcement that Sirius had gone supernova, and "'regrets any alarm that its announcement may have cause.'" Gentry reflects on his regret for his behavior, but allows Sharon to take him to her apartment where she "comforted him far into the night."[17]

As if playing out Gentry's prognostications of doom on stage, Elois Hays, a successful middle-aged Broadway actress, is going through rehearsals for a new play called *The North Wind*, which involves "four doomed characters" on the cusp of a new ice age. Like Gentry, her husband George, the play's producer, is a philanderer, and Elois is irritated by his fawning over the young ingénue Susan. The rehearsals are a disaster and Elois is on the verge of walking out. Instead, she has dinner with the young playwright, Fred Hampdon, and tells him how he can rewrite the drama to make it work. When she returns to the theatre, she catches George and Susan in flagrante. By August, the rewritten *The North Wind* is a surprising success, capturing the mood of the times. During the cast party at George and Elois's apartment, Elois wanders into Central Park where she encounters a group of "middle-age crazies," part of a strange phenomenon occurring where otherwise mild-mannered people inexplicably leave their homes in trance-like states and silently join others so compelled in public spaces. She decides to go to Fred Hampdon's hotel room and follow through on a longing desire she's held for the man since they talked about rewriting the play. But Hampdon has already hooked up—with George. When we return to Elois in November she's set to do an interview on the "Jerry Minton Show." Elois wants to talk about the vital issues facing the next century, but Minton is only interested in the scandal of her marriage.

FIVE. The Joy Machine *to the* Transcendental *Trilogy*   233

In April, Sally Krebs, the CNN reporter, is covering sectarian strife in the Middle East. Here Gunn anticipates aspects of the conflicts that are defining the twenty-first century and refers to it as a "fifty-year war."[18] Gunn imagines the following: "Tribalism, once stifled by nationalism and police power, reemerged throughout the Middle East and Africa, and inevitably the entire Middle East exploded, while Europe looked the other way and the United States, disillusioned, brought all of its forces except the news agencies back to the North American continent and began pursuing a policy of energy conservation and alternative sources."[19] August finds Krebs in Siberia, after covering a global summit meeting in Moscow, investigating an apparent spaceship siting in a remote village in the Tunguska region, where an unexplained explosion occurred in 1908. What she finds is a constructed effigy made by the villagers, a cargo cult of sorts. Similar constructions have sprung up in other remote areas throughout the world. While she's there, disaster has struck at the summit: the Russian president has been assassinated and "a new hard-line government has taken over"; a world political crisis is unfolding.[20] Later, Krebs is in Rio de Janeiro gazing at the giant statue of Christ the Redeemer. On the flight from Miami, Krebs witnesses the devastation deforestation is having on the Amazon basin; this may be the biggest of all catastrophes facing the twenty-first century. Krebs is met at the airport by a Bolivian man named Raul, who takes her on a tour of the city, both the wealthy districts and the favelas of the poor. Raul is a revolutionary, a member of a guerrilla group called "the Dark Road," and that night they blowup Christ the Redeemer: "For a moment the figure climbed before it pitched forward slowly, and, like Icarus shedding his feathers, crumbled to the ground in fragments beyond their line of vision."[21] This image foreshadows the capstone at the End-of-the-World Ball.

May finds mathematics professor Murray Smith-Ng meeting his graduate seminar students in the "Beer Cellar," a "smoke-filled student hangout" in a typical end of the semester soiree. The focus of his seminar has been on "the practical applications of catastrophe theory."[22] As the beer clouds his mind, Smith-Ng entertains fantasies of his two female students, the slender Calley and the buxom Lisa, fantasies he'd indulged throughout the semester; meanwhile, a male student named Lyle makes his own overtures to the professor. Smith-Ng predicts that the chances for catastrophe increase as the year moves forward to the millennium. When he returns home, personal catastrophe strikes: his wife has left a note saying she's leaving him; a friend had seen him in the Beer Cellar with the students, and she knows he's been fantasizing over the young women all semester.

In August, Smith-Ng is in Hawaii investigating a volcano that is about to blow. His calculations have led him to the conclusion that eruptions and earthquakes will trigger around the Pacific Ring of Fire. He'd spent the last few months having affairs with Calley and then Lisa, and is now deeply embarrassed by the flings. In early December, Smith-Ng is abducted off the street in San Francisco by a group of survivalists, awaiting Armageddon, who want to "retain [his] services as a catastrophe theorist."[23]

The character circuit culminates with Barbara Shepherd. On June 3 she finds herself at a decadent Manhattan party, where guests frolic naked and hook up randomly. After a number of early life successes, Barbara has slipped into a life of sex, drugs, and fringe celebrity. She is a lost soul, bored and vaguely suicidal. While having sex with a man she met at the party, Barbara has a revelation "'a slash of light—of enlightenment, like Saul on the road to Damascus. Everything became clear for an instant, but now I've lost it.'"[24] This leads Barbara to seek that sensation again, and she casts off her life of decadence. By late September, Barbara has joined a religious commune on the west coast, headed by a prophet named Isaiah, a man who summons his all-female band of disciples "to the service of God," by having them service Isaiah, a setup reminiscent of Pa and his daughters in *Kampus*. Barbara discovered Isaiah through his television broadcasts where he exhorts "sinners about the end of this world."[25] To join the commune, she gave up all her substantial material possessions, recalling the requirements of Hedonics, Inc. With wrists "bound to the handle of a pitchfork whose tines had been driven deep into the dirt floor of the horse stall," Barbara is about to be initiated. In a frenzy talking to "God," Isaiah beats her with a horsewhip and the inner voice tells him "'she is too foul to use as a woman is used.'" At this point, Barbara has had enough, "she would not be buggered for God!" and she uses her athleticism to fend off his attack: "she concentrated all her strength on the task at hand, as she had in the Olympic competition, pulled the pitchfork from the ground, and raised it just as Isaiah arrived."[26] Barbara becomes the cult's leader and transforms it into a feminist utopia. On Christmas day, Shepherd turns the flock over to a woman named Janet and departs for New York and the Twenty-First Century Conference, where she'll make a very public expression of her revelation.

The final chapter brings all these disparate characters together at the End-of-the-World Ball atop the World Trade Center on New Year's Eve. William Landis meets Elois Hays and exchanges pleasantries; Paul Gentry chats with Sally Krebs; Murray Smith-Ng encounters his former student Lyle, and while they discuss catastrophe theory, Landis and Hays join in.

At 10:30 p.m., Barbara Shepherd, "draped in white linen" speaks before "a gathering of true believers on the roof top of the skyscraper."[27] The celebrations continue until the appointed hour. Rumors are heard that something is going on on the rooftop and along with most of the other revelers, the main characters make their way to the roof. As the hour ticks down to midnight, Barbara Shepherd makes her final attempt at transcendence: "Barbara Shepherd turned and ran toward the back of the platform like the acrobat she once had been. As she reached the middle, she did a flip backward, landed on her feet, and flipped again. The second took her off the end of the platform. For an instant she seemed to disappear from view. Then her figure reappeared, propelled upward with surprising speed, head high and facing the audience with the composed features and confidence of a saint, rising, rising, clearing the railing that surrounded the roof top and floating free in the air beyond it. Her gown fluttered, her arms reached out and, like wings, seemed to support her body in the crystalline air, even to lift it toward the heaven she addressed."[28] At first this appears as if Gunn is dabbling in magical realism: the image of Barbara Shepherd floating above the Towers seems straight out of Gábriel García Marquez or Salman Rushdie. But Gunn is a scientific realist and Shepherd has merely leaped over the railing like an Olympian gymnast on the vault. At the stroke of midnight, "the figure of Barbara Shepherd faltered in the air before it fell, with growing velocity, glittering, through the night."[29] In the tradition of literary fiction, Gunn ends the novel on this sensational bit of irony.

The Millennium Blues is a novel with a great deal of interest, and now can be read as a reflection on the beginnings of the twenty-first century. Gunn worked on the novel for many years, trying to develop the characters perfectly. Here he succeeds. It is a fine attempt at literary fiction and deserves a wider readership.

Gift from the Stars

Gift from the Stars is Gunn's final story-sequence novel; his latest *Transcendental* trilogy goes back to the single-narrative space opera where Gunn started his novel writing career. The novel consists of six stories (the last two were published together in magazine form) that appeared in *Analog* beginning in September 1999 and concluding in the January/February 2005 issue. In an introduction by Gregory Benford, Benford makes a comparison between Gunn's method of story sequence and A. E. Van Vogt's, noting that "in Van Vogt this process led to gathering incoherence.

In Gunn, to expansive vistas."³⁰ *Gift from the Stars* is a novel that is in dialogue with *The Listeners* and with Carl Sagan's bestseller *Contact*. According to Gunn, Sagan had been sent galleys of *The Listeners* before publication and gave the book an approving blurb: "One of the very best fictional portrayals of contact with extra-terrestrial intelligence ever written."³¹ When Sagan became internationally famous for his *Cosmos* television series, he signed a seven-figure contract to write a science fiction novel. *Contact* was published in 1985 and later filmed in 1997. *Contact* itself was in dialogue with *The Listeners* and like Gunn's novel, Sagan created a realistic portrayal of scientists at work. When Gunn saw the film version, he had a mixed response. Although he enjoyed the film, he thought it had romanticized Sagan's portrayal of the scientists and, at the same time, he felt Sagan's method and purpose of the space journey too fantastical, both in the novel and in the film. In any case, the film inspired Gunn to re-examine the idea of first contact.

The novel is structured along the lines of a conspiracy theory. Reflecting back on Gunn's prior work, conspiracy is at the heart of much of it. Here, Gunn follows the pattern of the conspiracy theories harbored by UFO enthusiasts. In part one, "The Giftie," Adrian Mast, an aerospace engineer, is browsing in a used bookstore he frequents, where he finds a book titled *Gift from the Stars* in the Cults/New Age/UFO remainder section. Gunn emphasizes that Mast makes this discovery by accident. In other words, great discoveries often occur in the slippage between active searching and synchronicity. Flipping through the book, Mast becomes intrigued by an appendix filled with diagrams "for some kind of ship." Mast recognizes these as sophisticated and accurate "engineering drawings," not crude drawings from some amateur UFO enthusiast. Mast feels an aura of synchronicity that the book was in some way waiting for him to find it, that the author "wanted to hide a message that would be found only by someone capable of noticing and understanding it." Scrutinizing the designs more carefully, Mast realizes that they are "working designs, not concepts, and even, somehow, as if they were antiquated, like museum pieces or redesigns of historic airships such as the Wright brothers' first craft. It would work, all right, probably better than the original, but it hinted at the existence of methods far more effective." When Mast and Mrs. Farmstead, the bookstore owner, try to track down the author of the book, they run into a number of roadblocks. When they call the publisher, Joel Simpson, he insists he never published such a book. Mast and Mrs. Farmstead conclude it must have been deliberately suppressed. As if to confirm their fears, the bookstore is burnt down later that night.³²

FIVE. *The Joy Machine to the Transcendental Trilogy* 237

Mast and Mrs. Farmstead embark on a road trip to find the author. The first step is to track down Simpson at his home in northern Arizona. After Simpson catches them riffling through files in his garage, quick thinking Mrs. Farmstead fools him into believing they're agents sent to check up on him, and he tells them that the book's author, Peter Cavendish, is in a mental hospital in Topeka, Kansas—the famed Menninger Clinic, which, alas, left Topeka for Houston in 2003. At the clinic they ask Cavendish about the book; apparently, the ship designs were picked up by SETI in a transmission not unlike the message in *The Listeners*. In broken thoughts, Cavendish explains: "'Cosmic rays. Energetic stuff. Too energetic to be natural, the physicists told me. Figure it out, it makes a picture. Right? You've got to decipher the code. But they make it easy. They want you to figure it out.'"[33] Cavendish's attending psychiatrist ends the interview and dissuades the pair from pursuing things any further; that the book is merely a product of Cavendish's schizophrenic delusions. But as they prepare to leave, an orderly who's been tasked with letting "'them know if anybody came around asking about Mr. Cavendish'" tells them to follow him to "'Forbes Field, where a man has just arrived in an Air Force jet,'" and is waiting to speak with them. The man is William Makepeace, consultant "in charge of the Cavendish affair."[34] Makepeace's is to suppress Cavendish's discovery, as it would shake up the global world order. For one thing, the "antimatter collectors," à la Williamson's *Seetee Ship*, "would lead to the development of new energy systems," which would in turn lead to "cheap energy." Makepeace's deduction comes straight out of Asimov's robot story "Reason": "'Our experts predict that we could beam down energy from orbit at a fraction of the cost of current sources.'"[35] Anathema to the fossil fuel cartels. Mast and Mrs. Farmstead argue that this could usher forth a Golden Age and they want to reveal the secret. To which Makepeace threatens to discredit them, but suppression of information is no longer possible in the world of the internet. Remember Gunn was crafting these stories when the ubiquity of the internet was just starting to change everyone's lives. Mast and Farmstead have already released the details to the world.

The second chapter, "Pow'r," is set ten years later. Having developed the alien technologies, Earth now has cheap, ubiquitous power which has transformed the lives of all citizens of the globe, liberating people from the drudgery of everyday existence, and this has also shifted politics. The power has gone out of governments and is now concentrated in an international consortium called the Energy Board. Rejuvenation processes have been perfected and biogentic therapies have eradicated obesity and insanity. Life has, somewhat, settled into utopia, as it had in *The Listeners*, but this has also calcified into complacency. At the same time, violent crime and terrorism are actually on an upswing because people freed from drudgery may also be more prone to ideology. Another cost has been the space program: people are no longer interested in expanding into space. The frontier urge has diminished. Gunn is writing before the shuttles were officially mothballed.

As the story begins, Frances Farmstead is trying to track down Adrian Mast who has gone missing. Traveling to Mast's cabin in "rustic isolation," Farmstead entertains another conspiracy theory that he has been taken away: his morning coffee remains unfinished at the kitchen table. While Farmstead is investigating his computer, a young woman named Jessica Buhler appears, claiming to be Mast's girlfriend. In truth, she's an agent for Makepeace, who now represents the Energy Board. A mysterious fire burns Adrian's cabin to the ground as the two women escape, but not before Frances uncovers a clue that will take them to the abandoned Kennedy Space Center. Gunn describes the empty Space Center as "a junkyard that looked like an old Emshwiller painting."[36] There, they find Adrian and a crew of engineers building a spaceship prototype from the alien designs, joined by Cavendish, whose schizophrenia has been cured by biogenetics. Seeing the spaceship, Jessica Buhler has an epiphany, but she's already made the call to Makepeace, who sweeps in via covert helicopter. Makepeace arranges a video meeting between Mast and the Energy Board. In typical Gunn style, Mast penetrates to the heart of the problem: that people are making trouble because things are too easy. He convinces the Energy Board to allow them to build a full-size ship in Earth orbit, where those who long for the space frontier can pursue their dream. It's kind of a mix of Bill Johnson's intuitive reason, Amos Danton's heroic symbolism, and Robert MacDonald's quiet search for meaning.

"The Abyss" occurs five years later, as Mast, Farmstead, Buhler, Cavendish and two-hundred others construct the spaceship in Earth orbit, using the abandoned space station as a center for their operations, recalling imagery from *Station in Space*. Gunn pays homage to the genre and to the magazine where the story first appeared: "The ship looked as if it had been lifted from the cover of *Astounding Stories*, maybe the first installment of *The Skylark of Valeron*."[37] Little things have been going wrong as the construction nears its completion, and Frances Farmstead believes that someone is trying to sabotage the mission. She first suspects Jessica Buhler, which prompts Buhler to do a search of her own. Buhler finds someone's secret living quarters in an unused module of the station;

it turns out that module was only recently docked, apparently sent up to look like part of the original station. The saboteur is, in fact, Cavendish. But Cavendish is not really a saboteur; instead, he has programmed additional information from the alien message that will send the ship into deep space. When the ship departs, Cavendish and like-minded others stay behind, unable to face the terrors of the cave of night.

In the next story, "The Rabbit Hole," Mast and his crew find themselves trapped in a white hole. Gunn cleverly conveys the experience of time distortion; at one point, Mast is confronted by the crew's yet born children who present demands that they stop trying to get out of the white hole since their own existence would be annihilated, to which Mast retorts "'you're nothing but a pack of possibilities.'"[38] At another instance Mast meets another version of himself. They are surprised when Cavendish appears among them, as they thought he'd stayed behind in Earth orbit, but this Cavendish is merely a simulacrum programmed into the computer. They finally determine that the only answer to their problem is to exit from where they entered. An unhappy end to the mission. But when they exit the wormhole, they find themselves in another solar system: "if time was inverted, maybe space was too."[39]

In part five, "Uncreated Night," the ship finds itself among a Sargasso of ships orbiting a nondescript planet. Evidently, these are representatives from other advanced civilizations who received the same message. Some have been there for centuries or millennia. The story involves Mast and crew's attempt to make contact with the aliens who brought them there. Eventually, Adrian, Frances, and Jessica make their way onto the surface of the planet, where an entrance opens that allows them into a labyrinth of tunnels, recalling Pohl's *Gateway*. This leads them to a vast computer array at which point they realize that the planet is essentially a vast library. The Cavendish hologram appears and informs them that the aliens have linked with their ship's computer. He also informs them that the alien librarians are not the aliens they seek.

The final section, "Strange Shadows," begins where "Uncreated Night" left off. The alien library is uploading a vast quantity of information that can transform humankind into a galactic culture and further human evolution. However, this upload will take a significant amount of time and so they must decide if they will take as much information as they can get and depart or wait, what might take decades, for the entirety of information to be processed. There's a complication, though. The wormholes are collapsing, and so if they wait too long, their chance of returning to Earth may be lost. Meanwhile, the Cavendish simulacrum explains some of the background of the aliens. Here Gunn draws on a number of new ideas in theoretical physics. The aliens came from a planet similar to Earth some two billion years ago and contact with an extra-dimensional alien species from a dark matter galaxy that collided with the Milky Way, led to a new surge of evolutionary development. This "unseen hand" then moved the alien solar system to the center of the galaxy where they could serve as the fulcrum for further evolutionary development of species across the galaxy. The alien librarians are called the Enigmatics and they serve as intermediaries between the dark matter aliens, the Shadows, and the sentients of the Milky Way. The Enigmatics are dying out and the sentient species of the galaxy will be on their own. As the story concludes, the Cavendish hologram downloads itself into the Enigmatic library, hoping to become the new liaison between the Shadows and the species of our galaxy. After six months of data upload, "the *Ad Astra* broke loose from orbit and headed back toward the star-strewn galaxy to begin its long journey home."[40]

Gift from the Stars is a solid galactic adventure soundly based on current theory that sets out to blend Gunn's near-future approach with the possibilities of a breakthrough moment that transforms the human experience. It is in a different register than Gunn's most recent work, the *Trascendental* series, which is set much further along the timeline of the human future, but shows that Gunn in his later years is just as skilled at hard science space SF as he had been with social science fiction.

Transcendental, Transgalactic and *Transformation*

Gunn's most recent project is the *Transcendental* trilogy. So far, the first two books *Transcendental* and *Transgalactic* have been published. Gunn completed the final book, *Transformation*, as this study was being written, and generously offered me the opportunity to consider it here. The idea for *Transcendental* was inspired by Alexei and Cory Panshin's study of Golden Age science fiction *The World Beyond the Hill*. *Transcendental* was released to coincide with Gunn's Guest of Honor appearance at the 2013 World Science Fiction Convention in San Antonio. It was well-received. *Transgalactic* came out in March 2015, as this book was being drafted. *Transformation* will appear in the spring of 2017.

Transcendental is, in part, modeled on *The Canterbury Tales*. As the novel begins, a motley crew of space travelers are aboard the spaceship

Geoffrey on a quest to find the legendary Transcendental Machine. Gunn creates a cast of unusual alien characters, include a Dorian, an elephant-like being named Tordor; Xi, a treacherous weasel-like creature ; a flower-being from Mur; a birdlike Centauran whose species had committed genocide against the flower-beings; an eloquent Sirian whose planet is so hostile they've evolved in such a way that the father serves as host for parasitic newborns who eat their way out of the father's belly, a la Octavia Butler's "Bloodchild"; an A.I. shaped like a coffin; and a pair of asexual clones named Jon and Jan, whose story echoes Ursula K. Le Guin's "Nine Lives." But the central characters are a pair of humans named Riley and Asha. Riley is a veteran adventurer, a survivor of the wars. Asha is a former colonist from a generation starship who was taken captive by the galactics in the early stages of human expansion into space. In fact, humans have only been newly introduced into the galactic community, and their arrival has caused disruption to the relative peace and harmony that the other species of the galaxy had achieved after millennia of conflict in the past. Apparently, all of these beings have been brought together for the quest to find the Transcendental Machine.

The quest begins at the planet Terminal, a frontier planet. Riley is in the waiting room for the space elevator that will take the pilgrims up to geosynchronous orbit where they will embark on the spaceship *Geoffrey*. Raised on Mars, Riley had volunteered for the Interstellar Guard and had spent years fighting in the wars between humans and the galactics. An uneasy peace has been made, in part due to Transcendentalism, a new religion "sweeping the galaxy."[41] Riley is kind of a combination of the soldier Mandela from Joe Haldeman's *The Forever War* and William Gibson's cyberpunk hero Case from *Neuromancer*. When he returned from the wars, Riley followed the path of Gunn's various dreamers and "lost himself in the sim section of the pleasure-world habitat of Dante off Rigel."[42] Brought out of the simulation, Riley is hired by an unknown employer who wants him to go on the pilgrimage and make sure "the pilgrimage reaches the shrine."[43] Riley has been rigged with a "pedia," a microcomputer surgically connected to his brain.

The space elevator takes seven days to reach orbit and during the course of the trip, the pilgrims warily evaluate one another and form alliances. Riley makes an alliance with Tordor, a massive elephant-like creature from a heavy gravity planet, and next approaches the human woman Asha, but she's not interested in an alliance. The alliance making is an homage to Van Vogt's *The World of Null-A*, a central text in Gunn's teaching. As they near the *Geoffrey* an attempt at sabotage blows apart the space-elevator ribbon, which causes the "climber" (car) to drift into space. The *Geoffrey*, however, retrieves the errant climber before it drifts further out, and the pilgrims enter the ship and meet the captain, an adventurer named Ham, whom Riley knows from the wars.

As the *Geoffrey* makes its way to the nearest "Jump" portal, which allows a ship to pass "from one nexus to another across a fold of space,"[44] the pilgrims settle in and prepare to tell their stories: "The telling of stories or personal accounts was traditional for long trips."[45] This allows Gunn to create interesting and unusual alien cultures and world-build. But before the stories commence, the clone Jan is murdered. Riley is then taken before Ham and given additional details about the journey. For one thing, the *Geoffrey* doesn't know where it's going: after each Jump, the next set of coordinates are uploaded into the ship's pedia. Whomever knows the location of their final destination is on board the *Geoffrey*, but who that is, Ham doesn't know. The next Jump coordinates take the ship into the "Great Gulf," an immense expanse of near-empty space. As Asha informs Riley, "'In the historical past, five expeditions, each manned by a different species, set out, but only one returned.'"[46] So the *Geoffrey* is embarking deep into unknown territory, into the nether regions of the cave of night. During the long voyage in the Great Gulf, the pilgrims begin their tales, which are interspersed throughout the rest of the novel. Tordor and Xi, the weasel-like being, go first. Each story reveals details about Transcendentalism and the nature and purpose of the quest. Like Riley, Xi had been recruited by a group of "soft-spoken aliens" to find out "if the Prophet was on board the ship, and to learn whether the Transcendental Machine is real and how it worked and to bring it back."[47] Xi believes he has evidence that the Prophet is, indeed, aboard. After Tordor and Xi tell their stories, the tales are interrupted when the pilgrims realize that Captain Ham has locked them in, having the door to the pilgrims' hold welded shut.

As the story moves forward, Asha reveals herself to Riley as the Prophet. Asha had been born on the first human generation starship, the *Adastra*, shortly before the ship made first contact with aliens on its way to Alpha Centauri, when it was "intercepted by a galactic patrol ship."[48] Here Gunn's homage is to Murray Leinster's "Proxima Centauri," another of Gunn's prominent teaching texts. Taken to the "Galactic Council system" through a sequence of Jumps, the humans find another Earth ship and crew there before them; the *Vanguard* set out twenty years after the *Adastra* but had been captured first. Asha grew up on the *Adastra*, "orbiting the moon we humans named Hell, of the planet we named Hades."[49] The aliens took Asha's brother Pip and questioned him about humanity, to not much purpose, Pip was only thirteen. Later, her father petitioned for an audience before the council. A number of years passed before his return while Asha grew into adulthood. Meanwhile, one of the crew, a scientist named Ren, hacked into the council computer files and "downloaded their navigation charts." Her father was summoned before the council again and on his return he said they must escape: the aliens are "preparing for war with humanity," having determined "humanity was not only unfit for galactic membership but a danger to galactic civilization." To hide, the *Adastra* followed an "ancient chart" that took them into the unknown, eventually to the location of the Transcendental Machine, the very path the *Geoffrey* is now following. Nearly out of fuel, Ren led "a landing party to an Earth-like planet to check our location and make contact with possible aliens." The planet was in ruins, not unlike Coeurl's wasteland in Van Vogt's "Black Destroyer." Encountering a swarm of arachnoid aliens, the landing party was wiped out, with the exception of Asha and Ren, who fight their way to an intact building containing what appeared to be a shrine. As Ren fought off the arachnoids, Asha climbed inside the shrine hoping to hide, but found herself transported to "a remote room on a remote planet of our own spiral arm." She was also transformed into human perfection, "healthier than I have ever been, stronger, smarter, more capable—it's as if all of my potential as a person has been released from bondage." Readers might recognize a tribute to Aeysha from Rider Haggard's *She* here. From Asha's experience springs the purpose behind the pilgrimage.[50]

Events move forward from there. The birdlike Centauran is murdered by the Floran flower-being, leading to what is perhaps the most engaging traveler's tale as Gunn unfolds the evolution of the Florans. The Florans are collective beings, in this way similar to the aliens in "A Monster Named Smith," and had been victims of Centauran aggression millennia ago. 4107, as the Floran pilgrim is so named, has been sent to seek the Transcendental Machine: "'Out of this crisis I was grown, against every Floran instinct, to assume the reviled role of individual, to act alone and through my sacrifice find salvation for my sisters. I cannot describe my desolation, my grief, my anguished separation from my fellow Florans as I joined this voyage.'" Gunn creates a poignant hoped for destiny for the gentle flower-beings: 4107's goal in finding the Transcendental Machine is to "'remove the curse of sapience.'"[51]

Shortly after 4107's tale, the *Geoffrey*'s last jump takes them in proximity to a star. The captain announces that a small party can take the captain's barge "to explore one of the rocky planets in the habitable zone."[52]

Riley and Asha are joined by Tordor, Xi, 4107, and the coffin-shaped A.I. Interfacing with the barge's computer, the A.I. discovers that the ship only has "'enough hydrogen to get us to the surface of the planet.'" The *Geoffrey* has deserted them. Like the planet of the Transcendental Machine, this planet is covered with ruins from an ancient civilization. While the A.I. manufactures new hydrogen fuel from a body of water, the pilgrims investigate one of the ruined cities and encounter spider-like beings similar to those Asha encountered before, leading to a desperate chase back to the ship. Refueled, the pilgrims take the barge through the next nexus point—Asha has the coordinates—and hope to "beat the *Geoffrey* to the Transcendental Machine.'"[53] But first the A.I. tells its tale. Called Trey, the A.I. comes from a planet that was home to two warring sapient species, one on the land and the other from the sea. The A.I.'s were produced by the land sapients as "instruments of service and discovery" that were turned into "machines for destruction," in the tradition of Fred Saberhagen's Berserkers and Keith Laumer's Bolos, reprogrammed to seek out and destroy the sea sapients. For their part, the sea sapients developed biological weapons, and this resulted in extinction of both species, leaving only the machines. The A.I.'s settled into self-reflection, discovered that other sapients existed in the galaxy, and "set out to the stars," arriving only to find the "galaxy at war with humans." Trey, which means three, is the receptacle of a male of the land sapients and a female from the sea in frozen stasis, hence its coffin shape. The A.I. hopes the Transcendental Machine can restore its makers and "redeem" the fallen machines.[54]

When they arrive on the planet of the Transcendental Machine, they find the crew of the *Geoffrey* slaughtered. Tordor kills Xi when the weasel-creature tries to attack Asha after identifying her as the Prophet. Fighting off waves of attacking arachnoids as they march through the city, the pilgrims split up, with Tordor, Trey, and 4107 taking one route, and Riley and Asha another. Asha laments, "'I have grown attached to a machine and a flower. I hope they are very, very lucky.'"[55] Riley and Asha make their way to the shrine. As the quest concludes, Asha, and then Riley, go separately into the Transcendental Machine. The novel ends with an epilogue clearly suggesting a sequel. Riley "woke up," restored, transformed, and no longer encumbered by his pedia. His next task is to find his way back to Asha and once he finds her, "they would change the galaxy."[56]

Transgalactic follows Riley and Asha as they try to find one another after their transformations through the Transcendental Machine has reconstituted each of them on remote planets at different locations in the galaxy. Gunn modeled the narrative on *The Odyssey*. As in its predecessor, here Gunn creates an engaging story of galactic adventure. The narrative is somewhat structured on the pattern of *The Millennium Blues* in that chapters go back and forth between Riley's and Asha's adventures in trying to get back to one another.

The novel begins where *Transcendental* left off. Riley awakens and finds himself "in a featureless cube with a ceiling above his reach and the machine in the center"—the image here recalls Frank R. Paul's cover illustration of H.G. Wells's *When the Sleeper Wakes* for the Winter 1928 issue of *Amazing Stories Quarterly*. Like Asha, Riley has been transformed, with "newfound sensitivity of touch," among other physiological improvements. Riley realizes he's in some sort of "massive structure assembled to protect the remains of some ancient ruler or god for eternity," as he discovers what looks like a marsupial-like set of bones in a sarcophagus. In fact these are the bones of an ancestor species of the dinosaur sapients indigenous to the planet. Here Gunn pays tribute to Harry Harrison's *West of Eden*. To keep it safe, the Transcendental entities placed the portal in the existing temple. Using his enhanced senses, Riley finds a pathway out of the structure and into a tropical jungle. Riley's journey through the structure echoes Horn's flight through the caverns of Sunport in *Star Bridge* and the jungle recalls Gunn's youthful encounters with Tarzan. Asha awakens in a "centerpiece of a fountain" in a plaza as "several hundred aliens, somewhat humanoid in appearance, and without clothing" look on. On this world, the Machine is venerated as a holy shrine. Like Riley, she very quickly determines that she must find a way back to known space and reconnect.[57]

The next chapters follow Riley and Asha as they make contact with the local sentients and try to figure out ways to depart their respective planets. Riley befriends a local he names Rory, a species with a dinosaur-like appearance different than the bones in the temple, and in another temple finds a red sphere (depicted on the book jacket), which he surmises was the mechanism that brought the Machine's receiver to this world, and which gives him a means to get off the planet. It's a symbiotic ship which Riley is able to guide to the nearest nexus point. Asha calls her sentients the "Squeal," because of their whistling annunciation of their language. The Squeals evidently anticipate that Asha will select "one of them for a mate or consort or scapegoat," but she has other plans. Her pursuit by Squeal suitors mimics Penelope in *The Odyssey*. Asha soon recognizes a Dorian on the other side of the plaza. The Dorian is an Ambassador charged with preparing the Squeal's for eventual membership with the galactic community. There's some interesting interplay between Asha and this Dorian bureaucrat that fits wells with Gunn's previous scenes involving administrators at work. Asha makes a deal with the ambassador that will facilitate her own quest and contribute to the uplift of the Squeals: if the ambassador brings down the Captain's Barge from the starship orbiting the planet, then Asha can make her departure: "'I will pick a suitor, but instead of the fountain we will go to the Captains' Barge and depart. That single event, with everyone forced to look at the sky and envision the royal pair ascending into the heavens, will alter the psychology of the Squeal people, provide therapy for their aversion to space, and begin their journey to the stars."[58] Two chapters narrated by the Squeal and Rory allow Gunn to get inside the heads of these species similar to the tales told by the various sentients in *Transcendental*.

Asha makes her way through the nexus points to Federation Central, where she can access the master computers and, perhaps, locate Riley by searching for reports of an unusual being mysteriously appearing on some Federation world or in Federation space. Riley heads to Rigel, star of the pleasure-world Dante, a "habitat carved out of a moon of a onetime gas-giant planet," where he had once indulged in simulations and where he had first been hired for the pilgrimage. But Riley first heads to a companion habitat, once called Alighieri, "filled with thieves, organ snatchers, kidnappers, and assassins,"[59] recalling any number of space opera "frontier" scenes, such as C.L. Moore's Northwest Smith adventures. Riley enters a bar where he can log into the computer array and look for reports of Asha. Eventually, he journeys to Dante and seeks out Sharn, the doctor who fixed him up after the wars, became his lover, and, not yet known to him, surgically installed his pedia. Sharn has retreated into the dream tanks. Here again Gunn recreates themes explored in *The Joy Makers*, *The Dreamers*, and *The Joy Machine*. When Riley pulls her out of her tank, Sharn explains why she implanted the pedia in Riley's head: "You would have become a captive of your dreams, slowly drifting away into a simulacrum of paradise until you would die like a fetus absorbed back into the womb." To find out who was behind it all, Riley goes back into the tank, and discovers that it "was the Pedia itself," a master computer like Hedon or the Joy Machine, and since Riley has been through the Transcendental Machine, now no longer under the control of the Pedia, the Pedia wants him eliminated.[60] A word on what the Pedia (short for encyclopedia) is. Gunn's idea is that every technological species eventually develops artificial intelligence, a storehouse of knowledge and a guiding hand that makes becoming a galactic species possible. Humanity's Pedia is relatively young, compared to those of the Federation species, but it has kept humanity from destroying itself and brought them the stars.

Meanwhile, Asha works through the Federation bureaucracy to put forward the application of the Squeal's. By the end of this process, she is reunited with her father, who has become a human envoy to the Federation Council, and who now believes the Federation "'is the only force for peace and stability in the galaxy.'"[61] From her father, Asha finds that Ren, too, has returned; her brother Kip (Pip in the first novel) had been sent back to Earth. This gives Asha an insight as to where she'll find Riley.

Both make their way to Earth. Asha disembarks from a space elevator that deposits her on the island of Sri Lanka—an homage to Arthur C. Clarke and his novel *The Fountains of Paradise*. Conditions on Earth have been rectified, and the planet is now once more in ecological balance, and people live a utopian existence thanks to the guiding hand of the Pedia. But there are "ugly reminders of old mistakes": "craters of ancient nuclear explosions," "shattered ruins of ancient cities, destroyed by bombs or barbarian attacks over burning issues long forgotten," "soaring metropolises buried under rising seas," and "polar icecaps shrunken by the warming effect of ancient vegetation, accumulated since the beginnings of plant life itself, burned in an orgy of industrialization and released, in noxious fumes, into the atmosphere."[62] Riley first goes to the Moon, to a facility called "Lunar Research Project No.2, in search of Jan and Jon's origin clone, Jak Plus, named in homage to Hugo Gernsback's Ralph 124C 41+."

In Sri Lanka, Asha meets a woman named Latha (named after Latha Nair, founder of the Indian Gunn Centre) whose goal is to destroy the Pedia, by introducing a computer virus, the "Grand Poison," into the Pedia's programming, a la Kirk's standoff with the Joy Machine. Latha and her movement believe the Pedia has too much control. Riley talks with Jak Plus and another clone named Jer on the Moon, and unanswered questions are raised which will be answered in the final book. In his conversation with the clones, the idea is raised that humanity in some way may be the source of the Transcendental Machine, a possibility that resonates with the denouement of *This Fortress World*. Back on Earth, Latha doesn't intend to let Asha leave her compound, and Asha senses that the grand plan to destroy the Pedia won't work—that the Pedia knows and "allows them to continue so that rebellion won't grow into revolt."[63] But Asha could provide knowledge that could tip things, and so she must leave. Meanwhile, Riley enters Earth's atmosphere in a "one-person spaceship—little more than an escape pod" (189) which lands in Lake Mead, outside Las Vegas. He enters the city and makes his way along the refurbished strip in what amounts to a clever recasting of the funhouse scenes in *The Joy Makers*. Riley uses his enhanced capabilities to win a fortune at roulette, with the idea that will trigger a disruption that will take him to the Pedia—and to Asha. Asha herself arrives in Oakland, since San Francisco is now underwater, where she finds a clue that will take her to the Pedia's server farm near Salt Lake. There, Riley and Asha are reunited, and they enter an ancient building once called "the Utah Data Center." After encountering a series of illusions, including Tordor, *Geoffrey's* Captain Ham, and Ren, in the manner of the illusions D'glas faced on his way to Hedon, the pair find themselves in the master control room where they encounter an old man, "'a survivor of long ago, kept alive by the will of the machine I helped build.'" Asha and Riley reason that the Pedia needs to allow humanity to grow "'you're trying to distract humanity from its built-in mandate to grow and improve, and to dampen the unpredictable before it threatens the status quo.'" This debate is far more condensed as that in *The Joy Makers*—in part because there is another book to come—but it amounts to the same thing. However, the Pedia, which is ultimately a benign creation guiding humanity in the manner of Asimov's R. Daneel Olivaw, seems to agree with Riley's argument, and for the time being goes silent. As the novel ends, fire engulfs the Pedia building and Asha and Riley make their way outside with new "hope for humanity."[64]

Transformation finds Riley and Asha back on the Moon and Sri Lanka, respectively. Riley is working with Jak Plus to build a new Transcendental Machine which can provide instant communication and transport across the Federation—in many ways this technology resembles the Tubes of *Star Bridge* in terms of its ability to transcend the physics of time and space. Jak and Jer have tested the machine and both have experienced the physical restoration and enhancement the transformation provides. Asha has returned to Sri Lanka to tell Latha about the encounter with the Pedia in Utah and how they convinced the Pedia to loosen its benignly stultifying guidance so that humanity could continue to grow: "'It's what we told the Pedia. That the purpose of self-aware intelligence is to comprehend, to answer the big questions of existence: where did we come from, where are we going, where will it end, and what does it all mean?'"[65] She's also brought a link with the Pedia so it can communicate directly with the resistance.

Meanwhile, a number of Federation worlds on the fringes have gone "silent"—and it's feared that some sort of invasion from outside the Federation is picking off remote civilizations. This news has reawakened the Earth Pedia and it believes that Riley and Asha should go to Federation Central. They are joined by Latha's son Adithya and a portable Pedia in the shape of a medallion. At Federation Central they bring their plan before the Council, where they are reunited with Tordor, the Dorian. Like them, Tordor passed through the Transcendental Machine and had to make his way back to Federation Central. Tordor will also join the expedition. Whereas Gunn modeled the first two books on the *Canterbury Tales* and *The Odyssey* respectively, *Transformation* is modeled on Jason and the Argonauts.

What follows is a series of adventures on planets that have fallen victim to the invaders from outside the galaxy, much in the manner of Asimov's *Foundation's Edge*. Once again Gunn creates fascinating alien cultures. The first involves a star-faring civilization named Nepenthe, a species which had forgotten their origins. The Nepentheans evolved on an "orphan" world cast out of its solar system. They evolved in the interior of the planet in a sea kept warm by the molten core and kept from evaporating by layers of rock and ice overhead. At some point the Nepentheans developed technology and bore through the crust, becoming starfarers. Their story evokes Verne's and Burroughs' hollow Earth tales and Blish's "Surface Tension," in that the Nepentheans experience a similar Conceptual Breakthrough when they see the stars. Protected by a suit made of the red matter from the symbiotic ship, Riley investigates and he finds the ocean evaporated and heaps of Nepenthean bones. Complications ensue when Adithya releases a computer virus into the Pedia causing temporary disruption in communication. But Riley uses the red matter and the Pedia medallion to safely return to the ship. As Riley, Asha, Tordor, Adithya, and the Pedia make their search, Jer further develops the Transcendental portal technology and eventually transports herself to Federation Central. The Jer chapters are interspersed between the planetary expeditions.

The next stop takes the adventurers to a high-gravity world suitable for Tordor to explore. This world is the home of the Centaurans, quadruped creatures modeled after the mythical beasts. The Centaurans' encounter with the invader has not led to extinction, like the Nepentheans, but rather to an apparent loss of sentience; they have abandoned their technological civilization and reverted to being bovine prey for the planet's tiger-like predators. In an abandoned Centauran city Tordor finds a broadcasting station sending out a dissonant recording, which in some ways recalls the Joy Machine broadcast, although bringing discomfort not ecstasy. A timely rescue by Riley and crew saves Tordor from a pack of the predators.

It is Asha's turn to explore the planet of the Lemnians, humanoid bird-riders who live on an Earth-like planet. All of the Lemnians Asha encounters are female. Soon she discovers that the females have wiped out all males of the species with the exception of one, whom they have chained to a pallet where he can "service" the Lemnian females. Thus far, none have become impregnated, which will result in species extinction in another generation, recalling the alien-invasion theory in "The Girls who were Really Built." In this case, the invaders directive appeared as a revelation from God. Adithya is allowed down to find Asha and gets sexually involved with a Lemnian guard, before Riley arrives to facilitate another timely rescue.

From there, Riley and Tordor together go down to a waterworld called Oceanus where two intelligent species had evolved concurrently and had forged a peace for millennia. That peace is now broken. After a sequence of mishaps that takes Riley to a city on the ocean floor by a smaller tentacled creature, the more hostile of the two species, where he is soon freed by the friendlier mammalian leviathan creature, Asha and the red ship make another timely rescue. There next visit is to a world named Aerie where the sentient species lives on floating cities in the upper atmosphere, recalling the Laputans in *Gulliver's Travels*. The Aerieians themselves are winged humanoids, but Asha soon finds they have a social hierarchy, with a wingless underclass living in the bowels of the city. The problem here is that the Aerieians have forgotten about their technology and knowledge of their past, and the mechanisms that keep the cities afloat are running out of fuel. When the Aerieian rulers decide to execute Asha and Adithya by shoving them off the city's edge, their red material forms wings and they fly to safety, saving one of the wingless who helped them in the process.

As their voyage nears its end, the explorers realize that the attacks follow a straight line and after consulting the star charts, that line appears to be heading toward Federation Central. Following that pattern, the next populated star system is a planet called Extreme. Extreme is a planet orbiting between two stars which experiences cycles of extreme heat and extreme cold. Here Gunn pays tribute to Brian Aldiss's *Helliconia*. Currently the sentients of Extreme are in hibernation during a cold cycle and when the explorers go to the surface of the planet, they find what appears to be a shrine, but is in fact a radio telescope, which points them to a small object orbiting between the binary stars. This is the artifact of the invaders. As the novel concludes, the alien invader turns out to be an ancient artificial intelligence from another galaxy which has gone insane, and has come to our galaxy "only to serve."[66] But like many of its science fiction predecessors—Williamson's Humanoids, Saberhagen's Berserkers, Hedon—this A.I.'s service brings death. Before the invader can cause further damage, the red matter of the ship engulfs the planetoid. This was the purpose of the Transcendental Machine. Its makers anticipated the

Five. The Joy Machine *to the* Transcendental *Trilogy*

invasion from outside and spent a million years, with their memories uploaded into the fabric of the red material, to give one final gift to the sentients of our galaxy, by protecting them from this insane A.I.

Left only with a small habitat of red material, the crew await death. But as the novel closes, Asha's former lover Ren arrives, having followed them from Federation Central. Gunn leaves open the possibility of another sequel (at least in the draft I read), but his intention might also be to suggest that the sentients of the galaxy are now free to continue to evolve together and expand across the galaxy using the Transcendental portals, which they can now manufacture.

In the end, what Gunn has achieved in the *Transcendental* trilogy is the creation of a compelling wide-canvas galactic adventure comparable to Gregory Benford's *Galactic Center* series and Frederik Pohl's *Heechee* saga. The *Transcendental* trilogy takes a new look at Gunn's thinking about the ultimate technology, posing the argument that sentient species must evolve in partnership with their technologies, not become victims of their own creation's good intentions. The *Transcendental* trilogy provides new answers to the philosophical questions Gunn first explored in "Breaking Point" and *The Joy Makers*, and in many of the works he's written in the sixty plus years in between. Gunn leaves us with a fitting capstone to his phenomenal career. Although he may not be done yet. Like his longtime friends and colleagues, Jack Williamson and Pohl, Gunn proves that a nonagenarian can still write with a youthful vigor and a sense of wonder.

Six

The Scholarship

I'll conclude this study with a brief overview of James Gunn's contributions to the field of science fiction scholarship. As I remarked earlier, Gunn was one of the first critics to consider science fiction from an academic viewpoint, having written his master's thesis, *Modern Science Fiction A Critical Analysis* in 1951. It's worth mentioning that at the time, although Gunn's adviser John Hankins approved, one of the more traditional members of the KU English faculty considered science fiction "at best, sub-literary."[1] Incredibly, such attitudes still occasionally surface in academia. Portions of the thesis were published in the short-lived pulp magazine *Dynamic Science Fiction* in 1953 and 1954. It is unfortunate that the study did not find a book publisher—both Pohl and Altshuler, Gunn's agents, tried. Had Gunn's thesis been published as a book in the 1950s, or even in the 1960s when Advent published Blish's *The Issue at Hand* and Knight's *In Search of Wonder*, and found its way into the collections of university libraries across the globe, it would no doubt have had a similar foundational influence on the field of SF scholarship as J.O. Bailey's *Pilgrims Through Space and Time* and Kingsley Amis's *New Maps of Hell*. Instead, its impact can be seen in the work of those who were able to access the old issues of *Dynamic* or otherwise tracked down the KU thesis (Gary Wolfe's *The Known and the Unknown*, for example, reveals a familiarity; Wolfe was an undergraduate at KU) and in the way Gunn's early ideas formed the foundation of his own later work in the field, especially in *Alternate Worlds* and *The Road to Science Fiction*.

Gunn's primary purpose in *Modern Science Fiction* was to establish scholarly criteria for examining the emerging new genre. Gunn believed that SF had reached the point where it was time for it to be taken seriously by scholars; that it was no longer a mere fringe genre literature primarily for entertainment, but a literature that had reached a level of maturity that required critical interpretation. Gunn argued that SF needed three layers of inquiry to establish itself and for it to realize its full potentiality as a field of consequence: what is has been (history), what it is (contemporary analysis), and what it may become (theory). According to Gunn, J.O. Bailey had fulfilled the first point, and the purpose of his thesis was to consider the latter two. As Gunn was writing in the early 1950s, SF had reached the stage for critical self-reflection. Gunn was absolutely right on this assessment. And though SF criticism would very slowly begin to build a body of historical, biographical, critical, and theoretical work, by now there is a substantial library of SF scholarship and a growing interest in the field among academics and cultural critics. These works stand on the shoulders of Gunn, Bailey, Amis, Blish, Knight, and the small handful of other early SF scholars and critics.

The first section of *Modern Science Fiction* defines and explores "The Philosophy of Science Fiction." When Gunn was writing, science fiction was experiencing an upsurge in popularity due to the dropping of the atomic bombs and the growing public awareness about the prospects implicit in rocketry. Gunn argues that the rise in popularity can be problematic in that it exploits the low element of the field and that the newly initiated might ignore the serious element. Gunn wants to counter the common misconceptions that science fiction is pure escapism and that it hasn't yet developed a set of ideas and an aesthetic worthy of scholarly analysis. He then goes on to explain that science fiction is a literature of ideas; SF writers usually begin with an idea or concept: "If such-and such happened or such-and-such was invented, what would be the result?"[2] From that, character, style and plot are dependent. Gunn also argues that science fiction is not so much about individuals and their everyday problems, as most mainstream literature is about, but rather science fiction concerns itself with the species, its challenges, its growth, its evolution.

In the second half of the thesis, "The Plot Forms of Science Fiction," Gunn sets out to examine a number of stories and novels, primarily from the previous decade, within the theoretical framework he established in the prior section and within an anatomy of the various types of science fiction stories, e.g., "facing a problem raised by new technology," "aliens," "time," etc. Discussions of such now classic stories as Campbell's "Forgetfulness," Van Vogt's "Black Destroyer," Heinlein's, "By His Bootstraps," Asimov's "Nightfall," Kuttner and Moore's "Mimsy were the Borogoves," Tenn's "Child's Play," Clarke's "Rescue Party," Leiber's "Coming Attraction," and many others are illuminating.

Gunn's next major contributions to SF scholarship began when he returned to teaching in the KU English Department in the fall of 1970.

For the large lecture SF class he was teaching, Gunn created a series of lectures tracing the history of the field and its key ideas. These lectures eventually developed into the history *Alternate Worlds*, published by Prentice-Hall in 1975. Meanwhile, Gunn produced the *Literature of Science Fiction* film series, enormously important footage of many of the genre's major writers lecturing on the history, ideas, and techniques of the field. The *Lunch with John Campbell* film is particularly valuable, as Campbell died just a few months after filming. At that time, Gunn also participated in the formation of the Science Fiction Research Association at an organizational meeting in Toronto in 1971. As he reflected in the Foreword to *The Cambridge Companion to Science Fiction*: "That was where we were, in Toronto, caught between our pulp traditions ... and the realization that science fiction was capable of greater sophistication and that it was worthy of study, of scholarship, even of being taught to students."[3]

For many years, *Alternate Worlds* was, along with Brian Aldiss's eclectic *Billion Year Spree*, the standard history of the field. And for many it still is. A new translation will soon be published in China; and an unauthorized translation has been circulating in Chinese universities for years: along with translations of *The Road to Science Fiction* anthologies, it has become one of the primary gateways into English language SF for Chinese readers, students, and scholars. Whereas Aldiss begins *Billion Year Spree* with a focus on the Industrial Revolution as ground zero for the emergence of science fiction, culminating in the publication of Mary Shelley's *Frankenstein*, Gunn takes his origin story back further to the myths and early scientific developments of classic times and traces other texts up through the Renaissance to the Enlightenment. Gunn does not make any claims that texts such as Lucian of Samosata's "Icaromenippus" or Campanella's *The City of the Sun* are, in fact, science fiction, but rather these types of extraordinary and utopian tales are examples of how writers in other times took tentative steps toward imaginatively exploring the kinds of questions that are central to science fiction. This historical scope provides students with a deeper grasp of history that facilitates considering the broader scale and scope of science fiction texts. Gunn includes Shelley as part of this earlier, proto period. For Gunn, science fiction doesn't really begin until the emergence of Jules Verne and H.G. Wells. But Gunn also considers other nineteenth-century writers of importance, including Poe, Hawthorne, Bulwer-Lytton, and Edward Everett Hale. What's important throughout is the way Gunn frames science fiction within the broader spectrum of accelerated technological and scientific development that characterizes the nineteenth century. This shows that science fiction literature, in essence, *had to emerge* during this era of invention as a literary form that engages directly with these inventions, their consequences, and the future possibilities of further invention building upon them. Gunn sees this progression from an American lens, whereas Aldiss's history is firmly framed within a British and Continental sensibility. Therefore, Gunn focuses a great deal on the development of the American pulp magazines and how they created the environment from which Hugo Gernsback could launch the first science fiction magazine, *Amazing Stories*, in 1926. From there, Gunn traces the development of the genre from the magazine era to the New Wave. As an introduction and overview of the field, *Alternate Worlds* remains essential reading for any student of the genre.

Gunn's *The Road to Science Fiction* anthologies are also significant to the development of science fiction scholarship and criticism. As mentioned before, because they were published in mass market paperback editions, they were widely circulated in the science fiction marketplace, and because of the convenient size, they also ended up in classroom paperback racks not only in colleges, but in high schools and libraries as well. In this way, Gunn's academic historical approach to the field was distributed among youthful science fiction enthusiasts long before they had opportunity to take a science fiction course in college. The first volume, *The Road to Science Fiction: From Gilgamesh to Wells*, samples texts from the early proto era, beginning with Lucian and concluding with Wells's "The Star." In the introduction to this first volume Gunn lays out some of his key definitions of the genre: "Science fiction is the branch of literature that deals with the effects of change on people in the real world as it can be projected into the past, the future, or to distant places."[4] Later in the introduction, Gunn adds further clarification that technological change has been at the forefront of human experience since the Industrial Revolution and science fiction, then, is the "artistic response" to those technological changes.[5] This definition has, in many ways, become standard for the teaching and scholarship of the genre. Others have used it, modified it, and expanded it in various ways, but Gunn's pronouncement that science fiction is the literature of change remains one of the key definitions of the genre. Gunn also makes the point that science fiction is the "literature of the human species," meaning that science fiction focuses more on outcomes that will impact all of us rather than on the minute concerns of individuals. Therefore, in SF, an idea is often the hero of a story, rather than an individual. Thus, traditional criticism's charge that science fiction isn't, in general, "literary" because science fiction writers don't focus on or have the artistry to deeply delve into character misses the point that science fiction isn't about character, it's about ideas. And therefore, science fiction should be judged by a different set of criteria than how mundane mainstream fiction is evaluated. Volume 2, *From Wells to Heinlein*, traces the development of science fiction from the beginning of the twentieth century to the pre–War years of the Campbell era. In the introduction, Gunn expands his definition further to suggest that science fiction is "the literature that concerns itself with the condition and fate of the human species."[6] Here Gunn also emphasizes the importance of Darwin's theory of evolution in the formation of science fiction. Because of the way Darwin defined humanity as a species, rather than a unique creation of God, this laid the groundwork for SF's concern for the human species over the individual. As Gunn puts it, Darwin's theory "provided a scientific rationale for a process that had slowly enlarged the meaning of the word 'human' until it encompassed the entire species. The view of humanity as a species was not only characteristic of science fiction but essential to it."[7] Thus, science fiction can also be thought of in terms of an ecology. Gunn expanded these ideas further in a 1995 article in *Extrapolation* titled "The Worldview of Science Fiction," where he adds the points that science fiction "treats human beings as a species that has evolved as a result of environment" (an important element that Gunn eloquently explores in the *Transcendental* series) and that we are "a species upon whom the evolutionary process is still at work."[8] There Gunn also emphasizes human adaptability as a characteristic of SF. In the worldview of science fiction, humanity has "the intellectual ability to recognize its origins and the processes at work upon it, and even, sometimes, to choose a course other than that instilled by its environment."[9] Whereas mainstream fiction is, for the most part, preoccupied with the present "an apparent desire to freeze reality in its current state," as Gunn puts it, science fiction "incorporates a belief that the most important aspect of existence is a search for humanity's origins, its purpose, and its ultimate fate."[10] Volume 3, *From Heinlein to Here*, contains stories beginning with Asimov's "Reason" and ending with Joe Haldeman's "Tricentennial," taking things roughly up to the time of the volume's publication in 1979, and does not provide much more in terms of genre definition, but rather traces the genre development from the Golden Age to the New Wave. Volume 4, *From Here to Forever*, fills in some of the omissions from the earlier volumes. Two additional volumes, *The British Way* and *Around the World*, were published in the 1990s to cover the unique ways that science fiction has unfolded in other parts of the world. In total, the anthologies remain an important gateway into the history of the genre. Those involved with the Gunn Center for the Study of Science Fiction are looking into the prospect of developing another volume or two to trace the genre's development since the emergence of cyberpunk in the early 1980s.

Gunn's single-author study of Isaac Asimov, *Isaac Asimov: The Foundations of Science Fiction*, was another landmark in the development and legitimization of science fiction scholarship. Published by Oxford University Press in 1982, as previously mentioned, several of the chapters appeared in *Isaac Asimov's Science Fiction Magazine* in 1980 and 1981. Like *The Road to Science Fiction* in mass market paperback, these articles brought sophisticated academic criticism to the general science fiction reader. The Oxford series began with a book on Heinlein by H. Bruce Franklin in 1980 and was followed by a book on Wells by Frank McConnell the next year. The Heinlein and Asimov books, in particular, showed that the time was right for serious single-author studies of major science fiction writers. Unfortunately, Oxford didn't take the series any further, but other publishers to varying degree of scope, did for a time. It is only recently that a reemergence of single-author studies are making a new push in the field. Gunn's Asimov study provides an example going forward.

As Gunn further developed his thought on the study and teaching of SF, he also contributed to (and in the classroom applied) the conversation stemming from the ideas of Samuel R. Delany on the reading protocols necessary for readers to understand science fiction texts. Delany formulated his ideas in an essay published in *Analog* in 1979 titled "Science Fiction and 'Literature'—or, The Conscience of the King," which Gunn later reprinted in the critical anthology *Speculations on Speculation*. Delany made the point that reading science fiction requires a different set of reading expectations than that required for realistic fiction, and that many readers are simply unequipped to cope with the complexities built into even the more pedestrian texts in the genre. Delany further argues that over the course of the genre's development, it had built up a vocabulary and a set of semiotic signs that crossover from text to text and that readers unpack, often in their formative teen reading years, through immersive reading in the genre. Delany's classic example is Heinlein's phrase that "the door dilated" in *Beyond This Horizon* and how that developed into a standard image and later design.[11]

When Delany's article first came out, Gunn (who actually first heard Delany discuss the ideas at an MLA meeting) thought they were "so illuminating to the processes that I had found myself going through, and through which I had guided my students, that I adopted them myself."[12] In his teaching, Gunn demonstrates the reading protocols in a line by line reading of Philip Jose Farmer's "Sail On! Sail On!" In 1996, during the early days of internet ubiquity, Gunn got into an online debate with Damon Knight where Knight challenged the idea of science fiction reading protocols. This prompted Gunn to write an article titled "The Protocols of Science Fiction" where he restates Delany's argument and then shows the practical application of Delany's theory by taking us through the process by which he teaches Farmer's story. What's especially important about Gunn's essay is that it is one of the clearest examples of turning theory into application.

Another useful essay Gunn first published in 1986 is "Touchstones." Gunn argues that a science fiction touchstone is a story that we instantly recognize as "the right stuff," a story that "should contain, or even better epitomize, the element of discontinuity that makes the work science fiction." For Gunn, a touchstone "should bring the reader up short, cause a reevaluation of older ideas or an adjustment to new condition, make the reader think."[13] Gunn first applied the term to Tom Godwin's "The Cold Equations" in *The Road to Science Fiction Vol. 3*, where Gunn comments that the story forces the reader to "learn the rules and play the game." In this case, the rules of the game is that the physics of the universe don't allow for human sentiment; that space is hard.[14] In "Touchstones," Gunn provides many other examples, each illustrating the characteristics that make a science fiction story science fiction.

Many of Gunn's critical essays are collected in *Inside Science Fiction*, including "The Gatekeepers," where Gunn discusses the influential editors in the field; "The City and the Critics," which examines the cityscapes in Wells's *When the Sleeper Wakes*, Forster's "The Machine Stops," Zamyatin's *We*, and Asimov's *The Caves of Steel*—given Gunn's own city imagery in such works as *Star Bridge* and *The Immortals*, this essay is especially enticing; and a number of other critical and teaching essays. Gunn's book on the art of science fiction writing, *The Science of Science-Fiction Writing* also contains a number of essays of scholarly interest, including pieces on Wells, Heinlein, Asimov, and Kuttner and Moore. The book's chapters on the craft of writing are also of great interest for those who want insight into how the literary works they study are created. In addition to *Speculations on Speculation,* mentioned above, Gunn's *Reading Science Fiction*, co-edited with Marleen Barr and Matthew Candelaria, provides several worthwhile essays from scholars and writers ranging from H. Bruce Franklin's "What Is Science Fiction—and How It Grew" and Sherryl Vint and Mark Bould's controversial and contentious "There is No Such Thing as Science Fiction" to Gunn's own piece "Reading Science Fiction as Science Fiction." Gregory Benford's essay on "Physics Through Science Fiction" is a particularly insightful cross-disciplinary piece.

I'll end this chapter (and this book) with a brief comment about Gunn's most recent critical work, *Paratexts: Introductions to Science Fiction and Fantasy*. As mentioned, Gunn spent nearly two decades as a consulting editor for Easton Press, providing introductions and readers notes for the *Masterpieces of Science Fiction* and *Masterpieces of Fantasy* series, as well as introductions to his own books and to a series of signed first editions. Gunn brought these together in the *Paratexts* volume in 2013. What is valuable about the introductions is that they do what an introduction is supposed to do: introduce readers to the text and author and provide some preliminary illumination on the work to help the reader contextualize the novel at hand, or, in the case of bringing the introductions together in *Paratexts*, introducing potential readers to texts they were perhaps unaware of. What *Paratexts* does, then, is what Gunn has always sought to do in his scholarship (and his fiction, for that matter): to illuminate and teach, rather than to obfuscate and tear down.

That is what I hope this study has achieved: an illumination on the work, the life, and the wide range of contributions that James Gunn has made to the science fiction field. When I first discovered the first volume of *The Road to Science Fiction* in the paperback rack in my high school classroom thirty-four years ago, the same year I discovered science fiction, I never would have imagined that I would eventually meet James Gunn, take his Summer Institute courses, receive his insightful feedback on my scholarly work, have him become a dear, dear mentor and friend, and write the first study on the important contributions James Gunn has made to the field of science fiction as a writer, as a teacher, as a scholar, and as an advocate. For all you have done for science fiction, and for me, thank you Jim. May we continue your work to save the world through science fiction.

Chapter Notes

Chapter One

1. Patterson, *Robert A. Heinlein: In Dialogue with His Century, Vol. I*, 40.
2. Heinlein, Robert A. *To Sail Beyond the Sunset*, 205–25.
3. Graham, "Yours for the Revolution," 88–89, 163–67, 278–79, 295–98.
4. Pohl, *The Way the Future Was*, 2–3; Nadis, *The Man from Mars*, 7–8; Silverberg, "Sounding Brass, Tinkling Cymbal," 10; Williamson, *Wonder's Child*, 23.
5. Gunn, "James Gunn," 238.
6. *Ibid.*, 239.
7. *Ibid.*, 238.
8. Clarke, *Astounding Days*, 3–4.
9. Williamson, *Wonder's Child*, 49.
10. Pohl, *The Way the Future Was*, 1.
11. Asimov, *In Memory Yet Green*, 94–95.
12. Gunn, "The Magic of Imagination," 1.
13. *Ibid.*, 2.
14. Goulart, *Cheap Thrills*, 76.
15. Gunn, "James Gunn," 240.
16. Silverberg, *Other Spaces, Other Times*, 18.
17. Pohl, "Frederik Pohl," 340.
18. Gunn, *Star-Begotten*, 23.
19. Wells, "The Fall in America, 1937," 153.
20. Wells, "New Americans," 44.
21. Gunn, *Star-Begotten*, 15.
22. Kessel, "Buffalo," 282.
23. Gunn, *Star-Begotten*, 35.
24. *Ibid.*
25. Gunn, "James Gunn," 243.
26. *Ibid.* 23.
27. Gunn, *Star-Begotten*, 59.
28. *Ibid.*, 68–69.
29. Gunn, "James Gunn," 244.
30. Gunn, *Star-Begotten*, 77.
31. Gunn, email to the author, December 22, 2015.
32. Gunn, *Star-Begotten*, 80.
33. *Ibid.*, 89.
34. *Ibid.*, 88.
35. *Ibid.*, 82.
36. *Ibid.*, 97.
37. Gunn, "James Gunn," 247.
38. *Ibid.*
39. *Ibid.*
40. Letter from Smith to Gunn, April 13, 1949.
41. Gunn, *Star-Begotten*, 108.
42. Letter from Stoffel to Gunn, May 23, 1949.
43. Letter from Stoffel to Gunn, July 5, 1949.
44. Gunn, *Star-Begotten*, 103.
45. Gunn, "James Gunn," 247.
46. Gunn, *Star-Begotten*, 103.
47. Gunn, "James Gunn," 247.
48. Letter from Smith to Gunn, September 11, 1950.
49. Letter from Smith to Gunn, October 5, 1950.
50. Letter from Gunn to Smith, October 12, 1950.
51. *Ibid.*
52. Lyles, *Putting Dell on the Map*, 8.
53. Letter from Gunn to Ward, March 8, 1951.
54. *Ibid.*
55. Letter from Ward to Gunn, March 9, 1951.
56. Nicholls, "Conceptual Breakthrough," 254–7.
57. Gunn, "A Classic of Science Fiction," 3–5.
58. Letter from Ward to Gunn, April 17, 1951.
59. Letter from Gunn to Ward, April 20, 1951.
60. Letter from Ward to Gunn, April 25, 1951.
61. Letter from Gunn to Campbell, May 23, 1950.
62. Gunn, *Star-Begotten*, 112.

Notes—Chapter One

63. *Ibid.*, 115–16.
64. Letter from Gunn to Rev Mullins, undated, c. early 1952.
65. Gunn, *Star-Begotten*, 123–4.
66. Gunn, "James Gunn," 248.
67. Gunn, *Star-Begotten*, 125–6.
68. McKitterick, "Call to Arms," 138–9.
69. Gunn, *Star-Begotten*, 126.
70. Gunn, "James Gunn," 249.
71. Gunn, *Star-Begotten*, 128.
72. Gunn, "The Misogynist (Introduction)," 103–4.
73. Silverberg, *Tales from Super-Science Fiction*, 67.
74. Gunn, *Star-Begotten*, 131–32.
75. *Ibid.*, 129.
76. *Ibid.*, 135.
77. Letter from Williamson to Gunn, September 27, 1952.
78. Gunn, *Star-Begotten*, 135–6.
79. Silverberg, *Tales from Super-Science Fiction*, 67.
80. Silverberg, Review of *Future Imperfect*, 125.
81. Pohl, *Way the Future Was*, 148–96.
82. Letter from Williamson to Gunn, September 27, 1952.
83. Letter from Gunn to Williamson, November 6, 1952.
84. Letter from Williamson to Gunn, January 9, 1953.
85. Letter from Gunn to Williamson, April 7, 1953.
86. Letter from Gunn to Williamson, May 11, 1953.
87. Letter from Williamson to Gunn, May 13, 1953.
88. Williamson, *Wonder's Child*, 179.
89. Gunn, "Fred and Me," 165–6.
90. Letter from Williamson to Gunn, July 20, 1953.
91. Letter from Gunn to Williamson, July 22, 1953.
92. Letter from Gunn to Williamson, July 27, 1953.
93. Letter from Altshuler to Gunn, July 31, 1953.
94. Letter from Gunn to Williamson, September 10, 1953.
95. Letter from Gunn to Sheckley, September 30, 1953.
96. Letter from Williamson to Gunn, March 9, 1957.
97. Pohl, *Way the Future Was*, 196.
98. Gunn, *Star-Begotten*, 137.
99. Letter from Altshuler to Gunn, November 28, 1953.
100. Letter from Altshuler to Gunn, December 2, 1953.
101. Letter from Altshuler to Gunn, November 4, 1960.
102. Letter from Williamson to Gunn, January 28, 1955.
103. Gunn, "Introduction (*Some Dreams Are Nightmares*), xvi.
104. *Ibid.*, xvii.
105. Gunn, "James Gunn," 251.
106. *Ibid.*
107. Letter from Asimov to Gunn, May 23, 1959.
108. Letter from Gunn to Williamson, June 17, 1954.
109. Letter from Gunn to Williamson, June 23, 1954.
110. Letter from Williamson to Gunn, June 26, 1954.
111. Letter from Gunn to Sheckley, September 22, 1954.
112. Gunn, *Star-Begotten*, 148.
113. Letter from Gunn to Sheckley, August 3, 1955.
114. Letter from Gunn to Williamson, April 7, 1953.
115. Letter from Williamson to Gunn, October 22, 1955.
116. Williamson, *Wonder's Child*, 205.
117. Letter from Greenberg to Gunn, August 2, 1955.
118. Letter from Gunn to Altshuler, October 24, 1955.
119. Gunn, *Alternate Worlds*, 193.
120. *Ibid.*
121. Gunn, "Fred and Me," 165.
122. Ackerman, "The Odd Genre," 2.
123. Letter from Gunn to Greenberg, October 1, 1955.
124. Letter from Greenberg to Gunn, November 28, 1955.
125. Email to the author, July 8, 2015.
126. McCool, "Rising Son."
127. Clute, "James E. Gunn," 529.
128. Letter from Asimov to Gunn, December 19, 1960.
129. Malzberg, "Afterword to 'New Blood,'" 205.
130. Letter from Altshuler to Gunn, June 20, 1966.
131. Gunn, "Preface: *The Immortals*," xi.
132. Gunn, "James Gunn," 244.
133. Ellison, *The Other Glass Teat*, 189.
134. *Ibid.*
135. *Ibid.*
136. Gunn, *Star-Begotten*, 221–22.
137. Campbell, *The John W. Campbell Letters*, 493.
138. *Ibid.*
139. Gunn, "The Listeners (Introduction)," 278.

140. Letter from Altshuler to Gunn, September 9, 1967.
141. Letter from Gunn to Altshuler, September 12, 1967.
142. Qtd. in Bova, *Nebula Awards Showcase 2008*, 277.
143. Gunn, *Star-Begotten*, 180.
144. Gunn, "James Gunn," 254.
145. Gunn, *Star-Begotten*, 174.
146. Harrison, *Harry Harrison! Harry Harrison!*, 222.
147. *Ibid.*, 259–60.
148. *Ibid.*, 261.
149. Gunn, *Star-Begotten*, 239.
150. *Ibid.*, 187.
151. Williamson, "Science Fiction Comes to College," 68.
152. Gunn, "James Gunn," 255.
153. Gunn, *Star-Begotten*, 199.
154. Gunn, "James Gunn," 233.
155. Gunn, *Star-Begotten*, 192.
156. *Ibid.*, 193.
157. Allen, *Science Fiction: The Future*, ix.
158. Gunn, "On Style," 303–11.
159. Gunn, "Science Fiction and the Mainstream," 183–216.
160. Gunn, "Heroes, Heroines, Villains," 161–77.
161. Tenn, "Jazz Then, Musicology Now," 124.
162. Bova, "Teaching Science Fiction," 176–77.
163. Gunn, "Teaching Science Fiction Revisited," 176.
164. Bova, "Teaching the Teachers," 6.
165. Sawyer and Wright, "Design, Delivery and Evaluation," 221.
166. Gunn, *Star-Begotten*, 196.
167. Malzberg, "Afterword to 'New Blood,'" 206.
168. Gunn, *Star-Begotten*, 231.
169. Gunn, *Isaac Asimov*, 190.
170. *Ibid.*, 202–03.
171. *Ibid.*, 217.
172. Email to the author, April 18, 2013.
173. Srinarahari, "International Report from India," 29.
174. Gunn, *Star-Begotten*, 242.
175. *Ibid.*, 223.
176. *Ibid.*
177. *Ibid.*
178. *Ibid.*, 223–24.
179. Gunn, *Paratexts*, 32.
180. Letter from Gunn to Clarke, October 23, 1989.
181. Kessel, "James Gunn, Grand Master," 272.
182. *Ibid.*, 275.
183. Gunn, *Star-Begotten*, 247.
184. *Ibid.*
185. *Ibid.*, 250.
186. *Ibid.*, 261–62.
187. *Ibid.*, 266.
188. *Ibid.*, 280.
189. Pohl, "A Tribute to Gunn," 10.
190. Gunn, "2015 Science Fiction Hall of Fame Acceptance Speech," 34.
191. *Ibid.*

Chapter Two

1. Gunn, "Paradox," 140.
2. *Ibid.*, 144.
3. Gunn, "Mask of Peace," 56.
4. *Ibid.*
5. *Ibid.*, 62.
6. Gunn, "Slave of Venus," 107.
7. Gunn, "Communications," 108.
8. Gunn, *Star-Begotten*, 109.
9. Gunn, *Future Imperfect* (hereafter FI), 91.
10. FI, 94.
11. FI, 109.
12. FI, 110.
13. Gunn, "The Misogynist (Introduction), 105.
14. Email from Gunn to the author, February 3, 2015.
15. FI, 1.
16. FI, 2–5.
17. FI, 7.
18. Gunn, *Station in Space* (hereafter SS), 156.
19. FI, 7–8.
20. FI, 8.
21. Larbalestier, *Battle of the Sexes in Science Fiction*, 46.
22. FI, 9.
23. FI, 11–16.
24. Gunn, *Star-Begotten*, 102.
25. McAleer, *Arthur C. Clarke*, 88.
26. Letter from Sturgeon to Gunn, January 9, 1951.
27. Letter from Sturgeon to Gunn, January 14, 1952.
28. *Ibid.*
29. Letter from Gunn to Sturgeon, January 15, 1952.
30. Gunn, *Breaking Point* (hereafter BP), 13.
31. *Ibid.*
32. BP, 15.
33. BP, 25.
34. BP, 40–41.
35. Email from Gunn to the author, May 12, 2016

36. P. Williams, "Story Notes 'Baby is Three,'" 412.
37. BP, 43–49.
38. BP, 51.
39. BP, 51–52.
40. Anthony, *One and Wonder*, 62–63.
41. Gunn, *Witching Hour* (hereafter WH), 27.
42. WH, 11–21.
43. WH, 24–28.
44. Sutin, *Divine Invasions*, 20–23.
45. WH, 29–30.
46. Campbell, *Collected Editorials*, 217.
47. WH, 31–35.
48. WH, 35.
49. WH, 54–56.
50. Anthony, *One and Wonder*, 320.
51. WH, 73.
52. WH, 80.
53. Amis, *New Maps of Hell*, 114–23.
54. FI, 70–72.
55. FI, 74–75.
56. BP, 54.
57. BP, 61.
58. BP, 66.
59. BP, 74.
60. BP, 77.
61. Gunn, *This Fortress World* (hereafter TFW), 1.
62. TFW, 14–15
63. Knight, *In Search of Wonder*, 258.
64. TFW, 45–46.
65. TFW, 48.
66. Letter from Gunn to Greenberg, November 16, 1954.
67. TFW, 70.
68. TFW, 82–84.
69. TFW, 87.
70. TFW, 112–20.
71. TFW, 125–30.
72. TFW, 143.
73. TFW, 144–45.
74. TFW, 167–71.
75. TFW, 196.
76. TFW, 198–201.
77. Merril Reader's Report, September 28, 1954.
78. *Ibid.*
79. *Ibid.*
80. Letter from Altshuler to Gunn, November 2, 1954.
81. Bryant, "American Gods, American Dreaming," xx.
82. Gunn, "Afterword (*Star Bridge*), 297.
83. Williamson, "Breakdown," 113–54.
84. Williamson, *Wonder's Child*, 132–33.
85. *Ibid.*, 200–01.
86. *Ibid.*, 132.
87. Letter from Gunn to Williamson, October 9, 1953.
88. Gunn & Williamson, *Star Bridge* (hereafter SB), 11.
89. SB, 23.
90. Abbott, *Frontiers Past and Future*, 21.
91. SB, 31.
92. SB, 53.
93. SB, 27–28.
94. SB, 58.
95. SB, 57.
96. SB, 58.
97. *Ibid.*
98. SB, 66.
99. SB, 157.
100. SB, 69–71.
101. Carter, *Creation of Tomorrow*, 226.
102. SB, 71–72.
103. SB, 106.
104. SB, 115.
105. SB, 133–34.
106. Williamson, *Beyond Mars*, 55.
107. SB, 133–34.
108. SB, 141.
109. SB, 148–51.
110. SB, 152–53.
111. SB, 162.
112. SB, 195.
113. SB, 203.
114. SB, 214.
115. SB, 232.
116. SB, 271.
117. Suvin, *Metamorphoses of Science Fiction*, 63.
118. SB, 271.
119. SB, 273–84.

Chapter Three

1. Gunn, *Star-Begotten*, 113–14.
2. Gunn, "James Gunn," 258.
3. Gunn email to the author July 26, 2016.
4. Letter from Gunn to Altshuler, March 17, 1954.
5. Letter from Gunn to Altshuler, February 23, 1955.
6. Letter from Altshuler to Gunn, April 8, 1954.
7. Gunn, *The Joy Makers* (hereafter JM), 4–9.
8. JM, 10–13.
9. JM, 14–20.
10. JM, 20.
11. JM, 27–28.
12. JM, 29.
13. JM, 36–37.
14. JM, 42–43.

15. JM, 47–48.
16. JM, 45–68.
17. JM, 72–82.
18. JM, 82–83.
19. JM, 103–04.
20. JM, 111.
21. JM, 115
22. JM, 120.
23. JM, 123–24.
24. JM, 128.
25. JM, 130.
26. JM, 127.
27. JM, 131.
28. JM, 135–36.
29. JM, 138.
30. JM., 143–63.
31. JM, 171–73.
32. JM, 177–79.
33. JM, 178.
34. JM, 181–82.
35. Wells, *Experiment in Autobiography*, 2.
36. JM, 185.
37. JM, 189.
38. JM, 192–93.
39. JM, 193–99.
40. JM, 199–200.
41. Bostrom, *Superintelligence*, 134–35.
42. JM, 201.
43. Zebrowski, Introduction (*The Joy Makers*), xi.
44. Gunn, "James Gunn," 251.
45. Letter from Gunn to Altshuler, December 18, 1954.
46. Letter from Gunn to Greenberg, April 2, 1955.
47. Letter from Gunn to Altshuler, April 20, 1955.
48. Freeman, *You Will Go to the Moon*, 23.
49. Letter from Gunn to Altshuler, April 20, 1955.
50. Gunn, *Station in Space* (hereafter SS), 3.
51. SS, 6.
52. SS, 1–7.
53. SS, 9.
54. SS, 14.
55. SS, 12–13,
56. SS, 14.
57. SS, 16–17.
58. SS, 20.
59. SS, 28–30.
60. SS, 31–32.
61. SS, 35–37.
62. SS, 39–40.
63. SS, 41–42.
64. SS, 46–47.
65. SS, 56–57.
66. SS, 64.
67. SS, 69–70.
68. Gunn, *Star-Begotten*, 155.
69. *Ibid.*, 156.
70. Gordon, *How to Read a Novel*, 60.
71. *Ibid.*, 69.
72. SS, 73–77.
73. SS, 80–81.
74. SS, 89.
75. SS, 93–97.
76. SS, 106.
77. SS, 107.
78. SS, 108–109.
79. SS, 110–11.
80. SS, 111.
81. SS, 112–14.
82. SS, 131.
83. SS, 125.
84. SS, 154.
85. SS, 156.
86. Westfahl, *Islands in the Sky*, 24.
87. SS, 156.
88. Letter from Gunn to Altshuler, July 20, 1954.
89. Gunn, *The Immortals* (hereafter TI), 9–12.
90. TI, 37–39
91. TI, 48.
92. TI, 52–53
93. TI, 125.
94. TI, 107.
95. TI, 119.
96. TI, 124–25.
97. TI, 141.
98. Letter from Altshuler to Gunn, September 8, 1954.
99. Rejection slip from Gold, October 21, 1954.
100. Letter from Mills to Gunn, June 3, 1957.
101. Gunn, *Road to Science Fiction* Vol. 3, 139.
102. TI, 151.
103. TI, 160.
104. Gunn, *Star-Begotten*, 4.
105. TI, 170.
106. TI, 188.
107. TI, 200.
108. TI, 223–24.
109. TI, 232.
110. TI, 235.
111. TI, 252.
112. TI, 266.
113. TI, 276.
114. TI, 271.
115. TI, 286.
116. TI, 287.
117. TI, 288.
118. TI, 289–90.
119. TI, 297–98.
120. TI, 298.

121. Letter from Gunn to Altshuler, March 22, 1955.
122. FI, 17.
123. FI, 21–23.
124. Page, *Frederik Pohl*, 59.
125. FI, 38.
126. FI, 39–45.
127. Gunn, *Star-Begotten*, 143.
128. FI, 46–52.
129. BP, 95–111.
130. Letter from Altshuler to Gunn, July 18, 1957.
131. Gunn, *Star-Begotten*, 157.
132. FI, 89.
133. FI, 179.
134. *Ibid.*
135. Gunn, *The Burning* (hereafter TB), 2–5.
136. TB, 4–5.
137. TB, 6.
138. TB, 11.
139. TB, 12–13.
140. TB, 27.
141. TB, 18.
142. TB, 25.
143. TB, 40–44.
144. TB, 92–99.
145. TB, 125.
146. TB, 133.
147. TB, 142–48.

Chapter Four

1. Gunn, *The Listeners* (hereafter TL), 20–21.
2. Stableford, *Sociology of Science Fiction*, 117.
3. TL, 22–25.
4. TL, 38.
5. TL, 50–51.
6. TL, 54.
7. TL, 61.
8. TL, 75–84.
9. TL, 94.
10. TL, 96.
11. TL, 111–12.
12. TL, 136–40.
13. TL, 149–50.
14. TL, 165–66.
15. TL, 197.
16. TL, 211.
17. TL, 211–12.
18. Email to the author July 17, 2015.
19. Gunn, *The Magicians*, 27.
20. TM, 75.
21. TM, 141.
22. Letter from Gunn to Mills, January 7, 1972.
23. *Ibid.*
24. Letter from Ravage to Mills, March 14, 1972.
25. Letter from Gunn to Mills, August 8, 1973.
26. *Ibid.*
27. Letter from Gunn to Pohl, August 17, 1973.
28. Letter from Pohl to Gunn, September 7, 1973.
29. Gunn, *Kampus* (hereafter K), 1–11.
30. K,13–14
31. K, 14.
32. K, 14.
33. K, 17–21.
34. K, 53.
35. K, 86–90.
36. K, 96–105.
37. K, 109–111.
38. K, 123.
39. K, 152–58.
40. K, 164.
41. K, 173.
42. K, 175–78.
43. K, 182–86.
44. K, 208–217.
45. K, 229–32.
46. K, 233–44.
47. K, 254–78.
48. K, 284.
49. K, 305–308.
50. Letter from Williamson to Gunn, September 18, 1977.
51. Gunn, *The Dreamers* (hereafter TD), 7.
52. TD, 16.
53. TD, 23–24.
54. TD, 19.
55. TD, 30–36.
56. TD, 37–42.
57. TD, 52.
58. TD, 64.
59. TD, 70.
60. TD, 82.
61. TD, 96–97.
62. TD, 121.
63. TD, 153.
64. TD, 171.
65. TD, 174.
66. Gunn, *Science of Science-Fiction Writing*, 29–30.
67. Gunn, *Crisis!* (hereafter C), 15.
68. C, 18.
69. C, 25.
70. C, 55.
71. C, 64.
72. C. 96.
73. C, 118.
74. C, 123.

75. C, 132.
76. C, 144.
77. C, 150.
78. C, 151.

Chapter Five

1. Gunn, *Human Voices*, 220.
2. Gunn, *Star-Begotten*, 244–45.
3. *Ibid.*
4. Gunn, *Joy Machine*, 5–10.
5. *Ibid.*, 26–29.
6. *Ibid.*, 49.
7. *Ibid.*, 55.
8. *Ibid.*, 62.
9. *Ibid.*, 90–91.
10. *Ibid.*, 135.
11. *Ibid.*, 261–63.
12. Gunn, *Millennium Blues* (hereafter MB), 3.
13. MB, 1.
14. MB, 8.
15. MB, 17.
16. MB, 120.
17. MB, 126–27.
18. MB, 31.
19. *Ibid.*
20. MB, 90.
21. MB, 144.
22. MB, 42.
23. MB, 150.
24. MB, 54.
25. MB, 104.
26. MB, 108.
27. MB, 173.
28. MB, 182.
29. *Ibid.*
30. Benford, "Looking with a Wide Eye," 3.
31. Gunn, "Preface (*Gift from the Stars*), 1.
32. Gunn, *Gift from the Stars* (hereafter GS), 9–11.
33. GS, 24.
34. GS, 29–30.
35. GS, 31.
36. GS, 46.
37. GS, 61.
38. GS, 101.
39. GS, 108.
40. GS, 154.
41. Gunn, *Transcendental*, 47.
42. *Ibid.*, 70.
43. *Ibid.*, 77.
44. *Ibid.*, 43.
45. *Ibid.*, 30.
46. *Ibid.*, 91.
47. *Ibid.*, 132.
48. *Ibid.*, 175.
49. *Ibid.*, 176.
50. *Ibid.*, 180–85.
51. *Ibid.*, 212.
52. *Ibid.*, 217.
53. *Ibid.*, 250.
54. *Ibid.*, 258–60.
55. *Ibid.*, 280.
56. *Ibid.*, 302.
57. Gunn, *Transgalactic*, 10–18.
58. *Ibid.*, 58.
59. *Ibid.*, 86–88.
60. *Ibid.*, 122–28.
61. *Ibid.*, 113.
62. *Ibid.*, 147.
63. *Ibid.*, 188.
64. *Ibid.*, 214–17.
65. Gunn, *Transformation*, 7.
66. *Ibid.*, 240.

Chapter Six

1. Gunn email to the author, August 5, 2016.
2. Gunn, *Modern Science Fiction*, 5.
3. Gunn, "Foreword" *(Cambridge Companion)*, xv.
4. Gunn, *Road to Science Fiction Vol. 1*, 1.
5. *Ibid.*, 4.
6. Gunn, *Road to Science Fiction Vol. 2*, xi.
7. *Ibid.*, x.
8. Gunn, *Inside Science Fiction*, 73.
9. *Ibid.*
10. *Ibid.*, 74–75.
11. Delany, "Science Fiction and 'Literature,'" 95–117.
12. Gunn, *Insider Science Fiction*, 141.
13. Gunn, "Touchstones," 301.
14. Gunn, *Road to Science Fiction Vol. 3*, 213–15.

Bibliography

Abbott, Carl. *Frontiers Past and Future: Science Fiction and the American West.* Lawrence: University Press of Kansas, 2006.

Ackerman, Forrest J. "The Odd Genre." *If,* February 1956. 2–3, 116.

Allen, Dick, ed. *Science Fiction: The Future.* New York: Harcourt Brace Jovanovich, 1971.

Amis, Kingsley. *New Maps of Hell.* New York: Harcourt Brace, 1960.

Anthony, Piers. *One and Wonder: Piers Anthony's Remembered Stories.* E-book. Open Road Integrated Media, 2014.

Asimov, Isaac. *In Memory Yet Green: The Autobiography of Isaac Asimov, 1920–1954.* New York: Doubleday, 1979.

Benford, Gregory. "Looking with a Wide Eye." Introduction. *Gift from the Stars.* By James Gunn. Dallas: Benbella Books, 2005. 3–6.

Bostrom, Nick. *Superintelligence Paths, Dangers, Strategies.* Oxford: Oxford University Press, 2014.

Bova, Ben, ed. *Nebula Awards Showcase 2008.* New York: ROC, 2008.

———. "Teaching Science Fiction." *Analog,* June 1974. 5–8. 176–78.

———. "Teaching the Teachers." *Analog,* January 1976. 5–10.

Bryant, Edward. "American Gods, American Dreaming." Foreword. *Spider Island: The Collected Works of Jack Williamson, Volume Four.* Royal Oak: Haffner Press, 2002. xv-xxi.

Campbell, John W. *Collected Editorials from Analog.* Ed. Harry Harrison. New York: Doubleday, 1966.

———. *The John W. Campbell Letters Volume 1.* Eds. Perry Chapdelaine, Tony Chapdelaine, and George Hay. Franklin, TN: AC Projects, 1985.

Carter, Paul A. *The Creation of Tomorrow.* New York: Columbia University Press, 1977.

Clarke, Arthur C. *Astounding Days.* New York: Bantam, 1989.

Clute, John. "James E. Gunn." *The Encyclopedia of Science Fiction.* Eds. John Clute and Peter Nicholls. London: Orbit, 1993. 529.

Delany, Samuel R. "Science Fiction and 'Literature'—or, The Conscience of the King." *Speculations on Speculation.* Eds. James Gunn and Matthew Candelaria. Lanham: Scarecrow Press, 2005. 95–117.

Ellison, Harlan. *The Other Glass Teat: Further Essays of Opinion on Television.* New York: Pyramid Books, 1975.

Freeman, Mae and Ira. *You Will Go to the Moon.* New York: Random House, 1959.

Gordon, Caroline. *How to Read a Novel.* New York: Viking, 1957.

Goulart, Ron. *Cheap Thrills: An Informal History of the Pulp Magazines.* New Rochelle: Arlington House, 1972.

Graham, John, Ed. *"Yours for the Revolution": The Appeal to Reason, 1895–1922.* Lincoln: University of Nebraska Press, 1990.

Gunn, James. "Afterword (*Star Bridge*)." *Star Bridge* By Jack Williamson and James Gunn. New York: TOR, 2014. 295–98.

———. *Alternate Worlds: The Illustrated History of Science-Fiction.* New York: Prentice-Hall, 1975.

———. "The Boy with Five Fingers." *Startling Stories,* January 1953. 58–60.

———. *Breaking Point.* New York: DAW, 1972.

———. *The Burning.* New York: Dell, 1972.

———. "A Classic of Science Fiction." *Universe.* By Robert A. Heinlein. New York: Dell, 1951. 3–5.

———. "Communications." *Startling Stories,* September 1949. 100–20.

———. *Crisis!* New York: TOR, 1986.

_____. *The Dreamers*. [1980]. As *The Mind Master*. New York: Pocket, 1982.

_____. "Foreword." *The Cambridge Companion to Science Fiction*. Eds. Edward James and Farah Mendlesohn. Cambridge: Cambridge UP, 2003. xv-xviii.

_____. "Fred and Me." *Gateways*. Ed. Elizabeth Anne Hull. New York: Tor, 2010. 165–9.

_____. *Funny Side Up*. Ed., uncredited. New York: Dell, 1952.

_____. *Future Imperfect*. New York: Bantam, 1964.

_____. *Gift from the Stars*. Dallas: Benbella, 2005.

_____. "Heroes, Heroines, Villains: The Characters of Science Fiction." *The Craft of Science Fiction*. Ed. Reginald Bretnor. New York: Harper & Row, 1976. 161–77.

_____. *Human Voices*. Waterville: Five Star, 2002.

_____. *The Immortals* [1962]. New York: Pocket, 2004.

_____. *Inside Science Fiction*. Second Edition. Lanham: Scarecrow Press, 2006.

_____. "Introduction." *Some Dreams Are Nightmares*. New York: Scribner's, 1974.

_____. *Isaac Asimov: The Foundations of Science Fiction*. Revised Edition. Lanham: Scarecrow Press, 1996.

_____. "James Gunn." *Contemporary Authors Autobiography Series Volume 2*. Farmington Hills: Gale, 1985. 233–60.

_____. *The Joy Machine*. New York: Pocket, 1996.

_____. *The Joy Makers*. [1961]. New York: Bantam, 1971.

_____. *Kampus*. New York: Bantam, 1977.

_____. *The Listeners*. New York: Scribner's, 1972.

_____. "The Listeners (Introduction)." *Nebula Awards Showcase 2008*. Ed. Ben Bova. New York: ROC, 2008. 277–80.

_____. *The Magicians*. [1976]. New York: Signet, 1976.

_____. "The Magic of Imagination." Foreword. *The Teenage Tarzan: A Literary Analysis of Edgar Rice Burroughs'* Jungle Tales of Tarzan. By Stan Galloway. Jefferson: McFarland, 2010. 1–3.

_____. *Man and the Future*. Ed. Lawrence: University Press of Kansas, 1968.

_____. "The Man with Common Sense." *Amazing*, July 1950. 112–22.

_____. "Mask of Peace." *Future*, September 1951. 56–65.

_____. *The Millennium Blues*. Norwalk: Easton Press, 2001.

_____. "The Misogynist (Introduction)." *SF: Authors' Choice 4*. Ed. Harry Harrison. New York: Putnam's, 1974. 103–5.

_____. *Modern Science Fiction: A Critical Analysis*. Unpublished thesis, 1951.

_____. "On Style." *Those Who Can: A Science Fiction Reader*. Ed. Robin Scott Wilson. New York, Mentor, 1973. 303–11.

_____. "Open Warfare." *Galaxy*, May 1954. 106–28.

_____. "Paradox." *Thrilling Wonder Stories*, October 1949. 135–56.

_____. *Paratexts: Introductions to Science Fiction and Fantasy*. Lanham: Scarecrow Press, 2013.

_____. "Preface (*Gift from the Stars*)." *Gift from the Stars*. By James Gunn. Dallas: Benbella Books, 2005.

_____. "Preface: *The Immortals*." *The Immortals*. By James Gunn. New York: Pocket, 2004.

_____. "Private Enterprise." *Astounding*, July 1950. 63–77.

_____. *Reading Science Fiction*. Ed., with Marleen S. Barr and Matthew Candelaria. London: Palgrave, 2009.

_____. *The Road to Science Fiction Volume 1: From Gilgamesh to Wells*. Ed. New York: Mentor, 1977.

_____. *The Road to Science Fiction Volume 2: From Wells to Heinlein*. Ed. Lanham: Scarecrow, 1979, 2002.

_____. *The Road to Science Fiction Volume 3: From Heinlein to Here*. Ed. Lanham: Scarecrow Press, 1979, 2002.

_____. *The Road to Science Fiction Volume 4: From Here to Forever*. Ed. New York: Mentor, 1982.

_____. *The Road to Science Fiction Volume 5: The British Way*. Ed. Clarkson: White Wolf, 1998.

_____. *The Road to Science Fiction Volume 6: Around the World*. Ed. Clarkson: White Wolf, 1998.

_____. "Science Fiction and the Mainstream." *Science Fiction, Today and Tomorrow*. Ed. Reginald Bretnor. Baltimore: Penguin, 1974. 183–216.

_____. *The Science of Science-Fiction Writing*. Lanham: Scarecrow Press, 2000.

_____. "Slave Psychology." *Future*, January 1951. 60–69.

_____. "Slaves of Venus." *Planet Stories*, September 1952. 90–115.

_____. *Some Dreams Are Nightmares*. New York: Scribner's, 1974.

_____. *Speculations on Speculation: Theories of Science Fiction*. Ed., with Matthew Candelaria. Lanham: Scarecrow Press, 2005.

_____. *Star-Begotten: A Life Lived in Science Fiction*. Unpublished memoir (forthcoming from McFarland).
_____. *Station in Space*. New York: Bantam, 1958.
_____. *Star Bridge* [1955], and Jack Williamson. New York: TOR, 2014.
_____. "The Sun Came Up Last Night." *Science Fiction Quarterly*, August 1951. 8–36.
_____. "Teaching Science Fiction Revisited." *Analog*, November 1974. 5–10, 175–8.
_____. "These Things Are Sirius." *Thrilling Wonder Stories*, August 1951. 126–37.
_____. *This Fortress World* [1955]. New York: Berkley, 1979.
_____. "Touchstones." *Speculations on Speculation*. Eds. James Gunn and Matthew Candelaria. Lanham: Scarecrow Press, 2005. 301–309.
_____. *Transcendental*. New York: TOR, 2013.
_____. *Transgalactic*. New York: TOR, 2016.
_____. *Transformation*. New York: TOR, 2017.
_____. "2015 Science Fiction Hall of Fame Acceptance Speech." *Locus* 75:2 (August 2015). 34.
_____. *The Witching Hour*. New York: Dell, 1970.
_____. "Without Portfolio." *Astounding*, January 1955. 128–39.
_____. "A Word for Freedom." *If*, January 1954. 68–81.
Harrison, Harry. *Harry Harrison! Harry Harrison!*. New York: TOR, 2014.
Heinlein, Robert A. *To Sail Beyond the Sunset*. New York: Ace, 1987.
Kessel, John. "Buffalo." *The Pure Product*. By John Kessel. New York: TOR, 1997. 282–301.
_____. "James Gunn, Grand Master." *Nebula Awards Showcase 2008*. Ed. Ben Bova. New York: ROC, 2008. 269–275.
Knight, Damon. *In Search of Wonder*. Chicago: Advent, 1967.
Larbalestier, Justine. *The Battle of the Sexes in Science Fiction*. Middletown: Wesleyan UP, 2002.
Lyles, William H. *Putting Dell on the Map: A History of Dell Paperbacks*. Westport: Greenwood, 1983.
Malzberg, Barry. "Afterword to 'New Blood.'" *The End of Summer: Science Fiction of the Fifties*. Eds. Barry Malzberg and Bill Pronzini. New York: Ace, 1979. 205–06.
McAleer, Neil. *Arthur C. Clarke: The Authorized Biography*. Chicago: Contemporary Books, 1992.
McCool, John H. "Rising Son." kuhistory.com. Retrieved June 12, 2016.

McKitterick, Christopher. "Call to Arms." *Analog*, January 1996. 137–41.
Nadis, Fred. *The Man from Mars: Ray Palmer's Amazing Pulp Journey*. New York: Tarcher, 2013.
Nicholls, Peter. "Conceptual Breakthrough." *The Encyclopedia of Science Fiction*. Eds. John Clute and Peter Nicholls. London: Orbit, 1993. 254–7.
Page, Michael R. *Frederik Pohl*. Champaign: University of Illinois Press, 2015.
Patterson, William H., Jr. *Robert A Heinlein, In Dialogue with His Century Volume I: 1907–1948 Learning Curve*. New York: Tor, 2010.
Pohl, Frederik. "Frederik Pohl." *Contemporary Authors Volume 188*. Farmington Hills: Gale, 2001. 333–55.
_____. "A Tribute to Gunn." *LoneStarCon 3: The 71st World Science Fiction Convention*. Convention program. San Antonio, 2013.
_____. *The Way the Future Was*. New York: Ballantine, 1978.
Sawyer, Andy and Peter Wright. "Design, Delivery and Evaluation." *Teaching Science Fiction*. Eds. Andy Sawyer and Peter Wright. London: Palgrave Macmillan, 2011. 219–46.
Silverberg, Robert. *Other Spaces, Other Times*. New York: Nonstop Press, 2009.
_____. Review of *Future Imperfect*. *Amazing*, July 1964. 125.
_____. "Sounding Brass, Tinkling Cymbal." *Hell's Cartographers*. Eds. Brian W. Aldiss and Harry Harrison. New York: Harper & Row, 1975. 7–45.
_____. *Tales from Super-Science Fiction*. Ed. Royal Oak: Haffner Press, 2012.
Srinarahari, M.H. "International Report from India." *Locus* 72:2, June 2014. 28–29.
Stableford, Brian. *The Sociology of Science Fiction*. San Bernardino: Borgo Press, 1987.
Sutin, Lawrence. *Divine Invasions: A Life of Philip K. Dick*. New York: Citadel Twilight, 1989.
Suvin, Darko. *Metamorphoses of Science Fiction*. New Haven: Yale University Press, 1979.
Tenn, William. "Jazz Then, Musicology Now." *Dancing Naked: The Unexpurgated William Tenn*. Framingham: NESFA Press, 2004. 119–27.
Wells, H.G. *Experiment in Autobiography*. Boston: Little, Brown, 1934.
_____. "The Fall in America, 1937." *World Brain*. London: Meuthen, 1938. 153–67.
_____. "New Americans." *Collier's* 101: 6 (February 5, 1938). 14–15, 44.
Westfahl, Gary. *Islands in the Sky: The Space*

Station Theme in Science Fiction. Second Edition. Rockville: Borgo Press, 2009.

Williams, Paul. "Story Notes 'Baby is Three.'" *Baby is Three, Volume VI: The Complete Stories of Theodore Sturgeon.* By Theodore Sturgeon. Ed. Paul Williams. Berkeley: North Atlantic Books, 1999. 412–15.

Williamson, Jack. *Beyond Mars, Book 2.* El Cajon: Blackthorne Publishing, 1987.

_____. "Breakdown." *The Best of Jack Williamson.* New York: Ballantine, 1978. 113–54.

_____. "Science Fiction Comes to College." *Extrapolation,* May 1971. 68–71.

_____. *Wonder's Child: My Life in Science Fiction.* Dallas: Benbella, 2005.

Zebrowski, George. "Introduction (*The Joy Makers*)." *The Joy Makers.* By James Gunn. New York: Crown, 1984. ix–xi.

Index

Abbott, Carl 120
ABC "Movie of the Week" 51
Abelard Press 36, 39, 41–42
AboutSF 4, 7
"The Abyss" 238–239
"The Academic Viewpoint" 61
Ackerman, Forrest J. 35, 47–48, 57
"Ad Infinitum" *see* "Every Day Is Christmas"
administrative systems 50, 54, 80–81, 83, 149–163, 164, 188–197, 245–246
Adventures in Time and Space (Healy and McComas) 10, 24
Again, Dangerous Visions (Ellison) 58, 188
Against the Fall of Night (Clarke) 116
Aldiss, Brian 3, 9, 11, 63–64, 69, 73, 92, 250, 254–255
alien contact 77–78, 82–83, 91–96, 188–197, 235–251
alien invasion 77–82, 86–90, 104–105, 179–180, 250
Allen, Dick 60
Allen, L. David 10
Alternate Worlds 12, 31, 47, 60, 63, 66–67, 252, 254–255
Altshuler, Harry 38, 40–42, 44, 47, 51, 53–55, 117, 132, 149, 164, 168–169, 175, 179, 252
Alumni Magazine (KU) 48
Amazing Stories 9, 12, 18, 19, 25, 38, 77, 84, 225, 255
Amazing Stories Quarterly 245
The American Magazine 32
American News Corporation 48, 133
Amis, Kingsley 103, 252–253
"Among the Beautiful Bright Children" 59, 66, 214–216
Analog 10, 11, 14, 34, 61–62, 65, 67–68, 219, 225, 235, 257
Anderson, Poul 57, 69, 72, 106, 219
"The Angry Man" *see* "The Naked Sky"
"The Answer" 188, 193–195

Anthony, Piers 96, 101
"The Anti-Nuclear Conspiracy" 10
Anvil, Christopher 85
apocalyptic elements 15, 36, 85–86, 132–148, 163, 169–175, 178–187, 189, 200–213, 229–235
Apollo missions 59, 151
The Appeal to Reason 18
Apple II computer 201–203
Arecibo Observatory 190–197
"Arena" (Brown) 79
Argosy 37
"As the Wall Crumbles" (Scholes) 61
Asimov, Isaac 1, 9, 10, 14, 18, 23, 28–29, 40–41, 44, 47–48, 50, 57, 65, 67, 70, 72, 74, 78, 80, 82, 106–107, 115, 118, 122, 125–126, 130, 133, 163, 175, 183, 229, 231, 248, 249, 253, 256–257, 258
Associated Press 49
Astounding 18, 19, 23, 25, 31, 34, 38, 44, 46, 77–79, 82, 84, 86, 91, 92, 117, 118, 134, 164, 180, 228, 231, 238
Astounding Days (Clarke) 18
atomic bomb, atomic war 22, 36, 85–86, 106, 120, 149, 158–159, 161, 220, 247, 253
"An Author Watches His Brainchild Die on Television" 52

Baby and Child Care (Spock) 177
"Baby Is Three" (Sturgeon) 10, 95, 133
Bacigalupi, Paolo 3
Bacon, Francis 10
Bailey, J.O. 252–253
Bailey, Robin Wayne 72
Ballantine Books 77
Ballard, J.G. 92
Bantam Books 29, 52, 134, 148, 200–201
Barnard, Allan 32
Barr, Marleen 13, 73–74, 258
The Battle of the Sexes in Science Fiction (Larbalestier) 89

273

Baxter, Stephen 3
Bear, Greg 57
"The Beautiful Brew" 44, 56–57
Benford, Gregory 235–236, 251, 259
Berkeley, California 207, 212–213
The Best of Science Fiction (Conklin) 24
Bester, Alfred 35, 118, 119, 175
Beyond 35, 42, 44, 105, 199
Beyond Apollo (Malzberg) 64
Beyond Mars (Williamson) 32, 37, 126
Beyond This Horizon (Heinlein) 257
"The Big Wheel" 46, 149, 154–157, 161
Billion Year Spree (Aldiss) 63, 254
The Birth of a New Republic (Breuer and Williamson) 12
"The Bitterest Pill" (Pohl) 177
"Black Destroyer" (Van Vogt) 243, 253
Blackwood, Algernon 12
Blatty, William Peter 197
Blish, James 40–41, 52, 92, 117, 133, 249, 252–253
Bloch, Robert 33, 62
"Bloodchild" (Butler) 241
Blue Book 79
The Body Snatchers (Finney) 89, 104
Bonestell, Chesley 44, 148, 152
The Book of the New Sun (Wolfe) 108
Borgo Press 71
Bostrom, Nick 148
Boucher, Anthony 29, 33
Bould, Mark 258
Bova, Ben 61–62
"A Boy and His Dog" (Ellison) 185–186
"The Boy with Five Fingers" 34, 38, 85
Brackett, Leigh 106
Bradbury, Ray 10, 29–30, 36, 138–139, 142, 171, 177
Brave New World (Huxley) 137–138
Brazil (film) 169
"Breakdown" (Williamson) 118
"Breaking Point" 14, 24, 27, 30, 35, 38–39, 66, 80, 91–96, 102, 110, 161, 226, 251
Bretnor, Reginald 60
Breuer, Miles J. 1, 12
Brin, David 188
Bring the Jubilee (Moore) 133
Brown, Fredric 79
Brunner, John 58, 118
Bryant, Ed 117–118
Budrys, Algis 50, 169
"Buffalo" (Kessel) 20–21, 72
Bulwer Lytton, Edward 254
Burgess, Anthony 200
The Burning 14, 36, 43, 46, 57, 175, 180–187, 188, 189, 207, 211–212, 226, 227
Burroughs, Edgar Rice 9, 19, 29, 249
Butler, Octavia 180, 241
"By His Bootstraps" (Heinlein) 253

Cadigan, Pat 6
The Caine Mutiny (Wouk) 152
Callisto 141, 143
The Cambridge Companion to Science Fiction (James and Mendlesohn) 254
Campanella, Tomaso 254
Campbell, John W. 9, 19, 25, 31, 33, 36, 44, 45, 46, 53–54, 57–58, 61, 72, 77–79, 82, 85–86, 99, 104, 117, 118, 133–134, 143, 180, 183–184, 199, 228, 253, 254, 256
Campbell Award 3, 64–65, 70
Campbell Conference 1, 2, 3, 4, 13, 62, 64–65, 67, 70, 72, 75
Candelaria, Matthew 73, 258
Candide (Voltaire) 204, 207
Canterbury Tales 240–241
Carnival of Souls 102, 140
Carroll, Lewis 81
Carter, Paul 124
"The Cave of Night" 24, 44, 148, 150–152
The Caves of Steel (Asimov) 125–126, 258
Cerebus 144
Chalmers, Laurence 55–56
Chambers, Everett 51
Chandler, Raymond 19
Cheap Thrills (Goulart) 19
chemical memory and drugs 55–56, 132–148, 184, 186, 200–219, 227–229
Chicago 22, 24, 32–35, 47, 66, 93, 116, 198
"Child of the Sun" 67, 219, 221
"Childhood's End" (Clarke) 92
"Child's Play" (Tenn) 253
China 66–67, 83, 254
"Cinderella Story" 49
City (Simak) 133
"The City and the Critics" 258
"City of the Living Dead" (Manning and Pratt) 145
The City of the Sun (Campanella) 254
"The City on the Edge of Forever" (Ellison) 223
Clareson, Tom 62–63
Clarion workshops 60
Clarke, Arthur C. 9, 10, 18, 51, 69–70, 72, 74, 92, 116, 148, 149, 153, 154, 189, 196, 247, 253
Clement, Hal 69
Clifton, Mark 46
climate change 83, 120, 221, 230, 232, 247
Clingerman, Mildred 46
A Clockwork Orange (Burgess) 200, 206
Clute, John 50, 68–69
Cogswell, Theodore 169
"The Cold Equations" (Godwin) 149, 258
Cold War 83, 89, 107, 120, 150–151, 152, 157
Cole, Everett B. 85
Coleridge, Samuel Taylor 157
Collier's 20, 32, 40, 43–44, 77, 148–149

Collins, Suzanne 126
"Colony" (Dick) 105
Comic Inferno 103, 175, 189
"Coming Attraction" (Leiber) 35, 169, 253
communication 77–81, 86, 91–96, 119, 188–197, 213–219
"Communications" 25, 78–83, 149, 157
competent man 83, 91–96, 132–148, 149–163
computers 81, 93, 107–116, 130, 132–148, 170–171, 191–197, 202–203, 208–210, 212, 220, 227–229, 237, 239–251
Conboy, William A. 51
Conceptual Breakthrough 30, 106, 116, 249
Conjure Wife (Leiber) 86
Connell, Evan S. 27
The Conquest of Space (Ley) 152
consumerism 102–104, 175–178, 201–202
Contact (Sagan) 14, 26, 71, 236
Cosmopolitan 32
Cosmos (Sagan) 236
The Craft of Science Fiction (Bretnor) 60
Crafton, Allen 23–24
"Craphound" (Doctorow) 84
Crisis! 14, 43, 67–68, 135, 219–224, 231
Critical Explorations in Science Fiction and Fantasy series 65
cyberpunk 14, 218–219, 241, 257

Daily Kansan 21, 23
Dangerous Visions (Ellison) 54, 58
Darwin, Charles 256
Datlow, Ellen 3
"The Day the Magic Came Back" 71, 225–226
"Deadly Silence" 36, 45, 179–180
Death Race 2000 169
de Camp, L. Sprague 33
"The Defenders" (Dick) 36
Delany, Samuel R. 73, 117–118, 257–258
Dell paperbacks 14, 26, 28–33, 56
Del Rey, Lester 36, 37, 46, 91, 93, 175
The Demolished Man (Bester) 35
Denton, Bradley 3, 6
Desilu Playhouse 44
"The Diamond Lens" (O'Brien) 225
Dianetics 134, 136
Dick, Philip K. 36, 45, 54, 79, 89, 93, 98, 105, 134, 143, 148, 178, 184, 189
Dickson, Gordon R. 56–58, 61–62, 69, 113, 115
Dick Tracy Monthly 26, 32
Di Fate, Vincent 65
Disney magazine 32
Docking, George 50
Doc Savage 19
Dr. Seuss 135
Dr. Strangelove 159

Doctorow, Cory 3, 84
"Donor" 46, 164, 165–167, 169
Donovan's Brain (Siodmak) 164
Dozois, Gardner 9
Drake, Frank 54
The Dreamers 14, 43, 59, 66–67, 86, 112, 125, 184, 213–219, 226, 228, 229, 246
The Dream-Quest of Vellitt Boe (Johnson) 7
dreams 79–81, 91–96, 102, 125, 132–148, 150–163, 178–179, 182, 184, 210, 213–219, 227–229, 241, 246
Drumm, Chris 37
Duncan, Andy 3, 76
Dune (Herbert) 9, 115, 119
Dye, Charles 42
Dynamic 14, 31, 65, 72, 252
dystopian elements 15, 34, 46, 55–56, 102–104, 132–148, 167–177, 180–187, 200–213

Early Edition 68
Earth Abides (Stewart) 28
Earthman, Come Home (Blish) 117, 133
Eastern New Mexico University 1, 12, 47
Easton Press 69, 230, 259
Eaton Conference 13, 67, 75
economics 82–84, 121–131, 150–163, 189–197, 203, 221–222
Edwards, Carroll 27
Eiseley, Loren 51
Eisenhower, Dwight D. 49–50
"Elixir" 71, 164, 167–169
Ellison, Harlan 9, 40, 52–54, 56, 58–59, 62, 66, 147, 185, 188, 191–192, 214
Ellsworth, Fred 49
EMP Museum 72
Emshwiller, Ed 238
Encyclopædia Britannica 132
The Encyclopedia of Science Fiction (Nicholls and Clute) 50, 68–69
"End of the World" 11, 68, 220
"The End-of-the-World Ball" 229–230
Escape from New York 169
Esquire 200
"Every Day Is Christmas" 37–38, 102–104, 136
The Exorcist (Blatty) 197
The Exploration of Space (Clarke) 148
Extrapolation 59–60, 62, 256

A Face in the Crowd (Kazan) 222
Fahrenheit 451 (Bradbury) 138–140, 171
The Fall of the Towers (Delany) 118
falling away from science 106–116, 180–187, 191–193, 212, 225–226
Famous Fantastic Mysteries 20, 77
Fantastic 49, 179
Fantastic Adventures 77

Fantastic Universe 45, 46, 133
Fantasy (magazine) 46
Fantasy Book 77
Farmer, Philip Jose 69, 258
"The Father-Thing" (Dick) 105
"Feeding Time" 46
Fern, Paula 54
The Fifties: The End of Summer (Malzberg) 10, 50
Finney, Jack 89, 104
"The Fireman" (Bradbury) 29–30
"First Contact" (Leinster) 79, 93
First Fandom 17
Flaubert, Gustave 157
Follett, Ken 189
"Fondly Fahrenheit" (Bester) 175
The Forever War (Haldeman) 241
"Forgetfulness" (Campbell) 253
Forster, E.M. 126, 137, 144, 174, 176, 214, 258
Foundation (Asimov) 9, 23, 65, 78, 82, 106–107, 115, 118, 130, 133, 183
Foundation (journal) 60
Foundation's Edge (Asimov) 249
The Fountains of Paradise (Clarke) 247
"Fox Magic" (Johnson) 71
Frankenstein (Shelley) 11, 254
Frank Merriwell adventures 18, 19
Franklin, H. Bruce 257–258
"Freedom, Inc." *see* "Slaves of Venus"
Freeman, Mae, and Ira 149–150
From the Earth to the Moon (Verne) 60
frontier theme 78–84, 86, 120, 123, 141–148, 148–163, 182, 186–187, 223, 238–239, 241–244, 246
The Fugitive 51–52
Fuller, R. Buckminster 51
"The Function of Science Fiction" 47
Funny Side Up 32–33
Furies 144
Future (magazine) 25, 78, 81
Future Imperfect 38, 50, 88–89
Futurians 36, 141
"The Futurist" 25

G-8 and His Flying Aces 19
Gable, Clark 25
Gagarin, Yuri 150
Galactic Center series (Benford) 251
galactic empire 78–79, 106–131
Galaxy 14, 25, 26, 27, 29, 32, 34–35, 37–38, 41, 44, 46, 53, 55, 72, 77, 84, 85–86, 88–93, 95, 96–97, 101, 117, 125, 175, 180, 184, 189
Ganymede 141, 143
García Marquez, Gábriel 235
Garrett, Randall 85
"The Gatekeepers" 258
Gateway (Pohl) 64, 239

Gateways (Hull) 74
Gender/gender politics 51, 86–90, 161, 178–179, 185–186, 189, 221, 234, 249–250
genetic engineering/bio-technology 83, 164, 237–238
George, Christopher 52
Gernsback, Hugo 9, 12, 27, 247, 255
Gibson, William 141, 218, 241
Gift from the Stars 14, 26, 43, 71, 197, 235–240
"The Giftie" 236—237
"The Gingerbread Man" 71
Girard, Kansas 18, 19, 26, 179
"The Girl from Mars" (Breuer and Williamson) 12
"The Girls Who Were Really Built" 49, 145, 179–180, 250
Glenn, John 150–151
Gloriana (Moorcock) 64
Gnome Press 42–43, 116, 117
The Gods Themselves (Asimov) 65
Godwin, Tom 149, 258
Gold, Evelyn 33, 45, 47
Gold, Horace 27, 30, 35–36, 37, 45, 53, 72, 85, 88–93, 96, 101, 105, 117, 132, 133, 138, 168, 199
Golding, William 189
Goldman, Stephen 64, 68–69
The Golfer's Own Book 91
Goonan, Kathleen Ann 3
Gordon, Caroline 48, 157
Goulart, Ron 19
"The Gravity Business" 46
"Green Thumb" 48
Greenberg, Marty 42–43, 47–48, 109, 116, 117, 149
Grokking the Future (Hollister and Thompson) 60
Guam 22
"Guardian Angel" (Clarke) 92
Guardians of the Galaxy 128–129
Gulliver's Travels (Swift) 250
Gunn, Christopher "Kit" 27, 32, 56, 74, 86–87, 161, 178–179
Gunn, James: alumni work 48–49, 55; civil defense work 36, 50, 139; college education 21, 23–24, 27, 29, 84; collaboration with Williamson 32, 37–39, 42–43, 116–118; comic book writing 26, 32; fatherhood 26–27, 177–179; G.I. Bill 23–24; Grandmaster 72–73; Gunn's Law 5–6, 43, 65; Hollywood experiences 51–53, 67–68, 219; master's thesis 14, 27, 28, 31, 65, 72, 84, 86, 91, 157, 169, 252–253; naval experience 21–23, 50, 79–81, 153; on the value of science fiction 28, 31, 33–34, 43, 45, 47, 73, 75–76, 148–149, 225, 228, 252–255; overseas trips 21, 64, 66–

67; parents (J. Wayne and Elsie) 17, 37, 70, 74; Pilgrim Award 63, 117–118; radio writing 24; reading 18–19, 22, 24, 25, 153, 157; reading protocols of science fiction 60, 257–258; saving the world through science fiction concept 4, 6–7, 15, 34, 45, 73, 75, 228, 259; scholarship and criticism 14, 20, 23, 27, 31, 60–61, 63–65, 68–70, 72–73, 75, 157, 196, 199, 213, 252–259; SFRA presidency 59, 64; SFWA presidency 56, 59–62, 64; speaking engagements 21, 64, 66; story-sequence technique 43, 132–133, 188, 214, 235; teaching 5, 12, 14, 15, 20, 22, 23, 46–47, 48–49, 55–56, 59–63, 65, 67, 70–71, 73, 75–76, 84, 213, 225, 242, 254–259; teaching of writing 45, 48, 60, 71, 75, 258; touchstones critical concept 169, 258; university administration 14, 23, 40, 49–51, 53, 55–56, 81, 167–168, 180, 183–184, 188, 200–201; *Writing the Rockies* Lifetime Achievement Award 17

Gunn, James, themes in his fiction: administrative systems 50, 54, 80–81, 83, 149–163, 164, 188–197, 245–246; alien contact 77–78, 82–83, 91–96, 188–197, 235–251; alien invasion 77–82, 86–90, 104–105, 179–180, 250; apocalyptic elements 15, 36, 85–86, 132–148, 163, 169–175, 178–187, 189, 200–213, 229–235; big projects 81, 148–163, 188–197, 235–240; chemical memory and drugs 55–56, 132–148, 184, 186, 200–219, 227–229; climate change 83, 120, 221, 230, 232, 247; Cold War 83, 107, 150–151; communication 77–81, 86, 91–96, 119, 188–197, 213–219; competent man 83, 91–96, 132–148, 149–163; computers 81, 93, 107–116, 130, 132–148, 170–171, 191–197, 202–203, 208–210, 212, 220, 227–229, 237, 239–251; consumerism 102–104, 175–178, 201–202; dreams 79–81, 91–96, 102, 125, 132–148, 150–163, 178–179, 182, 184, 210, 213–219, 227–229, 241, 246; dystopian elements 15, 34, 46, 55–56, 102–104, 132–148, 167–177, 180–187, 200–213; economics 82–84, 121–131, 150–163, 189–197, 203, 221–222; falling away from science 106–116, 180–187, 191–193, 212, 225–226; frontier theme 78–84, 86, 120, 123, 141–148, 148–163, 182, 186–187, 223, 238–239, 241–244, 246; galactic empire 78–79, 106–131; genetic engineering/bio-technology 83, 164, 237–238; loneliness 80–81, 91–102, 105, 156–163, 188–197, 213–219; machines, technology 87, 89–90, 94, 106–116, 132–148, 175–177, 182, 208–210, 212; marriage/family life 86–91, 102–104, 148, 155–157, 161–163, 177–179, 188–190, 206, 214–219, 221, 232; mutation, human evolution 84–86, 120–131, 163–175, 240; paranoia 86–102, 104–105, 132–148, 175–179, 214–219, 236–240; politics 14, 46, 78–79, 82–83, 106–116, 121–131, 148–163, 181–187, 189–197, 199, 200–213, 237–239; psychology 79–81, 91–102, 104–105, 108–112, 132–148, 157–163, 176–177, 181–187, 188–190, 202, 214–219; recursivity 82, 85, 179, 194, 225, 228, 238; religion 78, 106–116, 145–148, 161, 181–187, 189–197, 210–211, 231–235, 241–251; robots/androids 91, 143–148, 175–177, 179, 205–206; ruinous cities 110–111, 164–177; shifting realities 94–96, 125, 132–148, 178–179, 184, 200–219, 239; telepathy/Telekinesis as theme 77–78, 96–102, 106–108, 112–116; underground movements 137–142, 175–177, 183–187, 211–212, 228–229; urban geographies 111, 125–127, 132–148, 166–175, 179–180, 214; virtual reality 107–116, 123, 132–148, 210, 213–219

Gunn, Jane 23, 26, 32–33, 35, 46, 50, 74, 86–90, 179
Gunn, John 18, 20, 26
Gunn, Kevin 44–45, 74, 161, 177–178
Gunn, Richard 17, 20, 37, 70, 74, 78, 164
Gunn Center for the Study of Science Fiction 1, 4, 11–13, 17, 34, 67, 70–72, 74–75, 256–257
Gunnison, Colorado 17

Haber, Heinz 148, 153
Haggard, Rider 19, 66, 243
Haldeman, Joe 3, 64, 72, 241, 256
Haldeman-Julius, Emanuel 18
Hale, Edward Everett 254
Halsey, Reese 67
Hamilton, Edmond 156
Hammett, Dashiell 19
Hankins, John 252
The Haploids (Sohl) 89
"Happy Birthday, Dear Jesus" (Pohl) 103
"Happy Is the Bride" *see* "The Reluctant Witch"
Harrison, Harry 53, 57–58, 64, 69, 86, 245
Harry Harrison! Harry Harrison! (Harrison) 57–58
Harvey Comics 26
Harvey, Herk 102, 140
Haskell Indian Institute 48
Hawthorne, Nathaniel 10, 254
"Hedonics, Inc." *see* "The Unhappy Man"
"The Hedonist" *see* "Name Your Pleasure"
Heechee saga (Pohl) 251
Heinlein, Robert A. 9, 10, 12, 17, 29–30,

278   Index

32, 70, 72, 83, 89, 107, 116, 117, 126, 149, 231, 253, 257
"Helen O'Loy" (Del Rey) 175
Helliconia trilogy (Aldiss) 250
Hemingway, Ernest 19, 24
Herbert, Frank 9, 115, 119, 122, 147
The Hidden Persuaders (Packard) 103
Hilton, James 211
"Hoax" 44–45, 149, 152–154
Hobbes, Thomas 212
Hoskins, Bob 49
"The House Dutiful" *see* "The Technological Revolution"
How to Read a Novel (Gordon) 157
"How-2" (Simak) 175
Hubbard, L. Ron 134
The Hucksters (Wakeman) 25
Hugo Award 47, 63, 65
Hull, Elizabeth Anne 3, 5, 13, 62
Human Voices 225
The Hunger Games (Collins) 126
Huxley, Aldous 137
Hyperion (Simmons) 119

"I Have No Mouth and I Must Scream" (Ellison) 147, 192
I, Robot (Asimov) 133, 175
"Icaromenippus" (Lucian) 254
Iceland 21, 66
If 44, 47, 53, 86, 104, 180, 184
"If I Forget Thee" 66, 214
The Iliad (Homer) 218–219, 249
The Immortal (novelization) 52
The Immortal (TV series) 51–53, 164, 167
"The Immortals" 49, 77, 171–175, 178, 180, 185, 227
The Immortals 10, 14, 15, 36, 43–46, 49–53, 71, 163–175, 179, 184–185, 189, 219, 258
"Imposter" (Dick) 143
In Search of Wonder (Knight) 252
India 67
Indian Association for Science Fiction Studies Conference 67
Infinity (magazine) 46
Infinity (paperback anthology) 49
Inside Science Fiction 71, 258
Intelligent Life in the Universe (Sagan and Shklovskii) 54
Intensive Institute on the Teaching of Science Fiction 1, 4, 5, 12, 22, 30, 33, 58, 62–64, 66–67, 70–71, 259
Inter-Century Seminar 50–51
Invasion from Mars: Interplanetary Stories (Welles) 29
Isaac Asimov: The Foundations of Science Fiction 257
Isaac Asimov's Science Fiction Magazine 65, 257

The Issue at Hand (Blish) 252
It's Your Atomic Age (Del Rey) 36

Jack Williamson Library 1, 12
Jakobsson, Eljer 55
James, M.R. 12
"Jazz Then, Musicology Now" (Klass) 61
The Jesus Incident (Herbert and Ransom) 147
Jianzhong, Guo 66
Johnson, Kij 1, 4, 6, 7, 13, 71, 75
Johnson, Samuel 212
The John W. Campbell Letters (Campbell) 53
The Joy Machine 14, 71, 139, 226–229, 246, 247, 249
The Joy Makers 14, 15, 43–44, 46, 50, 66, 91, 104, 112, 125, 132–148, 152, 160, 163, 164, 171, 177, 182, 184–186, 189, 205, 208, 210, 214–215, 216, 218, 223, 226–227, 246, 247, 248, 250, 251

Kampus 14, 15, 55, 66, 86, 112, 139, 140, 184–185, 199–213, 229, 234
Kansas City 2, 13, 17, 19, 20–21, 23, 24, 33, 34–36, 39, 45–47, 50, 62–63, 70, 101, 139, 151, 164–175, 179–180, 182, 198–199, 206–207
Kansas City City Hall 36, 139, 169–170
Kansas City Science Fiction and Fantasy Society 72
Kansas City Star 24, 27
Kansas Writers' Conference 45
Kazan, Elia 222
Kennedy Space Center 238
Kenneth Spencer Research Library 13–14, 67, 70
Kent State University 55
Kessel, John 3, 6, 13, 20, 72, 75
"Kindergarten" 46, 48
King, Stephen 102, 197–198
Klass, Phillip *see* William Tenn
Klein, Jay Kay 11
Knight, Damon 54, 57, 60, 72, 108, 111, 252–253, 258
The Known and the Unknown (Wolfe) 252
Koontz, Dean 198
Kornbluth, C.M. 35, 36, 49, 86, 103–104, 122, 127, 137, 141, 149, 169, 175
Kress, Nancy 3
Kubrick, Stanley 200
Kuttner, Henry 49, 133, 253, 258

Landis, Geoffrey 3
Lang, Fritz 57
Larbalestier, Justine 89
The Last Dangerous Visions (Ellison) 59, 66, 214
The Last Theorem (Clarke and Pohl) 74

"The Last Word" 45, 86
Laumer, Keith 244
Lawrence, Kansas 3, 12–13, 21, 23, 33, 46, 48–49, 56–57, 64–65, 67, 74, 100–102, 132, 164, 171–175, 178–187, 203–204, 206
Lazzarino, Alex 56–57
The Legion of Space (Williamson) 129
Le Guin, Ursula K. 73, 241
Leiber, Fritz 35, 86, 169, 253
Leinster, Murray 53, 79, 93, 149, 242
Lem, Stanislaw 91
"The Lens of Time" 71, 225
Level 7 (Roshwald) 159
Levin, Ira 179, 197
Ley, Willy 40, 44, 148, 152, 153, 154
"Life-Line" (Heinlein) 231
The Lifeship (Dickson and Harrison) 57–58
Limbo (Wolfe) 159
Lippman, Barry 63
"The Listeners" 54, 60, 188–191
The Listeners 14, 26, 43, 50, 55, 58, 64, 81, 86, 163, 188–197, 213, 223, 225, 229, 231, 236–238
Literature of Science Fiction film series 5, 56–58, 60, 63, 188, 254
Little Blue Books 18, 26
"Little Orphan Android" 46, 175–177, 208
Little Orphan Annie 176
Locus Awards 75
loneliness 80–81, 91–102, 105, 156–163, 188–197, 213–219
The Long Loud Silence (Tucker) 36
"The Long Rain" (Bradbury) 142
The Long Tomorrow (Brackett) 106
Los Angeles 11, 23, 50, 57, 221–223
Lost Horizon (Hilton) 211
Lottman, Eileen 52
Lowndes, Robert W. 31
Lucian of Samosata 10, 254–255
Lunch with John Campbell 57–58, 254

MacDonald, John D. 145
Machen, Arthur 12
"The Machine Stops" (Forster) 126, 137, 144, 174, 176, 214, 258
machines, technology 87, 89–90, 94, 106–116, 132–148, 175–177, 182, 208–210, 212
MacLeod, Ian 3
Macrolife (Zebrowski) 223
Mad Max 169
Magazine of Fantasy and Science Fiction 61, 77, 133, 168, 200
"The Magicians" 57, 197
The Magicians 42, 62, 105, 197–199, 201
Malzberg, Barry 10, 63–64
Man and the Future 51, 53, 231
Man in Orbit 44

Man in Space (Haber) 148
"Man of the Hour" 68, 221–222
"The Man Who Owned Tomorrow" 37
Man Will Conquer Space Soon! (Ley) 148
"The Man with Common Sense" 25, 84
The Man with the Strange Head (Breuer) 1, 12
Manning, Laurence 144–145
Marcuse, Herbert 204
marriage/family life 86–91, 102–104, 148, 155–157, 161–163, 177–179, 188–190, 206, 214–219, 221, 232
Mars 79, 121, 141, 143, 153, 160–163, 196, 241
Marshall, E.G. 44
The Martian (Weir) 151
The Martian Chronicles (Bradbury) 36
"The Martian Way" (Asimov) 80, 163
Marvin, Lee 44
Massachusetts Avenue 101
"Mask of Peace" 25, 78–79, 82, 106
Matheson, Richard 33
"Maturity" (Sturgeon) 31
McCaffrey, Anne 115, 122
McCarthy, Joseph 34, 46, 178, 181, 184
McConnell, Frank 257
McDevitt, Jack 3
McKitterick, Christopher 11, 12, 15, 34, 63, 70–71, 74, 75
"Medic" 44–45, 168–171, 179, 180
Menninger, Karl 51, 237
Mephistopheles 144
Merril, Judith 36, 47, 117
Merritt, A. 20
Merwin, Sam, Jr. 25, 79
"The Message" 188, 191–193
"Microcosmic God" (Sturgeon) 83
"The Midas Plague" (Pohl) 175–177
Miéville, China 3
The Millennium Blues 14, 71, 210, 229–235, 245
Mills, Robert 168–169, 200
"Mimsy Were the Borogoves" (Kuttner and Moore) 253
The Mirror of Infinity (Silverberg) 60
"The Misogynist" 25, 34, 38, 45, 86–90, 91, 103, 163, 178
Mr. and Mrs. Bridge (Connell) 27
Modern Drama (journal) 27
Modern Language Association 73–74, 257
Modern Masters of Science Fiction series 13, 65
Modern Science Fiction: A Critical Analysis 14, 31, 84, 169, 252–253
"A Monster Named Smith" 42, 104–105, 243
Montagu, Ashley 51
Moon 26, 32, 59, 83, 86, 149–150, 153, 196, 242, 247–248

The Moon Is a Harsh Mistress (Heinlein) 118
"The Moon Pool" (Merritt) 20
Moorcock, Michael 54, 64
Moore, C.L. 246, 253, 258
Moore, Ward 133
More Than Human (Sturgeon) 133
Morrow, James 3
Moskowitz, Sam 19
"Mother to the World" (Wilson) 55
Mount Oread 101–102, 172–174, 186
Muehlebach Hotel 62, 198–199
Mullins, Reverdy 24, 33
Murphy, Franklin 49–51
Mutant (Kuttner) 133
mutation, human evolution 84–86, 120–131, 163–175, 240

Naar, Joe 219
Nair, Latha 67, 247
"The Naked Sky" 46, 133, 142–148
"Name Your Pleasure" 44, 132–133, 137–142
Nebraska 1, 9–10, 120
Nebula Award 55, 57, 72
Nebula Awards Showcase 2008 (Bova) 72
Nebula Awards Ten 60–61
Nebula Winners Twelve (Dickson) 61
"Neosho's Choicest" *see* "The Girls Who Were Really Built"
Neuromancer (Gibson) 141, 218, 241
"New Americans" (Wells) 20
"New Blood" 10, 44, 164–165, 168, 173
The New Encyclopedia of Science Fiction 64, 68–69, 73
New Maps of Hell (Amis) 103, 252
New Wave 54, 92, 213, 255–256
New Worlds 54, 185
New York City 32–33, 35–41, 47, 53–54, 57–58, 72, 90, 92, 103, 117, 125, 126, 151, 220, 225, 230, 234–235
New York Daily News 32, 126
New York Times 72
Nicholls, Peter 30, 68–69
"Nightfall" (Asimov) 253
"Nine Lives" (Le Guin) 241
1984 (Orwell) 28, 177
Niven, Larry 9
"Not So Great an Enemy" *see* "Medic"
Nova 2 (Harrison) 53

O'Brien, Fitz-James 10, 225
Odd John (Stapledon) 83
The Odyssey (Homer) 244–245, 249
"The Old Folks" 53
"On the Foundations of Science Fiction" 65
On the Road (Kerouac) 207
"On the Robot Novels" 65

One and Wonder (Anthony) 101
O'Neill, Gerard 223
"Open Warfare" 25, 26, 34, 44, 84, 90–91
Operator #5 19
Orbit anthology series 54
Ordover, John 226
Orwell, George 28, 177
The Other Glass Teat (Ellison) 52
Outpost Mars (Kornbluth and Merril) 36
Oxford University Press 65, 257
Ozarks 38, 97–102

Packard, Vance 103
Pal, George 57
Palgrave Macmillan 74
Palmer, Raymond 18, 33, 36
Palumbo, Donald 13
Panshin, Alexei, and Cory 240
"Paradise" (Simak) 145
"Paradox" 25, 77–78, 79, 82, 105
Paramount Pictures 51–52, 226
paranoia 86–102, 104–105, 132–148, 175–179, 214–219, 236–240
Paratexts 69, 259
Paul, Frank R. 126, 245
Pebble in the Sky (Asimov) 28–29
Penguin Books 68–69, 73
Penthouse 200
"Pest House" 49
Philadelphia 40, 198
"Physics Through Science Fiction" (Benford) 259
Pilgrims Through Time and Space (Bailey) 252
The Pillars of the Earth (Follett) 189
"Pill Roller" 45
Piper, H. Beam 85
Pirates of Venus (Burroughs) 29
Planet of the Apes (film) 9
Planet Stories 25, 37, 77, 79
Playboy 179, 200
Pocket Book of Science Fiction (Wollheim) 22, 83
Pocket Books 71
Poe, Edgar Allan 254
Pohl, Frederik 3, 5, 9, 13, 14, 18, 19, 22, 35, 39, 47, 40, 53–55, 58, 62, 64, 69, 72, 74, 75, 77, 86, 103–104, 122, 127, 137, 141, 172, 175–177, 180, 184, 185, 201, 239, 251; as literary agent 27, 31, 33–43, 117, 252
politics 14, 46, 78–79, 82–83, 106–116, 121–131, 148–163, 181–187, 189–197, 199, 200–213, 237–239
Portales, New Mexico 12, 18, 37, 47
"Powder Keg" 48, 157–160
The Power (Robinson) 140
"The Power and the Glory" 53
"Pow'r" 237–238

Pratt, Fletcher 145
Prelude to Space (Clarke) 149
Prentice-Hall 60, 254
"Private Enterprise" 25, 82–83, 129
"The Protocols of Science Fiction" 258
"Proxima Centauri" (Leinster) 242
psi powers, psychic phenomena 14, 23, 36, 38, 96–102, 181–184
psychology 79–81, 91–102, 104–105, 108–112, 132–148, 157–163, 176–177, 181–187, 188–190, 202, 214–219
The Puppet Masters (Heinlein) 89

Quantum Leap 68
"The Rabbit Hole" 239

race/racism 51, 120–121, 130, 193–195
Racine, Wisconsin 26, 29–34, 86–87, 89
Ransom, Bill 147
Ravage, Alan 200
Reading Science Fiction 73, 258–259
"Reading Science Fiction as Science Fiction" 258–259
Reagan administration 10, 158
"Reason" (Asimov) 237, 256
"The Reason Is with Us" 38
recursivity 82, 85, 179, 194, 225, 228, 238
The Reefs of Space (Pohl and Williamson) 172, 185
Reich, Wilhelm 134, 210
religion 78, 106–116, 145–148, 161, 181–187, 189–197, 210–211, 231–235, 241–251
religious fundamentalism/fanaticism 46, 55, 106–116, 118, 181–187, 192–197, 210–211, 231, 236
"The Reluctant Witch" 14, 23, 36, 38, 44, 46, 56, 96–102, 104, 181
"The Reply" 188, 196–197
"Rescue Party" (Clarke) 253
Reynolds, Mack 33, 211
Riley, Frank 46
Ringworld (Niven) 9
The Road to Science Fiction 2, 10, 12, 20, 31, 63–64, 66–67, 71, 157, 169, 180, 225, 252, 254–259
"The Roads Must Roll" (Heinlein) 126
Robinson, Frank M. 140
robots/androids 91, 143–148, 175–177, 179, 205–206
Rocket Stories 77
Rocket to the Morgue (Boucher) 29
Roosevelt, Franklin D. 20
Rosemary's Baby (Levin) 197
Roshwald, Mordecai 159
ruinous cities 110–111, 164–177
Rushdie, Salman 235
Russ, Joanna 64
Russell, Ray 179

Saberhagen, Fred 244, 250
Sagan, Carl 14, 25–26, 54, 71, 236
"Sail On! Sail On!" (Farmer) 258
The Saint Mystery Magazine 45
'Salem's Lot (King) 198
San Francisco 22–23, 45, 120, 232, 234, 248
"Sane Asylum" 25, 79
Sargent, Pamela 3
Satellite 38
satire 14, 37, 86–91, 102–104, 122, 175–178, 199–213
Saturday Evening Post 77, 149
Sawyer, Robert 3
Scarecrow Press 71
Scholes, Robert 61, 65, 73
"Science Fiction and 'Literature'—or, The Conscience of the King" (Delany) 257–258
"Science Fiction and the Mainstream" 60
The Science Fiction Book Club 10, 55
Science Fiction Hall of Fame 72, 75
The Science Fiction Hall of Fame Volume I (Silverberg) 60
The Science Fiction Hall of Fame Volume IIA (Bova) 9
Science Fiction Quarterly 25, 83
Science Fiction Reader's Guide (Allen) 10
Science Fiction Research Association (SFRA) 12–13, 59, 61, 63–64, 67, 74–75, 117–118, 254
Science Fiction Studies 60
Science Fiction: The Future (Allen) 60
Science Fiction: Today and Tomorrow (Bretnor) 60
Science Fiction World 66
Science Fiction Writers of America (SFWA) 56, 59–60, 62, 64, 72
Science Fiction Writers Workshop 2, 4, 11, 13, 17, 62, 64, 70–71, 75–76
The Science of Science-Fiction Writing 71, 258
Science World 44
Scott Meredith Literary Agency 53
Scribner's 55, 188, 197, 200
Seattle, Washington 3–4, 72, 75
"Second Variety" (Dick) 143
Seetee Ship (Williamson) 237
Serling, Rod 57
SETI (Search for Extraterrestrial Intelligence) 54–55, 188–197, 237–238
"The Sex Opposite" (Sturgeon) 95
SF Author's Choice 4 (Harrison) 86
The Shadow 19
Shadow of Tomorrow (Pohl) 86
Shadow on the Hearth (Merril) 36
Shapley, Harlow 51
She (Haggard) 243
Sheckley, Robert 14, 38, 41, 45–48, 103

282 Index

Sheffield, Charles 3
Shelley, Mary 11, 254
shifting realities 94–96, 125, 132–148, 178–179, 184, 200–219, 239
"Shill" 44
Shklovskii, I.S. 54
"Shore Leave" (Sturgeon) 226
Shuch, Paul 55
Silverberg, Robert 9, 18, 19, 35, 37–38, 42, 60, 66, 214
Simak, Clifford D. 9, 33, 58, 133, 145, 175
Simmons, Dan 3, 119
"Sine of the Magus" *see* *The Magicians*
Siodmak, Curt 164
The Six Million Dollar Man 67, 219
Sixth Column (Heinlein) 107
"Skin Game" 48
The Skylark of Valeron" (Smith) 238
Slan (Van Vogt) 29
"Slave Psychology" 25, 81–82
"Slaves of Venus" 25, 79
Slonczewski, Joan 3
"The Small Assassin" (Bradbury) 177
Smith, Cordwainer 70
Smith, E.E. "Doc" 19, 126–127, 238
Smith, Lloyd 26–29, 34
The Sneetches (Dr. Seuss) 135
social science fiction 14, 43, 52, 72, 79, 86–90, 102–104, 132, 163–175, 180–187, 200–213, 219–224, 240
Sohl, Jerry 89
Solaris (Lem) 91–92
Some Dreams Are Nightmares 43
Soviet Union 49, 66, 83, 107, 150, 180, 220
Space Cadet (Heinlein) 32
"Space Is a Lonely Place" 48, 160–163, 168, 188
The Space Merchants (Pohl and Kornbluth) 35, 86, 103–104, 122, 127, 136, 137, 138, 141–142, 175
space opera 14, 43, 78–79, 106–131, 139,, 142, 197, 226–229, 235–251
Space Platform (Leinster) 149
Space Science Fiction 37–38, 91, 93
Specht, Bob 51
"Spectator Sport" (MacDonald) 145
Speculations on Speculation 73, 257–258
"Speech Sounds" (Butler) 180
The Spider 19
Spinrad, Norman 69
The Spire (Golding) 189
Spock, Benjamin 177
Sri Lanka 70, 247–248
Stableford, Brian 189
Stapledon, Olaf 83, 113
"The Star" (Wells) 10, 255
Star Bridge 14, 32, 37–39, 42–44, 78, 89, 104–106, 111–131, 132, 140, 183, 197, 245, 248, 258

Star Science Fiction anthologies (Pohl) 49, 77
Star Trek 9, 14, 51–52, 71, 114, 139, 149, 223, 226–229
Star Wars 201
Star Wars Initiative 158
The Stars My Destination (Bester) 118, 119
Starchild Trilogy (Pohl and Williamson) 39, 42, 172
Starship Troopers (Heinlein) 117
Startling Stories 25, 38, 46, 77, 79, 85, 116, 133
Station in Space 14, 40, 43–46, 48, 50, 80, 88, 148–163, 164, 183, 186, 189, 223, 238
The Stepford Wives (Levin) 179
Stewart, George R. 28
"The Stilled Patter" 46, 177–178
Stoffel, Albert 26
Stones, Eric 69
Straub, Peter 198
Structural Fabulation (Scholes) 61
A Study of History (Toynbee) 113
"The Stuff Itself" 65
Sturgeon, Theodore 9, 10, 14, 27, 30–31, 35, 38, 40, 58, 62, 70, 83, 91–92, 94–95, 133, 226, 229
Sturgeon Memorial Award 3, 65, 70–71
Sullivan, Walter 54
"The Sun Came Up Last Night" 25, 83
Super-Science Fiction 37–38, 102–103
"Surface Tension" (Blish) 249
"Survival Policy" 34, 38, 84–85, 91
Suvin, Darko 73, 130
Synergy (Zebrowski) 230

Takeoff (Kornbluth) 149
"Tales of the Spaceship *Geoffrey*" 74
Tarzan 18–19, 245
"Teaching Science Fiction" (Bova) 61
Teaching Science Fiction (Sawyer and Wright) 63
"Teaching Science Fiction Revisited" 61
Teaching Tomorrow (Williamson) 65
"The Technological Revolution" 49
"Teddy Bear" 46, 58, 178–179
telepathy/telekinesis as theme 77–78, 96–102, 106–108, 112–116
Tenn, William 50, 61, 103, 253
"There Is No Such Thing as Science Fiction" (Bould and Vint) 258
"These Things Are Sirius" 25, 83
They'd Rather Be Right (Clifton and Riley) 47
The Thirteenth Immortal (Silverberg) 42
This Fortress World 14, 33, 36–38, 41–43, 78, 89, 104–116, 119, 122, 125, 166, 183, 197, 216, 247
This Week (magazine) 43
Those Who Can (Wilson) 60

Three Mile Island 10
Thrilling Wonder Stories 25, 34, 44, 77, 83, 133
Thy Kingdom Come 24
"Tiger! Tiger!" 37, 39
Time (magazine) 30
The Time Machine (Wells) 106–107, 225
time travel 67–68, 219–225
"The Tinsel Screen" 65
"The Tolerance of Elmer Wilkey" 48
Tom Corbett, Space Cadet 32
Topeka, Kansas 51, 186, 237
TOR books 68, 75
To Sail Beyond the Sunset (Heinlein) 17
"Touch of the Match" 68, 222–223
Touchstone Pictures 71
"Touchstones" 258
Toynbee, Arnold 113, 119
Transcendental 15, 43, 74–76, 197, 235, 240–245, 256
Transformation 15, 17, 76, 240, 248–251
Transgalactic 76, 240, 244–248
"Trends" (Asimov) 231
"Trial by Fire" 53, 66, 180, 183–184
Triax (Silverberg) 66, 214
"Tricentennial" (Haldeman) 256
True Names (Vinge) 141
Truk Island 22–23
Truman, Harry 164
"Tsylana" 44, 46
Tucker, Wilson 36
TV Guide 52–53
Twilight Zone 90
2001: A Space Odyssey (Clarke) 69

UCLA 50–51
"Uncreated Night and Strange Shadows" 239–240
underground movements 137–142, 175–177, 183–187, 211–212, 228–229
Undersea series (Pohl and Williamson) 39
"The Unhappy Man" 44, 132, 134–137, 140
"Universe" (Heinlein) 9, 29–31, 116
University of Kansas (KU) 2, 4, 11, 14, 17, 21–23, 27, 30, 46–51, 55–58, 64, 69–72, 75, 84, 97, 100–102, 113, 172–175, 180–188, 200–206, 220, 231, 252–254; KU Medical Center 44, 49–50, 164, 167–171; student unrest at 55–56, 200–201
Unknown 199
The Unpublished Gunn 25
urban geographies 111, 125–127, 132–148, 166–175, 179–180, 214
U.S. Information Agency 66

Vance, Jack 84
Vanguard 49
Van Vogt, A.E. 9, 10, 23, 29, 45, 69, 72, 84, 122, 138, 235–236, 241, 243, 253

"Variations on a Robot" 65
Vault of the Ages (Anderson) 106
Venture 168, 200
Venus 79, 137, 141–148, 153, 220, 223
Verne, Jules 9, 19, 60, 249, 254
Vietnam era 55
Vinge, Vernor 3, 141
Vint, Sherryl 258
virtual reality 107–116, 123, 132–148, 210, 213–219
"The Voices" 58, 188, 190–191
Voltaire 204
von Braun, Wernher 148, 154
Vortex 77
The Voyage of the Space Beagle (Van Vogt) 29

"The Waiting" 188, 195–196
Wakeman, Frederic 25
Ward, David 69
Ward, Don 29–33
The War of the Worlds (Wells) 69, 80, 174
The Way the Future Was (Pohl) 38
We (Zamyatin) 258
We Are Not Alone (Sullivan) 54
"We Can Remember It for You Wholesale" (Dick) 134
"We *Must* Study Psi" (Campbell) 99
The Weapons Shops of Isher (Van Vogt) 84
Weir, Matt 151
Weird Tales 77
Welles, Orson 29
Wells, H.G. 6, 9, 10, 13, 15, 19, 20, 29, 45, 69, 72–73, 75, 80, 106, 126, 141, 146, 174, 225, 245, 254, 255, 257–258; "Open Conspiracy" 6, 20–21, 34, 45, 73, 75, 141
Wendroff, Gayle 56
Wescoe, W. Clarke 50, 55
Wescoe Hall 185
West of Eden (Harrison) 245
Western Printing and Lithography 14, 26, 27–34, 38, 42, 54, 89, 92
Westfahl, Gary 163
"What Is Science Fiction—and How It Grew" (Franklin) 258
"What's It Like Out There?" (Hamilton) 156
"When the Shoe Fits" *see* "Cinderella Story"
When the Sleeper Wakes (Wells) 126, 245, 258
Where Do We Go from Here? (Asimov) 44
"Wherever You May Be" *see* "The Reluctant Witch"
"Who Goes There?" (Campbell) 9, 104, 143
Whyte, William 208
"Will-of-the-Wisp" 68, 224
Williams, Nate 12, 75

Williams, Paul 95
Williamson, Jack 9, 12, 14, 18, 22, 32–33, 36–43, 45, 47, 58–59, 69, 72–73, 104, 116–131, 134, 172, 175, 177, 185, 213, 237, 250, 251
Willis, Connie 75
Wilson, Richard 55
Wilson, Robert Charles 3
Wilson, Robin Scott 60
"Witch Hunt" 54, 180, 184–187
"Witches Must Burn" 34, 42, 36, 53, 55, 180–184
The Witching Hour 36, 56
"With Folded Hands" (Williamson) 9, 134, 137, 175, 177
"Without Portfolio" 44, 83
Wolfe, Bernard 159
Wolfe, Gary K. 6, 13, 73, 75, 252
Wolfe, Gene 108
Wolfe, Thomas 19
Wollheim, Donald 22, 67, 70, 83, 219
"Woman of the Year" 68, 223–224
Wonder Stories 18, 19
Wonder Stories Quarterly 18
"A Word for Freedom" 86
"The Word Sweep" (Zebrowski) 180
The World Beyond the Hill (Panshin) 240

World Brain (Wells) 20
The World Inside (Silverberg) 214
The World of Null-A (Van Vogt) 23, 84–85, 241
World Science Fiction Convention (World Con) 2, 13, 17, 32–34, 36, 40–42, 45, 47, 56, 58, 63, 66, 74–75, 93, 116–117, 198, 240
World SF 64
World's Best Science Fiction (Wollheim) 67, 219
"The Worldview of Science Fiction" 256
World War II 13, 21–23, 51, 106

X Minus One 44, 91

Ye, Dong 67
Yeager, Chuck 150
You Will Go to the Moon (Freeman) 149–150
Yugoslavia 21, 66

Zamyatin, Yevgeny 258
Zane Grey's Western Magazine 29–30
Zebrowski, George 3, 148, 180, 223, 230
Zelazny, Roger 54
Zip Foster, Spaceman 32

www.ingramcontent.com/pod-product-compliance
Ingram Content Group UK Ltd.
Pitfield, Milton Keynes, MK11 3LW, UK
UKHW041928140426
5217IPUK00014B/365